What is Justice?

What is Justice?

Classic and
Contemporary Readings

SECOND EDITION

Edited by

Robert C. Solomon
Mark C. Murphy

NEW YORK • OXFORD
Oxford University Press
2000

Oxford University Press

Oxford   New York
Athens   Auckland   Bangkok   Bogotá   Buenos Aires   Calcutta
Cape Town   Chennai   Dar es Salaam   Delhi   Florence   Hong Kong   Istanbul
Karachi   Kuala Lumpur   Madrid   Melbourne   Mexico City   Mumbai
Nairobi   Paris   São Paulo   Singapore   Taipei   Tokyo   Toronto   Warsaw

and associated companies in
Berlin   Ibadan

Copyright © 2000 by Oxford University Press, Inc.

Published by Oxford University Press, Inc.,
198 Madison Avenue, New York, New York, 10016
http://www.oup-usa.org
1-800-334-4249

Library of Congress Cataloging-in-Publication Data

What is justice? : classic and contemporary readings / edited by
   Robert C. Solomon, Mark C. Murphy. — 2nd ed.
      p.   cm.
   Includes bibliographical references.
   ISBN 978-0-19-512810-9 (paper)

   1. Justice.   I. Solomon, Robert C.   II. Murphy, Mark C.
JC578.W47   2000
320′.01′1—dc21   99-22333
                                                        CIP

Printed in the United States of America
on acid-free paper

for
Thomas and Ann Murphy
and
Eugene and Kathryn Higgins

ACKNOWLEDGMENTS

We owe thanks to Jon Solomon, Victor Caston, Douglas Kellner, Kenneth Riley, and our editors at Oxford, Cynthia Read and Robert Miller. Mark Murphy would also like to thank the Erasmus Institute at the University of Notre Dame, which supported him with a fellowship leave during the period in which the second edition was revised.

CONTENTS

Part Three: Justice and Society

Part Four: Justice and Punishment

Part Five: The Contemporary Debate on Distributive Justice

What is Justice?

INTRODUCTION

"What is justice?" asked Socrates in Plato's *Republic,* and ever since, this has been one of the leading questions of philosophy and all social thinking. For Plato and for Aristotle after him, justice, in its most general sense, was the essential virtue, the summary virtue, the virtue most important for the "social animals" that we are, living together in ever-larger communities, cities, and nation-states. But even in the *Republic,* the answer to that question—the definition of *justice* (or rather, *dikaiosune*)—is at best controversial and provides no clear criteria for making the choices, just or unjust, that we make in everyday life. Socrates dispatches his various interlocutors and their proposed answers, such as "justice is giving and getting one's due," but it is not at all evident that, after rejecting such context-bound and merely conventional replies, Socrates is able to provide a single criterion that accounts for justice in its various contexts. He says in Book IV that justice is "doing one's own"—every person performing his or her proper role in the community—but it is by no means obvious how we should translate this into concrete decisions and policies.

We do become clear, though, on what justice is *not.* In one of the classic early exchanges in the *Republic,* the philosophical thug Thrasymachus argues the ultracynical line that justice always serves the interests of the rulers of the society, that justice is no more than "the advantage of the stronger." If you are an ordinary person, you are only hurting yourself by trying to live in accordance with justice. This shocking thesis is refuted by Socrates, right is properly distinguished from mere might, and Thrasymachus walks off in a huff. In Thrasymachus's abandoned place, Glaucon suggests a more modest thesis, that justice is ultimately a matter of self-interest, and that people adhere to its conventions only to avoid punishment. Socrates takes this suggestion much more seriously, but he ultimately insists that justice is not merely a matter of convention and, in the vulgar sense intended, it is not a matter of mere self-interest, either. But then Socrates spends the rest of the *Republic* taking us through a whirlwind of philosophical considerations as he speculates about metaphysics and human nature, praises (some of) the political ideals of ancient Greece, and introduces his own radical republicanism to show that justice must be counted as desirable for its own sake, that justice is harmony in the soul as it is harmony in the state, that justice is the rule of reason, and finally, that justice even "pays off" in the end, for the just person can ultimately suffer no harm—to his or her soul, at least. But what we do not get—what we thought we *would* get—is anything like an adequate criterion concerning what sorts of considerations we should use in evaluating this or that social arrangement or rule. Plato does tell us that responsibility should be delegated in accordance with ability and "place," but what about the distribution of wealth in society? As a spokesman for the aristocracy, Plato was disdainful of money and markets and said very little about them. How should the goods of society get distributed? What should we do about the poor? How much should a doctor or a lawyer or a soldier or a tradesman be paid? What Socrates seems to promise us is a standard of justice; what we get is an elaborate metaphor. But so it has been ever since with philosophical discussions of justice.

On the one hand, the question "What is justice?" is an invitation to the most abstract sort of philosophical speculation. What is the good society? What makes a government legitimate? What kind of creatures does God, or Nature, intend us to be? What is our essential relationship to our fellow human beings, and what obligations do we have to one another? Where did these obligations come from? On the other hand, the question of justice focuses our attention on the concrete problems of our times: Is it just for there to be poor people living virtually next to people who have more money than they could ever possibly spend? Is it fair that hard-working people of considerable talent go unrewarded, while others, smiled upon by fortune and raised with wealth and power, are constantly "rewarded" when they do no work and make no contribution to society whatever? Should the rich be taxed to help the poor? Should "unearned" income be taxed at the same rate as "earned" income? Should men and women receive the same wages for the same jobs, without regard to need? Should workers be paid, or students graded, on the basis of their efforts or their results? Do people whose ancestors were treated unfairly deserve compensation for what their grandparents suffered, and if so, from whom? What should a society do with those who break the law? Should we execute criminals for the most heinous crimes? A theory of justice has the extremely difficult task of bridging the abyss between the abstract and the eminently practical. No theory of justice can long remain on the luxurious level of philosophical speculation without diving down into the particularities of social life, but no attempt to solve the problems of daily politics can long sustain itself without reaching up to the heights of philosophy, struggling as Socrates struggled to come to grips with the definition of justice, with its essential nature and justification.

What is justice? The original meaning of the term, for instance in the Old Testament and the *Iliad,* is very much bound up with punishment, or more accurately, with retribution and revenge. But even by the time of Socrates and in the teachings of Jesus, revenge had clearly been separated from justice and was viewed as a vice instead of a virtue. The problem of punishment would remain a central concern of every society, but justice became more a matter of social harmony (in Plato) and reconciliation (in Christian ethics). In Plato, the ideal of justice was wholly bound up with the ideal community, while already in the Torah, as later in the Gospels and in the Koran, the idea of justice was bound up with belief in and obedience to a merciful (if also retributive) God. But even in ancient times, the concept of justice had particular application to the details of ordinary household life, to the question of fair wages and the distribution of rewards and honors. The particular concept of justice developed by Aristotle, for example, has much to do with fair exchange and "equality" (or, more accurately, proportion), or what we would call "desert," what a person deserves or has earned. The conception he offers also focuses on the notion of compensation when one is deprived of what he or she deserves. In modern times the focus of justice has come to be more and more concentrated on questions of distribution and exchange and, in particular, on questions of private property and individual liberty. But here, too, the apparent focus reveals a blur of competing images: How are we to reconcile the supposedly inalienable right of individuals to own private property with the tragic existence of misery and poverty in the same society, misery and poverty that are often not unrelated to precisely the same activities through which the wealthy obtained their property? How are we to reconcile the rights of individuals to hold on to property that they did not in any sense earn (e.g., obtained through inheritance or a lucky bet in the state lottery) with our insistence that people should earn and thus deserve what they get? Indeed, insofar as justice is a legal and moral right to hold on to what one (or one's family or community) already has, is it too far-fetched to suggest that, once again, we find ourselves faced, in neo-Thrasymachean language, with the rights of the stronger, the entitlement of the powerful and privileged to hold on to what they already have? What are the rights, in such a framework, of the poor and unpropertied? Or are we putting too much emphasis on property rights as the focus of justice? Are other rights and liberties not more important than the right to unlimited ownership? And is the overall public good not more important than the rights and liberties of any particular individual? Or should our focus be somewhere else as well, on the conception of universal equality, according to which it is any *difference* in the distribution of wealth that needs justification instead of the alternative presumption that established differences are, through their very establishment, legitimate, and that it is any redistribution (e.g., through taxes) that needs justification?

Such are the dimensions of the question "What is justice?" The very general issues that faced Socrates in the *Republic* are still with us now. Are our standards of justice, ultimately, in the interests of the stronger, the more established and more powerful citizens? Is faithfully following the principles of justice in any sense in one's own interest and to one's own advantage? Is our concept of justice really just a social convention, perhaps a matter of agreement among the members of this society but possibly quite different in others? Indeed, given the enormous amount of disagreement among us concerning the right conception of justice, can we suppose with any confidence that there is, ultimately, some single standard to be found? But in addition, there are all of those other, more specific and more urgent practical questions that need resolution. How should we think of punishment: as retaliation or retribution or mere public revenge against those who criminally assaulted us or violated our laws, or as a more future-oriented attempt to deter future crime and reform wayward citizens? How should we understand that very modern sense in which everyone is "created equal"? How do we (or can we) justify—and from what perspective should we view—the often enormous disparities between the rich and the poor? How do we weigh the importance of individual rights and liberties against the public good? And how much trust should we put in that peculiarly modern social institution—the free market—as a vehicle for assuring justice? Or is that the wrong way to look at the role of the market in society? Perhaps the market defines its own conception of justice and should not be treated as a mere means to other, possibly archaic conceptions. Perhaps the market replaces, or is incompatible with, the concept of justice. All of this presumes, of course, that there is an adequate answer to our original question, "What is justice?" Is it fairness? Is it equal treatment? Is it desert? Is it "getting one's due"? And does this concept of justice depend on a particular context, a particular set of social goals and conventions, or is it something bigger and more universal than that, perhaps provided by God or the intrinsic features of human nature?

Despite its obvious importance and eminent practicality, the question of justice seems to come and go as a central topic of concern. By the beginning of this century it had been eclipsed and had fallen out of favor in contemporary philosophy. Perhaps the rather expansive question of justice was put aside to make room for other moral and social questions that seemed to admit of more precision. Perhaps it was because social and political philosophy had been overshadowed for such a long time by metaphysics and theology and, more recently, dismissed as tangential to "mainstream" interests in epistemology and philosophy of language. Perhaps it was because the question of justice came to seem too practical to philosophers concerned with much more abstract questions and too immense to philosophers focused on seemingly more manageable issues. Perhaps it was because the interest in human nature fell under the anthropologist's or existentialist's ax or simply shifted into the social science departments. Perhaps it became too apparent that seemingly abstract theories of justice had long stood as façades for other more immediate concerns—the legitimation of a revolution or a dictatorship, or the defense of the status quo and the sanctity of private property, for example. Nevertheless, it is safe to say that the subject of justice, perhaps in somewhat altered form or as part of some related concern, perhaps in the guise of a shadow or even in its very absence, has been at the core of social thinking ever since Plato and Aristotle.

Today it is clear that the question of justice has returned to center stage in Anglo-American philosophy. In 1971 Harvard philosopher John Rawls published his epochal book, *A Theory of Justice,* and the old Socratic question has never been more alive. Only three years later, Rawls's younger colleague Robert Nozick published his own theory of justice, a very different sort of theory and something of a rejoinder to Rawls's. The difference between the two might be (and is often) characterized as the difference between a "liberal" and a "libertarian" theory, but such politically loaded designations do little to help philosophical understanding. In a nutshell, Rawls tried to find a proper ordering between equality and liberty with a particular concern for the needs of the least advantaged in society; Nozick was anxious to defend a particularly strong notion of "entitlement," such that a just world would be one in which everyone had just what he or she is entitled to, without reference to equality or inequality. But the dispute was, for all its interest and importance, only a recent and rather narrow manifestation of a three-thousand-year-old debate. Rawls's concern for universal equality and individual liberty would not have been intelligible to Plato and Aristotle, and Nozick's exclusive insistence on private property rights and virtually total neglect of any concept of community would have horrified them. But what was particularly revealing, as Alasdair MacIntyre observed, was that neither Rawls nor Nozick adequately acknowledged what the ancients—and many moderns—would consider the heart of justice, and that is the concept of *desert.* Moreover, both of them were only marginally concerned with questions of punishment and with questions of social status and honors that cannot be "cashed out" in economic terms. To be sure, the question of whether the state has the right to tax some people in order to help others in need—one of the central questions that arose from the Rawls and Nozick debate—is still a lively and emotional issue in days when the economic scene is extraordinarily volatile and Social Security seems on the verge of collapse, but the question of justice and the range of human concerns that it expresses are much more expansive than that, as many writers after Rawls and Nozick have stressed. We have tried to capture some of that expanse in this book.

What is justice? What are the origins of justice? What are the different types of justice and how do they relate to one another? Can we subsume our concern for the poor, our insistence that people earn what they have, and our need to punish those who break the law under a single, all-embracing criterion? Is there a single overriding concept of justice that encompasses all of our activities and crosses the borders of all cultures, no matter how socially different? Is justice, as Rawls (and Cicero long before him) argued, the leading virtue of societies—or are there other virtues more central, more important even than justice? Could justice be, in certain circumstances, dispensable, perhaps even irrelevant? What is the relationship between justice and the law—is there, or could there be, any justice apart from legal institutions? Is there some "natural" (or divine) law, from which our civil laws (at least, those worthy of respect) are derived? What or where are the sources of justice— in God or human nature, in our rational capacities to reason dispassionately and abstractly, in the history of (particular) human practices, in our search for social harmony and utility, or in the allegedly rock-bottom fact of individual freedom? Is justice conventional or natural? Does it consist primarily in respect for authority, respect for principles, or respect for persons? Can we conceive of a unifying answer that does justice to all of these, or is justice—as Socrates's interlocutors unsuccessfully insisted—whatever rules or rulers dominate a particular society at a particular time?

What are the definitive ingredients in justice? Is it need (as the Marxists say, "to each according to his needs")? Is it merit (as in Aristotle, for example, who one is and what one has done)? Is it equality (and in what sense is it true that all men—or, rather, all *people*—are created equal)? How much weight should tradition and the status quo have in determinations of justice? How much consideration should the history of injustice have in our current disputes over justice, or are they, too, "just history" and irrelevant to what is just and fair now? What pressures does the free enterprise system place on justice, or does that system embody a special theory of justice itself? Does the free enterprise system reward merit, as is often suggested by its promoters, or is it more a matter of luck? What are we to make of the concept of private property, which played such an enormous role in the development of British social philosophy but surprisingly little role elsewhere? (Rousseau suggested, in his "Discourse on the Origins of Inequality," that the invention of private property is tantamount to a crime against humanity, and Pierre Proudhon flatly asserted that "property is theft.") What are we to make of the notion of "rights" that has become so central to our own thinking about justice—and so prone to abuse? (Do ordinary citizens really have a right to possess and carry military assault weapons?) How do we measure these ingredients, need against merit against rights, in an adequate conception of justice? This is no abstract question, a mere plaything for the philosophers. Our public policy depends on an answer, and every citizen has a stake in it.

And what are we to make of punishment? Is it "natural" to want to punish someone who has wronged you, to hurt him or her as you have been hurt, or is retribution an invention of society and thus, perhaps, properly and strictly a function of the law? Should we punish people at all, or should we rather restrict our punitive efforts to deterring crime and reforming criminals? Or should we instead turn our attention to rooting out the conditions of crime, placing much more emphasis on rewards than punishments? Such are the questions of justice. Our current debates are but the most recent manifestations of a set of concerns that are as old as "civilized" society itself. Indeed, one might hypothesize that it is just that set of concerns that *defines* a society as civilized. It is with this in mind that we present the following selections, not as an attempt to answer Socrates's question, but in an effort to get a new generation engaged in one of the most important and practical philosophical activities of our time.

This book is divided into five parts, although not according to any single dimension or set of categories. Our aim has been to provide a wide variety of topics and selections of both historical and current interest ranging from the presuppositions of our own conceptions of justice and society (to be found, for example, in the United States Declaration of Independence and Bill of Rights) to the nature of justice as such (if there is such a thing), from the most basic obligations one citizen or one human being owes another to the relative roles of deterrence and retribution in the various theories of punishment.

Part One, "Classical Sources," provides a number of ancient discussions of justice, from which our contemporary conceptions and debates inevitably derive. It includes excerpts from the Bible (both Old and New Testaments) and the Koran, an excerpt from Homer's *Iliad* in which the primitive conception of justice as vengeance is uncompromisingly expressed, and a sizable selection from Plato's *Republic*. We have included most of Aristotle's discussion of justice in his *Nicomachean Ethics* and Saint Thomas Aquinas's later reflections on Aristotle, whom Aquinas calls "the Philosopher." To avoid provincial-ism—but not only for that reason—we have also included an expression of the Confucian view of justice in ancient China, according to Confucius's leading disciple, Mencius.

Part Two, "Justice and the Social Contract," concerns what is today the single most prevalent metaphor in the discussion of the conceptual and/or historical origins of justice, the idea of a "social contract." Whether this is supposed to be a historically real or a merely hypothetical event, the social contract is an agreement on the basis of which society was (or would be) founded by rational, autonomous human beings seeking a way to compromise their various and divisive particular interests in order to establish a society in which a fair balance between these interests can be achieved. Prior to such an agreement, so the harsh-est version of the story goes, there is an undisciplined "state of nature" in which individu-als are either hostile or indifferent to one another, do not cooperate, and consequently receive none of the benefits or securities made possible by civilized society. In particular, there is no justice, for justice, according to the defenders of this idea, is only an artificial virtue, a matter of social convention or invention and not a natural virtue at all. Social con-tract theory came to all but define social and political philosophy by the eighteenth century, particularly from the work of Thomas Hobbes, John Locke, and Jean-Jacques Rousseau, and as embodied in our own Declaration of Independence and Constitution. Today, the dual imagery of the social contract and the state of nature remains at the very core of our debates about justice, for example, in the more abstract form of what John Rawls calls "the origi-nal position." Indeed, David Gauthier holds that social contract is so deeply ingrained in our consciousness as to constitute a common ideology.

The selections in Part Two trace the development of modern social contract thinking, from Hobbes's, Locke's, and Rousseau's rival visions of the state of nature to Rawls's more abstract hypothetical choice conception of social justice. Not all of the authors in Part Two endorse the idea of the social contract, or the state of nature, or both. Robert Nozick, for instance, accepts the argument from the state of nature but rejects any reliance on any form of social contract, however hypothetical. Annette Baier admits that contractual relation-ships are important to justice, but argues that any reliance on contract as the central model for justice is bound to distort our account of justice between unequals—between young and old, strong and weak, healthy and sick. And in the deepest of all of these critiques, G. W. F. Hegel, modeling the state-of-nature scenarios employed by Hobbes and Rousseau, tries to show that the very idea of autonomous individuals in a presocial state of nature, even as a hypothetical precursor to society, makes no real sense and in any event is a disastrous start-ing point for social philosophy.

Part Three, "Justice and Society," moves beyond the discussion of the origins of justice into the more contemporary question of the role of justice and its justification in modern soci-ety. Quite apart from the origins of justice, what function does it play in our culture—or in any culture? Is it, as Hobbes insists, an attempt to guarantee security and safety? Is it, as Locke insists, primarily a matter of "convenience" and protection for our natural right to own property? The place and justification of the notion of private property, accordingly, is a cen-tral concern of Part Three, and along with the right to private property the notion of rights in general. So, too, the subject of the public good, the primary concern of that enormously influ-ential moral philosophy called "utilitarianism," is much at issue here. Is social utility in fact the primary object of justice? Is it possibly its *only* object? Or is it, as the critics of utilitari-anism have maintained, incompatible with and antithetical to justice?

The selections in Part Three begin with our own Declaration of Independence and the Bill of Rights (plus selected amendments) to our Constitution. We have then provided readings from John Locke, David Hume, and Adam Smith (his *Theory of the Moral Sentiments* as well as his better known and more influential *Wealth of Nations*) expressing the central concern with private property that characterized traditional modern British social philosophy. We have included an important selection from Kant's *Philosophy of Law*, another excerpt from Hegel (this time from his *Philosophy of Right*), and an excerpt each from Friedrich Engels and Karl Marx that are, predictably, deeply critical of the institution of private property and the injustices it engenders. And we have excerpted a substantial selection from the rightly famous and controversial fifth chapter of John Stuart Mill's *Utilitarianism*.

One of the key presuppositions of utilitarianism, but of most modern social philosophy as well, is that all people are in some essential sense *equal*. But this insistence on equality, as we have already warned, is not clearly compatible with several other crucial ingredients of justice. In particular, it is not obviously compatible with the inevitable inequalities that result from the operations of the free market and is clearly incompatible with the idea of individual merit, in which it is our differences that define justice rather than our similarities. And so to round out Part Three, we have included an excerpt from the Austrian economist Friedrich von Hayek, who argues that the liberties basic to the free market preclude efforts to ensure equality or recognize merit. In contrast, we have included an excerpt from Cambridge-Berkeley philosopher Bernard Williams's "The Idea of Equality," defending that notion. Finally, to put all of this in perspective, we have included a cross-cultural analysis of justice by British sociologist/philosopher David Miller—with the suggestion that there may be no one conception of justice that is valid in very different societies.

Part Four, "Justice and Punishment," involves a shifting of gears into the study of retributive rather than distributive justice—the logic of punishment. As we saw in Part One, justice has long been wrapped up with *punishment,* and punishment with *vengeance.* Contemporary discussions seem, for the most part, to have left vengeance by the wayside. In this part we attempt to correct this bit of historical repression, and to capture the main strands of current debates over the nature and justification of punishment while also keeping in mind the deep historical connections between revenge and retribution. We open with an examination of the Sardinian code of vengeance by Pietro Marongiu and Graeme Newman, and with Robert Nozick's careful attempt to distinguish retribution and revenge. We then consider several accounts of the justification of punishment—not only the historically prominent utilitarian views, argued for by Bentham and John Rawls, and the retributivist views, argued for by Kant and Michael Moore, but also interestingly divergent positions such as Hegel's view of punishment as self-chosen and Hampton's view of punishment as morally educative. We have also included Nietzsche's connection of punishment to the sentiment of resentment (*ressentiment*) and Robert Solomon's account of how undeserved the neglect of vengeance has been in discussions of justified retribution. We close the section with a consideration of that darkest of punishments, the death penalty: we consider both the majority opinion of the Supreme Court, upholding the constitutionality of the death penalty in *Gregg* v. *Georgia,* and the minority's dissent, and we take a look at the three distinct visions of the death penalty offered by Hugo Bedau, Ernest van den Haag, and Albert Camus.

Part Five, "The Contemporary Debate on Distributive Justice," includes a number of selections from and reactions to John Rawls's pioneering work on justice: this is only fitting, as the contemporary debate is largely a debate provoked by Rawls's work and carried out in the terms set by Rawls's account. We begin, then, with Rawls's own view, as laid out in his early "Justice as Fairness," in which some of the basic positions of the book are laid out, and follow with his development of two principles of justice from *A Theory of Justice.*

We then examine critical responses to Rawls's work. Ronald Dworkin and Thomas Nagel are sympathetic with Rawls's basic egalitarian orientation, but have some reservations about how Rawls formulates his view and develops some of his arguments. Robert Nozick, by contrast, is deeply critical of Rawls's view and offers in its stead an account of justice built on the intuitive idea that the justice of a distribution depends not on its structural features but on how it came about. Alasdair MacIntyre suggests that Rawls and Nozick are more alike than different, that their dismissal of desert leaves them open to arbitrariness and inconclusiveness in their arguments that match the arbitrariness and inconclusiveness in our contemporary public debates on justice. Michael Sandel, echoing Hegel's criticism of social contract thinking from Part Two, calls into question the sort of conception of self-hood presupposed by Rawls's view. And Susan Moller Okin wonders whether Rawls's view fails to reckon adequately with matters of gender, while ultimately concluding that a suitably emended Rawlsian view can provide a way for feminists to articulate clearly their criticisms of oppressive social structures. The book concludes, fittingly, with a return to Rawls. Rawls's most recent book on political philosophy, *Political Liberalism,* offers a reconception of the aims of political theory and a corresponding reinterpretation of the account of justice put forward twenty years earlier in *A Theory of Justice.* We include here a selection from an article that lays out a number of the basic ideas of the new Rawlsian view, which has predictably generated a great deal of debate and disagreement, reinvigorating the effort to answer the Socratic question.

This volume is arranged so that readers and instructors will have considerable freedom and flexibility in ordering selections. We have tried as much as possible to keep our own biases and opinions out of both the text and its structure and to avoid current, convenient political labels and other devices that would tend to prejudice the reader one way or another. Needless to say, such evenhandedness in editing, as in justice, is, however desirable, an ideal all but impossible to carry out in practice. But we hope that the result is as fair-minded and representative of the field—and as readable and enjoyable—as possible.

Part One: Classical Sources

Our concept of justice has a long, convoluted history, steeped in philosophy and theology and in ancient practices that no doubt preceded recorded history altogether. Every human society, no doubt, has possessed conceptions of right and wrong; the forbidden, permissible, and commendable; the way things ought to be and the way things ought not to be. The great religious texts of the West—the Old and New Testaments, and the Koran—are about justice, both human and divine, as well as about more spiritual and transcendent matters. The great Homeric epics were not just chauvinist adventure stories but morality tales and lessons in justice. And it is no accident that the question of justice as posed by Socrates in Plato's *Republic* marks something of an official beginning to Western philosophy.

In ancient Greece there were at least two different terms that might be translated into English as *justice: dikaiosune,* usually translated as "justice," and *ison,* better translated as "equality" (Gregory Vlastos, "Justice and Equality," in Brandt, *Social Justice*). The former is graphically represented in Homer's *Iliad.* What Menelaus and Agamemnon mean in the short excerpt that we have included from the *Iliad* is justice as vengeance, indeed justice as legitimate genocide! It is against this background of justice as retribution that we should read Plato's *Republic* and Socrates's inspired defense of what was in fact a radically new conception of justice, justice as social and psychic harmony. Similarly, we find the ferocity of the divine retribution in the Old Testament limited by considerations of justice: Abraham pleads with God, and receives God's assurance, that the innocent in Sodom and Gomorrah will not be punished with the guilty, that for the sake of ten innocents the scores of wicked will be spared. The well-known Old Testament injunction "an eye for an eye, a tooth for a tooth" is not an incitement to brutality but, quite the contrary, an attempt to limit vengeance and punishment to "measure for measure," harming just the culprit instead of, as in the *Iliad,* destroying his or her entire family, tribe, or city. Moving even further away from the vengeance mentality of the *Iliad* is Jesus's emphasis on mercy, on the idea that the righteous person be willing to forgo even this limited reprisal; the Koran, too, exhibits a close relationship between justice and retribution, but consistently tempers retribution with mercy. If even these attenuated connections between justice and retribution strike us—with our own strictly civilian emphasis on distributive justice—as uncivilized, we should remind ourselves that the circumstances in which the ancient codes of justice were formulated were anything but peaceful. That, indeed, makes the antiretributive shift in justice in the great Greek philosophers and in the New Testament all the more remarkable. It also makes the neglect of retribution (and vengeance) in contemporary discussions of justice curious.

Plato's conception of justice as republican community and harmony requires getting rid of the more warlike and cynical images of justice, and this explains the particular importance of the rather belligerent debate with Thrasymachus in Book I of the *Republic.* By the time that Aristotle picks up the discussion a generation later, in his *Nicomachean Ethics,* the centrality of civil justice and justice as a personal virtue, quite apart from questions of power and vengeance, has been established. Aristotle's conception of justice as equality may be easily misunderstood, for while Aristotle was no doubt more of a democrat than Plato and Socrates, he certainly did not have anything in mind like the egalitarian distribution defended by modern liberal and leftist philosophers. Indeed, Aristotle (like Socrates and Plato) was not concerned with what we call "distributive" (or "redistributive") justice at all, but rather with "commutative" justice, that is, the notion of a fair exchange. The central notion is "proportion," and what Aristotle has in mind by "equality" is not that people should be treated equally but rather the near-tautology that like cases should be treated alike and different cases treated differently. But with Aristotle, justice clearly completes the shift from retribution and vengeance to more "domesticated" virtues. We can see this lasting influence over a thousand years later, when Thomas Aquinas, reviewing, defending, and revising Aristotle from a Christian point of view, invokes the long tradition of Aristotelian "natural law," a conception of justice as arising out of the nature of human beings.

It is not just in the West that this struggle between warlike retribution and civil virtues takes place. It is, perhaps, with a due amount of Western humility that we should read Confucius and his disciple Mencius, who encouraged a sense of compassion and understanding when such sentiments were still struggling for recognition in the West, at about the time of Plato and Aristotle. But the Confucian conception of justice embodies another struggle, too, that makes itself evident in the ancient writings of the Mediterranean and the Middle East. That is the struggle for the recognition of a single ultimate authority, whether it be political or divine. In warlike worlds of scattered and mutually antagonistic tribes and city-states, the hunger for such a central authority had to be overwhelming. And so we should not be surprised by the authoritarianism of Plato's *Republic,* any more than we are shocked by the emphasis on divine authority and obedience to God in the Bible or the Koran. In ancient China, too, the appeal to justice was also an appeal to authority, like the appeal to the republic in Plato or to God in the Bible and in the Koran.

Homer, "Agamemnon's Plea for Justice," from the *Iliad* (ca. 800 B.C.)

Homer probably lived in Asia Minor around 800 BC, at least 400 years after the bitter war in Troy that he so vividly describes in the *Iliad*. There is considerable controversy about his life, his dates, his authorship, and indeed his very existence, for it has often been argued that there was no single poet named "Homer" who was the author of the *Iliad* and the *Odyssey*. The concept of justice as vengeance threads through the *Iliad* as part of its essential plot, from the opening offense of Agamemnon (kidnapping Apollo's priestess, Chryseis), for which Apollo takes his revenge, and Paris's taking of Helen (whom he had justly won as a prize from Aphrodite), to the wholesale act of revenge visited by the combined Greek forces on Paris's home-city of Troy. The action of the *Iliad* is largely defined by such acts of injustice and retribution, and in the brief passage that follows, Agamemnon summarizes a brutal ancient notion of justice (*dike*). The excerpt is taken from Book Six, in the midst of a ferocious battle between the Achaians and the Trojans.

Now Menelaos of the great war cry captured Adrestos
alive; for his two horses bolting over the level land
got entangled in a tamarisk growth, and shattered the curving
chariot at the tip of the pole; so they broken free went
on toward the city, where many beside stampeded in terror.
So Adrestos was whirled beside the wheel from the chariot
headlong into the dust on his face; and the son of Atreus,
Menelaos, with the far-shadowed spear in his hand, stood over him.
But Adrestos, catching him by the knees, supplicated:
'Take me alive, son of Atreus, and take appropriate ransom.
In my rich father's house the treasures lie piled in abundance;
bronze is there, and gold, and difficultly wrought iron,
and my father would make you glad with abundant repayment
were he to hear that I am alive by the ships of the Achaians.'
So he spoke, and moved the spirit inside Menelaos.
And now he was on the point of handing him to a henchman
to lead back to the fast Achaian ships; but Agamemnon
came on the run to join him and spoke his word of argument:
'Dear brother, o Menelaos, are you concerned so tenderly
with these people? Did you in your house get the best of treatment
from the Trojans? No, let not one of them go free of sudden

death and our hands; not the young man child that the mother carries
still in her body, not even he, but let all of Ilion's
people perish, utterly blotted out and unmourned for.'
     The hero spoke like this, and bent the heart of his brother
since he urged justice. Menelaos shoved with his hand Adrestos
the warrior back from him, and powerful Agamemnon
stabbed him in the side.

"Justice, Equality, and Desert," from the Bible (Old and New Testaments)

The books that we know as the Bible were written over a substantial period of time, by a great many writers, from the Five Books of Moses (the Pentateuch or Torah), which is now thought to have been written well before 1000 BC, to the last book of the New Testament, the book of Revelation, which was probably completed between 81 and 96 AD. What is presented in the Old and New Testaments is an unwavering standard of justice, one that lays down demands on the high and the low alike, and one that protects both the strong and the weak, the rich and the poor. God lays down His law for Adam and Eve; when it is broken by them, death enters the world, and Adam and Eve are cast out of Eden. The wickedness of Sodom and Gomorrah evokes God's destruction, but God promises Abraham that He will not sweep away the innocent with the guilty. With the New Testament, the emphasis on obedience to God's law through outward acts is supplemented by a further demand to conform one's attitudes and desires to God's commands, and to be forgiving and loving to those who do one wrong. To those who follow Christ, mercy for one's transgressions is promised; but to those who reject Him, the full force of divine punishment will be felt.

Genesis 3: 1–24

Now the serpent was more crafty than any of the wild animals the Lord God had made. He said to the woman, "Did God really say, 'You must not eat from any tree in the garden'?"

[2]The woman said to the serpent, "We may eat fruit from the trees in the garden, [3]but God did say, 'You must not eat fruit from the tree that is in the middle of the garden, and you must not touch it, or you will die.'"

[4]"You will not surely die," the serpent said to the woman. [5]"For God knows that when you eat of it your eyes will be opened, and you will be like God, knowing good and evil."

[6]When the woman saw that the fruit of the tree was good for food and pleasing to the eye, and also desirable for gaining wisdom, she took some and ate it. She also gave some to her husband, who was with her, and he ate it. [7]Then the eyes of both of them were opened, and they realized they were naked; so they sewed fig leaves together and made coverings for themselves.

[8]Then the man and his wife heard the sound of the Lord God as he was walking in the garden in the cool of the day, and they hid from the Lord God among the trees of the garden. [9]But the Lord God called to the man, "Where are you?"

[10]He answered, "I heard you in the garden, and I was afraid because I was naked; so I hid."

[11]And he said, "Who told you that you were naked? Have you eaten from the tree that I commanded you not to eat from?"

[12]The man said, "The woman you put here with me—she gave me some fruit from the tree, and I ate it."

[13]Then the Lord God said to the woman, "What is this you have done?"

The woman said, "The serpent deceived me, and I ate."

[14]So the Lord God said to the serpent, "Because you have done this,

> "Cursed are you above all the livestock
> and all the wild animals!
> You will crawl on your belly
> and you will eat dust
> all the days of your life.
> [15]And I will put enmity
> between you and the woman,
> and between your offspring and hers;
> he will crush your head,
> and you will strike his heel."

[16]To the woman he said,

> "I will greatly increase your pains in childbearing;
> with pain you will give birth to children.
> Your desire will be for your husband,
> and he will rule over you."

[17]To Adam he said, "Because you listened to your wife and ate from the tree about which I commanded you, 'You must not eat of it,'

> "Cursed is the ground because of you;
> through painful toil you will eat of it
> all the days of your life.
> [18]It will produce thorns and thistles for you,
> and you will eat the plants of the field.
> [19]By the sweat of your brow
> you will eat your food

> until you return to the ground,
> since from it you were taken;
> for dust you are
> and to dust you will return."

[20]Adam named his wife Eve, because she would become the mother of all the living.

[21]The Lord God made garments of skin for Adam and his wife and clothed them. [22]And the Lord God said, "The man has now become like one of us, knowing good and evil. He must not be allowed to reach out his hand and take also from the tree of life and eat, and live forever." [23]So the Lord God banished him from the Garden of Eden to work the ground from which he had been taken. [24]After he drove the man out, he placed on the east side of the Garden of Eden cherubim and a flaming sword flashing back and forth to guard the way to the tree of life.

Genesis 18: 20–33, 19: 1–28

[20]Then the Lord said, "The outcry against Sodom and Gomorrah is so great and their sin so grievous [21]that I will go down and see if what they have done is as bad as the outcry that has reached me. If not, I will know."

[22]The men turned away and went toward Sodom, but Abraham remained standing before the Lord. [23]Then Abraham approached him and said: "Will you sweep away the righteous with the wicked? [24]What if there are fifty righteous people in the city? Will you really sweep it away and not spare the place for the sake of the fifty righteous people in it? [25]Far be it from you to do such a thing—to kill the righteous with the wicked, treating the righteous and the wicked alike. Far be it from you! Will not the Judge of all the earth do right?"

[26]The Lord said, "If I find fifty righteous people in the city of Sodom, I will spare the whole place for their sake."

[27]Then Abraham spoke up again: "Now that I have been so bold as to speak to the Lord, though I am nothing but dust and ashes, [28]what if the number of the righteous is five less than fifty? Will you destroy the whole city because of five people?"

"If I find forty-five there," he said, "I will not destroy it."

[29]Once again he spoke to him, "What if only forty are found there?"

He said, "For the sake of forty, I will not do it."

[30]Then he said, "May the Lord not be angry, but let me speak. What if only thirty can be found there?"

He answered, "I will not do it if I find thirty there."

[31]Abraham said, "Now that I have been so bold as to speak to the Lord, what if only twenty can be found there?"

He said, "For the sake of twenty, I will not destroy it."

[32]Then he said, "May the Lord not be angry, but let me speak just once more. What if only ten can be found there?"

He answered, "For the sake of ten, I will not destroy it."

[33] When the Lord had finished speaking with Abraham, he left, and Abraham returned home.

The two angels arrived at Sodom in the evening, and Lot was sitting in the gateway of the city. When he saw them, he got up to meet them and bowed down with his face to the ground. [2]"My lords," he said, "please turn aside to your servant's house. You can wash your feet and spend the night and then go on your way early in the morning."

"No," they answered, "we will spend the night in the square."

[3]But he insisted so strongly that they did go with him and entered his house. He prepared a meal for them, baking bread without yeast, and they ate. [4]Before they had gone to bed, all the men from every part of the city of Sodom—both young and old—surrounded the house. [5]They called to Lot, "Where are the men who came to you tonight? Bring them out to us so that we can have sex with them."

[6]Lot went outside to meet them and shut the door behind him [7]and said, "No, my friends. Don't do this wicked thing. [8]Look, I have two daughters who have never slept with a man. Let me bring them out to you, and you can do what you like with them. But don't do anything to these men, for they have come under the protection of my roof."

[9]"Get out of our way," they replied. And they said, "This fellow came here as an alien, and now he wants to play the judge! We'll treat you worse than them." They kept bringing pressure on Lot and moved forward to break down the door.

[10]But the men inside reached out and pulled Lot back into the house and shut the door. [11]Then they struck the men who were at the door of the house, young and old, with blindness so that they could not find the door.

[12]The two men said to Lot, "Do you have anyone else here—sons-in-law, sons or daughters, or anyone else in the city who belongs to you? Get them out of here, [13]because we are going to destroy this place. The outcry to the Lord against its people is so great that he has sent us to destroy it."

[14]So Lot went out and spoke to his sons-in-law, who were pledged to marry his daughters. He said, "Hurry and get out of this place, because the Lord is about to destroy the city!" But his sons-in-law thought he was joking.

[15]With the coming of dawn, the angels urged Lot, saying, "Hurry! Take your wife and your two daughters who are here, or you will be swept away when the city is punished."

[16]When he hesitated, the men grasped his hand and the hands of his wife and of his two daughters and led them safely out of the city, for the Lord was merciful to them. [17]As soon as they had brought them out, one of them said, "Flee for your lives! Don't look back, and don't stop anywhere in the plain! Flee to the mountains or you will be swept away!"

[18]But Lot said to them, "No, my lords, please! [19]Your servant has found favor in your eyes, and you have shown great kindness to me in sparing my life. But I can't flee to the mountains; this disaster will overtake me, and I'll die. [20]Look, here is a town near enough to run to, and it is small. Let me flee to it—it is very small, isn't it? Then my life will be spared."

[21]He said to him, "Very well, I will grant this request too; I will not overthrow the town you speak of. [22]But flee there quickly, because I cannot do anything until you reach it." (That is why the town was called Zoar.)

[23]By the time Lot reached Zoar, the sun had risen over the land. [24]Then the Lord rained down burning sulfur on Sodom and Gomorrah—from the Lord out of the heavens. [25]Thus he overthrew those cities and the entire plain, including all those living in the cities—and also the vegetation in the land.

[26]But Lot's wife looked back, and she became a pillar of salt.

[27]Early the next morning Abraham got up and returned to the place where he had stood before the Lord. [28]He looked down toward Sodom and Gomorrah, toward all the land of the plain, and he saw dense smoke rising from the land, like smoke from a furnace.

Leviticus 24: 17–22

[17]" 'If anyone takes the life of a human being, he must be put to death. [18]Anyone who takes the life of someone's animal must make restitution—life for life. [19]If anyone injures his neighbor, whatever he has done must be done to him: [20]fracture for fracture, eye for eye, tooth for tooth. As he has injured the other, so he is to be injured. [21]Whoever kills an animal must make restitution, but whoever kills a man must be put to death. [22]You are to have the same law for the alien and the native-born. I am the Lord your God.'"

Matthew 5: 1–12, 38–42

Now when he saw the crowds, he went up on a mountainside and sat down. His disciples came to him, [2]and he began to teach them, saying:

> [3]"Blessed are the poor in spirit,
> for theirs is the kingdom of heaven.
> [4]Blessed are those who mourn,
> for they will be comforted.
> [5]Blessed are the meek,
> for they will inherit the earth.
> [6]Blessed are those who hunger and thirst for righteousness,
> for they will be filled.
> [7]Blessed are the merciful,
> for they will be shown mercy.
> [8]Blessed are the pure in heart,
> for they will see God.
> [9]Blessed are the peacemakers,
> for they will be called sons of God.
> [10]Blessed are those who are persecuted because of righteousness,
> for theirs is the kingdom of heaven.

[11]"Blessed are you when people insult you, persecute you and falsely say all kinds of evil against you because of me. [12]Rejoice and be glad, because great is your reward in heaven, for in the same way they persecuted the prophets who were before you. . . ."

[38]"You have heard that it was said, 'Eye for eye, and tooth for tooth.' [39]But I tell you, Do not resist an evil person. If someone strikes you on the right cheek, turn to him the other also. [40]And if someone wants to sue you and take your tunic, let him have your cloak as well. [41]If someone forces you to go one mile, go with him two miles. [42]Give to the one who asks you, and do not turn away from the one who wants to borrow from you."

Luke 15: 11–32

[11]Jesus continued: "There was a man who had two sons. [12]The younger one said to his father, 'Father, give me my share of the estate.' So he divided his property between them.

[13]"Not long after that, the younger son got together all he had, set off for a distant country and there squandered his wealth in wild living. [14]After he had spent everything, there was a severe famine in that whole country, and he began to be in need. [15]So he went

and hired himself out to a citizen of that country, who sent him to his fields to feed pigs. [16]He longed to fill his stomach with the pods that the pigs were eating, but no one gave him anything.

[17]"When he came to his senses, he said, 'How many of my father's hired men have food to spare, and here I am starving to death! [18]I will set out and go back to my father and say to him: Father, I have sinned against heaven and against you. [19]I am no longer worthy to be called your son; make me like one of your hired men.' [20]So he got up and went to his father.

"But while he was still a long way off, his father saw him and was filled with compassion for him; he ran to his son, threw his arms around him and kissed him.

[21]"The son said to him, 'Father, I have sinned against heaven and against you. I am no longer worthy to be called your son.'"

[22]"But the father said to his servants, 'Quick! Bring the best robe and put it on him. Put a ring on his finger and sandals on his feet. [23]Bring the fattened calf and kill it. Let's have a feast and celebrate. [24]For this son of mine was dead and is alive again; he was lost and is found.' So they began to celebrate."

[25]"Meanwhile, the older son was in the field. When he came near the house, he heard music and dancing. [26]So he called one of the servants and asked him what was going on. [27]'Your brother has come,' he replied, 'and your father has killed the fattened calf because he has him back safe and sound.'

[28]"The older brother became angry and refused to go in. So his father went out and pleaded with him. [29]But he answered his father, 'Look! All these years I've been slaving for you and never disobeyed your orders. Yet you never gave me even a young goat so I could celebrate with my friends. [30]But when this son of yours who has squandered your property with prostitutes comes home, you kill the fattened calf for him!'

[31]"'My son,' the father said, 'you are always with me, and everything I have is yours. [32]But we had to celebrate and be glad, because this brother of yours was dead and is alive again; he was lost and is found.'"

Matthew 25: 14–46

[14][Jesus said,] "Again, it will be like a man going on a journey, who called his servants and entrusted his property to them. [15]To one he gave five talents of money, to another two talents, and to another one talent, each according to his ability. Then he went on his journey. [16]The man who had received the five talents went at once and put his money to work and gained five more. [17]So also, the one with the two talents gained two more. [18]But the man who had received the one talent went off, dug a hole in the ground and hid his master's money.

[19]"After a long time the master of those servants returned and settled accounts with them. [20]The man who had received the five talents brought the other five. 'Master,' he said, 'you entrusted me with five talents. See, I have gained five more.'

[21]"His master replied, 'Well done, good and faithful servant! You have been faithful with a few things; I will put you in charge of many things. Come and share your master's happiness!'

[22]"The man with the two talents also came. 'Master,' he said, 'you entrusted me with two talents; see, I have gained two more.'

[23]"His master replied, 'Well done, good and faithful servant! You have been faithful

with a few things; I will put you in charge of many things. Come and share your master's happiness!'

[24]"Then the man who had received the one talent came. 'Master,' he said, 'I knew that you are a hard man, harvesting where you have not sown and gathering where you have not scattered seed. [25]So I was afraid and went out and hid your talent in the ground. See, here is what belongs to you.'

[26]"His master replied, 'You wicked, lazy servant! So you knew that I harvest where I have not sown and gather where I have not scattered seed? [27]Well then, you should have put my money on deposit with the bankers, so that when I returned I would have received it back with interest.

[28]" 'Take the talent from him and give it to the one who has the ten talents. [29]For everyone who has will be given more, and he will have an abundance. Whoever does not have, even what he has will be taken from him. [30]And throw that worthless servant outside, into the darkness, where there will be weeping and gnashing of teeth.'

[31]"When the Son of Man comes in his glory, and all the angels with him, he will sit on his throne in heavenly glory. [32]All the nations will be gathered before him, and he will separate the people one from another as a shepherd separates the sheep from the goats. [33]He will put the sheep on his right and the goats on his left.

[34]"Then the King will say to those on his right, 'Come, you who are blessed by my Father; take your inheritance, the kingdom prepared for you since the creation of the world. [35]For I was hungry and you gave me something to eat, I was thirsty and you gave me something to drink, I was a stranger and you invited me in, [36]I needed clothes and you clothed me, I was sick and you looked after me, I was in prison and you came to visit me.'

[37]"Then the righteous will answer him, 'Lord, when did we see you hungry and feed you, or thirsty and give you something to drink? [38]When did we see you a stranger and invite you in, or needing clothes and clothe you? [39]When did we see you sick or in prison and go to visit you?'

[40]"The King will reply, 'I tell you the truth, whatever you did for one of the least of these brothers of mine, you did for me.'

[41]"Then he will say to those on his left, 'Depart from me, you who are cursed, into the eternal fire prepared for the devil and his angels. [42]For I was hungry and you gave me nothing to eat, I was thirsty and you gave me nothing to drink, [43]I was a stranger and you did not invite me in, I needed clothes and you did not clothe me, I was sick and in prison and you did not look after me.'

[44]"They also will answer, 'Lord, when did we see you hungry or thirsty or a stranger or needing clothes or sick or in prison, and did not help you?'

[45]"He will reply, 'I tell you the truth, whatever you did not do for one of the least of these, you did not do for me.'

[46]"Then they will go away to eternal punishment, but the righteous to eternal life."

Plato, "Justice in the State and in the Soul," from the *Republic* (ca. 380 B.C)

In the *Republic* Plato (427–347 BC) canonized the question, "What is justice?," as one of the leading questions of philosophy. Plato portrays his teacher Socrates as engaging in casual conversation with some of his colleagues in the Athenian marketplace, during which (as often occurs in a Socratic dialogue) Socrates focuses the discussion on a matter of deep moral interest, that is, the definition of justice, and probes it extensively and critically—much to the frustration of some of his interlocutors. The conversation with Cephalus, which begins the discussion, is short and inconclusive. Cephalus suggests that justice is paying one's debts and giving to each his or her due, and Socrates quickly shows him that it would not be just to pay a debt—say, of arms—to a wicked or crazed man. Cephalus, a grand and kindly old man, makes it quite clear that he is not quite up to the rigors of a philosophical argument, and politely excuses himself from the discussion. The next excerpt is the famous exchange between Socrates and Thrasymachus, who argues that justice is nothing but the interests of the strong. Socrates catches Thrasymachus in a contradiction, and Thrasymachus, his conversation already punctuated by insults, leaves with a final rebuff. The subsequent dialogue with Glaucon—which in fact continues for the remainder of the book—concerns the question, "Why should one be just?" Using the fabled "Ring of Gyges" as his example, Glaucon suggests that people would not be just if they could in fact get away with being unjust. Socrates is determined to argue, against Glaucon's sincere skepticism, that it is good to be just, for its own sake, and good for the just person, as well. Finally, we have included a short excerpt from Book IV, in which Plato offers us his own theory of justice, the twin ideal of the various parts of the republic and the various parts of the individual soul each doing their own assigned tasks and working together in harmony.

We should note a problem of language here, which introduces an enormous problem for the study of justice, not only through the ages and among cultures but even within a single society. There are at least two different words employed by the Greeks whose meaning is akin to our concept of justice, yet neither of them translates easily and precisely into an English equivalent. The problem is as much political as linguistic. On the one hand, there is *to eson* or *isotes*, which means "equality," but which (according to the dean of Plato scholars Gregory Vlastos) is also the most common word for "justice." Then there is *dikaiosune*—the word that Plato and Aristotle use for justice, which more properly means "righteousness." Thus many of the odder things that Plato and Aristotle worry about, such as whether justice is complete virtue or only one of the virtues, and Plato's central thesis that justice is "performing the function(s) for which one's nature is best fitted," makes more sense with "righteousness" than with justice. But then, one might well wonder whether we are talking about what we think of as justice at all. Moreover, insofar as justice means "equality," it is more than odd that both Plato and Aristotle notoriously defend inegalitarian views of justice. For example, Plato sums up his dismissal of democracy in a single line: "distributing an odd sort of equality to equals and unequals" (*Republic*, 558c). Sir Karl Popper was thus driven to exasperation when he asked, "Why did Plato claim that justice meant inequality if, in general usage, it meant equality?" and answered, "To make propaganda for his totalitarian state" (*The Open Society and Its Enemies*, London, 1949, p. 79). The meaning of "equality" with respect to justice will be one of the continuing concerns of this volume, and we will discuss its particular difficulties in Greek philosophy when we come to Aristotle in the next selection. But the divergence of meaning and the problem of translation should be kept in mind when reading Plato, too, and any comparisons with what we would ordinarily say about justice should thus be cautiously considered. Indeed, it is clear that, even within the same culture and same language, the Greeks do not agree on the proper usage or interpretation of these sensitive terms; and neither, in our own culture and language, do we.

[Cephalus describes the benefits and burdens of old age to Socrates] if it is moderate and contented, then old age too is but moderately burdensome; if it is not, then both old age and youth are hard to bear.

I [Socrates, who is the narrator] wondered at his saying this and I wanted him to say more, so I urged him on by saying: Cephalus, when you say this, I don't think most people would agree with you; they think you endure old age easily not because of your manner of life but because you are wealthy, for the wealthy, they say, have many things to encourage them.

What you say is true, he said. They would not agree. And there is something in what they say, but not as much as they think. What Themistocles said is quite right: when a man from Seriphus was insulting him by saying that his high reputation was due to his city and not to himself, he replied that, had he been a Seriphian, he would not be famous, but neither would the other had he been an Athenian. The same can be applied to those who are not rich and find old age hard to bear—namely that a good man would not very easily bear old age in poverty, nor would a bad man, even if wealthy, be at peace with himself.

Did you inherit most of your wealth, Cephalus, I asked, or did you acquire it?

How much did I acquire, Socrates? As a moneymaker I stand between my grandfather and my father. My grandfather and namesake inherited about the same amount of wealth which I possess but multiplied it many times. My father, Lysanias, however, diminished that amount to even less than I have now. As for me, I am satisfied to leave to my sons here no less but a little more than I inherited.

The reason I asked, said I, is that you did not seem to me to be overfond of money, and this is generally the case with those who have not made it themselves. Those who have acquired it by their own efforts are twice as fond of it as other men. Just as poets love their own poems and fathers love their children, so those who have made their money are attached to it as something they have made themselves, besides using it as other men do. This makes them poor company, for they are unwilling to give their approval to anything but money.

What you say is true, he said.

It surely is, said I. Now tell me this much more: What is the greatest benefit you have received from the enjoyment of wealth?

I would probably not convince many people in saying this, Socrates, he said, but you must realize that when a man approaches the time when he thinks he will die, he becomes fearful and concerned about things which he did not fear before. It is then that the stories we are told about the underworld, which he ridiculed before—that the man who has sinned here will pay the penalty there—torture his mind lest they be true. Whether because of the weakness of old age, or because he is now closer to what happens there and has a clearer view, the man himself is filled with suspicion and fear, and he now takes account and examines whether he has wronged anyone. If he finds many sins in his own life, he awakes from sleep in terror, as children do, and he lives with the expectation of evil. However, the man who knows he has not sinned has a sweet and good hope as his constant companion, a nurse to his old age, as Pindar too puts it. The poet has expressed this charmingly, Socrates, that whoever lives a just and pious life

> Sweet is the hope that nurtures his heart,
> companion and nurse to his old age,
> a hope which governs the rapidly changing thoughts of mortals.

This is wonderfully well said. It is in this connection that I would say that wealth has its greatest value, not for everyone but for a good and well-balanced man. Not to have lied to or deceived anyone even unwillingly, not to depart yonder in fear, owing either sacrifices to a god or money to a man: to this wealth makes a great contribution. It has many other uses, but benefit for benefit I would say that its greatest usefulness lies in this for an intelligent man, Socrates.

Beautifully spoken, Cephalus, said I, but are we to say that justice or right is simply to speak the truth and to pay back any debt one may have contracted? Or are these same actions sometimes right and sometimes wrong? I mean this sort of thing, for example: everyone would surely agree that if a friend has deposited weapons with you when he was sane, and he asks for them when he is out of his mind, you should not return them. The man who returns them is not doing right, nor is one who is willing to tell the whole truth to a man in such a state.

What you say is correct, he answered.

This then is not a definition of right or justice, namely to tell the truth and pay one's debts.

It certainly is, said Polemarchus interrupting, if we are to put any trust in Simonides.

And now, said Cephalus, I leave the argument to you, for I must go back and look after the sacrifice.

Do I then inherit your role? asked Polemarchus.

You certainly do, said Cephalus laughing, and as he said it he went off to sacrifice.

Then do tell us, Polemarchus, said I, as the heir to the argument, what it is that Simonides stated about justice which you consider to be correct.

He stated, said he, that it is just to give to each what is owed to him, and I think he was right to say so.

Well now, I said, it is hard not to believe Simonides, for he is a wise and inspired man, but what does he mean? Perhaps you understand him, but I do not. Clearly he does not mean what we were saying just now, that anything he has deposited must be returned to a man who is not in his right mind; yet anything he has deposited is owing to him. Is that not so?—Yes.

But it is not to be returned to him at all if he is out of his mind when he asks for it?—That's true.

Certainly Simonides meant something different from this when he says that to return what is owed is just.

He did indeed mean something different by Zeus, said he. He believes that one owes it to one's friends to do good to them, and not harm.

I understand, said I, that one does not give what is owed or due if one gives back gold to a depositor, when giving back and receiving are harmful, and the two are friends. Is that not what you say Simonides meant?—Quite.

Well then, should one give what is due to one's enemies?

By all means, said he, what is in fact due to them, and I believe that is what is properly due from an enemy to an enemy, namely something harmful.

It seems, I said, that Simonides was suggesting the nature of the just poetically and in riddles. For he thought this to be just, to give to each man what is proper to him, and he called this what is due.—Surely. . . .

When you say friends, do you mean those whom a man believes to be helpful to him, or those who are helpful even if they do not appear to be so, and so with enemies?

Probably, he said, one is fond of those whom one thinks to be good and helpful to one, and one hates those whom one considers bad and harmful.

Surely people make mistakes about this, and consider many to be helpful when they are not, and often make the opposite mistake about enemies?—They do.

Then good men are their enemies, and bad people their friends?—Quite so.

And so it is just and right for these mistaken people to benefit the bad and harm the good?—It seems so.

But the good are just and able to do no wrong?—True.

But according to your argument it is just to harm those who do no wrong.

Never, Socrates, he said. It is the argument that is wrong.

It is just to harm the wrongdoers and to benefit the just?

That statement, Socrates, seems much more attractive than the other.

Then, Polemarchus, for many who are mistaken in their judgment it follows that it is just to harm their friends, for these are bad, and to benefit their enemies, who are good, and so we come to a conclusion which is the opposite of what we said was the meaning of Simonides.

That certainly follows, he said, but let us change our assumption; we have probably not defined the friend and the enemy correctly.

Where were we mistaken, Polemarchus?

When we said that a friend was one who was thought to be helpful.

How shall we change this now? I asked.

Let us state, he said, that a friend is one who is both thought to be helpful and also is; one who is thought to be, but is not, helpful is thought to be a friend but is not. And so also with the enemy.

According to this argument then, the good man will be a friend, and the bad man an enemy.—Yes.

You want us to add to what we said before about the just, namely that it is just to benefit one's friend and harm one's enemy; to this you want us to make an addition and say that it is just to benefit the friend who is good and to harm the enemy who is bad?

Quite so, he said. This seems to me to be well said.

But, I said, is it the part of the just man to harm anyone at all?

Why certainly, he said, those who are bad and one's enemies.

Do horses become better or worse when they are harmed?—Worse. . . .

Shall we not say so about men too, that when they are harmed they deteriorate in their human excellence?—Quite so.

And is not justice a human excellence?—Of course.

Then men who are harmed, my friend, necessarily become more unjust.—So it appears. . . .

Well then, can the just, by the practice of justice, make men unjust? Or, in a word, can good men, by the practice of their virtue, make men bad?—They cannot. . . .

It is not then the function of the just man, Polemarchus, to do harm to a friend or anyone else, but it is that of his opposite, the unjust man?—I think that you are entirely right, Socrates.

If, then, anyone tells us that it is just to give everyone his due, and he means by this that from the just man harm is due to his enemies and benefit due to his friends—the man who says that is not wise, for it is not true. We have shown that it is never just to harm anyone.—I agree. . . .

While we were speaking Thrasymachus often started to interrupt, but he was restrained by those who were sitting by him, for they wanted to hear the argument to the end. But when we paused after these last words of mine he could no longer keep quiet. He gathered himself together like a wild beast about to spring, and he came at us as if to tear us to pieces.

Polemarchus and I were afraid and flustered as he roared into the middle of our company: What nonsense have you two been talking, Socrates? Why do you play the fool in thus giving way to each other? If you really want to know what justice is, don't only ask questions and then score off anyone who answers, and refute him. You know very well that it is much easier to ask questions than to answer them. Give an answer yourself and tell us what you say justice is. And don't tell me that it is the needful, or the advantageous, or the beneficial, or the gainful, or the useful, but tell me clearly and precisely what you mean, for I will not accept it if you utter such rubbish.

His words startled me, and glancing at him I was afraid. I think if I had not looked at him before he looked at me, I should have been speechless. As it was I had glanced at him first when our discussion began to exasperate him, so I was able to answer him and I said, trembling: do not be hard on us, Thrasymachus, if we have erred in our investigation, he and I; be sure that we err unwillingly. You surely do not believe that if we were searching for gold we would be unwilling to give way to each other and thus destroy our chance of finding it, but that when searching for justice, a thing more precious than much gold, we mindlessly give way to one another, and that we are not thoroughly in earnest about finding it. You must believe that, my friend, for I think we could not do it. So it is much more seemly that you clever people should pity us than that you should be angry with us.

When he heard that he gave a loud and bitter laugh and said: By Heracles, that is just Socrates' usual irony. I knew this, and I warned these men here before that you would not be willing to answer any questions but would pretend ignorance, and that you would do anything rather than give an answer, if anyone questioned you. . . .

Listen then, said he. I say that the just is nothing else than the advantage of the stronger. Well, why don't you praise me? But you will not want to.

I must first understand your meaning, said I, for I do not know it yet. You say that the advantage of the stronger is just. What do you mean, Thrasymachus? Surely you do not mean such a thing as this: Poulydamas, the pancratist athlete, is stronger than we are; it is to his advantage to eat beef to build up his physical strength. Do you mean that this food is also advantageous and just for us who are weaker than he is?

You disgust me, Socrates, he said. Your trick is always to take up the argument at the point where you can damage it most.

Not at all, my dear sir, I said, but tell us more clearly what you mean.

Do you not know, he said, that some cities are ruled by a despot, others by the people, and others again by the aristocracy?—Of course.

And this element has the power and rules in every city?—Certainly.

Yes, and each government makes laws to its own advantage: democracy makes democratic laws, a despotism makes despotic laws, and so with the others, and when they have made these laws they declare this to be just for their subjects, that is, their own advantage, and they punish him who transgresses the laws as lawless and unjust. This then, my good man, is what I say justice is, the same in all cities, the advantage of the established government, and correct reasoning will conclude that the just is the same everywhere, the advantage of the stronger.

Now I see what you mean, I said. Whether it is true or not I will try to find out. But you too, Thrasymachus, have given as an answer that the just is the advantageous whereas you forbade that answer to me. True, you have added the words "of the stronger."

Perhaps, he said, you consider that an insignificant addition!

It is not clear yet whether or not it is significant. Obviously, we must investigate whether what you say is true. I agree that the just is some kind of advantage, but you add that it is the advantage of the stronger. I do not know. We must look into this.—Go on looking, he said.

We will do so, said I. Tell me, do you also say that obedience to the rulers is just?—I do.

And are the rulers in all cities infallible, or are they liable to error?—No doubt they are liable to error.

When they undertake to make laws, therefore, they make some correctly and make others incorrectly?—I think so.

"Correctly" means that they make laws to their own advantage, and "incorrectly" not to their own advantage. Or how would you put it?—As you do.

And whatever laws they make must be obeyed by their subjects, and this is just?—Of course.

Then, according to your argument, it is just to do not only what is to the advantage of the stronger, but also the opposite, what is not to their advantage.

What is that you are saying? he asked.

The same as you, I think, but let us examine it more fully. Have we not agreed that, in giving orders to their subjects, the rulers are sometimes in error as to what is best for themselves, yet it is just for their subjects to do whatever their rulers order. Is that much agreed?—I think so.

Think then also, said I, that you have agreed that it is just to do what is to the disadvantage of the rulers and the stronger whenever they unintentionally give orders which are bad for themselves, and you say it is just for the others to obey their given orders. Does it not of necessity follow, my wise Thrasymachus, that it is just to do the opposite of what you said? The weaker are then ordered to do what is to the disadvantage of the stronger.

Yes by Zeus, Socrates, said Polemarchus, that is quite clear.

Yes, if you bear witness for him, interrupted Cleitophon.

What need of a witness? said Polemarchus. Thrasymachus himself agrees that the rulers sometimes give orders that are bad for themselves, and that it is just to obey them.

Thrasymachus maintained that it is just to obey the orders of the rulers, Polemarchus.

He also said that the just was the advantage of the stronger, Cleitophon. Having established those two points he went on to agree that the stronger sometimes ordered the weaker, their subjects, to do what was disadvantageous to themselves. From these agreed premises it follows that what is of advantage to the stronger is no more just than what is not.

But, Cleitophon replied, he said that the advantage of the stronger is what the stronger believes to be of advantage to him. This the weaker must do, and that is what he defined the just to be. . . .

When we reached this point in our argument and it was clear to all that the definition of justice had turned into its opposite, Thrasymachus, instead of answering, said: Tell me, Socrates, do you have a nanny?

What's this? said I. Had you not better answer than ask such questions?

Because, he said, she is letting you go around with a snotty nose and does not wipe it when she needs to, if she leaves you without any knowledge of sheep or shepherds.

What is the particular point of that remark? I asked.

You think, he said, that shepherds and cowherds seek the good of their sheep or cattle, whereas their sole purpose in fattening them and looking after them is their own good and that of their master. Moreover, you believe that rulers in the cities, true rulers that is, have a different attitude towards their subjects than one has towards sheep, and that they think of anything else, night and day, than their own advantage. You are so far from understanding the nature of justice and the just, of injustice and the unjust, that you do not realize that the just is really another's good, the advantage of the stronger and the ruler, but for the inferior who obeys it is a personal injury. Injustice on the other hand exercises its power over those who are truly naive and just, and those over whom it rules do what is of advantage to the other, the stronger, and, by obeying him, they make him happy, but themselves not in the least.

You must look at it in this way, my naive Socrates: the just is everywhere at a disadvantage compared with the unjust. First, in their contracts with one another: wherever two such men are associated you will never find, when the partnership ends, the just man to have more than the unjust, but less. Then, in their relation to the city: when taxes are to be paid, from the same income the just man pays more, the other less; but, when benefits are to be received, the one gets nothing while the other profits much; whenever each of them holds a public office, the just man, even if he is not penalized in other ways, finds that his private affairs deteriorate through neglect while he gets nothing from the public purse because he is just; moreover, he is disliked by his household and his acquaintances whenever he refuses them an unjust favour. The opposite is true of the unjust man in every respect. I repeat what I said before: the man of great power gets the better deal. Consider him if you want to decide how much more it benefits him privately to be unjust rather than just. You will see this most easily if you turn your thoughts to the most complete form of injustice which brings the greatest happiness to the wrongdoer, while it makes those whom he wronged, and who are not willing to do wrong, most wretched. This most complete form is despotism; it does not appropriate other people's property little by little, whether secretly or by force, whether public or private, whether sacred objects or temple property, but appropriates it all at once.

When a wrongdoer is discovered in petty cases, he is punished and faces great opprobrium, for the perpetrators of these petty crimes are called temple robbers, kidnappers, housebreakers, robbers, and thieves, but when a man, besides appropriating the possessions of the citizens, manages to enslave the owners as well, then, instead of those ugly names he is called happy and blessed, not only by his fellow-citizens but by all others who learn that he has run through the whole gamut of injustice. Those who give injustice a bad name do so because they are afraid, not of practising but of suffering injustice.

And so, Socrates, injustice, if it is on a large enough scale, is a stronger, freer, and more powerful thing than justice and, as I said from the first, the just is what is advantageous to the stronger, while the unjust is to one's own advantage and benefit.

Having said this and poured this mass of close-packed words into our ears as a bath-man might a flood of water, Thrasymachus intended to leave, but those present did not let him, and made him stay for a discussion of his views. I too begged him to stay and I said: My dear Thrasymachus, after throwing such a speech at us, you want to leave before adequately instructing us or finding out whether you are right or not? Or do you think it a small thing to decide on a whole way of living, which, if each of us adopted it, would make him live the most profitable life?

Come then, Thrasymachus, I said, answer us from the beginning. You say that complete injustice is more profitable than complete justice?

I certainly do say that, he said, and I have told you why.

Well then, what about this: you call one of the two a virtue and the other a vice?—Of course.

That is, you call justice a virtue, and injustice a vice?

Is that likely, my good man, said he, since I say that injustice is profitable, and justice is not?

What then?—The opposite.

Do you call being just a vice?—No, but certainly high-minded foolishness.

And you call being unjust low-minded?—No, I call it good judgment.

You consider the unjust then, Thrasymachus, to be good and knowledgeable?

Yes, he said, those who are able to carry injustice through to the end, who can bring cities and communities of men under their power. Perhaps you think I mean purse-snatchers? Not that those actions too are not profitable, if they are not found out, but they are not worth mentioning in comparison with what I am talking about.

I am not unaware of what you mean, I said, but this point astonishes me: do you include injustice under virtue and wisdom, and justice among their opposites?—I certainly do.

That makes it harder, my friend, and it is not easy now to know what to say. If you had declared that injustice was more profitable, but agreed that it was a vice or shameful as some others do, we could have discussed it along the lines of general opinion. Now, obviously, you will say that it is fine and strong, and apply to it all the attributes which we used to apply to justice, since you have been so bold as to include it under virtue and wisdom.—Your guess, he said, is quite right.

We must not, however, shrink from pursuing our argument and looking into this, so long as I am sure that you mean what you say. For I do not think you are joking now, Thrasymachus, but are saying what you believe to be true.

What difference, said he, does it make to you whether I believe it or not? Is it not my argument you are refuting?

No difference, said I, but try to answer this further question: do you think that the just man wants to get the better of the just?

Never, said he, for he would not then be well mannered and simple, as he is now.

Does he want to overreach a just action?

Not a just action either, he said.

Would he want to get the better of an unjust man, and would he deem that just or not?
He would want to, he said, and he would deem it right, but he would not be able to.

That was not my question, said I, but whether the just man wants and deems it right to
outdo not a just man, but an unjust one?—That is so.

What about the unjust man? Would he deem it right to outdo the just man and the just
action?

Of course he does, he said, since he deems it right to get the better of everybody.

So the unjust man will get the better of another unjust man or an unjust action and he
will strive to get all he can from everyone?—That is so.

Let us put it this way, I said. The just man does not try to get the better of one like him
but of one unlike him, whereas the unjust man overreaches the like and the unlike?—Very
well put.

The unjust man, I said, is knowledgeable and good, and the just man is neither?—That
is well said too.

It follows, I said, that the unjust man is like the knowledgeable and the good, while the
just man is unlike them?

Of course that will be so, he said, being such a man he will be like such men, while
the other is not like them. . . .

Now Thrasymachus, I said, we found that the unjust man tries to get the better of both
those like and those unlike him. Did you not say so?—I did.

Yes, and the just man will not get the better of his like, but of one unlike him?—Yes.

The just man then, I said, resembles the wise and good, while the unjust resembles the
bad and ignorant?—It may be so.

Further, we agreed that each will be such as the man he resembles?—We did so agree.

So we find that the just man has turned out to be good and wise, and the unjust man
ignorant and bad.

Thrasymachus agreed to all this, not easily as I am telling it, but reluctantly and after
being pushed. It was summer and he was perspiring profusely. And then I saw something I
had never seen before: Thrasymachus blushing. After we had agreed that justice was virtue
and wisdom, and injustice vice and ignorance, I said: Very well, let us consider this as established . . .

Come now, consider this point next: There is a function of the soul which you could
not fulfill by means of any other thing, as for example: to take care of things, to rule, to
deliberate, and other things of the kind; could we entrust these things to any other agent
than the soul and say that they belong to it?—To no other.

What of living? Is that not a function of the soul?—It most certainly is.

So there is also an excellence of the soul?—We say so.

And, Thrasymachus, will the soul ever fulfill its function well if it is deprived of its
own particular excellence, or is this impossible?—Impossible.

It is therefore inevitable that the bad soul rules and looks after things badly and that
the good soul does all these things well.—Inevitable.

Now we have agreed that justice is excellence of the soul, and that injustice is vice of
soul?—We have so agreed.

The just soul and the just man, then, will live well, and the unjust man will live
badly.—So it seems, according to your argument.

Surely the one who lives well is blessed and happy, and the one who does not is the
opposite.—Of course.

So the just man is happy, and the unjust one is wretched.—So be it.

It profits no one to be wretched, but to be happy.—Of course.

And so, my good Thrasymachus, injustice is never more profitable than justice. . . .

I, before finding the answer to our first enquiry into the nature of justice, let that go and turned to investigate whether it was vice and ignorance or wisdom and virtue. Another argument came up after, the injustice was more profitable than justice, and I could not refrain from following this up and abandoning the previous one so that the result of our discussion for me is that I know nothing; for, when I do not know what justice is, I shall hardly know whether it is a kind of virtue or not, or whether the just man is unhappy or happy.

When I had said this I thought I had done with the discussion, but evidently this was only a prelude. Glaucon on this occasion too showed that boldness which is characteristic of him, and refused to accept Thrasymachus' abandoning the argument. He said: Do you, Socrates, want to appear to have persuaded us, or do you want truly to convince us that it is better in every way to be just than unjust?

I would certainly wish to convince you truly, I said, if I could. . . .

They say [Glaucon continued] that to do wrong is naturally good, to be wronged is bad, but the suffering of injury so far exceeds in badness the good of inflicting it that when men have done wrong to each other and suffered it, and have had a taste of both, those who are unable to avoid the latter and practise the former decide that it is profitable to come to an agreement with each other neither to inflict injury nor to suffer it. As a result they begin to make laws and covenants, and the law's command they call lawful and just. This, they say, is the origin and essence of justice; it stands between the best and the worst, the best being to do wrong without paying the penalty and the worst to be wronged without the power of revenge. The just then is a mean between two extremes; it is welcomed and honoured because of men's lack of the power to do wrong. The man who has that power, the real man, would not make a compact with anyone not to inflict injury or suffer it. For him that would be madness. This then, Socrates, is, according to their argument, the nature and origin of justice.

Even those who practice justice do so against their will because they lack the power to do wrong. This we could realize very clearly if we imagined ourselves granting to both the just and the unjust the freedom to do whatever they liked. We could then follow both of them and observe where their desires led them, and we would catch the just man redhanded travelling the same road as the unjust. The reason is the desire for undue gain which every organism by nature pursues as a good, but the law forcibly sidetracks him to honour equality. The freedom I just mentioned would most easily occur if these men had the power which they say the ancestor of the Lydian Gyges possessed. The story is that he was a shepherd in the service of the ruler of Lydia. There was a violent rainstorm and an earthquake which broke open the ground and created a chasm at the place where he was tending sheep. Seeing this and marvelling, he went down into it. He saw, besides many other wonders of which we are told, a hollow bronze horse. There were window-like openings in it; he climbed through them and caught sight of a corpse which seemed of more than human stature, wearing nothing but a ring of gold on its finger. This ring the shepherd put on and came out. He arrived at the usual monthly meeting which reported to the king on the state of the flocks, wearing the ring. As he was sitting among the others he happened to twist the hoop of the ring towards himself, to the inside of his hand, and as he did this he became invisible to those sitting near him and they went on talking as if he had gone. He marvelled at this and, fingering the ring, he turned the hoop outward again and became visible.

Perceiving this he tested whether the ring had this power and so it happened: if he turned the hoop inwards he became invisible, but was visible when he turned it outwards. When he realized this, he at once arranged to become one of the messengers to the king. He went, committed adultery with the king's wife, attacked the king with her help, killed him, and took over the kingdom.

Now if there were two such rings, one worn by the just man, the other by the unjust, no one, as these people think, would be so incorruptible that he would stay on the path of justice or bring himself to keep away from other people's property and not touch it, when he could with impunity take whatever he wanted from the market, go into houses and have sexual relations with anyone he wanted, kill anyone, free all those he wished from prison, and do the other things which would make him like a god among men. His actions would be in no way different from those of the other and they would both follow the same path. This, some would say, is a great proof that no one is just willingly but under compulsion, so that justice is not one's private good, since wherever either thought he could do wrong with impunity he would do so. Every man believes that injustice is much more profitable to himself than justice, and any exponent of this argument will say that he is right. The man who did not wish to do wrong with that opportunity, and did not touch other people's property, would be thought by those who knew it to be very foolish and miserable. They would praise him in public, thus deceiving one another, for fear of being wronged. So much for my second topic.

As for the choice between the lives we are discussing, we shall be able to make a correct judgment about it only if we put the most just man and the most unjust man face to face; otherwise we cannot do so. By face to face I mean this: let us grant to the unjust the fullest degree of injustice and to the just the fullest justice, each being perfect in his own pursuit. First, the unjust man will act as clever craftsmen do—a top navigator for example or physician distinguishes what his craft can do and what it cannot; the former he will undertake, the latter he will pass by, and when he slips he can put things right. So the unjust man's correct attempts at wrongdoing must remain secret; the one who is caught must be considered a poor performer, for the extreme of injustice is to have a reputation for justice, and our perfectly unjust man must be granted perfection in injustice. We must not take this from him, but we must allow that, while committing the greatest crimes, he has provided himself with the greatest reputation for justice; if he makes a slip he must be able to put it right; he must be a sufficiently persuasive speaker if some wrongdoing of his is made public; he must be able to use force, where force is needed, with the help of his courage, his strength, and the friends and wealth with which he has provided himself.

Having described such a man, let us now in our argument put beside him the just man, simple as he is and noble, who, as Aeschylus put it, does not wish to appear just but to be so. We must take away his reputation, for a reputation for justice would bring him honour and rewards, and it would then not be clear whether he is what he is for justice's sake or for the sake of rewards and honour. We must strip him of everything except justice and make him the complete opposite of the other. Though he does no wrong, he must have the greatest reputation for wrongdoing so that he may be tested for justice by not weakening under ill repute and its consequences. Let him go his incorruptible way until death with a reputation for injustice throughout his life, just though he is, so that our two men may reach the extremes, one of justice, the other of injustice, and let them be judged as to which of the two is the happier.

Whew! My dear Glaucon, I said, what a mighty scouring you have given those two characters, as if they were statues in a competition. . . .

Besides this, Socrates, look at another kind of argument which is spoken in private, and also by the poets, concerning justice and injustice. All go on repeating with one voice that justice and moderation are beautiful, but certainly difficult and burdensome, while incontinence and injustice are sweet and easy, and shameful only by repute and by law. They add that unjust deeds are for the most part more profitable than just ones. They freely declare, both in private and in public, that the wicked who have wealth and other forms of power are happy. They honour them but pay neither honour nor attention to the weak and the poor, though they agree that these are better men than the others.

What men say about the gods and virtue is the most amazing of all, namely that the gods too inflict misfortunes and a miserable life upon many good men, and the opposite fate upon their opposites. . . .

[from Book IV, where Socrates defines justice as "doing one's own"]
. . . everyone must pursue one occupation of those in the city, that for which his nature best fitted him.—Yes, we kept saying that [Glaucon replied].

Further, we have heard many people say, and have often said ourselves, that justice is to perform one's own task and not to meddle with that of others.—We have said that.

This then, my friend, I said, when it happens, is in some way justice, to do one's own job. And do you know what I take to be a proof of this?—No, tell me.

Look at it this way and see whether you agree: you will order your rulers to act as judges in the courts of the city?—Surely.

And will their exclusive aim in delivering judgment not be that no citizen should have what belongs to another or be deprived of what is his own?—That would be their aim.

That being just?—Yes.

In some way then possession of one's own and the performance of one's own task could be agreed to be justice.—That is so.

Consider then whether you agree with me in this: if a carpenter attempts to do the work of a cobbler, or a cobbler that of a carpenter, and they exchange their tools and the esteem that goes with the job, or the same man tries to do both, and all the other exchanges are made, do you think that this does any great harm to the city?—No.

But I think that when one who is by nature a worker or some other kind of money-maker is puffed up by wealth, or by the mob, or by his own strength, or some other such thing, and attempts to enter the warrior class, or one of the soldiers tries to enter the group of counsellors and guardians, though he is unworthy of it, and these exchange their tools and the public esteem, or when the same man tries to perform all these jobs together, then I think you will agree that these exchanges and this meddling bring the city to ruin.—They certainly do.

The meddling and exchange between the three established orders does very great harm to the city and would most correctly be called wickedness.—Very definitely.

And you would call the greatest wickedness worked against one's own city injustice?—Of course.

That then is injustice. And let us repeat that the doing of one's own job by the money-making, auxiliary, and guardian groups, when each group is performing its own task in the city, is the opposite, it is justice and makes the city just.—I agree with you that this is so.

Do not let us, I said, take this as quite final yet. If we find that this quality, when existing in each individual man, is agreed there too to be justice, then we can assent to this—for what can we say?—but if not, we must look for something else. For the present, let us complete that examination which we thought we should make, that if we tried to observe justice in something larger which contains it, this would make it easier to observe it in the individual. We thought that this larger thing was a city, and so we established the best city we could, knowing well that justice would be present in the good city. It has now appeared to us there, so let us now transfer it to the individual and, if it corresponds, all will be well. But if it is seen to be something different in the individual, then we must go back to the city and examine this new notion of justice. By thus comparing and testing the two, we might make justice light up like fire from the rubbing of firesticks, and when it has become clear, we shall fix it firmly in our own minds.—You are following the path we set, and we must do so.

Well now, when you apply the same name to a thing whether it is big or small, are these two instances of it like or unlike with regard to that to which the same name applies?—They are alike in that, he said.

So the just man and the just city will be no different but alike as regards the very form of justice.—Yes, they will be.

Now the city was thought to be just when the three kinds of men within it each performed their own task, and it was moderate and brave and wise because of some other qualities and attitudes of the same groups.—True.

And we shall therefore deem it right, my friend, that the individual have the same parts in his own soul, and through the same qualities in those parts will correctly be given the same names.—That must be so. . . .

Well, then, I said, we are surely compelled to agree that each of us has within himself the same parts and characteristics as the city? Where else would they come from? It would be ridiculous for anyone to think that spiritedness has not come to be in the city from individuals who are held to possess it, like the inhabitants of Thrace and Scythia and others who live to the north of us, or that the same is not true of the love of learning which one would attribute most to our part of the world, or the love of money which one might say is conspicuously displayed by the Phoenicians and the Egyptians.—Certainly, he said.

This then, is the case, I said, and it is not hard to understand.—No indeed.

But this is: whether we do everything with the same part of our soul, or one thing with one of the three parts, and another with another. Do we learn with one part of ourselves, get angry with another, and with some third part desire the pleasures of food and procreation and other things closely akin to them, or, when we set out after something, do we act with the whole of our soul in each case? This will be hard to determine satisfactorily.—I think so too. . . .

The position of the spirited part seems the opposite of what we thought a short time ago. Then we thought of it as something appetitive, but now we say it is far from being that; in the civil war of the soul it aligns itself far more with the reasonable part.—Very much so.

Is it different from that also, or is it some part of reason, so that there are two parts of the soul instead of three, the reasonable and the appetitive? Or, as we had three separate parts holding our city together, the money-making, the auxiliary and the deliberative, so in the soul the spirited is a third part, by nature the helper of reason, if it has not been corrupted by a bad upbringing?—It must be a third part.

Yes, I said, if it now appears to be different from the reasonable part, as earlier from the appetitive part.

It is not difficult, he said, to show that it is different. One can see this in children; they are full of spirit from birth, whereas a few of them seem to me never to acquire a share of reason, while the majority do not do so until late.

By Zeus, I said, that is very well put. One can see this also in animals. Besides, our earlier quotation from Homer bears witness to it, where he says:

Striking his chest, he addressed his heart,

for clearly Homer represents the part which reasons about the better and the worse course, and which strikes his chest, as different from that which is angry without reasoning.—You are definitely right.

We have now made our difficult way through a sea of argument to reach this point, and we have fairly agreed that the same kinds of parts, and the same number of parts, exist in the soul of each individual as in our city.—That is so.

It necessarily follows that the individual is wise in the same way, and in the same part of himself, as the city.—Quite so.

And the part which makes the individual brave is the same as that which makes the city brave, and in the same manner, and everything which makes for virtue is the same in both?—That necessarily follows.

Moreover, Glaucon, I think we shall say that a man is just in the same way as the city is just.—That too is inevitable.

We have surely not forgotten that the city was just because each of the three classes in it was fulfilling its own task.—I do not think, he said, that we have forgotten that.

We must remember then that each one of us within whom each part is fulfilling its own task will himself be just and do his own work.—We must certainly remember this.

Therefore it is fitting that the reasonable part should rule, it being wise and exercising foresight on behalf of the whole soul, and for the spirited part to obey it and be its ally.—Quite so.

Aristotle, "The Various Types of Justice," from the *Nicomachean Ethics* (ca. 322 B.C.)

Aristotle (364–322 BC) was born in Macedonia, but spent most of his life in Athens, where he was a student of Plato and later the teacher of Alexander the Great. In the *Nicomachean Ethics*—a set of lecture notes, likely edited by Aristotle's son Nicomachus—Aristotle gives us a complicated account of a complex concept of justice. He begins by dividing justice into two categories, a general concept of justice as "the lawful" (though this does not necessarily mean obedience to the laws of any particular state), and a particular concept as "the fair and equal." Once again, as in the case of Plato, we should keep in mind the more literal meaning of *dikaiosune* as "righteousness," which makes more sense of Aristotle's claim that "this form of justice . . . is complete virtue, . . . not absolutely, but in relation to our neighbor." He then divides particular justice into "distributive" and "rectificatory" justice, and it becomes clear that at this point he is analyzing a notion that is much closer to our own notion(s) of justice as fairness. One of Aristotle's key terms here is that of "grasping" (*pleonexia*), which is something along the lines of what we mean by "greedy," clearly a vice to the Greek mind. Aristotle also makes much of the opposition between justice and injustice, for it is often through particular acts of injustice that we become clear about justice. Distributive justice is, for Aristotle, primarily concerned with what people *deserve*. Aristotle is also particularly concerned with the justice of transactions—a form of rectificatory (or commutative) justice, whether such "voluntary" matters as buying, selling, or lending, or such "involuntary" matters as being the victim of an insult, theft, or assassination. It is in the discussion of distributive justice that Aristotle's peculiar and perhaps perverse notion of "equality" enters into the argument. What Aristotle means by "equality," he makes quite clear to us, is really *proportion,* or specifically what he calls *geometrical* proportion. What he means is that equals deserve equal but unequals deserve unequal, in proportion to their merit. Thus Vlastos describes the "acrobatic linguistic posture" of Aristotle, and Plato, too, in trying to say that an "equal" distribution, to be just, is almost always an *unequal* one ("Justice and Equality," in Brandt, *Social Justice,* p. 32). Emphasizing again the importance of the concept of equality in Greek thinking, Vlastos adds, "the meritarian view of justice paid reluctant homage to the equalitarian one by using the language of equality to assert the justice of inequality" (ibid.).

Central to Aristotle's overall argument (and the content into which his discussion of justice fits in the *Ethics*) is the idea of justice as a state of character, a cultivated set of dispositions, attitudes, and good habits. It is not an abstract scheme or principle. In its particular manifestation, justice is concerned with good judgment and a sense of fairness. It is a virtue of particular importance, naturally, to those who rule and those who judge. In rectificatory justice, the justice of exchanges, such judgment again involves a sense of equality, here not as proportion but as straightforward equivalence. (Aristotle misleadingly calls it "arithmetical" as opposed to "geometrical.") It involves equality in the sense that two men who are before the court for the same crime are to be considered equals "before the law," even if they are very different otherwise. It is this sense of equality, too, that enters into considerations of punishment. Aristotle says, for example, that a man who has wounded or slain another man should receive a penalty, by which means "the judge tries to equalize things . . . taking away from the gain of the assailant." But notice that there is no clear indication of whether the penalty in such cases is to be conceived as retribution or retaliation, or as some other sort of redress or equalization. (Indeed, the very notion of rectificatory as opposed to retributive justice seems to obscure any such query.) Finally, Aristotle briefly discusses his famous doctrine that justice—like all virtues—is a "mean between extremes."

5. Justice

5.1   The Definition of Justice

5.11   JUSTICE AS A STATE OF CHARACTER

The questions we must examine about justice and injustice are these: What sorts of actions are they concerned with? What sort of mean is justice? What are the extremes between which justice is intermediate? Let us examine them by the same type of investigation that we used in the topics discussed before.

We see that the state everyone means in speaking of justice is the state that makes us doers of just actions, that makes us do justice and wish what is just. In the same way they mean by injustice the state that makes us do injustice and wish what is unjust. Let us also, then, [follow the common beliefs and] begin by assuming this in outline.

Since justice is a state, its relation to just actions is different from the relation of a capacity to its activities

For what is true of sciences and capacities is not true of states. For while one and the same capacity or science seems to have contrary activities, a state that is a contrary has no contrary activities. Health, e.g., only makes us do healthy actions, not their contraries; for we say we are walking in a healthy way if [and only if] we are walking in the way a healthy person would.

States may be studied by reference to their contraries

Often one of a pair of contrary states is recognized from the other contrary; and often the states are recognized from their subjects. For if, e.g., the good state is evident, the bad state becomes evident too; and moreover the good state becomes evident from the things that have it, and the things from the state. For if, e.g., the good state is thickness of flesh, then the bad state will necessarily be thinness of flesh, and the thing that produces the good state will be what produces thickness of flesh.

It follows, usually, that if one of a pair of contraries is spoken of in more ways than one, so is the other; if, e.g., what is just is spoken of in more ways than one, so is what is unjust.

5.12   THE TYPES OF JUSTICE AND INJUSTICE

Now it would seem that justice and injustice are both spoken of in more ways than one, but since the different ways are closely related, their homonymy is unnoticed, and is less clear than it is with distant homonyms where the distance in appearance is wide (e.g., the bone below an animal's neck and what we lock doors with are called keys homonymously).

5.13   JUSTICE AS LAWFULNESS AND JUSTICE AS FAIRNESS

Let us, then, find the number of ways an unjust person is spoken of. Both the lawless person and the greedy and unfair person seem to be unjust; and so, clearly, both the lawful and the fair person will be just. Hence what is just will be both what is lawful and what is fair, and what is unjust will be both what is lawless and what is unfair.

5.14   THE GOODS AND EVILS RELEVANT TO FAIRNESS

Since the unjust person is greedy, he will be concerned with goods—not with all goods, but only with those involved in good and bad fortune, goods which are, [considered] unconditionally, always good, but for this or that person not always good. Though human beings pray for these and pursue them, they are wrong; the right thing is to pray that what is good unconditionally will also be good for us, but to choose [only] what is good for us.

Now the unjust person [who chooses these goods] does not choose more in every case; in the case of what is bad unconditionally he actually chooses less. But since what is less bad also seems to be good in a way, and greed aims at more of what is good, he seems to be greedy. In fact he is unfair; for unfairness includes [all these actions], and is a common feature [of his choice of the greater good and of the lesser evil].

5.2   General Justice

5.21   IT REQUIRES OBSERVANCE OF LAW

Since, as we saw, the lawless person is unjust and the lawful person is just, it clearly follows that whatever is lawful is in some way just; for the provisions of legislative science are lawful, and we say that each of them is just. Now in every matter they deal with the laws aim either at the common benefit of all, or at the benefit of those in control, whose control rests on virtue or on some other such basis. And so in one way what we call just is whatever produces and maintains happiness and its parts for a political community.

5.22   THE SCOPE OF LAW EXTENDS TO ALL THE VIRTUES . . .

Now the law instructs us to do the actions of a brave person—not to leave the battle-line, e.g., or to flee, or to throw away our weapons; of a temperate person—not to commit adultery or wanton aggression; of a mild person—not to strike or revile another; and similarly requires actions that express the other virtues, and prohibits those that express the vices. The correctly established law does this correctly, and the less carefully framed one does this worse.

5.23   . . . AND HENCE GENERAL JUSTICE IS COMPLETE VIRTUE

This type of justice, then, is complete virtue, not complete virtue unconditionally, but complete virtue in relation to another. And this is why justice often seems to be supreme among the virtues, and "neither the evening star nor the morning star is so marvellous," and the proverb says "And in justice all virtue is summed up."

Moreover, justice is complete virtue to the highest degree because it is the complete exercise of complete virtue. And it is the complete exercise because the person who has justice is able to exercise virtue in relation to another, not only in what concerns himself; for many are able to exercise virtue in their own concerns but unable in what relates to another.

And hence Bias seems to have been correct in saying that ruling will reveal the man, since a ruler is automatically related to another, and in a community. And for the same reason justice is the only virtue that seems to be another person's good, because it is related to another; for it does what benefits another, either the ruler or the fellow-member of the community.

The worst person, therefore, is the one who exercises his vice towards himself and his friends as well [as towards others]. And the best person is not the one who exercises virtue [only] towards himself, but the one who [also] exercises it in relation to another, since this is a difficult task.

This type of justice, then, is the whole, not a part, of virtue, and the injustice contrary to it is the whole, not a part, of vice.

At the same time our discussion makes clear the difference between virtue and this type of justice. For virtue is the same as justice, but what it is to be virtue is not the same as what it is to be justice. Rather, in so far as virtue is related to another, it is justice, and in so far as it is a certain sort of state unconditionally it is virtue.

5.3   Special Justice Contrasted with General

5.31   SPECIAL JUSTICE MUST BE A VIRTUE DISTINCT FROM GENERAL JUSTICE

But we are looking for the type of justice, since we say there is one, that consists in a part of virtue, and correspondingly for the type of injustice that is a part [of vice].

Here is evidence that there is this type of justice and injustice:

First, if someone's activities express the other vices—if, e.g., cowardice made him throw away his shield, or irritability made him revile someone, or ungenerosity made him fail to help someone with money—what he does is unjust, but not greedy. But when one acts from greed, in many cases his action expresses none of these vices—certainly not all of them; but it still expresses some type of wickedness, since we blame him, and [in particular] it expresses injustice. Hence there is another type of injustice that is a part of the whole, and a way for a thing to be unjust that is a part of the whole that is contrary to law.

Moreover, if A commits adultery for profit and makes a profit, while B commits adultery because of his appetite, and spends money on it to his own loss, B seems intemperate rather than greedy, while A seems unjust, not intemperate. Clearly, then, this is because A acts to make a profit.

Further, we can refer every other unjust action to some vice—to intemperance if he committed adultery, to cowardice if he deserted his comrade in the battle-line, to anger if he struck someone. But if he made an [unjust] profit, we can refer it to no other vice except injustice.

Hence evidently (a) there is another type of injustice, special injustice, besides the whole of injustice; and (b) it is synonymous with the whole, since the definition is in the same genus. For (b) both have their area of competence in relation to another. But (a) special injustice is concerned with honour or wealth or safety, or whatever single name will include all these, and aims at the pleasure that results from making a profit; but the concern of injustice as a whole is whatever concerns the excellent person.

Clearly, then, there is more than one type of justice, and there is another type besides [the type that is] the whole of virtue; but we must still grasp what it is, and what sort of thing it is.

5.32   THE DISTINCTION REFLECTS THE DISTINCTION BETWEEN WHAT IS LAWLESS AND WHAT IS UNFAIR

What is unjust is divided into what is lawless and what is unfair, and what is just into what is lawful and what is fair. The [general] injustice previously described, then, is concerned with what is lawless. But what is unfair is not the same as what is lawless, but related to it as part to whole, since whatever is unfair is lawless, but not everything lawless is unfair. Hence also the type of injustice and the way for a thing to be unjust [that expresses unfairness] are not the same as the type [that expresses lawlessness], but differ as parts from wholes. For this injustice [as unfairness] is a part of the whole of injustice, and similarly justice [as fairness] is a part of the whole of justice.

Hence we must describe special [as well as general] justice and injustice, and equally this way for a thing to be just or unjust.

5.33   A DETAILED DESCRIPTION OF GENERAL JUSTICE IS UNNECESSARY, SINCE IT IS SIMPLY THE WHOLE OF VIRTUE

Let us, then, set to one side the type of justice and injustice that corresponds to the whole of virtue, justice being the exercise of the whole of virtue, and injustice of the whole of vice, in relation to another.

And it is evident how we must distinguish the way for a thing to be just or unjust that expresses this type of justice and injustice; for the majority of lawful actions, we might say, are the actions resulting from virtue as a whole. For the law instructs us to express each virtue, and forbids us to express each vice, in how we live. Moreover, the actions producing the whole of virtue are the lawful actions that the laws prescribe for education promoting the common good.

We must wait till later, however, to determine whether the education that makes an individual an unconditionally good man is a task for political science or for another science; for, presumably, being a good man is not the same as being every sort of good citizen.

5.34   BUT A DETAILED DESCRIPTION OF SPECIAL JUSTICE IS NEEDED

Special justice, however, and the corresponding way for something to be just [must be divided].

One species is found in the distribution of honours or wealth or anything else that can be divided among members of a community who share in a political system; for here it is possible for one member to have a share equal or unequal to another's.

Another species concerns rectification in transactions. This species has two parts, since one sort of transaction is voluntary, and one involuntary. Voluntary transactions include selling, buying, lending, pledging, renting, depositing, hiring out—these are called voluntary because the origin of these transactions is voluntary. Some involuntary ones are secret, e.g. theft, adultery, poisoning, pimping, slave-deception, murder by treachery, false witness; others are forcible, e.g. assault, imprisonment, murder, plunder, mutilation, slander, insult.

5.4   *Justice in Distribution*

5.41   JUSTICE, FAIRNESS AND EQUALITY

Since the unjust person is unfair, and what is unjust is unfair, there is clearly an intermediate between the unfair [extremes], and this is what is fair; for in any action where too much and too little are possible, the fair [amount] is also possible. And so if what is unjust is unfair, what is just is fair (*ison*), as seems true to everyone even without argument.

And since what is equal (*ison*) [and fair] is intermediate, what is just is some sort of intermediate. And since what is equal involves at least two things [equal to each other], it follows that what is just must be intermediate and equal, and related to some people. In so far as it is intermediate, it must be between too much and too little; in so far as it is equal, it involves two things; and in so far as it is just, it is just for some people. Hence what is just requires four things at least; the people for whom it is just are two, and the [equal] things that are involved are two.

5.42 HOW EQUALITY IS DETERMINED

Equality for the people involved will be the same as for the things involved, since [in a just arrangement] the relation between the people will be the same as the relation between the things involved. For if the people involved are not equal, they will not [justly] receive equal shares; indeed, whenever equals receive unequal shares, or unequals equal shares, in a distribution, that is the source of quarrels and accusations.

This is also clear from considering what fits a person's worth. For everyone agrees that what is just in distributions must fit some sort of worth, but what they call worth is not the same; supporters of democracy say it is free citizenship, some supporters of oligarchy say it is wealth, others good birth, while supporters of aristocracy say it is virtue.

5.43 JUSTICE IS PROPORTIONATE EQUALITY

Hence what is just [since it requires equal shares for equal people] is in some way proportionate. For proportion is special to number as a whole, not only to numbers consisting of [abstract] units, since it is equality of ratios and requires at least four terms. . . . This is the sort of proportion that mathematicians call geometrical, since in geometrical proportion the relation of whole to whole is the same as the relation of each [part] to each [part]. But this proportion [involved in justice] is not continuous, since there is no single term for both the person and the item.

What is just, then, is what is proportionate, and what is unjust is what is counter-proportionate. Hence [in an unjust action] one term becomes more and the other less; and this is indeed how it turns out in practice, since the one doing injustice has more of the good, and the victim less. With an evil the ratio is reversed, since the lesser evil, compared to the greater, counts as a good; for the lesser evil is more choiceworthy than the greater, what is choiceworthy is good, and what is more choiceworthy is a greater good.

This, then, is the first species of what is just.

5.5 Justice in Rectification

5.51 IT IS DISTINCT FROM DISTRIBUTIVE JUSTICE

The other way of being just is the rectificatory, found in transactions both voluntary and involuntary; and this way of being just belongs to a different species from the first.

For what is just in distribution of common assets will always fit the proportion mentioned above, since distribution from common funds will also fit the ratio to one another of different people's deposits. Similarly, the way of being unjust that is opposed to this way of being just is what is counter-proportionate. On the other hand, what is just in transactions is certainly equal in a way, and what is unjust is unequal; but still it fits numerical proportion, not the [geometrical] proportion of the other species.

5.52 IT INVOLVES NUMERICAL PROPORTION AND EQUALITY

For here it does not matter if a decent person has taken from a base person, or a base person from a decent person, or if a decent or a base person has committed adultery. Rather, the law looks only at differences in the harm [inflicted], and treats the people involved as equals, when one does injustice while the other suffers it, and one has done the harm while the other has suffered it. Hence the judge tries to restore this unjust situation to equality, since it is unequal.

These apply to other wrongs besides theft

For [not only both when one steals from another but also] and when one is wounded and the other wounds him, or one kills and the other is killed, the action and the suffering are unequally divided [with profit for the offender and loss for the victim]; and the judge tries to restore the [profit and] loss to a position of equality, by subtraction from [the offender's] profit. For in such cases, stating it without qualification, we speak of profit for, e.g., the attacker who wounded his victim, even if that is not the proper word for some cases, and of loss for the victim who suffers the wound. At any rate, when what was suffered has been measured, one part is called the [victim's] loss, and the other the [offender's] profit.

In fact, however, these names 'loss' and 'profit' are derived from voluntary exchange. For having more than one's own share is called making a profit, and having less than what one had at the beginning is called suffering a loss, e.g. in buying and selling and in other transactions permitted by law. And when people get neither more nor less, but precisely what belongs to them, they say they have their own share, and make neither a loss nor a profit.

5.53 HENCE RECTIFICATORY JUSTICE IS A MEAN

Hence what is equal is intermediate between more and less; profit and loss are more and less in contrary ways, since more good and less evil is profit, and the contrary is loss; and the intermediate area between [profit and loss], we have found, is what is equal, which we say is just. Hence what is just in rectification is what is intermediate between loss and profit.

This is confirmed by the judge's rectificatory role in justice

Hence parties to a dispute resort to a judge, and an appeal to a judge is an appeal to what is just; for the judge is intended to be a sort of living embodiment of what is just. Moreover, they seek the judge as an intermediary, and in some cities they actually call judges mediators, assuming that if they are awarded an intermediate amount, the award will be just. If, then, the judge is an intermediary, what is just is in some way intermediate.

5.54 RECTIFICATORY JUSTICE IS ADMINISTERED BY RESTORING NUMERICAL EQUALITY

The judge restores equality, as though a line [AB] had been cut into unequal parts [AC and CB], and he removed from the larger part [AC] the amount [DC] by which it exceeds the half [AD] of the line [AB], and added this amount [DC] to the smaller part [CB]. And when the whole [AB] has been halved [into AD and DB], then they say that each person has what is properly his own, when he has got an equal share. This is also why it is called just (*dikaion*), because it is a bisection (*dicha*), as though we said bisected (*dichaion*), and the judge (*dikastes*) is a bisector (*dichastes*).

What is equal [in this case] is intermediate, by numerical proportion, between the larger [AC] and the smaller line [CB]. For when [the same amount] is subtracted from one of two equal things and added to the other, then the one part exceeds the other by the two parts; for if a part had been subtracted from the one, but not added to the other, the larger part would have exceeded the smaller by just one part. Hence the larger part exceeds the intermediate by one part, and the intermediate from which [a part] was subtracted [exceeds the smaller] by one part.

In this way, then, we will recognize what we must subtract from the one who has more and add to the one who has less [to restore equality]; for to the one who has less we must add the amount by which the intermediate exceeds what he has, and from the greatest amount [which the one who has more has] we must subtract the amount by which it exceeds the intermediate.

5.64 MONEY IS DESIGNED TO SECURE PROPORTIONATE RECIPROCITY, BY FACILITATING EXCHANGE

This is why all items for exchange must be comparable in some way. Currency came along to do exactly this, and in a way it becomes an intermediate, since it measures everything, and so measures excess and deficiency—how many shoes are equal to a house.

Hence, as builder is to shoemaker, so must the number of shoes be to a house; for if this does not happen, there will be no exchange and no association, and the proportionate equality will not be reached unless they are equal in some way. Everything, then, must be measured by some one measure, as we said before.

Exchange rests on need, and hence is facilitated by money
In reality, this measure is need, which holds everything together; for if people required nothing, or needed things to different extents, there would be either no exchange or not the same exchange. . . .

5.7 Political Justice

5.71 CONDITIONS FOR POLITICAL JUSTICE

We have previously described, then, the relation of reciprocity to what is just. We must now notice that we are looking not only for what is just unconditionally but also for what is just in a political association. This is found among associates in a life aiming at self-sufficiency, who are free and either proportionately or numerically equal.

Hence those who lack these features have nothing politically just in their relations, though they have something just in so far as it is similar [to what is politically just].

For what is just is found among those who have law in their relations. Where there is law, there is injustice, since the judicial process is judgement that distinguishes what is just from what is unjust. Where there is injustice there is also doing injustice, though where there is doing injustice there need not also be injustice. And doing injustice is awarding to oneself too many of the things that, [considered] unconditionally, are good, and too few of the things that, [considered] unconditionally, are bad.

5.72   THE NATURE OF POLITICAL JUSTICE EXPLAINS WHY INDIVIDUALS
ARE TEMPTED TO DO INJUSTICE

This is why we allow only reason, not a human being, to be ruler; for a human being awards himself too many goods and becomes a tyrant, but a ruler is a guardian of what is just and hence of what is equal [and so must not award himself too many goods].

If a ruler is just, he seems to profit nothing by it. For since he does not award himself more of what, [considered] unconditionally, is good if it is not proportionate to him, he seems to labour for another's benefit; that is why justice is said, as we also remarked before, to be another person's good. Hence some payment [for ruling] should be given; this is honour and privilege, and the people who are unsatisfied by these are the ones who become tyrants.

5.73   FORMS SIMILAR TO POLITICAL JUSTICE

What is just for a master and a father is similar to this, not the same. For there is no unconditional injustice in relation to what is one's own; one's own possession, or one's child until it is old enough and separated, is as though it were a part of oneself, and no one decides to harm himself. Hence there is no injustice in relation to them, and so nothing politically unjust or just either. For we found that what is politically just must conform to law, and apply to those who are naturally suited for law, hence to those who have equality in ruling and being ruled. [Approximation to this equality] explains why relations with a wife more than with children or possessions allow something to count as just—for that is what is just in households; still, this too is different from what is politically just.

5.74   JUSTICE BY NATURE AND BY LAW

One part of what is politically just is natural, and the other part legal. What is natural is what has the same validity everywhere alike, independent of its seeming so or not. What is legal is what originally makes no difference [whether it is done] one way or another, but makes a difference whenever people have laid down the rule—e.g. that a mina is the price of a ransom, or that a goat rather than two sheep should be sacrificed; and also laws passed for particular cases, e.g. that sacrifices should be offered to Brasidas; and enactments by decree.

Variations may seem to show there is no natural justice
Now it seems to some people that everything just is merely legal, since what is natural is unchangeable and equally valid everywhere—fire, e.g., burns both here and in Persia—while they see that what is just changes [from city to city].

However, variations are consistent with the existence of natural justice
This is not so, though in a way it is so. With us, though presumably not at all with the gods, there is such a thing as what is natural, but still all is changeable; despite the change there is such a thing as what is natural and what is not.

What sort of thing that [is changeable and hence] admits of being otherwise is natural, and what sort is not natural, but legal and conventional, if both natural and legal are changeable? It is clear in other cases also, and the same distinction [between the natural and the unchangeable] will apply; for the right hand, e.g., is naturally superior, even though it is possible for everyone to become ambidextrous.

The sorts of things that are just by convention and expediency are like measures. For measures for wine and for corn are not of equal size everywhere, but in wholesale markets they are bigger, and in retail smaller. Similarly, the things that are just by human [enactment] and not by nature differ from place to place, since political systems also differ; still, only one system is by nature the best everywhere.

"Justice, Retribution, and Mercy," from the Koran

The Qur'an, or Koran, the holy book of half a billion Muslims, is said to be an exact transcription of a tablet that exists for all eternity in heaven, revealed to Mohammed in the seventh century over a period of some twenty years. Technically, the text is untranslatable from the original Arabic, so what is offered here is, according to Islam, a piece of paraphrase into English. The Holy Book of Islam has a great deal to say about justice, and the key to this justice is submission (or Islam) and the fear of God (Allah). Allah is described as "terrible in his retribution" but yet "all-forgiving and compassionate." The ultimate standard of justice is belief itself, but with belief and obedience comes a system of divine demands concerning the details of daily life. A central theme in the Koran, both as a matter of practical concern and as a metaphor, is the *debt,* for ancient, just as modern Arab and Middle Eastern culture, was rich in commerce and trading. The metaphor of debt is also central to the conception of justice: for example, we are told that thieves are to have their hands cut off "as a recompense for what they have earned." The concepts of vengeance and retribution are prevalent, but they are tempered throughout by mercy. The biblical injunction of "a life for a life, an eye for an eye" is repeated, but with the qualification that "whosoever forgoes it [that is, retaliation] . . . that shall be for him an expiation."

And fear the Day
When ye shall be
Brought back to God.
Then shall every soul

Be paid what it earned,
And none shall be
Dealt with unjustly.

O ye who believe!
When ye deal with each other,
In transactions involving
Future obligations
In a fixed period of time,
Reduce them to writing
Let a scribe write down
Faithfully as between
The parties: let not the scribe
Refuse to write: as God
Has taught him,
So let him write.
Let him who incurs
The liability dictate,
But let him fear
His Lord God,
And not diminish
Aught of what he owes.
If the party liable
Is mentally deficient,
Or weak, or unable
Himself to dictate,
Let his guardian
Dictate faithfully.
And get two witnesses,
Out of your own men,
And if there are not two men,
Then a man and two women,
Such as ye choose,
For witnesses,
So that if one of them errs,
The other can remind her.
The witnesses
Should not refuse
When they are called on
(For evidence).
Disdain not to reduce
To writing (your contract)
For a future period,
Whether it be small
Or big: it is juster
In the sight of God,
More suitable as evidence,
And more convenient

To prevent doubts
Among yourselves
But if it be a transaction
Which ye carry out
On the spot among yourselves,
There is no blame on you
If ye reduce it not
To writing.
But take witnesses
Whenever ye make
A commercial contract;
And let neither scribe
Nor witness suffer harm.
If ye do (such harm),
It would be wickedness
In you. So fear God;
For it is God
That teaches you.
And God is well acquainted
With all things. . . .

O ye who believe!
Stand out firmly
For God, as witnesses
To fair dealing, and let not
The hatred of others
To you make you swerve
To wrong and depart from
Justice. Be just: that is
Next to Piety: and fear God.
For God is well-acquainted
With all that ye do.

To those who believe
And do deeds of righteousness
Hath God promised forgiveness
And a great reward.
Those who reject faith
And deny Our Signs
Will be Companions
Of Hell-fire.

O ye who believe!
Call in remembrance
The favour of God
Unto you when
Certain men formed the design
To stretch out

Their hands against you,
But (God) held back
Their hands from you:
So fear God. And on God
Let Believers put
(All) their trust. . . .

As to the thief,
Male or female,
Cut off his or her hands:
A punishment by way
Of example, from God,
For their crime:
And God is Exalted in Power.

But if the thief repent
After his crime,
And amend his conduct,
God turneth to him
In forgiveness; for God
Is Oft-forgiving, Most Merciful.

Knowest thou not
That to God (alone)
Belongeth the dominion
Of the heavens and the earth?
He punisheth whom He pleaseth,
And He forgiveth whom He pleaseth:
And God hath power
Over all things. . . .

Therefore fear not men,
But fear Me, and sell not
My Signs for a miserable price.
If any do fail to judge
By (the light of) what God
Hath revealed, they are
(No better than) Unbelievers.

We ordained therein for them:
"Life for life, eye for eye,
Nose for nose, ear for ear,
Tooth for tooth, and wounds
Equal for equal." But if
Any one remits the retaliation
By way of charity, it is
An act of atonement for himself.
And if any fail to judge

By (the light of) what God
Hath revealed, they are
(No better than) wrong-doers. . . .

    O ye who believe!
God doth but make a trial of you
In a little matter
Of game well within reach
Of your hands and your lances,
That He may test
Who feareth Him unseen:
Any who transgress
Thereafter, will have
A grievous penalty.

O ye who believe!
Kill not game
While in the Sacred
Precincts or in pilgrim garb.
If any of you doth so
Intentionally, the compensation
Is an offering, brought
To the Ka'ba, of a domestic animal
Equivalent to the one he killed,

As adjudged by two just men
Among you; or by way
Of atonement, the feeding
Of the indigent; or its
Equivalent in fasts: that he
May taste of the penalty
Of his deed. God
Forgives what is past:
For repetition God will
Exact from him the penalty.
For God is Exalted,
And Lord of Retribution.

Lawful to you is the pursuit
Of water-game and its use
For food,—for the benefit
Of yourselves and those who
Travel; but forbidden
Is the pursuit of land-game;—
As long as ye are
In the Sacred Precincts
Or in pilgrim garb.
And fear God, to Whom
Ye shall be gathered back. . . .

Know ye that God
Is strict in punishment
And that God is
Oft-forgiving, Most Merciful.

Thomas Aquinas, "The Nature of Justice," from *Summa Theologica* (1274)

Thomas Aquinas (1224–1274) synthesized the Christianity of the Catholic Church with Aristotle's ethics and metaphysics, and the result was a theology that has held sway in the Catholic Church for many centuries since. In the following passages, Aquinas examines and defends "the Philosopher"—that is, Aristotle—with respect to his analysis of justice, against a number of objections that might be (and in some cases were in fact) raised against the view. (Some of these objections Aristotle could not have even conceived, grounded as they are in Christian understandings of the human good.) He considers, in particular, Aristotle's defense of desert in distributive justice, whether each person should get "his right," Aristotle's insistence that justice (as "righteousness") is essentially a virtue directed at relations with other people, whether there is both general and particular justice, whether justice is about the passions, and whether justice is a mean between extremes. Finally, Aquinas considers the issue of whether distributive justice should be, as it is on the Aristotelian view, concerned exclusively with desert, or whether it is more properly conceived in terms of need and benevolence (as Augustine had argued) or in terms of generosity (as Cicero's view suggested).

Of Justice

We must now consider justice. Under this head there are twelve points of inquiry: (1) What is justice? (2) Whether justice is always towards another? (3) Whether it is a virtue? (4) Whether it is the will as its subject? (5) Whether it is a general virtue? (6) Whether, as a general virtue, it is essentially the same as every virtue? (7) Whether there is a particular justice? (8) Whether particular justice has a matter of its own? (9) Whether it is about pas-

From *Summa Theologica* by Thomas Aquinas, © McGraw-Hill Publishing Company. Reprinted by permission of Glencoe / McGraw-Hill Educational Division, Macmillan / McGraw-Hill School Publishing Company.

sions or about operations only? (10) Whether the mean of justice is an objective mean? (11) Whether the act of justice is to render to everyone his own? (12) Whether justice is the chief of the moral virtues?

First Article

Is Justice Fittingly Defined as Being the Perpetual and Constant Will to Render to Each One His Right?

We proceed thus to the First Article:

Obj. 1. It would seem that lawyers have unfittingly defined justice as being "the perpetual and constant will to render to each one his right." For, according to the Philosopher, justice is a habit which makes a man "capable of doing what is just and of being just in action and in intention." Now, "will" denotes a power or also an act. Therefore, justice is unfittingly defined as being a will.

Obj. 2. Further, rectitude of the will is not the will; else if the will were its own rectitude, it would follow that no will is unrighteous. Yet, according to Anselm, justice is rectitude. Therefore, justice is not the will.   .

Obj. 3. Further, no will is perpetual save God's. If, therefore, justice is a perpetual will, in God alone will there be justice.

Obj. 4. Further, whatever is perpetual is constant, since it is unchangeable. Therefore, it is needless in defining justice to say that it is both perpetual and constant.

Obj. 5. Further, it belongs to the ruler to give each one his right. Therefore, if justice gives each one his right, it follows that it is in none but the ruler, which is absurd.

Obj. 6. Further, Augustine says that "justice is love serving God alone." Therefore, it does not render to each one what is his.

I answer that The aforesaid definition of justice is fitting if understood aright. For, since every virtue is a habit, that is, the principle of a good act, a virtue must needs be defined by means of the good act bearing on the matter proper to that virtue. Now, the proper matter of justice consists of those things that belong to our intercourse with other men, as shall be shown further on. Hence the act of justice in relation to its proper matter and object is indicated in the words, "Rendering to each one his right," since, as Isidore says, "a man is said to be just because he respects the right [*jus*] of others."

Now, in order that an act bearing upon any matter whatever be virtuous; it should be voluntary, stable, and firm, because the Philosopher says that, in order for an act to be virtuous, it needs first of all to be done knowingly; secondly, to be done by choice and for a due end; thirdly, to be done resolutely. Now the first of these is included in the second, since "what is done through ignorance is involuntary." Hence the definition of justice mentions first the will, in order to show that the act of justice must be voluntary, and mention is made afterwards of its constancy and perpetuity in order to indicate the firmness of the act.

Accordingly, this is a complete definition of justice, save that the act is mentioned instead of the habit, which takes its species from that act, because habit implies relation to act. And if anyone would reduce it to the proper form of a definition, he might say that "justice is a habit whereby a man renders to each one his due by a constant and perpetual will"; this is about the same definition as that given by the Philosopher, who says that "justice is a habit whereby a man is said to be capable of doing just actions in accordance with his choice."

Second Article

Is Justice Always Towards Another?

We proceed thus to the Second Article:

Obj. 1. It would seem that justice is not always towards another. For the Apostle says that "the justice of God is by faith in Jesus Christ." Now, faith does not concern the dealings of one man with another. Neither, therefore, does justice.

Obj. 2. Further, according to Augustine, "It belongs to justice that man should direct to the service of God his authority over the things that are subject to him." Now the sensitive appetite is subject to man, according to Genesis 4:7, where it is written: "The lust thereof," viz., of sin, "shall be under you, and you shall have dominion over it." Therefore, it belongs to justice to have dominion over one's own appetite, so that justice is towards oneself.

Obj. 3. Further, the justice of God is eternal. But nothing else is co-eternal with God. Therefore, justice is not essentially towards another.

Obj. 4. Further, man's dealings with himself need to be rectified no less than his dealings with another. Now, man's dealings are rectified by justice, according to Proverbs 11:5, "The justice of the upright shall make his way prosperous." Therefore, justice is about our dealings, not only with others but also with ourselves.

On the contrary, Tully says that "the object of justice is to keep men together in society and mutual intercourse." Now this implies relationship of one man to another. Therefore, justice is concerned only about our dealings with others.

I answer that, As stated above, since justice by its name implies equality, it denotes essentially relation to another, for a thing is equal, not to itself, but to another. And, inasmuch as it belongs to justice to rectify human acts, as stated above, this otherness which justice demands must needs be between beings capable of action. Now, actions belong to ultimate objects of attribution and wholes and, properly speaking, not to parts and forms or powers, for we do not say properly that the hand strikes, but a man with his hand, nor that heat makes a thing hot, but fire by heat, although such expressions may be employed metaphorically. Hence justice, properly speaking, demands a distinction of ultimate objects of attribution and consequently is only in one man towards another. Nevertheless, in one and the same man we may speak metaphorically of his various principles of action, such as reason and the irascible and the concupiscible appetites, as though they were so many agents, so that metaphorically in one and the same man there is said to be justice insofar as the reason commands the irascible and concupiscible, and these obey reason, and in general insofar as to each part of man is ascribed what is becoming to it. Hence the Philosopher calls this "metaphorical justice."

Fifth Article

Is Justice a General Virtue?

We proceed thus to the Fifth Article:

Obj. 1. It would seem that justice is not a general virtue. For justice is specified with the other virtues, according to Wis. 8:7, "She teaches temperance and prudence and justice and fortitude." Now, the general is not specified or reckoned together with the species contained under the same general. Therefore, justice is not a general virtue.

Obj. 2. Further, as justice is accounted a cardinal virtue, so are temperance and fortitude. Now, neither temperance nor fortitude is reckoned to be a general virtue. Therefore, neither should justice in any way be reckoned a general virtue.

Obj. 3. Further, justice is always towards others, as stated above. But a sin committed against one's neighbor cannot be a general sin because it is distinguished from sin committed against oneself. Therefore, neither is justice a general virtue.

On the contrary, The Philosopher says that "justice is every virtue."

I answer that, Justice, as stated above, directs man in his relations with other men. Now, this may happen in two ways: first, as regards his relation with individuals; secondly, as regards his relations with others in general, insofar as a man who serves a community serves all those who are included in that community. Accordingly, justice in its proper acceptation can be directed to another in both these senses. Now, it is evident that all who are included in a community stand in relation to that community as parts to a whole, while a part, as such, belongs to a whole, so that whatever is the good of a part can be directed to the good of the whole. It follows, therefore, that the good of any virtue, whether such virtue direct man in relation to himself or in relation to certain other individual persons, is referable to the common good, to which justice directs, so that all acts of virtue can pertain to justice insofar as it directs man to the common good. It is in this sense that justice is called a general virtue. And since it belongs to the law to direct to the common good, as stated above, it follows that the justice which is in this way styled general is called legal justice, because thereby man is in harmony with the law which directs the acts of all the virtues to the common good.

Seventh Article

Is There a Particular Besides a General Justice?

We proceed thus to the Seventh Article:

Obj. 1. It would seem that there is not a particular besides a general justice. For there is nothing superfluous in the virtues, as neither is there in nature. Now, general justice directs man sufficiently in all his relations with other men. Therefore, there is no need for a particular justice. . . .

Obj. 3. Further, between the individual and the general public stands the household community. Consequently, if in addition to general justice there is a particular justice corresponding to the individual, for the same reason there should be a domestic justice directing man to the common good of a household, and yet this is not the case. Therefore, neither should there be a particular besides a legal justice.

Reply Obj. 1. Legal justice does indeed direct man sufficiently in his relations towards others. As regards the common good, it does so immediately, but as to the good of the individual, it does so mediately. Wherefore there is need for particular justice to direct a man immediately to the good of another individual.

Reply Obj. 3. The household community, according to the Philosopher, differs in respect of a threefold fellowship namely, of husband and wife, father and son, master and slave, in each of which one person is, as it were, part of the other. Wherefore, between such persons, there is not justice simply but a species of justice, viz., domestic justice, as stated in *Ethics* V, 6.

Ninth Article

Is Justice About the Passions?

We proceed thus to the Ninth Article:

Obj. 1. It would seem that justice is about the passions. For the Philosopher says that "moral virtue is about pleasure and pain." Now, pleasure, or delight, and pain are passions, as stated above when we were treating of the passions. Therefore, justice, being a moral virtue, is about the passions.

Obj. 2. Further, justice is the means of rectifying a man's operations in relation to another man. Now, such like operations cannot be rectified unless the passions be rectified, because it is owing to disorder of the passions that there is disorder in the aforesaid operations; thus sexual lust leads to adultery, and over-much love of money leads to theft. Therefore, justice must needs be about the passions.

Obj. 3. Further, even as particular justice is towards another person, so is legal justice. Now, legal justice is about the passions, else it would not extend to all the virtues, some of which are evidently about the passions. Therefore, justice is about the passions.

On the contrary, The Philosopher says that justice is about operations.

I answer that, The true answer to this question may be gathered from a twofold source. First, from the subject of justice, i.e., from the will, whose movements or acts are not passions, as stated above, for it is only the sensitive appetite whose movements are called passions. Hence justice is not about the passions, as are temperance and fortitude, which are about the irascible and concupiscible appetite. Secondly, on the part of the matter, because justice is about a man's relations with another, and we are not directed immediately to another by the internal passions. Therefore, justice is not about the passions.

Reply Obj. 1. Not every moral virtue is about pleasure and pain as its proper matter, since fortitude is about fear and daring, but every moral virtue is directed to pleasure and pain, as to ends to be acquired. For, as the Philosopher says, "pleasure and pain are the principal end in respect of which we say that this is an evil, and that a good," and in this way too they belong to justice, since "a man is not just unless he rejoice in just actions."

Reply Obj. 2. External operations are means, as it were, between external things, which are their matter, and internal passions, which are their origin. Now, it happens sometimes that there is one of these without there being a defect in the other. Thus, a man may steal another's property, not through the desire to have the thing but through the will to hurt the man; or, vice versa, a man may covet another's property without wishing to steal it. Accordingly, the directing of operations, insofar as they tend towards external things, belongs to justice, but insofar as they arise from the passions, it belongs to the other moral virtues, which are about the passions. Hence, justice hinders theft of another's property insofar as stealing is contrary to the equality that should be maintained in external things, while liberality hinders it as resulting from an immoderate desire for wealth. Since, however, external operations take their species, not from the internal passions but from external things as being their objects, it follows that external operations are essentially the matter of justice rather than of the other moral virtues.

Reply Obj. 3. The common good is the end of each individual member of a community, just as the good of the whole is the end of each part. On the other hand, the good of one individual is not the end of another individual; wherefore legal justice, which is directed to the common good, is more capable of extending to the internal passions, whereby man is disposed in some way or other in himself, than is particular justice, which is directed to the good of another individual, although legal justice extends chiefly to other virtues in the point of their external operations, insofar, to wit, as "the law commands us to perform the actions of a courageous person, . . . the actions of a temperate person . . . and the actions of a gentle person."

Tenth Article

Is the Mean of Justice an Objective Mean?

We proceed thus to the Tenth Article:

Obj. 1. It seems that the mean of justice is not the mean of some object. For the concept of a genus is preserved in all its species. But moral virtue is defined in the *Ethics* as "a willed habit which observes a mean determined in relation to us by reason." Therefore, just so, there is in justice a rational mean, not an objective one.

Obj. 2. Further, in things that are good simply, there is neither excess nor defect, and consequently neither is there a mean, as is clearly the case with the virtues according to *Ethics* II, 6. Now, justice is about things that are good simply, as stated in *Ethics* V. Therefore, in justice there is not an objective mean.

Obj. 3. Further, the reason why the other virtues are said to observe the rational and not an objective mean is because, in their case, the mean varies according to different persons, since what is too much for one is too little for another. Now, this is also the case in justice, for one who strikes a prince does not receive the same punishment as one who strikes a private individual. Therefore, just so, justice does not possess an objective mean but a rational one.

On the contrary, The Philosopher says that the mean of justice is to be taken according to arithmetical proportion, which is an objective mean.

I answer that, As stated above, the other moral virtues are chiefly concerned with the passions, the regulation of which is gauged entirely by the measure of the very man who is the subject of those passions, insofar as his anger and desire are as much as they ought to be in various circumstances. Hence, the mean in such like virtues is measured not by the proportion of one thing to another but merely by comparison with the virtuous man himself, so that with them the mean is only that which is fixed by reason in our regard.

On the other hand, the matter of justice is external operation, insofar as an operation or the thing used in that operation is duly proportonate to another person; wherefore the mean of justice consists in a certain proportion of equality between the external thing and the external person. Now, equality is the real mean between greater and less, as stated in *Metaphysics* IX; wherefore justice observes the mean objectively.

Reply Obj. 1. This objective mean is also the rational mean; wherefore justice satisfies the conditions of a moral virtue.

Reply Obj. 2. We may speak in two ways of a thing being good simply. First, a thing may be good in every way; thus the virtues are good, and there is neither mean nor extremes in things that are simply good in this sense. Secondly, a thing is said to be simply good through being good absolutely, i.e., in its nature, although it may become evil through being abused. Such are riches and honors, and in the like it is possible to find excess, deficiency, and mean as regards men, who can use them well or ill, and it is in this sense that justice is about things that are good simply.

Reply Obj. 3. The injury inflicted bears a different proportion to a ruler from that which it bears to a private person; wherefore each injury needs to be equalized by punishment in a different way, and this implies an objective and not merely a rational diversity.

Eleventh Article

Is the Act of Justice to Render to Each One His Own?

We proceed thus to the Eleventh Article:

Obj. 1. It would seem that the act of justice is not to render to each one his own. For Augustine ascribes to justice the act of succoring the needy. Now, in succoring the needy, we give them what is not theirs but ours. Therefore, the act of justice does not consist in rendering to each one his own.

Obj. 2. Further, Tully says that "beneficence, which we may call kindness or liberality, belongs to justice." Now, it pertains to liberality to give to another of one's own, not of what is his. Therefore, the act of justice does not consist in rendering to each one his own.

Obj. 3. Further, it belongs to justice not only to distribute things duly but also to repress injurious actions, such as murder, adultery, and so forth. But the rendering to each one of what is his seems to belong solely to the distribution of things. Therefore, the act of justice is not sufficiently described by saying that it consists in rendering to each one his own.

On the contrary, Ambrose says, "It is justice that renders to each one what is his and claims not another's property; it disregards its own profit in order to preserve the common equity."

I answer that, As stated above, the matter of justice is an external operation, insofar as either it or the thing we use by it is made proportionate to some other person to whom we are related by justice. Now, each man's own is that which is due to him according to equality of proportion. Therefore, the proper act of justice is nothing else than to render to each one his own.

Reply Obj. 1. Since justice is a cardinal virtue, other secondary virtues, such as mercy, liberality, and the like, are connected with it, as we shall state further on. Wherefore, to succor the needy, which belongs to mercy or pity, and to be liberally beneficent, which pertains to liberality, are by a kind of reduction ascribed to justice as to their principal virtue.

This suffices for the *Reply* to the *Second Objection.*

Reply Obj. 3. As the Philosopher states, in matters of justice, the name of profit is extended to whatever is excessive, and whatever is deficient is called loss. The reason for this is that justice is first of all and more commonly exercised in voluntary interchanges of things, such as buying and selling, wherein those expressions are properly employed, and yet they are transferred to all other matters of justice. The same applies to the rendering to each one of what is his own.

Mencius, "Justice and Humanity," from *On the Mind*

Mencius (ca. 372–ca. 298 BC) was a disciple of the great Chinese philosopher Confucius. Mencius lived and worked about the same time as Plato and Aristotle, and he developed a sensitive and elaborate philosophy of what would much later (in the eighteenth century in Europe) be identified as a theory of moral sentiments. He emphasizes the importance of justice in a ruler and the equal importance of respect and obedience in the ruler's followers. Confucius himself lived from 551 to 479 BC, and his philosophy emphasized above all the importance of "uprightness" in the prince, and obedience and "gentlemanliness" in his subjects. He introduced two key terms into Chinese thought and ordinary language: the idea of *li*, or rules of conduct, and that of *ren*, benevolent love, or what later Western thinkers would similarly call *agape*. The ideal of justice was an upright ruler with the pious obedience and adulation of the people. It is worth noting that this ideal was, above all, personal—a matter of the character and virtue of the prince and his subjects—and not merely a matter of law and rules as such. A just state, according to the Confucians, would be the envy of surrounding tyrannical states, and people would flock from tyranny to justice. The insistence on obedience and loyalty undercut any suggestion that an unjust ruler should be overthrown, but Confucius assured us that justice would triumph, nevertheless. (In what follows, the word *mind* might be better read as *soul*, suggesting deep spirituality and selfhood rather than simply our intellectual faculties.)

6.1

Mencius said, "It is a feeling common to all mankind that they cannot bear to see others suffer. The Former Kings had such feelings, and it was this that dictated their policies. One could govern the entire world with policies dictated by such feelings, as easily as though one turned it in the palm of the hand.

"I say that all men have such feelings because, on seeing a child about to fall into a well, everyone has a feeling of horror and distress. They do not have this feeling out of sympathy for the parents, or to be thought well of by friends and neighbours, or from a sense of dislike at not being thought a feeling person. Not to feel distress would be contrary to all human feeling. Just as not to feel shame and disgrace and not to defer to others and not to have a sense of right and wrong are contrary to all human feeling. This feeling of distress (at the suffering of others) is the first sign of Humanity. This feeling of shame and disgrace is the first sign of Justice. This feeling of deference to others is the first sign of propriety. This sense of right and wrong is the first sign of wisdom. Men have these four innate feelings just as they have four limbs. To possess these four things, and to protest that one is incapable of fulfilling them, is to deprive oneself. To protest that the ruler is incapable of doing so is to deprive him. since all have these four capacities within themselves, they should know how to develop and to fulfil them. They are like a fire about to burst into flame, or a spring about to gush forth from the ground. If, in fact, a ruler can fully realize them, he has all that is needed to protect the entire world. But if he does not realize them fully, he lacks what is needed to serve even his own parents."

6.2

Mencius said, "All men have things they cannot tolerate, and if what makes this so can be fully developed in the things they can tolerate, the result is Humanity. All men have things they will not do, and if what makes this so can be fully developed in the things they will do, then Justice results. If a man can fully exploit the thing in his mind which makes him not wish to harm others, then Humanity will result in overwhelming measure. If a man can fully exploit the thing in his mind which makes him reluctant to break through or jump over (other people's) walls, Justice will ensue in overwhelming measure." . . .

6.9

If the prince is a man of Humanity then nothing in his state but will be Humane. If the prince is a man of Justice, then nothing in his state but will be Just.

6.19

The difference between a man and an animal is slight. The common man disregards it altogether, but the True Gentleman guards the distinction most carefully. Shun understood all living things, but saw clearly the relationships that exist uniquely among human beings. These relationships proceed from Humanity and Justice, it is not because of these relationships that we proceed towards Humanity and Justice.

6.20

Mencius said, "Bull Mountain was once beautifully wooded. But, because it was close to a large city, its trees all fell to the axe. What of its beauty then? However, as the days passed things grew, and with the rains and the dews it was not without greenery. Then came the cattle and goats to graze. That is why, today, it has that scoured-like appearance. On seeing it now, people imagine that nothing ever grew there. But this is surely not the true nature of a mountain? And so, too, with human beings. Can it be that any man's mind naturally lacks Humanity and Justice? If he loses his sense of the good, then he loses it as the mountain lost its trees. It has been hacked away at—day after day—what of its beauty then?

"However, as the days pass he grows, and, as with all men, in the still air of the early hours his sense of right and wrong is at work. If it is barely perceptible, it is because his actions during the day have disturbed or destroyed it. Being disturbed and turned upside down the 'night airs' can barely sustain it. If this happens he is not far removed from the animals. Seeing a man so close to an animal, people cannot imagine that once his nature was different—but this is surely not the true nature of the man? Indeed, if nurtured aright, anything will grow, but if not nurtured aright anything will wither away. Confucius said, 'Hold fast to it, and you preserve it; let it go and you destroy it; it may come and go at any time no one knows its whereabouts.' Confucius was speaking of nothing less than the mind."

6.21

Mencius said, "I am fond of fish, but, too, I am fond of bear's paws. If I cannot have both, then I prefer bear's paws. I care about life, but, too, I care about Justice. If I cannot have both, then I choose Justice. I care about life, but then there are things I care about more than life. For that reason I will not seek life improperly. I do not like death, but then there are things I dislike more than death. For that reason there are some contingencies from which I will not escape.

"If men are taught to desire life above all else, then they will seize it by all means in their power. If they are taught to hate death above all else, then they will avoid all contingencies by which they might meet it. There are times when one might save one's life, but only by means that are wrong. There are times when death can be avoided, but only by means that are improper. Having desires above life itself and having dislikes greater than death itself is a type of mind that all men possess—it is not only confined to the worthy. What distinguishes the worthy is that he ensures that he does not lose it.

"Even though it be a matter of life or death to him, a traveller will refuse a basket of rice or a dish of soup if offered in an insulting manner. But food that has been trampled upon, not even a beggar will think fit to eat. And yet a man will accept emoluments of ten thousand *chung* regardless of the claims of propriety and Justice. And what does he gain by that? Elegant palaces and houses, wives and concubines to wait on him, and the allegiance of the poor among his acquaintance! I was previously speaking of matters affecting life and death, where even there under certain conditions one will not accept relief, but this is a matter of palaces and houses, of wives and concubines, and of time-serving friends. Should we not stop such things? This is what I mean by 'losing the mind with which we originally were endowed.'"

6.42

Mencius said, "The abilities men have which are not acquired by study are part of their endowment of good. The knowledge men have which is not acquired by deep thought is part of their endowment of good. Every baby in his mother's arms knows about love for his parents. When they grow up, they know about the respect they must pay to their elder brothers. The love for parents is Humanity. The respect for elders is Justice. It is nothing more than this, and it is so all over the world."

Part Two: Justice and the Social Contract

The ancient Greeks were already fascinated by the idea of prehistory, as no doubt were all intelligent people who had any sense of history. So, too, the ancient Greeks already had some idea of an implicit contract that bound citizens to their city-states, although they did not have (and likely did not miss) the concepts of individuality and legal autonomy that underlie such discussions in modern philosophy. Some sense of what is now called the social contract can be found in Plato (e.g., in the *Protagoras* and the *Crito*), and later in Lucretius there is interesting speculation about life "before" the formation of society. It has been argued (e.g., by Alasdair MacIntyre) that the ancient Greeks did not see such speculations as essential to the justification of their society or their conceptions of justice; indeed, they would not have seen these as requiring justification at all. But by the time that social contract theory emerged as the central speculative doctrine of modern social philosophy in the seventeenth and eighteenth centuries, justification was the heart of it. What justifies the state's right to take away our property, in the form of taxes, or to induct young men and women into state service, for instance, in wartime? What justifies the state's making and enforcing of laws and punishing those who violate them? What makes the state—what makes a government—*legitimate?* One answer, perhaps the dominant answer in Western (and Eastern) political philosophy, is that it is just. But once again: What is justice? And how do states and governments rightfully claim to be just?

The very popular and influential modern answer (which would not have made much sense to Plato and his colleagues) is that states and governments are legitimate insofar as they are formed and supported by the mutual agreement of the citizens of such a state, and illegitimate if not. But from this it seems not much of a step (especially to those who see "the state" and "society" as inseparable) to suggest that society itself is justified and legitimated only insofar as it is agreed upon and supported by its members. What, though, does it mean to talk about the historical formation of a society? We can understand, for instance, the formation of the United States of America as a nation through the drafting of a constitution, but it should be said that much of the structure of American society (if not the form of government) was already in place during the colonial, prerevolutionary days. The colonials for the most part shared a European ancestry, a language, a general if somewhat fractious sense of what social and economic life should be in this new world. The Constitution established a (form of) government; it did not form a society. Indeed, most societies exist for many years before drafting any such document or making any appeal to the "consent of the governed." England and France, for example, existed many centuries under hereditary monarchies, devoid of any democratic institutions, before their modern, quasi-social contract status was established.

But the actuality of a historical as opposed to a merely hypothetical agreement need not be much of an issue for social contract theorists. What is important is the *conception* of society as a network of voluntarily accepted obligations given to us by that notion, and that conception is of particular importance with respect to questions of justice. Whatever anthropologists may tell us about the actual state of prehistoric humans in the wild, we should conceive of society as voluntarily constructed by and composed of rational, autonomous human beings who saw and still see their way to compromising their various and often divisive self-interests to establish a society in which both their own and others' interests can be furthered. Justice is the content of this agreement. Before the establishment of such an agreement, there is no justice.

Social contract theory receives its first well worked out expression in Thomas Hobbes's seventeenth-century work *Leviathan*. In that work Hobbes famously contrasts the comparatively secure lot of subjects under a political authority, a sovereign, with their remarkably brutal and unhappy situation in "the natural condition of mankind." Before the formation of society, he tells us, life is a war of all against all, horrible and short. In this condition, force and fraud are "cardinal virtues," and justice and injustice have no relevance at all. The social contract, then, is designed to provide for mutual security and safety. John Locke develops a much more benign view of the state of nature, with industrious individuals planting and building and working to make their world a better, more comfortable place. Locke's social contract, accordingly, is designed primarily to protect the fruits of these individual's labors and the property on which it depends. Jean-Jacques Rousseau, again by way of contrast, develops an ebullient conception of our natural state and suggests that in nature, as opposed to contemporary civil society, we were free and happy. Society has corrupted us and made us dependent and miserable. But despite our alleged natural happiness, human freedom and reason brought us out of nature and into the oppressive strictures of society. It is in response to this degenerate sense of society that the social contract plays a central role in Rousseau's philosophy. In opposition to the corrupted and unjust forms of society that he sees around him, Rousseau suggests a very different conception of society, based not on the power of a few and the deception (and stupidity) of the rest but on the social contract, in which all citizens "impose the law on themselves" and cultivate a public moral life together.

It is in conscientious contrast with Hobbes and Rousseau in particular that the German philosopher G. W. F. Hegel presents his own allegorical representation of presocial beings, as two "self-consciousnesses" meet on an abstract and unembellished stage in the absence of any social setting or any sense of mutual belonging. In the famous "master and slave" section of his book, the *Phenomenology of Spirit,* Hegel argues (or rather, shows) that two people even in such a state of abstraction could never be indifferent to one another, as Rousseau holds that they are, and if the immediate result of such a meeting is hostility, this is not to be explained, as in Hobbes, by mutual selfishness. What people want and demand from each other—indeed what makes them "self-consciousnesses" at all—is mutual recognition, some shared sense of themselves. And if the "master-slave" conception turns out to be inadequate, that is because the very idea of individual self-consciousness is inadequate as well. Hegel's point is that the idea of autonomous individuals in a presocial state of nature makes no real sense and gives us an unintelligible picture of the nature of society.

Today, the theory of the social contract and the state of nature form the very core of the debates about justice. John Rawls postulates an "original position," not as any possible historical circumstance but as a rational model within which we can understand and justify the central principles of justice. The idea is that in the original position we find ourselves behind a "veil of ignorance" and thus do not know any specific facts about ourselves that would lead us to prefer one social arrangement over another out of sheer self-interest. If we do not know whether we are rich or poor, for example, then we will not (he argues) endorse a view of society or justice in which we would—if we turned out to be poor—be seriously handicapped or find our way to self-improvement hopelessly blocked. The original position, for Rawls, is supposed to be an abstract scenario by means of which one can model a reasonable social choice rather than a hypothesis about human nature, and the social contract is a hypothetical agreement generated from rational deliberations rather than anything like a possible historical document.

Robert Nozick accepts the idea of a state of nature as abstract scenario but rejects Rawls's reliance on the social contract, however hypothetical. What speculation about the state of nature teaches us, suggests Nozick, is the need for some minimal state, a state that functions as a protective association to secure property, enforce contracts, and defend individual rights—but little beyond this. Such a state need not arise, however, through the mutual understanding and agreement of its various members. It would rather evolve, through trial and error, possibly without the full recognition of any of its members. Borrowing a famous metaphor from Adam Smith, Nozick says that an "invisible hand" would lead to the creation of such a state, through a progression of unsatisfactory protective associations, without the conscious formation of such a structure by its members.

The final two selections take a step back and attempt to gain some perspective on social contract thinking. David Gauthier argues that the social contract is now so deeply ingrained in our consciousness as to form an ideology, and he tries to bring out precisely what the idea of the social contract as justifying social relationships assumes. His aim is not to endorse the social contract ideology, but only to lay it bare—though it should be noted that in his own first-order work on justice, Gauthier works squarely within the social contract tradition. Annette Baier, by contrast, is sharply critical of the hegemony of social contract thinking. While there is some place for thinking about justice in terms of contract, Baier argues that this place is limited solely to relationships between autonomous, fully functioning adults, with the result that any relationship of massive inequality or dependence is bound to be horribly distorted (or ignored) by social contract thinking. If Baier is right, then any attempt to account for justice in contractarian terms alone will inevitably be incomplete.

Thomas Hobbes, "The State of Nature and the Laws of Nature," from *Leviathan* (1651)

Leviathan, the masterpiece of Thomas Hobbes (1588–1679), is the classic source of modern social contract theory. In the excerpt that follows, Hobbes famously describes human life in the state of nature—that is, that condition in which human relations are not regulated by any sort of civil authority—as "solitary, poor, nasty, brutish, and short." Humans are, Hobbes thinks, predominantly self-interested, and essentially equal (though by this equality claim he means nothing more than that each person possesses sufficient mental and physical powers to pose a credible threat to every other person). In the absence of a political authority, the selfish motivation and natural equality of human beings is bound to degenerate into a war of all against all: while for each person aggressiveness is a less risky strategy to adopt than peacefulness, everyone's being warlike guarantees that the state of nature will be a very unpleasant place. What's more, Hobbes thinks, all humans also have tendencies toward vanity, and hostilities will erupt from people's insisting on deference from others. (It is on this latter point, in particular, that Rousseau will complain that Hobbes takes the vices that humans cultivate in civil society and projects them back into the state of nature. It is also on this point that Hegel will insist that humans in the state of nature are not presocial, but already bound to each other in mutual chains of recognition.) In this war of all against all, there is neither justice nor injustice, and no property rights to be respected. It is in the face of this terrible insecurity and universal fear that a mutual social compact becomes a recognizable rational necessity, and Hobbes spells out the conditions for such a compact below.

Chapter Thirteen

Of the Natural Condition of Mankind as Concerning Their Felicity and Misery

Men by nature equal. Nature has made men so equal in the faculties of the body and mind as that, though there be found one man sometimes manifestly stronger in body or of quicker mind than another, yet, when all is reckoned together, the difference between man and man is not so considerable as that one man can thereupon claim to himself any benefit to which another may not pretend as well as he. For as to the strength of body, the weakest has strength enough to kill the strongest, either by secret machination or by confederacy with others that are in the same danger with himself.

And as to the faculties of the mind, setting aside the arts grounded upon words, and especially that skill of proceeding upon general and infallible rules called science—which ' very few have and but in few things, as being not a native faculty born with us, nor attained, as prudence, while we look after somewhat else—I find yet a great equality among men than that of strength. For prudence is but experience, which equal time equally bestows on all men in those things they equally apply themselves unto. That which may perhaps make such equality incredible is but a vain conceit of one's own wisdom, which almost all men think they have in a greater degree than the vulgar—that is, than all men but themselves and a few others whom, by fame or for concurring with themselves, they approve. For such is the nature of men that howsoever they may acknowledge many others to be more witty or more eloquent or more learned, yet they will hardly believe there be many so wise as themselves; for they see their own wit at hand and other men's at a distance. But this proves rather that men are in that point equal than unequal. For there is not ordinarily a greater sign of the equal distribution of anything than that every man is contented with his share.

From equality proceeds diffidence. From this equality of ability arises equality of hope in the attaining of our ends. And therefore if any two men desire the same thing, which nevertheless they cannot both enjoy, they become enemies; and in the way to their end, which is principally their own conservation, and sometimes their delectation only, endeavor to destroy or subdue one another. And from hence it comes to pass that where an invader has no more to fear than another man's single power, if one plant, sow, build, or possess a convenient seat, others may probably be expected to come prepared with forces united to dispossess and deprive him, not only of the fruit of his labor, but also of his life or liberty. And the invader again is in the like danger of another.

From diffidence war. And from this diffidence of one another there is no way for any man to secure himself so reasonable as anticipation—that is, by force or wiles to master the persons of all men he can, so long till he see no other power great enough to endanger him; and this is no more than his own conservation requires, and is generally allowed. Also, because there be some that take pleasure in contemplating their own power in the acts of conquest, which they pursue farther than their security requires, if others that otherwise would be glad to be at ease within modest bounds should not by invasion increase their power, they would not be able, long time, by standing only on their defense, to subsist. And by consequence, such augmentation of dominion over men being necessary to a man's conservation, it ought to be allowed him.

Again, men have no pleasure, but on the contrary a great deal of grief, in keeping company where there is no power able to overawe them all. For every man looks that his companion should value him at the same rate he sets upon himself; and upon all signs of contempt or undervaluing naturally endeavors, as far as he dares (which among them that have no common power to keep them in quiet is far enough to make them destroy each other), to extort a greater value from his contemners by damage and from others by the example.

So that in the nature of man we find three principal causes of quarrel: first, competition; secondly, diffidence; thirdly, glory.

The first makes men invade for gain, the second for safety, and the third for reputation. The first use violence to make themselves masters of other men's persons, wives, children, and cattle; the second, to defend them; the third, for trifles, as a word, a smile, a different opinion, and any other sign of undervalue, either direct in their persons or by reflection in their kindred, their friends, their nation, their profession, or their name.

Out of civil states, there is always war of every one against every one. Hereby it is manifest that, during the time men live without a common power to keep them all in awe, they are in that condition which is called war, and such a war as is of every man against every man. For WAR consists not in battle only, or the act of fighting, but in a tract of time wherein the will to contend by battle is sufficiently known; and therefore the notion of *time* is to be considered in the nature of war as it is in the nature of weather. For as the nature of foul weather lies not in a shower or two of rain but in an inclination thereto of many days together, so the nature of war consists not in actual fighting but in the known disposition thereto during all the time there is no assurance to the contrary. All other time is peace.

The incommodities of such a war. Whatsoever, therefore, is consequent to a time of war where every man is enemy to every man, the same is consequent to the time wherein men live without other security than what their own strength and their own invention shall furnish them withal. In such condition there is no place for industry, because the fruit thereof is uncertain: and consequently no culture of the earth; no navigation nor use of the commodities that may be imported by sea; no commodious building; no instruments of moving and removing such things as require much force; no knowledge of the face of the earth; no account of time; no arts; no letters; no society; and, which is worst of all, continual fear and danger of violent death; and the life of man solitary, poor, nasty, brutish, and short.

It may seem strange to some man that has not well weighed these things that nature should thus dissociate and render men apt to invade and destroy one another; and he may therefore, not trusting to this inference made from the passions, desire perhaps to have the same confirmed by experience. Let him therefore consider with himself—when taking a journey he arms himself and seeks to go well accompanied, when going to sleep he locks his doors, when even in his house he locks his chests, and this when he knows there be laws and public officers, armed, to revenge all injuries shall be done him—what opinion he has of his fellow subjects when he rides armed, of his fellow citizens when he locks his doors, and of his children and servants when he locks his chests. Does he not there as much accuse mankind by his actions as I do by my words? But neither of us accuse man's nature in it. The desires and other passions of man are in themselves no sin. No more are the actions that proceed from those passions till they know a law that forbids them, which, till laws be made, they cannot know, nor can any law be made till they have agreed upon the person that shall make it.

It may peradventure be thought there was never such a time nor condition of war as this, and I believe it was never generally so over all the world; but there are many places where they live so now. For the savage people in many places of America, except the government of small families, the concord whereof depends on natural lust, have no government at all and live at this day in that brutish manner as I said before. Howsoever, it may be perceived what manner of life there would be where there were no common power to fear by the manner of life which men that have formerly lived under a peaceful government use to degenerate into a civil war.

But though there had never been any time wherein particular men were in a condition of war one against another, yet in all times kings and persons of sovereign authority, because of their independency, are in continual jealousies and in the state and posture of gladiators, having their weapons pointing and their eyes fixed on one another—that is, their forts, garrisons, and guns upon the frontiers of their kingdoms, and continual spies upon their neighbors—which is a posture of war. But because they uphold thereby the industry of their subjects, there does not follow from it that misery which accompanies the liberty of particular men.

In such a war nothing is unjust. To this war of every man against every man, this also is consequent: that nothing can be unjust. The notions of right and wrong, justice and injustice, have there no place. Where there is no common power, there is no law; where no law, no injustice. Force and fraud are in war the two cardinal virtues. Justice and injustice are none of the faculties neither of the body nor mind. If they were, they might be in a man that were alone in the world, as well as his senses and passions. They are qualities that relate to men in society, not in solitude. It is consequent also to the same condition that there be no propriety, no dominion, no *mine* and *thine* distinct; but only that to be every man's that he can get, and for so long as he can keep it. And thus much for the ill condition which man by mere nature is actually placed in, though with a possibility to come out of it consisting partly in the passions, partly in his reason.

The passions that incline men to peace. The passions that incline men to peace are fear of death, desire of such things as are necessary to commodious living, and a hope by their industry to obtain them. And reason suggests convenient articles of peace, upon which men may be drawn to agreement. These articles are they which otherwise are called the Laws of Nature, whereof I shall speak more particularly in the two following chapters.

Chapter Fourteen

Of the First and Second Natural Laws, and of Contracts

Right of nature what. The right of nature, which writers commonly call *jus naturale,* is the liberty each man has to use his own power, as he will himself, for the preservation of his own nature—that is to say, of his own life—and consequently of doing anything which, in his own judgment and reason, he shall conceive to be the aptest means thereunto.

Liberty what. By LIBERTY is understood, according to the proper signification of the word, the absence of external impediments; which impediments may oft take away part of a man's power to do what he would, but cannot hinder him from using the power left him according as his judgment and reason shall dictate to him.

A law of nature what. A LAW OF NATURE, *lex naturalis,* is a precept or general rule, found out by reason, by which a man is forbidden to do that which is destructive of his life or takes away the means of preserving the same and to omit that by which he thinks it may be best preserved. For though they that speak of this subject used to confound *jus* and *lex, right* and *law,* yet they ought to be distinguished.

Difference of right and law. RIGHT consists in liberty to do or to forbear, whereas LAW determines and binds to one of them; so that law and right differ as much as obligation and liberty, which in one and the same matter are inconsistent.

Naturally every man has right to every thing. And because the condition of man, as has been declared in the precedent chapter, is a condition of war of every one against every one—in which case everyone is governed by his own reason and there is nothing he can make use of that may not be a help unto him in preserving his life against his enemies—it follows that in such a condition every man has a right to everything, even to one another's body. And therefore, as long as this natural right of every man to everything endures, there can be no security to any man, how strong or wise soever he be, of living out the time which nature ordinarily allows men to live.

The fundamental law of nature. And consequently it is a precept or general rule of reason *that every man ought to endeavor peace, as far as he has hope of obtaining it; and when he cannot obtain it, that he may seek and use all helps and advantages of war.* The first branch of which rule contains the first and fundamental law of nature, which is *to seek peace and follow it.* The second, the sum of the right of nature, which is, *by all means we can to defend ourselves.*

The second law of nature. From this fundamental law of nature, by which men are commanded to endeavor peace, is derived this second law: *that a man be willing, when others are so too, as far forth as for peace and defense of himself he shall think it necessary, to lay down this right to all things, and be contented with so much liberty against other men as he would allow other men against himself.* For as long as every man holds this right of doing anything he likes, so long are all men in the condition of war. But if other men will not lay down their right as well as he, then there is no reason for anyone to divest himself of his, for that were to expose himself to prey, which no man is bound to, rather than to dispose himself to peace. This is that law of the gospel: *whatsoever you require that others should do to you, that do ye to them.* And that law of all men, *quod tibi fieri non vis, alteri ne feceris.*

What it is to lay down a right. To *lay down* a man's *right* to anything is to *divest* himself of the *liberty* of hindering another of the benefit of his own right to the same. For he that renounces or passes away his right gives not to any other man a right which he had not before—because there is nothing to which every man had not right by nature—but only stands out of his way, that he may enjoy his own original right without hindrance from him, not without hindrance from another. So that the effect which redounds to one man by another man's defect of right is but so much diminution of impediments to the use of his own right original. Right is laid aside either by simply renouncing it or by transferring it to another.

Renouncing a right, what it is. By *simply* RENOUNCING, when he cares not to whom the benefit thereof redounds.

Transferring right what. Obligation. By TRANSFERRING, when he intends the benefit thereof to some certain person or persons.

Duty. Injustice. And when a man has in either manner abandoned or granted away his right, then he is said to be OBLIGED or BOUND not to hinder those to whom such right is granted or abandoned from the benefit of it; and that he *ought,* and it is his DUTY, not to make void that voluntary act of his own; and that such hindrance is INJUSTICE and INJURY as being *sine jure,* the right being before renounced or transferred. So that *injury* or *injustice* in the controversies of the world is somewhat like to that which in the disputations of scholars is called *absurdity.* For as it is there called an absurdity to contradict what one maintained in the beginning, so in the world it is called injustice and injury voluntarily to undo that which from the beginning he had voluntarily done. The way by which a man either simply renounces or transfers his right is a declaration or signification by some voluntary and sufficient sign or signs that he does so renounce or transfer, or has so renounced or transferred, the same to him that accepts it. And these signs are either words only or actions only; or as it happens most often, both words and actions. And the same are the BONDS by which men are bound and obliged—bonds that have their strength, not from their own nature, for nothing is more easily broken than a man's word, but from fear of some evil consequence upon the rupture.

Not all rights are alienable. Whensoever a man transfers his right or renounces it, it is either in consideration of some right reciprocally transferred to himself or for some other good he hopes for thereby. For it is a voluntary act; and of the voluntary acts of every man, the object is some *good to himself.* And therefore there be some rights which no man can be understood by any words or other signs to have abandoned or transferred. As, first, a man cannot lay down the right of resisting them that assault him by force to take away his life, because he cannot be understood to aim thereby at any good to himself. The same may be said of wounds and chains and imprisonment, both because there is no benefit consequent to such patience as there is to the patience of suffering another to be wounded or imprisoned, as also because a man cannot tell, when he sees men proceed against him by violence, whether they intend his death or not. And, lastly, the motive and end for which this renouncing and transferring of right is introduced is nothing else but the security of a man's person in his life and in the means of so preserving life as not to be weary of it. And therefore if a man by words or other signs seem to despoil himself of the end for which those signs were intended, he is not to be understood as if he meant it or that it was his will, but that he was ignorant of how such words and actions were to be interpreted.

Contract what. The mutual transferring of right is that which men call CONTRACT.

There is difference between transferring of right to the thing and transferring, or tradition—that is, delivery—of the thing itself. For the thing may be delivered together with the translation of the right, as in buying and selling with ready money or exchange of goods or lands, and it may be delivered some time after.

Covenant what. Again, one of the contractors may deliver the thing contracted for on his part and leave the other to perform his part at some determinate time after and in the meantime be trusted, and then the contract on his part is called PACT or COVENANT; or both parts may contract now to perform hereafter, in which cases he that is to perform in time to come, being trusted, his performance is called *keeping of promise* or faith, and the failing of performance, if it be voluntary, *violation of faith.*

Free gift. When the transferring of right is not mutual, but one of the parties transfers in hope to gain thereby friendship or service from another or from his friends, or in hope to gain the reputation of charity or magnanimity, or to deliver his mind from the pain of compassion, or in hope of reward in heaven—this is not contract but GIFT, FREE GIFT, GRACE, which words signify one and the same thing. . . .

Covenants of mutual trust, when invalid. If a covenant be made wherein neither of the parties perform presently but trust one another, in the condition of mere nature, which is a condition of war of every man against every man, upon any reasonable suspicion, it is void; but if there be a common power set over them both, with right and force sufficient to compel performance, it is not void. For he that performs first has no assurance the other will perform after, because the bonds of words are too weak to bridle men's ambition, avarice, anger, and other passions without the fear of some coercive power which in the condition of mere nature, where all men are equal and judges of the justness of their own fears, cannot possibly be supposed. And therefore he which performs first does but betray himself to his enemy, contrary to the right he can never abandon of defending his life and means of living.

But in a civil estate, where there is a power set up to constrain those that would otherwise violate their faith, that fear is no more reasonable; and for that cause, he which by the covenant is to perform first is obliged so to do.

The cause of fear which makes such a covenant invalid must be always something arising after the covenant made, as some new fact or other sign of the will not to perform; else it cannot make the covenant void. For that which could not hinder a man from promising ought not to be admitted as a hindrance of performing. . . .

Covenants how made void. Men are freed of their covenants two ways: by performing or by being forgiven. For performance is the natural end of obligation, and forgiveness the restitution of liberty, as being a retransferring of that right in which the obligation consisted.

Covenants extorted by fear are valid. Covenants entered into by fear, in the condition of mere nature, are obligatory. For example, if I covenant to pay a ransom or service for my life to an enemy, I am bound by it; for it is a contract, wherein one receives the benefit of life, the other is to receive money or service for it; and consequently, where no other law, as in the condition of mere nature, forbids the performance, the covenant is valid. Therefore prisoners of war, if trusted with the payment of their ransom, are obliged to pay it; and if a weaker prince make a disadvantageous peace with a stronger, for fear, he is bound to keep it; unless, as has been said before, there arises some new and just cause of fear to renew the war. And even in commonwealths, if I be forced to redeem myself from a thief by promising him money, I am bound to pay it till the civil law discharge me. For whatsoever I may lawfully do without obligation, the same I may lawfully covenant to do through fear; and what I lawfully covenant, I cannot lawfully break.

The former covenant to one makes void the later to another. A former covenant makes void a later. For a man that has passed away his right to one man today has it not to pass tomorrow to another; and therefore the later promise passes no right, but is null.

A man's covenant not to defend himself is void. A covenant not to defend myself from force by force is always void. For, as I have showed before, no man can transfer or lay down his right to save himself from death, wounds, and imprisonment, the avoiding whereof is the only end of laying down any right; and therefore the promise of not resisting force in no covenant transfers any right, nor is obliging. For though a man may covenant thus: *unless I do so or so, kill me,* he cannot covenant thus: *unless I do so or so, I will not resist you when you come to kill me.* For man by nature chooses the lesser evil, which is danger of death in resisting, rather than the greater, which is certain and present death in not resisting. And this is granted to be true by all men, in that they lead criminals to execution and prison with armed men, notwithstanding that such criminals have consented to the law by which they are condemned.

No man obliged to accuse himself. A covenant to accuse oneself, without assurance of pardon, is likewise invalid. For in the condition of nature, where every man is judge, there is no place for accusation; and in the civil state, the accusation is followed with punishment, which, being force, a man is not obliged not to resist. The same is also true of the accusation of those by whose condemnation a man falls into misery, as of a father, wife, or benefactor. For the testimony of such an accuser, if it be not willingly given, is presumed to be corrupted by nature, and therefore not to be received; and where a man's testimony is not to be credited, he is not bound to give it. Also accusations upon torture are not to be reputed as testimonies. For torture is to be used but as means of conjecture and light in the further examination and search of truth; and what is in that case confessed tends to the ease of him that is tortured, not to the informing of the torturers, and therefore ought not to have the credit of a sufficient testimony; for whether he deliver himself by true or false accusation, he does it by the right of preserving his own life.

The end of an oath. The force of words being, as I have formerly noted, too weak to hold men to the performance of their covenants, there are in man's nature but two imaginable helps to strengthen it. And those are either a fear of the consequence of breaking their word, or a glory or pride in appearing not to need to break it. This latter is a generosity too rarely found to be presumed on, especially in the pursuers of wealth, command, or sensual pleasure—which are the greatest part of mankind. The passion to be reckoned upon is fear, whereof there be two very general objects: one, the power of spirits invisible; the other, the power of those men they shall therein offend. Of these two, though the former be the greater power, yet the fear of the latter is commonly the greater fear. The fear of the former is in every man his own religion, which has place in the nature of man before civil society. The latter has not so, at least not place enough to keep men to their promises, because in the condition of mere nature the inequality of power is not discerned but by the event of battle. So that before the time of civil society, or in the interruption thereof by war, there is nothing can strengthen a covenant of peace agreed on against the temptations of avarice, ambition, lust, or other strong desire but the fear of that invisible power, which they everyone worship as God and fear as a revenger of their perfidy.

The form of an oath. All therefore that can be done between two men not subject to civil power is to put one another to swear by the God he fears, which *swearing* or OATH is a *form of speech, added to a promise, by which he that promises signifies that, unless he perform, he renounces the mercy of his God, or calls to him for vengeance on himself.* Such was the heathen form, *Let Jupiter kill me else, as I kill this beast.* So is our form, *I shall do thus and thus, so help me God.* And this, with the rites and ceremonies which everyone uses in his own religion, that the fear of breaking faith might be the greater.

No oath but by God. By this it appears that an oath taken according to any other form or rite than his that swears is in vain and no oath, and that there is no swearing by anything which the swearer thinks not God. For though men have sometimes used to swear by their kings, for fear or flattery, yet they would have it thereby understood they attributed to them divine honor. And that swearing unnecessarily by God is but profaning of his name; and swearing by other things, as men do in common discourse, is not swearing but an impious custom gotten by too much vehemence of talking.

An oath adds nothing to the obligation. It appears also that the oath adds nothing to the obligation. For a covenant, if lawful, binds in the sight of God without the oath as much as with it; if unlawful, binds not at all, though it be confirmed with an oath.

Chapter Fifteen

Of Other Laws of Nature

The third law of nature, justice. From that law of nature by which we are obliged to transfer to another such rights as, being retained, hinder the peace of mankind, there follows a third, which is this: *that men perform their covenants made;* without which covenants are in vain and but empty words, and, the right of all men to all things remaining, we are still in the condition of war.

Justice and injustice what. And in this law of nature consists the fountain and original of JUSTICE. For where no covenant has preceded there has no right been transferred, and every man has right to every thing; and consequently no action can be unjust. But when a covenant is made, then to break it is *unjust;* and the definition of INJUSTICE is no other than *the not performance of covenant.* And whatsoever is not unjust is *just.*

Justice and propriety begin with the constitution of commonwealth. But because covenants of mutual trust, where there is a fear of not performance on either part, as has been said in the former chapter, are invalid, though the original of justice be the making of covenants, yet injustice actually there can be none till the cause of such fear be taken away, which, while men are in the natural condition of war, cannot be done. Therefore, before the names of just and unjust can have place, there must be some coercive power to compel men equally to the performance of their covenants by the terror of some punishment greater than the benefit they expect by the breach of their covenant, and to make good that propriety which by mutual contract men acquire in recompense of the universal right they abandon; and such power there is none before the erection of a commonwealth. And this is also to be gathered out of the ordinary definition of justice in the Schools, for they say that *justice is the constant will of giving to every man his own.* And therefore where there is no *own*—that is, no propriety—there is no injustice; and where there is no coercive power erected—that is, where there is no commonwealth—there is no propriety, all men having right to all things; therefore, where there is no commonwealth, there nothing is unjust. So that the nature of justice consists in keeping of valid covenants; but the validity of covenants begins not but with the constitution of a civil power sufficient to compel men to keep them; and then it is also that propriety begins.

Justice not contrary to reason. The fool hath said in his heart, there is no such thing as justice; and sometimes also with his tongue, seriously alleging that, every man's conservation and contentment being committed to his own care, there could be no reason why every man might not do what he thought conduced thereunto; and therefore also to make or not make, keep or not keep covenants was not against reason when it conduced to one's benefit. He does not therein deny that there be covenants and that they are sometimes broken, sometimes kept, and that such breach of them may be called injustice and the observance of them justice; but he questions whether injustice, taking away the fear of God—for the same fool hath said in his heart which dictates to every man his own good, and particularly then when it conduces to such a benefit as shall put a man in a condition to neglect not only the dispraise and revilings, but also the power of other men. The kingdom of God is gotten by violence; but what if it could be gotten by unjust violence? Were it against reason so to get it, when it is impossible to receive hurt by it? And if it be not against reason, it is not against justice, or else justice is not to be approved for good. From such reasoning as this, successful wickedness has obtained the name of virtue. . . .

This specious reasoning is nevertheless false.

For the question is not of promises mutual where there is no security of performance on either side—as when there is no civil power erected over the parties promising—for such promises are no covenants; but either where one of the parties has performed already or where there is a power to make him perform, there is the question whether it be against reason—that is, against the benefit of the other—to perform or not. And I say it is not against reason. For the manifestation whereof we are to consider, first, that when a man does a thing which, notwithstanding anything can be foreseen and reckoned on, tends to his own destruction, howsoever some accident which he could not expect, arriving, may turn it to his benefit, yet such events do not make it reasonably or wisely done. Secondly, that in a condition of war, wherein every man to every man, for want of a common power to keep them all in awe, is an enemy, there is no man who can hope by his own strength or wit to defend himself from destruction without the help of confederates, where everyone expects the same defense by the confederation that anyone else does; and therefore he which declares he thinks it reason to deceive those that help him can in reason expect no other means of safety than what can be had from his own single power. He, therefore, that breaks his covenant, and consequently declares that he thinks he may with reason do so, cannot be received into any society that unite themselves for peace and defense, but by the error of them that receive him; nor, when he is received, be retained in it without seeing the danger of their error, which errors a man cannot reasonably reckon upon as the means of his security; and therefore if he be left or cast out of society he perishes, and if he live in society, it is by the errors of other men, which he could not foresee nor reckon upon, and consequently against the reason of his preservation; and so, as all men that contribute not to his destruction, forbear him only out of ignorance of what is good for themselves.

As for the instance of gaining the secure and perpetual felicity of heaven by any way, it is frivolous, there being but one way imaginable, and that is not breaking but keeping of covenant.

And for the other instance of attaining sovereignty by rebellion, it is manifest that, though the event follow, yet because it cannot reasonably be expected, but rather the contrary, and because by gaining it so others are taught to gain the same in like manner the

attempt thereof is against reason. Justice, therefore—that is to say, keeping of covenant—
is a rule of reason by which we are forbidden to do anything destructive to our life, and consequently a law of nature. . . .

Justice of men and justice of actions what. The names of just and unjust, when they are
attributed to men, signify one thing, and when they are attributed to actions, another. When
they are attributed to men, they signify conformity or inconformity of manners to reason.
But when they are attributed to actions, they signify the conformity or inconformity to reason, not of manners or manner of life, but of particular actions. A just man, therefore, is he
that takes all the care he can that his actions may be all just; and an unjust man is he that neglects it. And such men are more often in our language styled by the names of righteous and
unrighteous than just and unjust, though the meaning be the same. Therefore a righteous man
does not lose that title by one or a few unjust actions that proceed from sudden passion or
mistake of things or persons; nor does an unrighteous man lose his character for such actions
as he does or forbears to do for fear, because his will is not framed by the justice but by the
apparent benefit of what he is to do. That which gives to human actions the relish of justice
is a certain nobleness or gallantness of courage, rarely found, by which a man scorns to be
beholden for the contentment of his life to fraud or breach of promise. This justice of the
manners is that which is meant where justice is called a virtue and injustice a vice.

But the justice of actions denominates men, not just, but *guiltless;* and the injustice of
the same, which is also called injury, gives them but the name of *guilty.*

Justice of manners, and justice of actions. Again, the injustice of manners is the disposition or aptitude to do injury, and is injustice before it proceed to act and without
supposing any individual person injured. But the injustice of an action—that is to say,
injury—supposes an individual person injured—namely, him to whom the covenant was
made—and therefore many times the injury is received by one man when the damage
redounds to another. As when the master commands his servant to give money to a stranger:
if it be not done, the injury is done to the master, whom he had before covenanted to obey;
but the damage redounds to the stranger, to whom he had no obligation and therefore could
not injure him. And so also in commonwealths private men may remit to one another their
debts but not robberies or other violences whereby they are endamaged; because the detain-
ing of debt is an injury to themselves, but robbery and violence are injuries to the person of
the commonwealth.

Nothing done to a man by his own consent can be injury. Whatsoever is done to a man,
conformable to his own will signified to the doer, is no injury to him. For if he that does it
has not passed away his original right to do what he please by some antecedent covenant,
there is no breach of covenant and therefore no injury done him. And if he have, then his
will to have it done, being signified, is a release of that covenant, and so again there is no
injury done him.

Justice commutative and distributive. Justice of actions is by writers divided into *commutative* and *distributive;* and the former they say consists in proportion arithmetical, the
latter in proportion geometrical. Commutative, therefore, they place in the equality of value
of the things contracted for, and distributive in the distribution of equal benefit to men of
equal merit. As if it were injustice to sell dearer than we buy, or to give more to a man than
he merits. The value of all things contracted for is measured by the appetite of the contractors, and therefore the just value is that which they be contented to give. And merit (besides
that which is by covenant, where the performance on one part merits the performance of the
other part, and falls under justice commutative, not distributive) is not due by justice, but
is rewarded of grace only. And therefore this distinction, in the sense wherein it uses to be
expounded, is not right. To speak properly, commutative justice is the justice of a contrac-

tor—that is, a performance of covenant in buying and selling, hiring and letting to hire, lending and borrowing, exchanging, bartering, and other acts of contract.

And distributive justice, the justice of an arbitrator—that is to say, the act of defining what is just. Wherein, being trusted by them that make him arbitrator, if he perform his trust, he is said to distribute to every man his own; and this is indeed just distribution, and may be called, though improperly, distributive justice, but more properly equity, which also is a law of nature, as shall be shown in due place. . . .

The sixth, facility to pardon. A sixth law of nature is this: *that upon caution of the future time, a man ought to pardon the offenses past of them that, repenting, desire it.* For PARDON is nothing but granting of peace, which, though granted to them that persevere in their hostility, be not peace but fear, yet, not granted to them that give caution of the future time, is sign of an aversion to peace, and therefore contrary to the law of nature.

The seventh, that in revenges men respect only the future good. A seventh is *that in revenges*—that is, retribution of evil for evil—*men look not at the greatness of the evil past, but the greatness of the good to follow.* Whereby we are forbidden to inflict punishment with any other design than for correction of the offender or direction of others. For this law is consequent to the next before it that commands pardon upon security of the future time. Besides, revenge without respect to the example and profit to come is a triumph or glorying in the hurt of another, tending to no end; for the end is always somewhat to come, and glorying to no end is vainglory and contrary to reason; and to hurt without reason tends to the introduction of war, which is against the law of nature and is commonly styled by the name of *cruelty.*

The eighth, against contumely. And because all signs of hatred or contempt provoke to fight, insomuch as most men choose rather to hazard their life than not to be revenged, we may in the eighth place for a law of nature set down this precept: *that no man by deed, word, countenance, or gesture declare hatred or contempt of another.* The breach of which law is commonly called *contumely.*

The ninth, against pride. The question who is the better man has no place in the condition of mere nature, where, as has been shown before, all men are equal. The inequality that now is has been introduced by the laws civil. I know that Aristotle in the first book of his *Politics,* for a foundation of his doctrine, makes men by nature some more worthy to command, meaning the wiser sort such as he thought himself to be for his philosophy, others to serve, meaning those that had strong bodies but were not philosophers as he; as if master and servant were not introduced by consent of men but by difference of wit, which is not only against reason but also against experience. For there are very few so foolish that had not rather govern themselves than be governed by others; nor when the wise in their own conceit contend by force with them who distrust their own wisdom, do they always, or often, or almost at any time, get the victory. If nature therefore have made men equal, that equality is to be acknowledged; or if nature have made men unequal, yet because men that think themselves equal will not enter into conditions of peace but upon equal terms, such equality must be admitted. And therefore for the ninth law of nature, I put this: *that every man acknowledge another for his equal by nature.* The breach of this precept is *pride.* . . .

The eleventh, equity. Also if *a man be trusted to judge between man and man,* it is a precept of the law of nature *that he deal equally between them.* For without that, the controversies of men cannot be determined but by war. He, therefore, that is partial in judgment does what in him lies to deter men from the use of judges and arbitrators, and consequently, against the fundamental law of nature, is the cause of war.

The observance of this law, from the equal distribution to each man of that which in reason belongs to him, is called EQUITY and, as I have said before, distributive justice.

John Locke, "The State of Nature and the Social Contract," from *Second Treatise of Government* (1690)

John Locke (1632–1704) wrote his two treatises on government to respond to the political theory of Robert Filmer, who in the *Patriarcha* understands all political authority in terms of an original bestowal of political authority upon Adam and its transmission to certain of Adam's heirs. In the first of his two treatises, Locke demolishes Filmer's views, showing that Filmer's account is both wildly implausible in itself and now entirely unhelpful in answering questions about authority. But upon finishing the destructive side of his response, Locke is left with a serious question: how is he to understand the source of property and authority? His answer is akin to Hobbes's: that we can best understand the origin and nature of political authority through examining the situation of prepolitical individuals, who through an agreement confer political authority on rulers. But while the concepts of the state of nature and the social contract loom as large in Locke's view as in Hobbes's, Locke wants to distance his view from the Hobbesian account: there is little of the utter selfishness and mutual hostility of Hobbes's horrifying portrait, but rather a picture of individuals with natural rights (including the right to property; see Part Three) who usually respect such rights but run into trouble trying to enforce them against wayward offenders. It is to acknowledge and enforce these natural rights that political authority is instituted by contract.

Of the State of Nature

4.   To understand political power right and derive it from its original, we must consider what state all men are naturally in, and that is a state of perfect freedom to order their actions and dispose of their possessions and persons as they think fit, within the bounds of the law of nature, without asking leave or depending upon the will of any other man.

A state also of equality, wherein all the power and jurisdiction is reciprocal, no one having more than another; there being nothing more evident than that creatures of the same species and rank, promiscuously born to all the same advantages of nature and the use of the same faculties, should also be equal one amongst another without subordination or subjection; unless the lord and master of them all should, by any manifest declaration of his will, set one above another, and confer on him by an evident and clear appointment an undoubted right to dominion and sovereignty.

5.   This equality of men by nature the judicious Hooker looks upon as so evident

in itself and beyond all question that he makes it the foundation of that obligation to mutual love amongst men on which he builds the duties we owe one another, and from whence he derives the great maxims of justice and charity. His words are:

> The like natural inducement hath brought men to know that it is no less their duty to love others than themselves; for seeing those things which are equal must needs all have one measure; if I cannot but wish to receive good, even as much at every man's hands as any man can wish unto his own soul, how should I look to have any part of my desire herein satisfied unless myself be careful to satisfy the like desire, which is undoubtedly in other men, being of one and the same nature? To have anything offered them repugnant to this desire must needs in all respects grieve them as much as me; so that, if I do harm, I must look to suffer, there being no reason that others should show greater measure of love to me than they have by me showed unto them; my desire therefore to be loved of my equals in nature, as much as possibly may be, imposeth upon me a natural duty of bearing to them-ward fully the like affection; from which relation of equality between ourselves and them that are as ourselves, what several rules and canons natural reason hath drawn, for direction of life, no man is ignorant. (*Of the Laws of Ecclesiastical Polity,* Book I)

6.   But though this be a state of liberty, yet it is not a state of license; though man in that state have an uncontrollable liberty to dispose of his person or possessions, yet he has not liberty to destroy himself, or so much as any creature in his possession, but where some nobler use than its bare preservation calls for it. The state of nature has a law of nature to govern it, which obliges every one; and reason, which is that law, teaches all mankind who will but consult it that, being all equal and independent, no one ought to harm another in his life, health, liberty, or possessions; for men being all the workmanship of one omnipotent and infinitely wise Maker—all the servants of one sovereign master, sent into the world by his order, and about his business—they are his property whose workmanship they are, made to last during his, not one another's, pleasure; and being furnished with like faculties, sharing all in one community of nature, there cannot be supposed any such subordination among us that may authorize us to destroy another, as if we were made for one another's uses as the inferior ranks of creatures are for ours. Every one, as he is bound to preserve himself and not to quit his station wilfully, so by the like reason, when his own preservation comes not in competition, ought he, as much as he can, to preserve, the rest of mankind, and may not, unless it be to do justice to an offender, take away or impair the life, or what tends to the preservation of the life, the liberty, health, limb, or goods of another.

7.   And that all men may be restrained from invading others' rights and from doing hurt to one another, and the law of nature be observed, which wills the peace and preservation of all mankind, the execution of the law of nature is, in that state, put into every man's hands, whereby everyone has a right to punish the transgressors of that law to such a degree as may hinder its violation; for the law of nature would, as all other laws that concern men in this world, be in vain if there were nobody that in that state of nature had a power to execute that law and thereby preserve the innocent and restrain offenders. And if anyone in the state of nature may punish another for any evil he has done, everyone may do so; for in that state of perfect equality, where naturally there is no superiority or jurisdiction of one over another, what any may do in prosecution of that law, everyone must needs have a right to do.

8.   And thus in the state of nature one man comes by a power over another; but yet no absolute or arbitrary power to use a criminal, when he has got him in his hands, according to the passionate heats or boundless extravagance of his own will; but only to retribute

to him, so far as calm reason and conscience dictate, what is proportionate to his trans-gression, which is so much as may serve for reparation and restraint; for these two are the only reasons why one man may lawfully do harm to another, which is that we call punish-ment. In transgressing the law of nature, the offender declares himself to live by another rule than that of reason and common equity, which is that measure God has set to the actions of men for their mutual security; and so he becomes dangerous to mankind, the tie which is to secure them from injury and violence being slighted and broken by him. Which being a trespass against the whole species and the peace and safety of it provided for by the law of nature, every man upon this score, by the right he has to preserve mankind in general, may restrain, or, where it is necessary, destroy things noxious to them, and so may bring such evil on any one who has transgressed that law, as may make him repent the doing of it and thereby deter him, and by his example others, from doing the like mischief. And in this case, and upon this ground, *every man has a right to punish the offender and be exe-cutioner of the law of nature.* . . .

10.   Besides the crime which consists in violating the law and varying from the right rule of reason, whereby a man so far becomes degenerate and declares himself to quit the principles of human nature and to be a noxious creature, there is commonly injury done to some person or other, and some other man receives damage by his transgression; in which case he who has received any damage has, besides the right of punishment common to him with other men, a particular right to seek reparation from him that has done it; and any other person, who finds it just, may also join with him that is injured and assist him in recovering from the offender so much as may make satisfaction for the harm he has suf-fered.

11.   From these two distinct rights—the one of punishing the crime for restraint and preventing the like offense, which right of punishing is in everybody; the other of tak-ing reparation, which belongs only to the injured party—comes it to pass that the magis-trate, who by being magistrate has the common right of punishing put into his hands, can often, where the public good demands not the execution of the law, remit the punishment of criminal offenses by his own authority, but yet cannot remit the satisfaction due to any private man for the damage he has received. That he who has suffered the damage has a right to demand in his own name, and he alone can remit; the damnified person has this power of appropriating to himself the goods or service of the offender by right of self-preservation, as every man has a power to punish the crime to prevent its being committed again, by the right he has of preserving all mankind and doing all reasonable things he can in order to that end; and thus it is that every man, in the state of nature, has a power to kill a murderer, both to deter others from doing the like injury, which no reparation can com-pensate, by the example of the punishment that attends it from everybody, and also to secure men from the attempts of a criminal who, having renounced reason—the common rule and measure God has given to mankind—has, by the unjust violence and slaughter he has committed upon one, declared war against all mankind, and therefore may be destroyed as a lion or a tiger, one of those wild savage beasts with whom men can have no society nor security. And upon this is grounded that great law of nature, "Whoso sheddeth man's blood, by man shall his blood be shed." And Cain was so fully convinced that every one had a right to destroy such a criminal that, after the murder of his brother, he cries out, "Every one that findeth me, shall slay me"; so plain was it written in the hearts of mankind.

12.   By the same reason may a man in the state of nature punish the lesser breaches of that law. It will perhaps be demanded: with death? I answer: Each transgression may be punished to that degree and with so much severity as will suffice to make it an ill bargain

to the offender, give him cause to repent, and terrify others from doing the like. Every offense that can be committed in the state of nature may in the state of nature be also punished equally, and as far forth as it may in a commonwealth; for though it would be beside my present purpose to enter here into the particulars of the law of nature, or its measures of punishment, yet it is certain there is such a law, and that, too, as intelligible and plain to a rational creature and a studier of that law as the positive laws of commonwealths, nay, possibly plainer, as much as reason is easier to be understood than the fancies and intricate contrivances of men, following contrary and hidden interests put into words; for so truly are a great part of the municipal laws of countries, which are only so far right as they are founded on the law of nature, by which they are to be regulated and interpreted. . . .

14.   It is often asked as a mighty objection, "Where are or ever were there any men in such a state of nature?" To which it may suffice as an answer at present that since all princes and rulers of independent governments all through the world are in a state of nature, it is plain the world never was, nor ever will be, without numbers of men in that state. I have named all governors of independent communities, whether they are, or are not, in league with others; for it is not every compact that puts an end to the state of nature between men, but only this one of agreeing together mutually to enter into one community and make one body politic; other promises and compacts men may make one with another and yet still be in the state of nature. The promises and bargains for truck, etc., between the two men in the desert island, mentioned by Garcilasso de la Vega, in his history of Peru, or between a Swiss and an Indian in the woods of America, are binding to them, though they are perfectly in a state of nature in reference to one another; for truth and keeping of faith belongs to men as men, and not as members of society. . . .

Of the State of War

16.   The state of war is a state of enmity and destruction; and, therefore, declaring by word or action, not a passionate and hasty but a sedate, settled design upon another man's life, puts him in a state of war with him against whom he has declared such an intention, and so has exposed his life to the other's power to be taken away by him or anyone that joins with him in his defense and espouses his quarrel; it being reasonable and just I should have a right to destroy that which threatens me with destruction; for, by the fundamental law of nature, man being to be preserved as much as possible when all cannot be preserved, the safety of the innocent is to be preferred; and one may destroy a man who makes war upon him, or has discovered an enmity to his being, for the same reason that he may kill a wolf or a lion, because such men are not under the ties of the common law of reason, have no other rule but that of force and violence, and so may be treated as beasts of prey, those dangerous and noxious creatures that will be sure to destroy him whenever he falls into their power.

17.   And hence it is that he who attempts to get another man into his absolute power does thereby put himself into a state of war with him, it being to be understood as a declaration of a design upon his life; for I have reason to conclude that he who would get me into his power without my consent would use me as he pleased when he got me there, and destroy me, too, when he had a fancy to it; for nobody can desire to have me in his absolute power unless it be to compel me by force to that which is against the right of my freedom, i.e., make me a slave. To be free from such force is the only security of my preservation; and reason bids me look on him as an enemy to my preservation who would take

away that freedom which is the fence to it; so that he who makes an attempt to enslave me thereby puts himself into a state of war with me. He that, in the state of nature, would take away the freedom that belongs to any one in that state must necessarily be supposed to have a design to take away everything else, that freedom being the foundation of all the rest; as he that, in the state of society, would take away the freedom belonging to those of that society or commonwealth must be supposed to design to take away from them everything else, and so be looked on as in a state of war.

18. · This makes it lawful for a man to kill a thief who has not in the least hurt him, nor declared any design upon his life any farther than, by the use of force, so to get him in his power as to take away his money, or what he pleases, from him; because using force where he has no right to get me into his power, let his pretense be what it will, I have no reason to suppose that he who would take away my liberty would not, when he had me in his power, take away everything else. And therefore it is lawful for me to treat him as one who has put himself into a state of war with me, i.e., kill him if I can; for to that hazard does he justly expose himself whoever introduces a state of war and is aggressor in it.

19.   And here we have the plain difference between the state of nature and the state of war which, however some men have confounded, are as far distant as a state of peace, good-will, mutual assistance, and preservation, and a state of enmity, malice, violence, and mutual destruction are one from another. Men living together according to reason, without a common superior on earth with authority to judge between them, is properly the state of nature. But force, or a declared design of force, upon the person of another, where there is no common superior on earth to appeal to for relief, is the state of war; and it is the want of such an appeal [that] gives a man the right of war even against an aggressor, though he be in society and a fellow subject. Thus a thief, whom I cannot harm but by appeal to the law for having stolen all that I am worth, I may kill when he sets on men to rob me but of my horse or coat; because the law, which was made for my preservation, where it cannot interpose to secure my life from present force, which, if lost, is capable of no reparation, permits me my own defense and the right of war, a liberty to kill the aggressor, because the aggressor allows not time to appeal to our common judge, nor the decision of the law, for remedy in a case where the mischief may be irreparable. Want of a common judge with authority puts all men in a state of nature; force without right upon a man's person makes a state of war both where there is and is not a common judge.

20.   But when the actual force is over, the state of war ceases between those that are in society and are equally on both sides subjected to the fair determination of the law, because then there lies open the remedy of appeal for the past injury and to prevent future harm. But where no such appeal is, as in the state of nature, for want of positive laws and judges with authority to appeal to, the state of war once begun continues with a right to the innocent party to destroy the other whenever he can, until the aggressor offers peace and desires reconciliation on such terms as may repair any wrongs he has already done and secure the innocent for the future; nay, where an appeal to the law and constituted judges lies open, but the remedy is denied by a manifest perverting of justice and a barefaced wresting of the laws to protect or indemnify the violence or injuries of some men, or party of men, there it is hard to imagine anything but a state of war; for wherever violence is used and injury done, though by hands appointed to administer justice, it is still violence and injury, however colored with the name, pretenses, or forms of law, the end whereof being to protect and redress the innocent by an unbiased application of it to all who are under it; wherever that is not bona fide done, war is made upon the sufferers, who having no appeal on earth to right them, they are left to the only remedy in such cases—an appeal to heaven.

21.   To avoid this state of war—wherein there is no appeal but to heaven, and wherein every the least difference is apt to end, where there is no authority to decide between the contenders—is one great reason of men's putting themselves into society and quitting the state of nature; for where there is an authority, a power on earth from which relief can be had by appeal, there the continuance of the state of war is excluded, and the controversy is decided by that power. Had there been any such court, any superior jurisdiction on earth, to determine the right between Jephthah and the Ammonites, they had never come to a state of war; but we see he was forced to appeal to heaven: "The Lord the Judge," says he, "be judge this day between the children of Israel and the children of Ammon" (Judges xi. 27.), and then prosecuting and relying on his appeal, he leads out his army to battle. And, therefore, in such controversies where the question is put, "Who shall be judge?" it cannot be meant, "who shall decide the controversy"; every one knows what Jephthah here tells us, that "the Lord the Judge" shall judge. Where there is no judge on earth, the appeal lies to God in heaven. That question then cannot mean: who shall judge whether another has put himself in a state of war with me, and whether I may, as Jephthah did, appeal to heaven in it? Of that I myself can only be judge in my own conscience, as I will answer it, at the great day, to the supreme Judge of all men. . . .

Of the Beginning of Political Societies

95.   Men being, as has been said, by nature all free, equal, and independent, no one can be put out of this estate and subjected to the political power of another without his own consent. The only way whereby any one divests himself of his natural liberty and puts on the bonds of civil society is by agreeing with other men to join and unite into a community for their comfortable, safe, and peaceable living one amongst another, in a secure enjoyment of their properties and a greater security against any that are not of it. This any number of men may do, because it injures not the freedom of the rest; they are left as they were in the liberty of the state of nature. When any number of men have so consented to make one community or government, they are thereby presently incorporated and make one body politic wherein the majority have a right to act and conclude the rest.

96.   For when any number of men have, by the consent of every individual, made a community, they have thereby made that community one body, with a power to act as one body, which is only by the will and determination of the majority; for that which acts any community being only the consent of the individuals of it, and it being necessary to that which is one body to move one way, it is necessary the body should move that way whither the greater force carries it, which is the consent of the majority; or else it is impossible it should act or continue one body, one community, which the consent of every individual that united into it agreed that it should; and so every one is bound by that consent to be concluded by the majority. And therefore we see that in assemblies impowered to act by positive laws, where no number is set by that positive law which impowers them, the act of the majority passes for the act of the whole and, of course, determines, as having by the law of nature and reason the power of the whole.

97.   And thus every man, by consenting with others to make one body politic under one government, puts himself under an obligation to every one of that society to submit to the determination of the majority and to be concluded by it; or else this original compact, whereby he with others incorporates into one society, would signify nothing, and be no compact, if he be left free and under no other ties than he was in before in the state of

nature. For what appearance would there be of any compact? What new engagement if he were no further tied by any decrees of the society than he himself thought fit and did actually consent to? This would be still as great a liberty as he himself had before his compact, or any one else in the state of nature has who may submit himself and consent to any acts of it if he thinks fit.

98.   For if the consent of the majority shall not in reason be received as the act of the whole and conclude every individual, nothing but the consent of every individual can make anything to be the act of the whole; but such a consent is next to impossible ever to be had if we consider the infirmities of health and avocations of business which in a number, though much less than that of a commonwealth, will necessarily keep many away from the public assembly. To which, if we add the variety of opinions and contrariety of interests which unavoidably happen in all collections of men, the coming into society upon such terms would be only like Cato's coming into the theatre only to go out again. Such a constitution as this would make the mighty leviathan of a shorter duration than the feeblest creatures, and not let it outlast the day it was born in; which cannot be supposed till we can think that rational creatures should desire and constitute societies only to be dissolved; for where the majority cannot conclude the rest, there they cannot act as one body, and consequently will be immediately dissolved again.

99.   Whosoever, therefore, out of a state of nature unite into a community must be understood to give up all the power necessary to the ends for which they unite into society to the majority of the community, unless they expressly agreed in any number greater than the majority. And this is done by barely agreeing to unite into one political society, which is all the compact that is, or needs be, between the individuals that enter into or make up a commonwealth. And thus that which begins and actually constitutes any political society is nothing but the consent of any number of freemen capable of a majority to unite and incorporate into such a society. And this is that, and that only, which did or could give beginning to any lawful government in the world.

Jean-Jacques Rousseau, "From the State of Nature to Citizenship," from *A Discourse on the Origins of Inequality* (1754) and *On the Social Contract* (1762)

Jean-Jacques Rousseau (1712–1778) wrote two discourses for the Academy in Dijon in the early 1750s. The first, on the arts and sciences, argued the eccentric thesis that the development of the arts and sciences actually contributed to the degeneracy of human civilization rather than to its improvement, and yet the Academy gave him the much-coveted prize for it. The second *Discourse,* on the origins of inequality, did not win a prize but established its young Swiss author as one of the foremost social critics in France. The second *Discourse* offers us an exuberant portrait of life in the state of nature, where happy and healthy individuals wander the earth, picking up plentiful food as they wish, sleeping comfortably where they will, and taking what they need from life's natural abundance, each hardly even aware of the others. It is quite a contrast with Hobbes's unhappy creatures, who feel compelled to enter society to protect themselves and their meager provisions. Rousseau's theory bears at least one essential similarity to Locke's theory, for he, too, agrees that it is the protection of private property that forces these happy natural individuals into the conventions of society. Rousseau, however, thought it was not entirely an improvement in the human situation. The invention of private property, and the grotesque inequalities that followed from it, resulted in a catastrophe for humanity, the end of our primeval happiness and independence. It is from the institution of private property that all of our unhappiness arises, the artificiality and competitiveness of contemporary society, the perverse differences between the rich and the poor, between those in power and those without it. But we do live in society, and there is no going back to nature. So what kind of society should it be, and what are its foundations? It is here that Rousseau offers his own version of the social contract, not as a vehicle for controlling each other or protecting ourselves or our property, but as a way for each of us to "give the law to ourselves," and thereby elevate us from our mere humanity to the morally illustrious condition of *citizenship.*

From *A Discourse on the Origins of Inequality*

As long as we are ignorant of natural man, it is futile for us to attempt to determine the law he has received or which is best suited to his constitution. All that we can see very clearly regarding this law is that, for it to be law, not only must the will of him who is obliged by it be capable of knowing submission to it, but also, for it to be natural, it must speak directly by the voice of nature.

Leaving aside therefore all the scientific books which teach us only to see men as they have made themselves, and meditating on the first and most simple operations of the human soul, I believe I perceive in it two principles that are prior to reason, of which one makes us ardently interested in our well-being and our self-preservation, and the other inspires in us a natural repugnance to seeing any sentient being, especially our fellow man, perish or suffer. It is from the conjunction and combination that our mind is in a position to make regarding these two principles, without the need for introducing that of sociability, that all the rules of natural right appear to me to flow; rules which reason is later forced to reestablish on other foundations, when, by its successive developments, it has succeeded in smothering nature.

In this way one is not obliged to make a man a philosopher before making him a man. His duties toward others are not uniquely dictated to him by the belated lessons of wisdom; and as long as he does not resist the inner impulse of compassion, he will never harm another man or even another sentient being, except in the legitimate instance where, if his preservation were involved, he is obliged to give preference to himself. By this means, an end can also be made to the ancient disputes regarding the participation of animals in the natural law. For it is clear that, lacking intelligence and liberty, they cannot recognize this law; but since they share to some extent in our nature by virtue of the sentient quality with which they are endowed, one will judge that they should also participate in natural right, and that man is subject to some sort of duties toward them. It seems, in effect, that if I am obliged not to do any harm to my fellow man, it is less because he is a rational being than because he is a sentient being: a quality that, since it is common to both animals and men, should at least give the former the right not to be needlessly mistreated by the latter. . . .

In considering human society from a tranquil and disinterested point of view it seems at first to manifest merely the violence of powerful men and the oppression of the weak. The mind revolts against the harshness of the former; one is inclined to deplore the blindness of the latter. And since nothing is less stable among men than those external relationships which chance brings about more often than wisdom, and which are called weakness or power, wealth or poverty, human establishments appear at first glance to be based on piles of shifting sand. It is only in examining them closely, only after having cleared away the dust and sand that surround the edifice, that one learns to respect its foundations. . . .

I conceive of two kinds of inequality in the human species: one which I call natural or physical, because it is established by nature and consists in the difference of age, health, bodily strength, and qualities of mind or soul. The other may be called moral or political inequality, because it depends on a kind of convention and is established, or at least authorized, by the consent of men. This latter type of inequality consists in the different privileges enjoyed by some at the expense of others, such as being richer, more honored, more powerful than they, or even causing themselves to be obeyed by them.

There is no point in asking what the source of natural inequality is, because the answer would be found enunciated in the simple definition of the word. There is still less of a point in asking whether there would not be some essential connection between the two inequalities, for that would amount to asking whether those who command are necessarily better than those who obey, and whether strength of body or mind, wisdom or virtue are always found in the same individuals in proportion to power or wealth. Perhaps this is a good question for slaves to discuss within earshot of their masters, but it is not suitable for reasonable and free men who seek the truth.

Precisely what, then, is the subject of this discourse? To mark, in the progress of things, the moment when, right taking the place of violence, nature was subjected to the law. To explain the sequence of wonders by which the strong could resolve to serve the weak, and the people to buy imaginary repose at the price of real felicity.

The philosophers who have examined the foundations of society have all felt the necessity of returning to the state of nature, but none of them has reached it. Some have not hesitated to ascribe to man in that state the notion of just and unjust, without bothering to show that he had to have that notion, or even that it was useful to him. Others have spoken of the natural right that everyone has to preserve what belongs to him, without explaining what they mean by "belonging." Others started out by giving authority to the stronger over the weaker, and immediately brought about government, without giving any thought to the time that had to pass before the meaning of the words "authority" and "government" could exist among men. Finally, all of them, speaking continually of need, avarice, oppression, desires, and pride, have transferred to the state of nature the ideas they acquired in society. They spoke about savage man, and it was civil man they depicted. It did not even occur to most of our philosophers to doubt that the state of nature had existed, even though it is evident from reading the Holy Scriptures that the first man, having received enlightenment and precepts immediately from God, was not himself in that state; and if we give the writings of Moses the credence that every Christian owes them, we must deny that, even before the flood, men were ever in the pure state of nature, unless they had fallen back into it because of some extraordinary event: a paradox that is quite awkward to defend and utterly impossible to prove.

Let us therefore begin by putting aside all the facts, for they have no bearing on the question. The investigations that may be undertaken concerning this subject should not be taken for historical truths, but only for hypothetical and conditional reasonings, better suited to shedding light on the nature of things than on pointing out their true origin, like those our physicists make everyday with regard to the formation of the world. . . .

When I strip that being, thus constituted, of all the supernatural gifts he could have received and of all the artificial faculties he could have acquired only through long progress; when I consider him, in a word, as he must have left the hands of nature, I see an animal less strong than some, less agile than others, but all in all, the most advantageously organized of all. I see him satisfying his hunger under an oak tree, quenching his thirst at the first stream, finding his bed at the foot of the same tree that supplied his meal; and thus all his needs are satisfied.

Accustomed from childhood to inclement weather and the rigors of the seasons, acclimated to fatigue, and forced, naked and without arms, to defend their lives and their prey against other ferocious beasts, or to escape them by taking flight, men develop a robust and nearly unalterable temperament.

Since the savage man's body is the only instrument he knows, he employs it for a variety of purposes that, for lack of practice, ours are incapable of serving. And our industry deprives us of the force and agility that necessity obliges him to acquire. If he had had an axe, would his wrists break such strong branches? If he had had a sling, would he throw a stone with so much force? If he had had a ladder, would he climb a tree so nimbly? If he had had a horse, would he run so fast? Give a civilized man time to gather all his machines around him, and undoubtedly he will easily overcome a savage man. But if you want to see an even more unequal fight, pit them against each other naked and disarmed, and you will soon realize the advantage of constantly having all of one's forces at one's disposal, of always being ready for any event, and of always carrying one's entire self, as it were, with one.

Hobbes maintains that man is naturally intrepid and seeks only to attack and to fight. On the other hand, an illustrious philosopher thinks . . . that nothing is as timid as man in the state of nature, and that he is always trembling and ready to take flight at the slightest sound he hears or at the slightest movement he perceives. That may be the case with regard to objects with which he is not acquainted. And I do not doubt that he is frightened by all the new sights that present themselves to him every time he can neither discern the physical good and evil he may expect from them nor compare his forces with the dangers he must run: rare circumstances in the state of nature, where everything takes place in such a uniform manner and where the face of the earth is not subject to those sudden and continual changes caused by the passions and inconstancy of peoples living together. But since a savage man lives dispersed among the animals and, finding himself early on in a position to measure himself against them, he soon makes the comparison; and, aware that he surpasses them in skillfulness more than they surpass him in strength, he learns not to fear them any more. Pit a bear or a wolf against a savage who is robust, agile, and courageous, as they all are, armed with stones and a hefty cudgel, and you will see that the danger will be at least equal on both sides, and that after several such experiences, ferocious beasts, which do not like to attack one another, will be quite reluctant to attack a man, having found him to be as ferocious as themselves. . . .

Therefore we must take care not to confuse savage man with the men we have before our eyes. Nature treats all animals left to their own devices with a predilection that seems to show how jealous she is of that right. The horse, the cat, the bull, even the ass, are usually taller, and all of them have a more robust constitution, more vigor, more strength, and more courage in the forests than in our homes. They lose half of these advantages in becoming domesticated; it might be said that all our efforts at feeding them and treating them well only end in their degeneration. It is the same for man himself. In becoming habituated to the ways of society and a slave, he becomes weak, fearful, and servile; his soft and effeminate lifestyle completes the enervation of both his strength and his courage. Let us add that the difference between the savage man and the domesticated man should be still greater than that between the savage animal and the domesticated animal; for while animal and man have been treated equally by nature, man gives more comforts to himself than to the animals he tames, and all of these comforts are so many specific causes that make him degenerate more noticeably. . . .

So far I have considered only physical man. Let us now try to look at him from a metaphysical and moral point of view. . . .

Every animal has ideas, since it has senses; up to a certain point it even combines its ideas, and in this regard man differs from an animal only in degree. Some philosophers have even suggested that there is a greater difference between two given men than between a given man and an animal. Therefore it is not so much understanding which causes the specific distinction of man from all other animals as it is his being a free agent. Nature commands every animal, and beasts obey. Man feels the same impetus, but he knows he is free to go along or to resist; and it is above all in the awareness of this freedom that the spirituality of his soul is made manifest. . . .

. . . But if the difficulties surrounding all these questions should leave some room for dispute on this difference between man and animal, there is another very specific quality which distinguishes them and about which there can be no argument: the faculty of self-perfection, a faculty which, with the aid of circumstances, successively develops all the others, and resides among us as much in the species as in the individual. On the other hand, an animal, at the end of a few months, is what it will be all its life; and its species, at the end of a thousand years, is what it was in the first of those thousand years. Why is man alone subject to becoming an imbecile? Is it not that he thereby returns to his primitive state, and that, while the animal which has acquired nothing and which also has nothing to lose, always retains its instinct, man, in losing through old age or other accidents all that his *perfectibility* has enabled him to acquire, thus falls even lower than the animal itself? It would be sad for us to be forced to agree that this distinctive and almost unlimited faculty is the source of all man's misfortunes; that this is what, by dint of time, draws him out of that original condition in which he would pass tranquil and innocent days; that this is what, through centuries of giving rise to his enlightenment and his errors, his vices and his virtues, eventually makes him a tyrant over himself and nature. . . .

Whatever these origins may be, it is clear, from the little care taken by nature to bring men together through mutual needs and to facilitate their use of speech, how little she prepared them for becoming habituated to the ways of society, and how little she contributed to all that men have done to establish the bonds of society. In fact, it is impossible to imagine why, in that primitive state, one man would have a greater need for another man than a monkey or a wolf has for another of its respective species; or, assuming this need, what motive could induce the other man to satisfy it; or even, in this latter instance, how could they be in mutual agreement regarding the conditions. I know that we are repeatedly told that nothing would have been so miserable than man in that state; and if it is true, as I believe I have proved, that it is only after many centuries that men could have had the desire and the opportunity to leave that state, that would be a charge to bring against nature, not against him whom nature has thus constituted. But if we understand the word *miserable* properly, it is a word which is without meaning or which signifies merely a painful privation and suffering of the body or the soul. Now I would very much like someone to explain to me what kind of misery can there be for a free being whose heart is at peace and whose body is in good health? I ask which of the two, civil or natural life, is more likely to become insufferable to those who live it? We see about us practically no people who do not complain about their existence; many even deprive themselves of it to the extent they are able, and the combination of divine and human laws is hardly enough to stop this disorder. I ask if anyone has ever heard tell of a savage who was living in liberty ever dreaming of complaining about his life and of killing himself. Let the judgment therefore be made with less pride on which side real misery lies. On the other hand, nothing would have been so miserable as savage man, dazzled by enlightenment, tormented by passions, and reasoning about a state different from his own. It was by a very wise providence that the latent faculties he possessed should develop only as the occasion to exercise them presents itself, so that they would be neither superfluous nor troublesome to him beforehand, nor underdeveloped and useless in time of need. In instinct alone, man had everything he needed in order to live in the state of nature; in a cultivated reason, he has only what he needs to live in society. . . .

Above all, let us not conclude with Hobbes that because man has no idea of goodness he is naturally evil; that he is vicious because he does not know virtue; that he always refuses to perform services for his fellow men he does not believe he owes them; or that, by virtue of the right, which he reasonably attributes to himself, to those things he needs, he foolishly imagines himself to be the sole proprietor of the entire universe. Hobbes has very clearly seen the defect of all modern definitions of natural right, but the consequences he draws from his own definition show that he takes it in a sense that is no less false. Were he to have reasoned on the basis of the principles he establishes, this author should have said that since the state of nature is the state in which the concern for our self-preservation is the least prejudicial to that of others, that state was consequently the most appropriate for peace and the best suited for the human race. He says precisely the opposite, because he had wrongly injected into the savage man's concern for self-preservation the need to satisfy a multitude of passions which are the product of society and which have made laws necessary. . . .

Hobbes did not see that the same cause preventing savages from using their reason, as our jurists claim, is what prevents them at the same time from abusing their faculties, as he himself maintains. Hence we could say that savages are not evil precisely because they do not know what it is to be good; for it is neither the development of enlightenment nor the restraint imposed by the law, but the calm of the passions and the ignorance of vice which prevents them from doing evil. *So much more profitable to these is the ignorance of vice than the knowledge of virtue is to those.* Moreover, there is another principle that Hobbes failed to notice, and which, having been given to man in order to mitigate, in certain circumstances, the ferocity of his egocentrism or the desire for self-preservation before this egocentrism of his came into being, tempers the ardor he has for his own well-being by an innate repugnance to seeing his fellow men suffer. I do not believe I have any contradiction to fear in granting the only natural virtue that the most excessive detractor of human virtues was forced to recognize. I am referring to pity, a disposition that is fitting for beings that are as weak and as subject to ills as we are; a virtue all the more universal and all the more useful to man in that it precedes in him any kind of reflection, and to natural that even animals sometimes show noticeable signs of it. . . .

Reason is what engenders egocentrism, and reflection strengthens it. Reason is what turns man in upon himself. Reason is what separates him from all that troubles him and afflicts him. Philosophy is what isolates him and what moves him to say in secret, at the sight of a suffering man, "Perish if you will; I am safe and sound." No longer can anything but danger to the entire society trouble the tranquil slumber of the philosopher and yank him from his bed. His fellow man can be killed with impunity underneath his window. He has merely to place his hands over his ears and argue with himself a little in order to prevent nature, which rebels within him, from identifying him with the man being assassinated. Savage man does not have this admirable talent, and for lack of wisdom and reason he is always seen thoughtlessly giving in to the first sentiment of humanity. When there is a riot or a street brawl, the populace gathers together; the prudent man withdraws from the scene. It is the rabble, the women of the marketplace, who separate the combatants and prevent decent people from killing one another.

It is therefore quite certain that pity is a natural sentiment, which, by moderating in each individual the activity of the love of oneself, contributes to the mutual preservation of the entire species. Pity is what carries us without reflection to the aid of those we see suffering. Pity is what, in the state of nature, takes the place of laws, mores, and virtue, with the advantage that no one is tempted to disobey its sweet voice. Pity is what will prevent every robust savage from robbing a weak child or an infirm old man of his hard-earned subsistence, if he himself expects to be able to find his own someplace else. Instead of the sublime maxim of reasoned justice, *Do unto others as you would have them do unto you,* pity inspires all men with another maxim of natural goodness, much less perfect but perhaps more useful than the preceding one: *Do what is good for you with as little harm as possible to others.* In a word, it is in this natural sentiment, rather than in subtle arguments that one must search for the cause of the repugnance at doing evil that every man would experience, even independently of the maxims of education. Although it might be appropriate for Socrates and minds of his stature to acquire virtue through reason, the human race would long ago have ceased to exist, if its preservation had depended solely on the reasonings of its members. . . .

The first person who, having enclosed a plot of land, took it into his head to say *this is mine* and found people simple enough to believe him, was the true founder of civil society. What crimes, wars, murders, what miseries and horrors would the human race have been spared, had someone pulled up the stakes or filled in the ditch and cried out to his fellow men: "Do not listen to this impostor. You are lost if you forget that the fruits of the earth belong to all and the earth to no one!" But it is quite likely that by then things had already reached the point where they could no longer continue as they were. For this idea of property, depending on many prior ideas which could only have arisen successively, was not formed all at once in the human mind. It was necessary to make great progress, to acquire much industry and enlightenment, and to transmit and augment them from one age to another, before arriving at this final stage in the state of nature. Let us therefore take things farther back and try to piece together under a single viewpoint that slow succession of events and advances in knowledge in their most natural order. . . .

Having previously wandered about the forests and having assumed a more fixed situation, men slowly came together and united into different bands, eventually forming in each country a particular nation, united by mores and characteristic features, not by regulations and laws, but by the same kind of life and foods and by the common influence of the climate. Eventually a permanent proximity cannot fail to engender some intercourse among different families. Young people of different sexes live in neighboring huts; the passing intercourse demanded by nature soon leads to another, through frequent contact with one another, no less sweet and more permanent. People become accustomed to consider different objects and to make comparisons. Imperceptibly they acquire the ideas of merit and beauty which produce feelings of preference. By dint of seeing one another, they can no longer get along without seeing one another again. A sweet and tender feeling insinuates itself into the soul and at the least opposition becomes an impetuous fury. Jealousy awakens with love; discord triumphs, and the sweetest passion receives sacrifices of human blood.

In proportion as ideas and sentiments succeed one another and as the mind and heart are trained, the human race continues to be tamed, relationships spread and bonds are tightened. People grew accustomed to gather in front of their huts or around a large tree; song and dance, true children of love and leisure, became the amusement or rather the occupation of idle men and women who had flocked together. Each one began to look at the others and to want to be looked at himself, and public esteem had a value. The one who sang or danced the best, the handsomest, the strongest, the most adroit or the most eloquent became the most highly regarded. And this was the first step toward inequality and, at the same time, toward vice. From these first preferences were born vanity and contempt on the one hand, and shame and envy on the other. And the fermentation caused by these new leavens eventually produced compounds fatal to happiness and innocence.

As soon as men had begun mutually to value one another, and the idea of esteem was formed in their minds, each one claimed to have a right to it, and it was no longer possible for anyone to be lacking it with impunity. From this came the first duties of civility, even among savages; and from this every voluntary wrong became an outrage, because along with the harm that resulted from the injury, the offended party saw in it contempt for his person, which often was more insufferable than the harm itself. Hence each man punished the contempt shown him in a manner proportionate to the esteem in which he held himself; acts of revenge became terrible, and men became bloodthirsty and cruel. This is precisely the stage reached by most of the savage people known to us; and it is for want of having made adequate distinctions among their ideas or of having noticed how far these peoples already were from the original state of nature that many have hastened to conclude that man is naturally cruel, and that he needs civilization in order to soften him. On the contrary, nothing is so gentle as man in his primitive state, when, placed by nature at an equal distance from the stupidity of brutes and the fatal enlightenment of civil man, and limited equally by instinct and reason to protecting himself from the harm that threatens him, he is restrained by natural pity from needlessly harming anyone himself, even if he has been harmed. For according to the axiom of the wise Locke, *where there is no property, there is no injury*. . . .

From the cultivation of land, there necessarily followed the division of land; and from property once recognized, the first rules of justice. For in order to render everyone what is his, it is necessary that everyone can have something. Moreover, as men began to look toward the future and as they saw that they all had goods to lose, there was not one of them who did not have to fear reprisals against himself for wrongs he might do to another. This origin is all the more natural as it is impossible to conceive of the idea of property arising from anything but manual labor, for it is not clear what man can add, beyond his own labor, in order to appropriate things he has not made. It is labor alone that, in giving the cultivator a right to the product of the soil he has tilled, consequently gives him a right, at least until the harvest, and thus from year to year. With this possession continuing uninterrupted, it is easily transformed into property. . . .

Things in this state could have remained equal, if talents had been equal, and if the use of iron and the consumption of foodstuffs had always been in precise bàlance. But this proportion, which was not maintained by anything, was soon broken. The strongest did the most work; the most adroit turned theirs to better advantage: the most ingenious found ways to shorten their labor. The farmer had a greater need for iron, or the blacksmith had a greater need for wheat; and in laboring equally, the one earned a great deal while the other barely had enough to live. Thus it is that natural inequality imperceptibly manifests itself together with inequality occasioned by the socialization process. Thus it is that the differences among men, developed by those of circumstances, make themselves more noticeable, more permanent in their effects, and begin to influence the fate of private individuals in the same proportion.

Thus we find here all our faculties developed, memory and imagination in play, egocentrism looking out for its interests, reason rendered active, and the mind having nearly reached the limit of the perfection of which it is capable. We find here all the natural qualities put into action, the rank and fate of each man established not only on the basis of the quantity of goods and the power to serve or harm, but also on the basis of mind, beauty, strength or skill, on the basis of merit or talents. And since these qualities were the only ones that could attract consideration, he was soon forced to have them or affect them. It was necessary, for his advantage, to show himself to be something other than what he in fact was. Being something and appearing to be something became two completely different things; and from this distinction there arose grand ostentation, deceptive cunning, and all the vices that follow in their wake. On the other hand, although man had previously been free and independent, we find him, so to speak, subject, by virtue of a multitude of fresh needs, to all of nature and particularly to his fellowmen, whose slave in a sense he becomes even in becoming their master; rich, he needs their services; poor, he needs their help; and being midway between wealth and poverty does not put him in a position to get along without them. It is therefore necessary for him to seek incessantly to interest them in his fate and to make them find their own profit, in fact or in appearance, in working for his. This makes him two-faced and crooked with some, imperious and harsh with others, and puts him in the position of having to abuse everyone he needs when he cannot make them fear him and does not find it in his interests to be of useful service to them. Finally, consuming ambition, the zeal for raising the relative level of his fortune, less out of real need than in order to put himself above others, inspires in all men a wicked tendency to harm one another, a secret jealousy all the more dangerous because, in order to strike its blow in greater safety, it often wears the mask of benevolence; in short, competition and rivalry on the one hand, opposition of interest[s] on the other, and always the hidden desire to profit at the expense of someone else. All these ills are the first effect of property and the inseparable offshoot of incipient inequality. . . .

From *On The Social Contract*

I want to inquire whether there can be some legitimate and sure rule of administration in the civil order, taking men as they are and laws as they might be. I will always try in this inquiry to bring together what right permits with what interest prescribes, so that justice and utility do not find themselves at odds with one another. . . .

Man is born free, and everywhere he is in chains. He who believes himself the master of others does not escape being more of a slave than they. How did this change take place? I have no idea. What can render it legitimate? I believe I can answer this question.

Were I to consider only force and the effect that flows from it, I would say that so long as a people is constrained to obey and does obey, it does well. As soon as it can shake off the yoke and does shake it off, it does even better. For by recovering its liberty by means of the same right that stole it, either the populace is justified in getting it back or else those who took it away were not justified in their actions. But the social order is a sacred right which serves as a foundation for all other rights. Nevertheless, this right does not come from nature. It is therefore founded upon convention. Before coming to that, I ought to substantiate what I just claimed.

The most ancient of all societies and the only natural one, is that of the family. Even so children remain bound to their father only so long as they need him to take care of them. As soon as the need ceases, the natural bond is dissolved. Once the children are freed from the obedience they owed the father and their father is freed from the care he owed his children, all return equally to independence. If they continue to remain united, this no longer takes place naturally but voluntarily, and the family maintains itself only by means of convention.

This common liberty is one consequence of the nature of man. Its first law is to see to his maintenance; its first concerns are those he owes himself; and, as soon as he reaches the age of reason, since he alone is the judge of the proper means of taking care of himself, he thereby becomes his own master.

The family therefore is, so to speak, the prototype of political societies; the leader is the image of the father, the populace is the image of the children, and, since all are born equal and free, none give up their liberty except for their utility. The entire difference consists in the fact that in the family the love of the father for his children repays him for the care he takes for them, while in the state, where the leader does not have love for his peoples, the pleasure of commanding takes the place of this feeling. . . .

The strongest is never strong enough to be master all the time, unless he transforms force into right and obedience into duty. Hence the right of the strongest, a right that seems like something intended ironically and is actually established as a basic principle. But will no one explain this word to me? Force is a physical power; I fail to see what morality can result from its effects. To give in to force is an act of necessity, not of will. At most, it is an act of prudence. In what sense could it be a duty?

Let us suppose for a moment that there is such a thing as this alleged right. I maintain that all that results from it is an inexplicable mish-mash. For once force produces the right, the effect changes places with the cause. Every force that is superior to the first succeeds to its right. As soon as one can disobey with impunity, one can do so legitimately; and since the strongest is always right, the only thing to do is to make oneself the strongest. For what kind of right is it that perishes when the force on which it is based ceases? If one must obey because of force, one need not do so out of duty; and if one is no longer forced to obey one is no longer obliged. Clearly then, this word "right" adds nothing to force. It is utterly meaningless here.

Let us then agree that force does not bring about right, and that one is obliged to obey only legitimate powers. Thus my original question keeps returning.

Since no man has a natural authority over his fellow man, and since force does not give rise to any right, conventions therefore remain the basis of all legitimate authority among men.

If, says Grotius, a private individual can alienate his liberty and turn himself into the slave of a master, why could not an entire people alienate its liberty and turn itself into the subject of a king? There are many equivocal words here which need explanation, but let us confine ourselves to the word *alienate*. To alienate is to give or to sell. A man who makes himself the slave of someone else does not give himself; he sells himself, at least for his subsistence. But why does a people sell itself? Far from furnishing his subjects with their subsistence, a king derives his own from them alone, and, according to Rabelais, a king does not live cheaply. Do subjects then give their persons on the condition that their estate will also be taken? I fail to see what remains for them to preserve.

It will be said that the despot assures his subjects of civil tranquility. Very well. But what do they gain, if the wars his ambition drags them into, if his insatiable greed, if the oppressive demands caused by his ministers occasion more grief for his subjects than their own dissensions would have done? What do they gain, if this very tranquility is one of their miseries? A tranquil life is also had in dungeons; is that enough to make them desirable? The Greeks who were locked up in the Cyclops' cave lived a tranquil existence as they awaited their turn to be devoured.

To say that a man gives himself gratuitously is to say something absurd and inconceivable. Such an act is illegitimate and null, if only for the fact that he who commits it does not have his wits about him. To say the same thing of an entire populace is to suppose a populace composed of madmen. Madness does not bring about right.

Even if each person can alienate himself, he cannot alienate his children. They are born men and free. Their liberty belongs to them; they alone have the right to dispose of it.

Before they have reached the age of reason, their father can, in their name, stipulate conditions for their maintenance and for their well-being. But he cannot give them irrevocably and unconditionally, for such a gift is contrary to the ends of nature and goes beyond the rights of paternity. For an arbitrary government to be legitimate, it would therefore be necessary in each generation for the people to be master of its acceptance or rejection. But in that event this government would no longer be arbitrary.

Renouncing one's liberty is renouncing one's dignity as a man, the rights of humanity and even its duties. There is no possible compensation for anyone who renounces everything. Such a renunciation is incompatible with the nature of man. Removing all morality from his actions is tantamount to taking away all liberty from his will. Finally, it is a vain and contradictory convention to stipulate absolute authority on one side and a limitless obedience on the other. Is it not clear that no commitments are made to a person from whom one has the right to demand everything? And does this condition alone not bring with it, without equivalent or exchange, the nullity of the act? For what right would my slave have against me, given that all he has belongs to me, and that, since his right is my right, my having a right against myself makes no sense? . . .

Even if I were to grant all that I have thus far refuted, the supporters of despotism would not be any better off. There will always be a great difference between subduing a multitude and ruling a society. If scattered men, however many they may be, were successively enslaved by a single individual, I see nothing there but a master and slaves; I do not see a people and its leader. It is, if you will, an aggregation, but not an association. There is neither a public good nor a body politic there. Even if that man had enslaved half the world, he is always just a private individual. His interest, separated from that of others, is never anything but a private interest. If this same man is about to die, after his passing his empire remains scattered and disunited, just as an oak tree dissolves and falls into a pile of ashes after fire has consumed it. . . .

In fact, if there were no prior convention, then, unless the vote were unanimous, what would become of the minority's obligation to submit to the majority's choice, and where do one hundred who want a master get the right to vote for ten who do not? The law of majority rule is itself an established convention, and presupposes unanimity on at least one occasion.

I suppose that men have reached the point where obstacles that are harmful to their maintenance in the state of nature gain the upper hand by their resistance to the forces that each individual can bring to bear to maintain himself in that state. Such being the case, that original state cannot subsist any longer, and the human race would perish if it did not alter its mode of existence.

For since men cannot engender new forces, but merely unite and direct existing ones, they have no other means of maintaining themselves but to form by aggregation a sum of forces that could gain the upper hand over the resistance, so that their forces are directed by means of a single moving power and made to act in concert.

This sum of forces cannot come into being without the cooperation of many. But since each man's force and liberty are the primary instruments of his maintenance, how is he going to engage them without hurting himself and without neglecting the care that he owes himself? This difficulty, seen in terms of my subject, can be stated in the following terms:

"Find a form of association which defends and protects with all common forces the person and goods of each associate, and by means of which each one, while uniting with all, nevertheless obeys only himself and remains as free as before?" This is the fundamental problem for which the social contract provides the solution.

The clauses of this contract are so determined by the nature of the act that the least modification renders them vain and ineffectual, that, although perhaps they have never been formally promulgated, they are everywhere the same, everywhere tacitly accepted and acknowledged. Once the social compact is violated, each person then regains his first rights and resumes his natural liberty, while losing the conventional liberty for which he renounced it.

These clauses, properly understood, are all reducible to a single one, namely the total alienation of each associate, together with all of his rights, to the entire community. For first of all, since each person gives himself whole and entire, the condition is equal for everyone; and since the condition is equal for everyone, no one has an interest in making it burdensome for the others.

Moreover, since the alienation is made without reservation, the union is as perfect as possible, and no associate has anything further to demand. For if some rights remained with private individuals, in the absence of any common superior who could decide between them and the public, each person would eventually claim to be his own judge in all things, since he is on some point his own judge. The state of nature would subsist and the association would necessarily become tyrannical or hollow.

Finally, in giving himself to all, each person gives himself to no one. And since there is no associate over whom he does not acquire the same right that he would grant others over himself, he gains the equivalent of everything he loses, along with a greater amount of force to preserve what he has.

If, therefore, one eliminates from the social compact whatever is not essential to it, one will find that it is reducible to the following terms. *Each of us places his person and all his power in common under the supreme direction of the general will; and as one we receive each member as an indivisible part of the whole.*

At once, in place of the individual person of each contracting party, this act of association produces a moral and collective body composed of as many members as there are voices in the assembly, which receives from this same act its unity, its common *self,* its life and its will. This public person, formed thus by union of all the others formerly took the name *city,* and at present takes the name *republic* or *body politic,* which is called *state* by its members when it is passive, *sovereign* when it is active, *power* when compared to others like itself. As to the associates, they collectively take the name *people;* individually they are called *citizens,* insofar as participants in the sovereign authority, and *subjects,* insofar as they are subjected to the laws of the state. But these terms are often confused and mistaken for one another. It is enough to know how to distinguish them when they are used with absolute precision.

This formula shows that the act of association includes a reciprocal commitment between the public and private individuals, and that each individual, contracting, as it were, with himself, finds himself under a twofold commitment: namely as a member of the sovereign to private individuals, and as a member of the state toward the sovereign. But the maxim of civil law that no one is held to commitments made to himself cannot be applied here, for there is a considerable difference between being obligated to oneself, or to a whole of which one is a part.

It must be further noted that the public deliberation that can obligate all the subjects to the sovereign, owing to the two different relationships in which each of them is viewed, cannot, for the opposite reason, obligate the sovereign to itself, and that consequently it is contrary to the nature of the body politic that the sovereign impose upon itself a law it could not break. Since the sovereign can be considered under but one single relationship, it is then in the position of a private individual contracting with himself. Whence it is apparent that there neither is nor can be any type of fundamental law that is obligatory for the people as a body, not even the social contract. This does not mean that the whole body cannot perfectly well commit itself to another body with respect to things that do not infringe on this contract. For in regard to the foreigner, it becomes a simple being, an individual.

However, since the body politic or the sovereign derives its being exclusively from the sanctity of the contract, it can never obligate itself, not even to another power, to do anything that derogates from the original act, such as alienating some portion of itself or submitting to another sovereign. Violation of the act whereby it exists would be self-annihilation, and whatever is nothing produces nothing.

As soon as this multitude is thus united in a body, one cannot harm one of the members without attacking the whole body. It is even less likely that the body can be harmed without the members feeling it. Thus duty and interest equally obligate the two parties to come to one another's aid, and the same men should seek to combine in this two-fold relationship all the advantages that result from it.

For since the sovereign is formed entirely from the private individuals who make it up, it neither has nor could have an interest contrary to theirs. Hence, the sovereign power has no need to offer a guarantee to its subjects, since it is impossible for a body to want to harm all of its members, and, as we will see later, it cannot harm any one of them in particular. The sovereign, by the mere fact that it exists, is always all that it should be.

But the same thing cannot be said of the subjects in relation to the sovereign, for which, despite their common interest, their commitments would be without substance if it did not find ways of being assured of their fidelity.

In fact, each individual can, as a man, have a private will contrary to or different from the general will that he has as a citizen. His private interest can speak to him in an entirely different manner than the common interest. His absolute and naturally independent existence can cause him to envisage what he owes the common cause as a gratuitous contribution, the loss of which will be less harmful to others than its payment is burdensome to him. And in viewing the moral person which constitutes the state as a being of reason because it is not a man, he would enjoy the rights of a citizen without wanting to fulfill the duties of a subject, an injustice whose growth would bring about the ruin of the body politic.

Thus, in order for the social compact to avoid being an empty formula, it tacitly entails the commitment—which alone can give force to the others—that whoever refuses to obey the general will will be forced to do so by the entire body. This means merely that he will be forced to be free. For this is the sort of condition that, by giving each citizen to the homeland, guarantees him against all personal dependence—a condition that produces the skill and the performance of the political machine, and which alone bestows legitimacy upon civil commitments. Without it such commitments would be absurd, tyrannical and subject to the worst abuses.

This passage from the state of nature to the civil state produces quite a remarkable change in man, for it substitutes justice for instinct in his behavior and gives his actions a moral quality they previously lacked. Only then, when the voice of duty replaces physical impulse and right replaces appetite, does man, who had hitherto taken only himself into account, find himself forced to act upon other principles and to consult his reason before listening to his inclinations. Although in this state he deprives himself of several of the advantages belonging to him in the state of nature, he regains such great ones. His faculties are exercised and developed, his ideas are broadened, his feelings are ennobled, his entire soul is elevated to such a height that, if the abuse of this new condition did not often lower his status to beneath the level he left, he ought constantly to bless the happy moment that pulled him away from it forever and which transformed him from a stupid, limited animal into an intelligent being and a man.

Let us summarize this entire balance sheet so that the credits and debits are easily compared. What man loses through the social contract is his natural liberty and an unlimited right to everything that tempts him and that he can acquire. What he gains is civil liberty and the proprietary ownership of all he possesses. So as not to be in error in these compensations, it is necessary to draw a careful distinction between natural liberty (which is limited solely by the force of the individual involved) and civil liberty (which is limited by the general will), and between possession (which is merely the effect of the force or the right of the first occupant) and proprietary ownership (which is based solely on a positive title).

To the preceding acquisitions could be added the acquisition in the civil state of moral liberty, which alone makes man truly the master of himself. For to be driven by appetite alone is slavery, and obedience to the law one has prescribed for oneself is liberty. But I have already said too much on this subject, and the philosophical meaning of the word *liberty* is not my subject here.

The first and most important consequence of the principles established above is that only the general will can direct the forces of the state according to the purpose for which it was instituted, which is the common good. For if the opposition of private interests made necessary the establishment of societies, it is the accord of these same interests that made it possible. It is what these different interests have in common that forms the social bond, and, were there no point of agreement among all these interests, no society could exist. For it is utterly on the basis of this common interest that society ought to be governed.

I therefore maintain that sovereignty is merely the exercise of the general will, it can never be alienated, and that the sovereign, which is only a collective being, cannot be represented by anything but itself.

G. W. F. Hegel, "Master and Slave," from *Phenomenology of Spirit* (1807)

G. W. F. Hegel (1770–1831) finished writing his monumental *Phenomenology of Spirit* in 1806, as he watched the "world spirit" in action as Napoleon completed his destruction of the Holy Roman Empire just a few miles away from the University of Jena, where Hegel was teaching. That sense of a new world beginning inspired Hegel, and so many other young philosophers and poets, and the *Phenomenology* was above all an expression of the new sense of internationalism and the hopes for justice that accompanied it. The "master and slave" parable reprinted here occurs early in the book, as a thought-experiment concerning the most primitive possible human relationship, abstracted from all social concerns, nothing but the unembellished meeting of two primal people, two "self-consciousnesses." What would it be like? A mutually defensive Hobbesian attack, born of selfishness and insecurity? A mere matter of Rousseauian indifference, as each of them went about its merry way? Hegel suggests that the primary concern of any two self-conscious beings would be their mutual *recognition*, a need to establish what they are—in their own and in each other's eyes. But then the very idea of two autonomous, independent beings is already undermined, for they gain their existence, their sense of selfhood, not from within themselves but from and through each other. That is the point of the Hegelian parable, and throughout the *Phenomenology* we are treated to repeated refutations of the various claims of individualism, the very idea that it makes sense to talk about *individuals* apart from the contexts of society. (For an attempt to bring out the nature of the individualism presupposed in social contract thinking, see the selection from Gauthier later in Part Two.) As the parable develops, the two beings struggle, each vying to be recognized as the superior of the other. Fighting for mutual recognition, one loses and, rather than lose its life (and, for the other, rather than lose the one witness to its victory), it becomes a slave, wholly dependent on the other, the master. But the parable takes a perverse twist, which would have considerable influence on other philosophers to follow in their own speculations about power and dependency. The master, who is supposedly independent, becomes dependent on the slave for the very means of its existence, and the slave, who is supposedly dependent on the master, finds that it is, in fact, very much in control of its life in a way that the master no longer is. In the language of justice, it is the slave that deserves recognition, but this will be possible only if the spartan framework of the master-slave relationship is relinquished in favor of a much more sociable and *natural* conception of human community.

From Hegel's *Phenomenology of Spirit*, translated by A. V. Miller and published by Oxford University Press, 1977. Reprinted by permission of Oxford University Press.

178.   Self-consciousness exists in and for itself when, and by the fact that, it so exists
for another; that is, it exists only in being acknowledged. The Notion of this its unity in its
duplication embraces many and varied meanings. Its moments, then, must on the one hand
be held strictly apart, and on the other hand must in this differentiation at the same time also
be taken and known as not distinct, or in their opposite significance. The twofold significance of the distinct moments has in the nature of self-consciousness to be infinite, or
directly the opposite of the determinateness in which it is posited. The detailed exposition
of the Notion of this spiritual unity in its duplication will present us with the process of
Recognition. . . .

186.   Self-consciousness is, to begin with, simple being-for-self, self-equal
through the exclusion from itself of everything else. For it, its essence and absolute object
is "I", and in this immediacy, or in this [mere] being, of its being-for-self, it is an *individual*. What is "other" for it is an unessential, negatively characterized object. But the "other"
is also a self-consciousness; one individual is confronted by another individual. Appearing
thus immediately on the scene, they are for one another like ordinary objects, *independent*
shapes, individuals submerged in the being [or immediacy] of *Life*—for the object in its
immediacy is here determined as Life. They are, *for each other,* shapes of consciousness
which have not yet accomplished the movement of absolute abstraction, of rooting-out all
immediate being, and of being merely the purely negative being of self-identical consciousness; in other words, they have not as yet exposed themselves to each other in the
form of pure being-for-self, or as self-consciousness. Each is indeed certain of its own self,
but not of the other, and therefore its own self-certainty still has no truth. For it would have
truth only if its own being-for-self had confronted it as an independent object, or, what is
the same thing, if the object had presented itself as this pure self-certainty. But according
to the Notion of recognition this is possible only when each is for the other what the other
is for it, only when each in its own self through its own action, and again through the action
of the other, achieves this pure abstraction of being-for-self.

187.   The presentation of itself, however, as the pure abstraction of self-consciousness consists in showing itself as the pure negation of its objective mode, or in showing that it is not attached to any specific *existence*, not to the individuality common to existence as such, that it is not attached to life. This presentation is a twofold action: action on
the part of the other, and action on its own part. In so far as it is the action of the *other,* each
seeks the death of the other. But in doing so, the second kind of action, action on its own
part, is also involved; for the former involves the staking of its own life. Thus the relation
of the two self-conscious individuals is such that they prove themselves and each other
through a life-and-death struggle. They must engage in this struggle, for they must raise
their certainty of being *for themselves* to truth, both in the case of the other and in their own
case. And it is only through staking one's life that freedom is won; only thus is it proved
that for self-consciousness, its essential being is not [just] being, not the *immediate* form in
which it appears, not its submergence in the expanse of life, but rather that there is nothing
present in it which could not be regarded as a vanishing moment, that it is only pure *being-
for-self.* The individual who has not risked his life may well be recognized as a *person,* but
he has not attained to the truth of this recognition as an independent self-consciousness.
Similarly, just as each stakes his own life, so each must seek the other's death, for it values
the other no more than itself; its essential being is present to it in the form of an "other," it
is outside of itself and must rid itself of its self-externality. The other is an *immediate* consciousness entangled in a variety of relationships, and it must regard its otherness as a pure
being-for-self or as an absolute negation.

188.   This trial by death, however, does away with the truth which was supposed to issue from it, and so, too, with the certainty of self generally. For just as life is the *natural* setting of consciousness, independence without absolute negativity, so death is the *natural* negation of consciousness, negation without independence, which thus remains without the required significance of recognition. Death certainly shows that each staked his life and held it of no account, both in himself and in the other; but that is not for those who survived this struggle. They put an end to their consciousness in its alien setting of natural existence, that is to say, they put an end to themselves, and are done away with as *extremes* wanting to be *for themselves,* or to have an existence of their own. But with this there vanishes from their interplay the essential moment of splitting into extremes with opposite characteristics; and the middle term collapses into a lifeless unity which is split into lifeless, merely immediate, unopposed extremes; and the two do not reciprocally give and receive one another back from each other consciously, but leave each other free only indifferently, like things. Their act is an abstract negation, not the negation coming from consciousness, which supersedes in such a way as to preserve and maintain what is superseded, and consequently survives its own supersession.

189.   In this experience, self-consciousness learns that life is as essential to it as pure self-consciousness. In immediate self-consciousness the simple "I" is absolute mediation, and has as its essential moment lasting independence. The dissolution of that simple unity is the result of the first experience; through this there is posited a pure self-consciousness, and a consciousness which is not purely for itself but for another, i.e. is a merely *immediate* consciousness, or consciousness in the form of *thinghood.* Both moments are essential. Since to begin with they are unequal and opposed, and their reflection into a unity has not yet been achieved, they exist as two opposed shapes of consciousness; one is the independent consciousness whose essential nature is to be for itself, the other is the dependent consciousness whose essential nature is simply to live or to be for another. The former is lord, the other is bondsman.

190.   The lord is the consciousness that exists *for itself,* but no longer merely the Notion of such a consciousness. Rather, it is a consciousness existing *for itself* which is mediated with itself through another consciousness, i.e. through a consciousness whose nature it is to be bound up with an existence that is independent, or thinghood in general. The lord puts himself into relation with both of these moments, to a *thing* as such, the object of desire, and to the consciousness for which thinghood is the essential characteristic. And since he is (a) *qua* the Notion of self-consciousness an immediate relation of *being-for-self,* but (b) is now at the same time mediation, or a being-for-self which is for itself only through another, he is related (a) immediately to both, and (b) mediately to each through the other. The lord relates himself mediately to the bondsman through a being [a thing] that is independent, for it is just this which holds the bondsman in bondage; it is his chain from which he could not break free in the struggle, thus proving himself to be dependent, to possess his independence in thinghood. But the lord is the power over this thing, for he proved in the struggle that it is something merely negative; since he is the power over this thing and this again is the power over the other [the bondsman], it follows that he holds the other in subjection. Equally, the lord relates himself mediately to the thing through the bondsman; the bondsman, *qua* self-consciousness in general, also relates himself negatively to the thing, and takes away its independence; but at the same time the things is independent *vis-à-vis* the bondsman, whose negating of it, therefore, cannot go the length of being altogether done with it to the point of annihilation; in other words, he only *works* on it. For the lord, on the other hand, the *immediate* relation becomes through this mediation the sheer nega-

tion of the thing, or the enjoyment of it. What desire failed to achieve, he succeeds in doing, viz. to have done with the thing altogether, and to achieve satisfaction in the enjoyment of it. Desire failed to do this because of the thing's independence; but the lord, who has interposed the bondsman between it and himself, takes to himself only the dependent aspect of the thing and has the pure enjoyment of it. The aspect of its independence he leaves to the bondsman, who works on it.

191.   In both of these moments the lord achieves his recognition through another consciousness; for in them, that other consciousness is expressly something unessential, both by its working on the thing, and by its dependence on a specific existence. In neither case can it be lord over the being of the thing and achieve absolute negation of it. Here, therefore, is present this moment of recognition, viz. that the other consciousness sets aside its own being-for-self, and in so doing itself does what the first does to it. Similarly, the other moment too is present, that this action of the second is the first's own action; for what the bondsman does is really the action of the lord. The latter's essential nature is to exist only for himself; he is the sheer negative power for whom the thing is nothing. Thus he is the pure, essential action in this relationship, while the action of the bondsman is impure and unessential. But for recognition proper the moment is lacking, that what the lord does to the other he also does to himself, and what the bondsman does to himself he should also do to the other. The outcome is a recognition that is one-sided and unequal.

192.   In this recognition the unessential consciousness is for the lord the object, which constitutes the *truth* of his certainty of himself. But it is clear that this object does not correspond to its Notion, but rather that the object in which the lord has achieved his lordship has in reality turned out to be something quite different from an independent consciousness. What now really confronts him is not an independent consciousness, but a dependent one. He is, therefore, not certain of *being-for-self* as the truth of himself. On the contrary, his truth is in reality the unessential consciousness and its unessential action.

193.   The *truth* of the independent consciousness is accordingly the servile consciousness of the bondsman. This, it is true, appears at first *outside* of itself and not as the truth of self-consciousness. But just as lordship showed that its essential nature is the reverse of what it wants to be, so too servitude in its consummation will really turn into the opposite of what it immediately is; as a consciousness forced back into itself, it will withdraw into itself and be transformed into a truly independent consciousness.

194.   We have seen what servitude is only in relation to lordship. But it is a self-consciousness, and we have now to consider what as such it is in and for itself. To begin with, servitude has the lord for its essential reality; hence the *truth* for it is the independent consciousness that is *for itself*. However, servitude is not yet aware that this truth is implicit in it. But it does in fact contain within itself this truth of pure negativity and being-for-self, for it has experienced this its own essential nature. For this consciousness has been fearful, not of this or that particular thing or just at odd moments, but its whole being has been seized with dread. In that experience it has been quite unmanned, has trembled in every fibre of its being, and everything solid and stable has been shaken to its foundations. But this pure universal movement, the absolute melting-away of everything stable, is the simple, essential nature of self-consciousness, absolute negativity, *pure being-for-self*, which consequently is *implicit* in this consciousness. This moment of pure being-for-self is also *explicit* for the bondsman, for in the lord it exists for him as his *object*. Furthermore, his consciousness is not this dissolution of everything stable merely in principle; in his service he *actually* brings this about. Through his service he rids himself of his attachment to natural existence in every single detail; and gets rid of it by working on it.

195.   However, the feeling of absolute power both in general, and in the particular form of service, is only implicitly this dissolution, and although the fear of the lord is indeed the beginning of wisdom, consciousness is not therein aware that it is a being-for-self. Through work, however, the bondsman becomes conscious of what he truly is. In the moment which corresponds to desire in the lord's consciousness, it did seem that the aspect of unessential relation to the thing fell to the lot of the bondsman, since in that relation the thing retained its independence. Desire has reserved to itself the pure negating of the object and thereby its unalloyed feeling of self. But that is the reason why this satisfaction is itself only a fleeting one, for it lacks the side of objectivity and permanence. Work, on the other hand, is desire held in check, fleetingness staved off; in other words, work forms and shapes the thing. The negative relation to the object becomes its *form* and something *permanent*, because it is precisely for the worker that the object has independence. This *negative* middle term or the formative *activity* is at the same time the individuality or pure being-for-self of consciousness which now, in the work outside of it, acquires an element of permanence. It is in this way, therefore, that consciousness, *qua* worker, comes to see in the independent being [of the object] its *own* independence.

196.   But the formative activity has not only this positive significance that in it the pure being-for-self of the servile consciousness acquires an existence; it also has, in contrast with its first moment, the negative significance of *fear*. For, in fashioning the thing, the bondsman's own negativity, his being-for-self, becomes an object for him only through his setting at nought the existing *shape* confronting him. But this objective *negative* moment is none other than the alien being before which it has trembled. Now, however, he destroys this alien negative moment, posits *himself* as a negative in the permanent order of things, and thereby becomes *for himself*, someone existing on his own account. In the lord, the being-for-self is an "other" for the bondsman, or is only *for* him [i.e. is not his own]; in fear, the being-for-self is present in the bondsman himself; in fashioning the thing, he becomes aware that being-for-self belongs to *him*, that he himself exists essentially and actually in his own right. The shape does not become something other than himself through being made external to him; for it is precisely this shape that is his pure being-for-self, which in this externality is seen by him to be the truth. Through this rediscovery of himself by himself, the bondsman realizes that it is precisely in his work wherein he seemed to have only an alienated existence that he acquires a mind of his own. For this reflection, the two moments of fear and service as such, as also that of formative activity, are necessary, both being at the same time in a universal mode. Without the discipline of service and obedience, fear remains at the formal stage, and does not extend to the known real world of existence. Without the formative activity, fear remains inward and mute, and consciousness does not become explicitly *for itself*. If consciousness fashions the thing without that initial absolute fear, it is only an empty self-centred attitude; for its form or negativity is not negativity per se, and therefore its formative activity cannot give it a consciousness of itself as essential being. If it has not experienced absolute fear but only some lesser dread, the negative being has remained for it something external, its substance has not been infected by it through and through. Since the entire contents of its natural consciousness have not been jeopardized, determinate being still *in principle* attaches to it; having a "mind of one's own" is self-will, a freedom which is still enmeshed in servitude. Just as little as the pure form can become essential being for it, just as little is that form, regarded as extended to the particular, a universal formative activity, an absolute Notion; rather it is a skill which is master over some things, but not over the universal power and the whole of objective being.

John Rawls, "The Original Position," from *A Theory of Justice* (1971)

John Rawls (1921–) rejuvenated the metaphor of the state of nature as well as the theory of the social contract in his *A Theory of Justice,* published to great acclaim (and with much anticipation) in 1971. Rawls's version of the state of nature, however, has nothing to do with men and women tripping around in primeval forests, whether indifferent or hostile to each other. Like Hobbes and Locke, Rawls finds extraordinarily attractive the idea that the best way to determine the nature of just social arrangements is through the device of the social contract. Since none of us actually enters into a society by way of an agreement, though, this contract must be *hypothetical:* we have to ask what social arrangements we *would* agree to. The "original position" is Rawls's account of the conditions under which we enter into this hypothetical agreement, just as in Hobbes and Locke the state of nature is the set of circumstances under which people originally set up political authority. Particularly ingenious is Rawls's way of guaranteeing that the agreement will be a fair one: he suggests that we imagine that while in the original position we are behind a "veil of ignorance," in which we do not know any particular details about ourselves. We do not know whether we are born rich or poor; healthy or ill; white, brown, red, or black. We do not know who our parents are. We do not know what our sex is. We do not know who our children are. Thus, Rawls says, whatever social arrangements we agree to will be fair, for none of us can try to skew the distribution of benefits and burdens dictated by the agreement in his or her own favor. All that we have to go on are certain very general facts about human psychology and the economic consequences of different types of social structures. What we must do, then, is to choose rationally on the basis of the various possibilities: the fairness of the original position translates into the justice of the chosen social arrangements. (The following excerpt offers Rawls's account of the design of the original position; Rawls's arguments from the original position to a specific conception of justice are presented in Part Five.)

The circumstances of justice may be described as the normal conditions under which human cooperation is both possible and necessary. Thus, as I noted at the outset, although a society is a cooperative venture for mutual advantage, it is typically marked by a conflict as well as an identity of interests. There is an identity of interests since social cooperation makes possible a better life for all than any would have if each were to try to live solely by his own efforts. There is a conflict of interests since men are not indifferent as to how the greater benefits produced by their collaboration are distributed, for in order to pursue their ends they each prefer a larger to a lesser share. Thus principles are needed for choosing among the various social arrangements which determine this division of advantages and for underwriting an agreement on the proper distributive shares. These requirements define the role of justice. The background conditions that give rise to these necessities are the circumstances of justice.

These conditions may be divided into two kinds. First, there are the objective circumstances which make human cooperation both possible and necessary. Thus, many individuals coexist together at the same time on a definite geographical territory. These individuals are roughly similar in physical and mental powers; or at any rate, their capacities are comparable in that no one among them can dominate the rest. They are vulnerable to attack, and all are subject to having their plans blocked by the united force of others. Finally, there is the condition of moderate scarcity understood to cover a wide range of situations. Natural and other resources are not so abundant that schemes of cooperation become superfluous, nor are conditions so harsh that fruitful ventures must inevitably break down. While mutually advantageous arrangements are feasible, the benefits they yield fall short of the demands men put forward.

The subjective circumstances are the relevant aspects of the subjects of cooperation, that is, of the persons working together. Thus while the parties have roughly similar needs and interests, or needs and interests in various ways complementary, so that mutually advantageous cooperation among them is possible, they nevertheless have their own plans of life. These plans, or conceptions of the good, lead them to have different ends and purposes, and to make conflicting claims on the natural and social resources available. Moreover, although the interests advanced by these plans are not assumed to be interests in the self, they are the interests of a self that regards its conception of the good as worthy of recognition and that advances claims in its behalf as deserving satisfaction. I shall emphasize this aspect of the circumstances of justice by assuming that the parties take no interest in one another's interests. I also suppose that men suffer from various shortcomings of knowledge, thought, and judgment. Their knowledge is necessarily incomplete, their powers of reasoning, memory, and attention are always limited, and their judgment is likely to be distorted by anxiety, bias, and a preoccupation with their own affairs. Some of these defects spring from moral faults, from selfishness and negligence; but to a large degree, they are simply part of men's natural situation. As a consequence individuals not only have different plans of life but there exists a diversity of philosophical and religious belief, and of political and social doctrines.

Now this constellation of conditions I shall refer to as the circumstances of justice. Hume's account of them is especially perspicuous and the preceding summary adds nothing essential to his much fuller discussion. For simplicity I often stress the condition of moderate scarcity (among the objective circumstances), and that of mutual disinterest, or individuals taking no interest in one another's interests (among the subjective circumstances). Thus, one can say, in brief, that the circumstances of justice obtain whenever mutually disinterested persons put forward conflicting claims to the division of social advantages under conditions of moderate scarcity. Unless these circumstances existed there would be no occasion for the virtue of justice, just as in the absence of threats of injury to life and limb there would be no occasion for physical courage.

Several clarifications should be noted. First of all, I shall, of course, assume that the persons in the original position know that these circumstances of justice obtain. This much they take for granted about the conditions of their society. A further assumption is that the parties try to advance their conception of the good as best they can, and that in attempting to do this they are not bound by prior moral ties to each other. . . .

The situation of the persons in the original position reflects certain constraints. The alternatives open to them and their knowledge of their circumstances are limited in various ways. These restrictions I refer to as the constraints of the concept of right since they hold for the choice of all ethical principles and not only for those of justice. If the parties were to acknowledge principles for the other virtues as well, these constraints would also apply.

I shall consider first the constraints on the alternatives. There are certain formal conditions that it seems reasonable to impose on the conceptions of justice that are to be allowed on the list presented to the parties. I do not claim that these conditions follow from the concept of right, much less from the meaning of morality. I avoid an appeal to the analysis of concepts at crucial points of this kind. There are many constraints that can reasonably be associated with the concept of right, and different selections can be made from these and counted as definitive within a particular theory. The merit of any definition depends upon the soundness of the theory that results; by itself, a definition cannot settle any fundamental question.

The propriety of these formal conditions is derived from the task of principles of right in adjusting the claims that persons make on their institutions and one another. If the principles of justice are to play their role, that of assigning basic rights and duties and determining the division of advantages, these requirements are natural enough. Each of them is suitably weak and I assume that they are satisfied by the traditional conceptions of justice. These conditions do, however, exclude the various forms of egoism, as I note below, which shows that they are not without moral force. This makes it all the more necessary that the conditions not be justified by definition or the analysis of concepts, but only by the reasonableness of the theory of which they are a part. I arrange them under five familiar headings.

First of all, principles should be general. That is, it must be possible to formulate them without the use of what would be intuitively recognized as proper names, or rigged definite descriptions. Thus the predicates used in their statement should express general properties and relations. Unfortunately deep philosophical difficulties seem to bar the way to a satisfactory account of these matters. I shall not try to deal with them here. In presenting a theory of justice one is entitled to avoid the problem of defining general properties and relations and to be guided by what seems reasonable. Further, since the parties have no specific information about themselves or their situation, they cannot identify themselves anyway. Even if a person could get others to agree, he does not know how to tailor principles to his advantage. The parties are effectively forced to stick to general principles, understanding the notion here in an intuitive fashion.

The naturalness of this condition lies in part in the fact that first principles must be capable of serving as a public charter of a well-ordered society in perpetuity. Being unconditional, they always hold (under the circumstances of justice), and the knowledge of them must be open to individuals in any generation. Thus, to understand these principles should not require a knowledge of contingent particulars, and surely not a reference to individuals or associations. Traditionally the most obvious test of this condition is the idea that what is right is that which accords with God's will. But in fact this doctrine is normally supported by an argument from general principles. For example, Locke held that the fundamental principle of morals is the following: if one person is created by another (in the theological sense), then that person has a duty to comply with the precepts set to him by his creator. This principle is perfectly general and given the nature of the world on Locke's view, it singles out God as the legitimate moral authority. The generality condition is not violated, although it may appear so at first sight.

Next, principles are to be universal in application. They must hold for everyone in virtue of their being moral persons. Thus I assume that each can understand these principles and use them in his deliberations. This imposes an upper bound of sorts on how complex they can be, and on the kinds and number of distinctions they draw. Moreover, a principle is ruled out if it would be self-contradictory, or self-defeating, for everyone to act upon it. Similarly, should a principle be reasonable to follow only when others conform to a different one, it is also inadmissible. Principles are to be chosen in view of the consequences of everyone's complying with them. . . .

A third condition is that of publicity, which arises naturally from a contractarian standpoint. The parties assume that they are choosing principles for a public conception of justice. They suppose that everyone will know about these principles all that he would know if their acceptance were the result of an agreement. Thus the general awareness of their universal acceptance should have desirable effects and support the stability of social cooperation. The difference between this condition and that of universality is that the latter leads one to assess principles on the basis of their being intelligently and regularly followed by everyone. But it is possible that all should understand and follow a principle and yet this fact not be widely known or explicitly recognized. The point of the publicity condition is to have the parties evaluate conceptions of justice as publicly acknowledged and fully effective moral constitutions of social life. The publicity condition is clearly implicit in Kant's doctrine of the categorical imperative insofar as it requires us to act in accordance with principles that one would be willing as a rational being to enact as law for a kingdom of ends. He thought of this kingdom as an ethical commonwealth, as it were, which has such moral principles for its public charter.

A further condition is that a conception of right must impose an ordering on conflicting claims. This requirement springs directly from the role of its principles in adjusting competing demands. There is a difficulty, however, in deciding what counts as an ordering. It is clearly desirable that a conception of justice be complete, that is, able to order all the claims that can arise (or that are likely to in practice). And the ordering should in general be transitive; if, say, a first arrangement of the basic structure is ranked more just than a second, and the second more just than a third, then the first should be more just than the third. These formal conditions are natural enough, though not always easy to satisfy. But is trial by combat a form of adjudication? After all, physical conflict and resort to arms result in an ordering; certain claims do win out over others. The main objection to this ordering is not that it may be intransitive. Rather, it is to avoid the appeal to force and cunning that the principles of right and justice are accepted. Thus I assume that to each according to his threat advantage is not a conception of justice. It fails to establish an ordering in the required sense, an ordering based on certain relevant aspects of persons and their situation which are independent from their social position, or their capacity to intimidate and coerce.

The fifth and last condition is that of finality. The parties are to assess the system of principles as the final court of appeal in practical reasoning. There are no higher standards to which arguments in support of claims can be addressed; reasoning successfully from these principles is conclusive. If we think in terms of the fully general theory which has principles for all the virtues, then such a theory specifies the totality of relevant considerations and their appropriate weights, and its requirements are decisive. They override the demands of law and custom, and of social rules generally. We are to arrange and respect social institutions as the principles of right and justice direct. Conclusions from these principles also override considerations of prudence and self-interest. This does not mean that these principles insist upon self-sacrifice; for in drawing up the conception of right the parties take their interests into account as best they can. The claims of personal prudence are already given an appropriate weight within the full system of principles. The complete scheme is final in that when the course of practical reasoning it defines has reached its conclusion, the question is settled. The claims of existing social arrangements and of self-interest have been duly allowed for. We cannot at the end count them a second time because we do not like the result.

Taken together, then, these conditions on conceptions of right come to this: a conception of right is a set of principles, general in form and universal in application, that is to be publicly recognized as a final court of appeal for ordering the conflicting claims of moral persons. . . .

The idea of the original position is to set up a fair procedure so that any principles agreed to will be just. The aim is to use the notion of pure procedural justice as a basis of theory. Somehow we must nullify the effects of specific contingencies which put men at odds and tempt them to exploit social and natural circumstances to their own advantage. Now in order to do this I assume that the parties are situated behind a veil of ignorance. They do not know how the various alternatives will affect their own particular case and they are obliged to evaluate principles solely on the basis of general considerations.

It is assumed, then, that the parties do not know certain kinds of particular facts. First of all, no one knows his place in society, his class position or social status; nor does he know his fortune in the distribution of natural assets and abilities, his intelligence and strength, and the like. Nor, again, does anyone know his conception of the good, the particulars of his rational plan of life, or even the special features of his psychology such as his aversion to risk or liability to optimism or pessimism. More than this, I assume that the parties do not know the particular circumstances of their own society. That is, they do not know its economic or political situation, or the level of civilization and culture it has been able to achieve. The persons in the original position have no information as to which generation they belong. These broader restrictions on knowledge are appropriate in part because questions of social justice arise between generations as well as within them, for example, the question of the appropriate rate of capital saving and of the conservation of natural resources and the environment of nature. There is also, theoretically anyway, the question of a reasonable genetic policy. In these cases too, in order to carry through the idea of the original position, the parties must not know the contingencies that set them in opposition. They must choose principles the consequences of which they are prepared to live with whatever generation they turn out to belong to.

As far as possible, then, the only particular facts which the parties know is that their society is subject to the circumstances of justice and whatever this implies. It is taken for granted, however, that they know the general facts about human society. They understand political affairs and the principles of economic theory; they know the basis of social organization and the laws of human psychology. Indeed, the parties are presumed to know whatever general facts affect the choice of the principles of justice. There are no limitations on general information, that is, on general laws and theories, since conceptions of justice must be adjusted to the characteristics of the systems of social cooperation which they are to regulate, and there is no reason to rule out these facts. It is, for example, a consideration against a conception of justice that, in view of the laws of moral psychology, men would not acquire a desire to act upon it even when the institutions of their society satisfied it. For in this case there would be difficulty in securing the stability of social cooperation. It is an important feature of a conception of justice that it should generate its own support. That is, its principles should be such that when they are embodied in the basic structure of society men tend to acquire the corresponding sense of justice. Given the principles of moral learning, men develop a desire to act in accordance with its principles. In this case a conception of justice is stable. This kind of general information is admissible in the original position.

The notion of the veil of ignorance raises several difficulties. Some may object that the exclusion of nearly all particular information makes it difficult to grasp what is meant by the original position. Thus it may be helpful to observe that one or more persons can at any time enter this position, or perhaps, better, simulate the deliberations of this hypothetical situation, simply by reasoning in accordance with the appropriate restrictions. . . .

These remarks show that the original position is not to be thought of as a general assembly which includes at one moment everyone who will live at some time; or, much less, as an assembly of everyone who could live at some time. It is not a gathering of all actual or possible persons. To conceive of the original position in either of these ways is to stretch fantasy too far; the conception would cease to be a natural guide to intuition. In any case, it is important that the original position be interpreted so that one can at any time adopt its perspective. It must make no difference when one takes up this viewpoint, or who does so: the restrictions must be such that the same principles are always chosen. The veil of ignorance is a key condition in meeting this requirement. It insures not only that the information available is relevant, but that it is at all times the same. . . .

I have assumed throughout that the persons in the original position are rational. In choosing between principles each tries as best he can to advance his interests. But I have also assumed that the parties do not know their conception of the good. This means that while they know that they have some rational plan of life, they do not know the details of this plan, the particular ends and interests which it is calculated to promote. How, then, can they decide which conceptions of justice are most to their advantage? Or must we suppose that they are reduced to mere guessing? To meet this difficulty, I postulate that they accept the account of the good touched upon in the preceding chapter: they assume that they would prefer more primary social goods rather than less. Of course, it may turn out, once the veil of ignorance is removed, that some of them for religious or other reasons may not, in fact, want more of these goods.

But from the standpoint of the original position, it is rational for the parties to suppose that they do want a larger share, since in any case they are not compelled to accept more if they do not wish to, nor does a person suffer from a greater liberty. Thus even though the parties are deprived of information about their particular ends, they have enough knowledge to rank the alternatives. They know that in general they must try to protect their liberties, widen their opportunities, and enlarge their means for promoting their aims whatever these are. Guided by the theory of the good and the general facts of moral psychology, their deliberations are no longer guesswork. They can make a rational decision in the ordinary sense.

The concept of rationality invoked here, with the exception of one essential feature, is the standard one familiar in social theory. Thus in the usual way, a rational person is thought to have a coherent set of preferences between the options open to him. He ranks these options according to how well they further his purposes; he follows the plan which will sat-

isfy more of his desires rather than less, and which has the greater chance of being successfully executed. The special assumption I make is that a rational individual does not suffer from envy. He is not ready to accept a loss for himself if only others have less as well.
He is not downcast by the knowledge or perception that others have a larger index of primary social goods. Or at least this is true as long as the differences between himself and
others do not exceed certain limits, and he does not believe that the existing inequalities are
founded on injustice or are the result of letting chance work itself out for no compensating
social purpose.

Robert Nozick, "From Anarchy to the Minimal State," from *Anarchy, State, and Utopia* (1974)

Anarchy, State, and Utopia, written by Rawls's Harvard colleague Robert·Nozick
(1938–), was published only three years after *A Theory of Justice,* and in addition to
the notoriety that it achieved in its own right, it formed an obvious pole of opposition and a staging area for attacks on Rawls and the welfare liberal tradition. Nozick
employs the state of nature imagery invoked by Rawls, but for him, too, this is more
than anything else a thought-experiment by which to establish the various rational
possibilities for the construction of, and justification of, society. Or, more properly,
it is a question of the justification of the *state,* not society as such, for Nozick is
wisely abstemious on the question of the natural condition of society and human
communities. What justifies the existence of state power, and how much state
power is justified? To answer these questions, Nozick raises some neo-Lockean
issues about the protection of property and whether we could assure ourselves of
mutual security without the imposition of a state. He considers the possibility of various "protective associations" and whether they might do the job, and argues that,
by necessity but not by design, a state—if only a *minimal* state—would be the
inevitable product of these various efforts.

Individuals in Locke's state of nature are in "a state of perfect freedom to order their actions and dispose of their possessions and persons as they think fit, within the bounds of the law of nature, without asking leave or dependency upon the will of any other man." The bounds of the law of nature require that "no one ought to harm another in his life, health, liberty, or possessions." Some persons transgress these bounds, "invading others' rights and . . . doing hurt to one another," and in response people may defend themselves or others against such invaders of rights. The injured party and his agents may recover from the offender "so much as may make satisfaction for the harm he has suffered"; "everyone has a right to punish the transgressors of that law to such a degree as may hinder its violation"; each person may, and may only "retribute to [a criminal] so far as calm reason and conscience dictate, what is proportionate to his transgression, which is so much as may serve for reparation and restraint."

There are "inconveniences of the state of nature" for which, says Locke, "I easily grant that civil government is the proper remedy." To understand precisely what civil government remedies, we must do more than repeat Locke's list of the inconveniences of the state of nature. We also must consider what arrangements might be made within a state of nature to deal with these inconveniences—to avoid them or to make them less likely to arise or to make them less serious on the occasions when they do arise. Only after the full resources of the state of nature are brought into play, namely all those voluntary arrangements and agreements persons might reach acting within their rights, and only after the effects of these are estimated, will we be in a position to see how serious are the inconveniences that yet remain to be remedied by the state, and to estimate whether the remedy is worse than the disease.

In a state of nature, the understood natural law may not provide for every contingency in a proper fashion, and men who judge in their own case will always give themselves the benefit of the doubt and assume that they are in the right. They will overestimate the amount of harm or damage they have suffered, and passions will lead them to attempt to punish others more than proportionately and to exact excessive compensation. Thus private and personal enforcement of one's rights (including those rights that are violated when one is excessively punished) leads to feuds, to an endless series of acts of retaliation and exactions of compensation. And there is no firm way to *settle* such a dispute, to *end* it and to have both parties know it is ended. Even if one party *says* he'll stop his acts of retaliation, the other can rest secure only if he knows the first still does not feel entitled to gain recompense or to exact retribution, and therefore entitled to try when a promising occasion presents itself. Any method a single individual might use in an attempt irrevocably to bind himself into ending his part in a feud would offer insufficient assurance to the other party; tacit agreements to stop also would be unstable. Such feelings of being mutually wronged can occur even with the clearest right and with joint agreement on the facts of each person's conduct; all the more is there opportunity for such retaliatory battle when the facts or the rights are to some extent unclear. Also, in a state of nature a person may lack the power to enforce his rights; he may be unable to punish or exact compensation from a stronger adversary who has violated them.

Protective Associations

How might one deal with these troubles within a state of nature? Let us begin with the last. In a state of nature an individual may himself enforce his rights, defend himself, exact compensation, and punish (or at least try his best to do so). Others may join with him in his defense, at his call. They may join with him to repulse an attacker or to go after an aggressor because they are public spirited, or because they are his friends, or because he has helped them in the past, or because they wish him to help them in the future, or in exchange for something. Groups of individuals may form mutual-protection associations: all will answer the call of any member for defense or for the enforcement of his rights. In union there is strength. . . .

A mutual-protection association might attempt to deal with conflict among its own members by a policy of nonintervention. But this policy would bring discord within the association and might lead to the formation of subgroups who might fight among themselves and thus cause the breakup of the association. This policy would also encourage potential aggressors to join as many mutual-protection associations as possible in order to gain immunity from retaliatory or defensive action, thus placing a great burden on the adequacy of the initial screening procedure of the association. Thus protective associations (almost all of those that will survive which people will join) will not follow a policy of nonintervention; they will use some procedure to determine how to act when some members claim that other members have violated their rights. Many arbitrary procedures can be imagined (for example, act on the side of that member who complains first), but most persons will want to join associations that follow some procedure to find out which claimant is correct. When a member of the association is in conflict with nonmembers, the association also will want to determine in some fashion who is in the right, if only to avoid constant and costly involvement in each member's quarrels, whether just or unjust. The inconvenience of everyone's being on call, whatever their activity at the moment or inclinations or comparative advantage, can be handled in the usual manner by division of labor and exchange. Some people will be *hired* to perform protective functions, and some entrepreneurs will go into the business of selling protective services. Different sorts of protective policies would be offered, at different prices, for those who may desire more extensive or elaborate protection.

An individual might make more particular arrangements or commitments short of turning over to a private protective agency all functions of detection, apprehension, judicial determination of guilt, punishment, and exaction of compensation. Mindful of the dangers of being the judge in his own case, he might turn the decision as to whether he has indeed been wronged, and to what extent, to some other neutral or less involved party. In order for the occurrence of the social effect of justice's being seen to be done, such a party would have to be generally respected and thought to be neutral and upright. Both parties to a dispute may so attempt to safeguard themselves against the appearance of partiality, and both might even agree upon the *same* person as the judge between them, and agree to abide by his decision. (Or there might be a specified process through which one of the parties dissatisfied with the decision could appeal it.) But, for obvious reasons, there will be strong tendencies for the above-mentioned functions to converge in the same agent or agency.

Presumably what drives people to use the state's system of justice is the issue of ultimate enforcement. Only the state can enforce a judgment against the will of one of the parties. For the state does not *allow* anyone else to enforce another system's judgment. So in any dispute in which both parties cannot agree upon a method of settlement, or in any dispute in which one party does not trust another to abide by the decision (if the other contracts to forfeit something of enormous value if he doesn't abide by the decision, by what agency is *that* contract to be enforced?), the parties who wish their claims put into effect will have no recourse permitted by the state's legal system other than to use that very legal system. This may present persons greatly opposed to a given state system with particularly poignant and painful choices. (If the state's legal system enforces the results of certain arbitration procedures, people may come to agree—supposing they abide by this agreement—without any actual direct contact with what they perceive to be officers or institutions of the state. But this holds as well if they sign a contract that is enforced only by the state.)

The Dominant Protective Association

Initially, several different protective associations or companies will offer their services in the same geographical area. What will occur when there is a conflict between clients of different agencies? Things are relatively simple if the agencies reach the same decision about the disposition of the case. (Though each might want to exact the penalty.) But what happens if they reach different decisions as to the merits of the case, and one agency attempts to protect its client while the other is attempting to punish him or make him pay compensation? Only three possibilities are worth considering:

    1.   In such situations the forces of the two agencies do battle. One of the agencies always wins such battles. Since the clients of the losing agency are ill protected in conflicts with clients of the winning agency, they leave their agency to do business with the winner.

    2.   One agency has its power centered in one geographical area, the other in another. Each wins the battles fought close to its center of power, with some gradient being established. People who deal with one agency but live under the power of the other either move closer to their own agency's home headquarters or shift their patronage to the other protective agency. (The border is about as conflictful as one between states.)

    In neither of these two cases does there remain very much geographical interspersal. Only one protective agency operates over a given geographical area.

    3.   The two agencies fight evenly and often. They win and lose about equally, and their interspersed members have frequent dealings and disputes with each other. Or perhaps without fighting or after only a few skirmishes the agencies realize that such battling will occur continually in the absence of preventive measures. In any case, to avoid frequent, costly, and wasteful battles the two agencies, perhaps through their executives, agree to resolve peacefully those cases about which they reach differing judgments. They agree to set up, and abide by the decisions of, some third judge or court to which they can turn when their respective judgments differ. (Or they might establish rules determining which agency has jurisdiction under which circumstances.) Thus emerges a system of appeals courts and agreed upon rules about jurisdiction and the conflict of laws. Though different agencies operate, there is one unified federal judicial system of which they all are components.

    In each of these cases, almost all the persons in a geographical area are under some common system that judges between their competing claims and *enforces* their rights. Out of anarchy, pressed by spontaneous groupings, mutual-protection associations, division of labor, market pressures, economies of scale, and rational self-interest there arises something very much resembling a minimal state or a group of geographically distinct minimal states. Why is this market different from all other markets? Why would a virtual monopoly arise in this market without the government intervention that elsewhere creates and maintains it? The worth of the product purchased, protection against others, is *relative:* it depends upon how strong the others are. Yet unlike other goods that are comparatively evaluated, maximal competing protective services cannot coexist; the nature of the service brings different agencies not only into competition for customers' patronage, but also into violent conflict with each other. Also, since the worth of the less than maximal product declines disproportionately with the number who purchase the maximal product, customers will not stably settle for the lesser good, and competing companies are caught in a declining spiral. Hence the three possibilities we have listed.

Our story above assumes that each of the agencies attempts in good faith to act within the limits of Locke's law of nature. But one "protective association" might aggress against other persons. Relative to Locke's law of nature, it would be an outlaw agency. What actual counterweights would there be to its power? (What actual counterweights are there to the power of a state?) Other agencies might unite to act against it. People might refuse to deal with the outlaw agency's clients, boycotting them to reduce the probability of the agency's intervening in their own affairs. This might make it more difficult for the outlaw agency to get clients; but this boycott will seem an effective tool only on very optimistic assumptions about what cannot be kept secret, and about the costs to an individual of partial boycott as compared to the benefits of receiving the more extensive coverage offered by an "outlaw" agency. If the "outlaw" agency simply is an *open* aggressor, pillaging, plundering, and extorting under no plausible claim of justice, it will have a harder time than states. For the state's claim to legitimacy induces its citizens to believe they have some duty to obey its edicts, pay its taxes, fight its battles, and so on; and so some persons cooperate with it voluntarily. An openly aggressive agency could not depend upon, and would not receive, any such voluntary cooperation, since persons would view themselves simply as its victims rather than as its citizens.

Invisible-Hand Explanations

How, if at all, does a dominant protective association differ from the state? Was Locke wrong in imagining a compact necessary to establish civil society? As he was wrong in thinking that an "agreement," or "mutual consent," was needed to establish the "invention of money." Within a barter system, there is great inconvenience and cost to searching for someone who has what you want and wants what you have, even at a marketplace, which, we should note, needn't become a marketplace by everyone's expressly agreeing to deal there. People will exchange their goods for something they know to be more generally wanted than what they have. For it will be more likely that they can exchange this for what they want. For the same reasons others will be more willing to take in exchange this more generally desired thing. Thus persons will converge in exchanges on the more marketable goods, being willing to exchange their goods for them; the more willing, the more they know others who are also willing to do so, in a mutually reinforcing process. (This process will be reinforced and hastened by middlemen seeking to profit in facilitating exchanges, who themselves will often find it most expedient to offer more marketable goods in exchange.) For obvious reasons, the goods they converge on, via their individual decisions, will have certain properties: initial independent value (else they wouldn't begin as more marketable), physically enduring, non-perishable, divisible, portable, and so forth. No express agreement and no social contract fixing a medium of exchange is necessary.

Is the Dominant Protective Association a State?

Have we provided an invisible-hand explanation of the state? There are at least two ways in which the scheme of private protective associations might be thought to differ from a minimal state, might fail to satisfy a minimal conception of a state: (1) it appears to allow some people to enforce their own rights, and (2) it appears not to protect all individuals within its domain. . . .

. . . A state claims a monopoly on deciding who may use force when; it says that only it may decide who may use force and under what conditions; it reserves to itself the sole right to pass on the legitimacy and permissibility of any use of force within its boundaries; furthermore it claims the right to punish all those who violate its claimed monopoly. The monopoly may be violated in two ways: (1) a person may use force though unauthorized by the state to do so, or (2) though not themselves using force a group or person may set themselves up as an alternative authority (and perhaps even claim to be the sole legitimate one) to decide when and by whom the use of force is proper and legitimate. . . .

We may proceed, for our purposes, by saying that a necessary condition for the existence of a state is that it (some person or organization) announce that, to the best of its ability (taking into account costs of doing so, the feasibility, the more important alternative things it should be doing, and so forth), it will punish everyone whom it discovers to have used force without its express permission. (This permission may be a particular permission or may be granted via some general regulation or authorization.) This still won't quite do: the state may reserve the right to forgive someone, ex post facto; in order to punish they may have not only to discover the "unauthorized" use of force but also prove via a certain specified procedure of proof that it occurred, and so forth. But it enables us to proceed. The protective agencies, it seems, do not make such an announcement, either individually or collectively. *Nor does it seem morally legitimate for them to do so.* So the system of private protective associations, if they perform no morally illegitimate action, appears to lack any monopoly element and so appears not to constitute or contain a state. To examine the question of the monopoly element, we shall have to consider the situation of some group of persons (or some one person) living within a system of private protective agencies who refuse to join any protective society; who insist on judging for themselves whether their rights have been violated, and (if they so judge) on personally enforcing their rights by punishing and/or exacting compensation from those who infringed them.

The second reason for thinking the system described is not a state is that, under it (apart from spillover effects) only those paying for protection get protected; furthermore, differing degrees of protection may be purchased. External economies again to the side, no one pays for the protection of others except as they choose to; no one is required to purchase or contribute to the purchasing of protection for others. Protection and enforcement of people's rights is treated as an economic good to be provided by the market, as are other important goods such as food and clothing. However, under the usual conception of a state, each person living within (or even sometimes traveling outside) its geographical boundaries gets (or at least, is entitled to get) its protection. Unless some private party donated sufficient funds to cover the costs of such protection (to pay for detectives, police to bring criminals into custody, courts, and prisons), or unless the state found some service it could charge for that would cover these costs, one would expect that a state which offered protection so broadly would be redistributive. It would be a state in which some persons paid more so that others could be protected. And indeed the most minimal state seriously discussed by the mainstream of political theorists, the night-watch-man state of classical liberal theory, appears to be redistributive in this fashion. Yet how can a protection agency, a business, charge some to provide its product to others? (We ignore things like some partially paying for others because it is too costly for the agency to refine its classification of, and charges to, customers to mirror the costs of the services to them.)

Thus it appears that the dominant protective agency in a territory not only lacks the requisite monopoly over the use of force, but also fails to provide protection for all in its territory; and so the dominant agency appears to fall short of being a state. But these appearances are deceptive. . . .

Behavior in the Process

We have argued that even someone who foresees that a protective association will become dominant may not forbid others to join up. But though no one may be forbidden to join up, might not everyone *choose* to stay out, in order to avoid the state at the end of the process? Might not a population of anarchists realize how individual efforts at hiring protection will lead, by an invisible-hand process, to a state, and because they have historical evidence and theoretical grounds for the worry that the state is a Frankenstein monster that will run amuck and will not stay limited to minimal functions, might not they each prudentially choose not to begin along that path? If told to anarchists, is the invisible-hand account of how the state arises a self-defeating prophecy? . . .

We have described a process whereby individuals in an area separately sign up for personal protection with different business enterprises which provide protective services, all but one of the agencies being extinguished or all coming to some modus vivendi, and so on. To what degree, if any, does this process fit what Locke envisioned as individuals "agreeing with other men to join and unite into a community," consenting "to make one community or government," compacting to make up a commonwealth? The process looks nothing like unanimous joint agreement to create a government or state. No one, as they buy protective services from their local protective agency, has in mind anything so grand. But perhaps joint agreement where each has in mind that the others will agree and each intends to bring about the end result of this is not necessary for a Lockean compact. I myself see little point to stretching the notion of "compact" so that each pattern or state of affairs that arises from the disparate voluntary actions of separately acting individuals is viewed as arising from a *social compact,* even though no one had the pattern in mind or was acting to achieve it. Or, if the notion is so stretched, this should be made clear that the notion is such that each of the following arises from a social compact: the total state of affairs constituted by who is married to, or living with, whom; the distribution on a given evening in a given city of who is in what movie theater, sitting where; the particular traffic pattern on a state's highways on a given day; the set of customers of a given grocery store on a given day and the particular pattern of purchase they make, and so on. Far be it from me to claim that this wider notion is of no interest; that a state can arise by a process that fits this wider notion (without fitting the narrower one) is of very great interest indeed!

The view we present here should not be confused with other views. It differs from social compact views in its invisible-hand structure. It differs from views that "de facto might makes state (legal) right" in holding that enforcement rights and rights to oversee this enforcement exist independently and are held by all rather than confined to one or a small group, and that the process of accumulating sole effective enforcement and overseeing power may take place without anyone's rights being violated; that a state may arise by a process in which no one's rights are violated. Shall we say that a state which has arisen from a state of nature by the process described has replaced the state of nature which therefore no longer exists, or shall we say that it exists within a state of nature and hence is compatible with one? No doubt, the first would better fit the Lockean tradition; but the state arises

so gradually and imperceptibly out of Locke's state of nature, without any great or fundamental breach of continuity, that one is *tempted* to take the second option, disregarding
Locke's incredulousness: ". . . unless any one will say the state of nature and civil society are one and the same thing, which I have never yet found any one so great a patron of
anarchy as to affirm."

David Gauthier, "The Presuppositions of the Social Contract," from "The Social Contract as Ideology" (1977)

David Gauthier (1932–), in the selection that follows, is concerned to lay bare the
deep structure of the ideology concerning social relationships shared by those persons inhabiting social institutions derived from Western Europe. In Gauthier's view,
this ideology is one that conceives all social relationships as contractual in nature,
the result of agreement—rather than, say, given by tradition, discovered in nature,
or laid down by God. At the root of such thinking, argues Gauthier, is a presupposed
picture of human nature: that the essential characteristics of human beings can be
understood apart from society; that human beings are appropriative, concerned to
gain possessions; and that they are maximizing agents, concerned to make themselves as well off as possible. Social relationships are justifiable, according to this
ideology, only insofar as they would be agreed to by beings thus understood.
Gauthier is not, here, arguing in favor of this conception; he is only trying to get at
the deep structure of our cultural conception of justifiable social relationships. But,
as he suggests, the hold that the social contract ideology has on us often makes it
difficult for us to conceive genuine alternatives to it.

The conception of social relationships as contractual lies at the core of our ideology. Indeed,
that core is constituted by the intersection of this conception with the correlative concep-

tions of human activity as appropriative and of rationality as utility-maximizing. My concern is to clarify this thesis and to enhance its descriptive plausibility as a characterization of our ideology, but to undermine its normative plausibility as ideologically effective.

. . . The thesis refers to our ideology. There are two terms here which require immediate clarification; the first is "our." Philosophers habitually use the first-person plural pronoun; its use demands specification. Who are "we"? In this essay, first-person plural references are intended to denote those persons who have inhabited Western Europe, who are descended from such inhabitants, or who live or have lived in social structures developed from those of Western Europe during the past three to four hundred years. I am supposing, without further defense, that these persons share certain ideas and certain ways of thinking and behaving that permit the attribution to them of an ideology.

"Ideology" is the second term which requires clarification. It has not been employed with great consistency or clarity by social thinkers. It picks out some aspect of our consciousness, frequently pejoratively, whether because of its allegedly derivative character (superstructure) or its allegedly misleading character (false consciousness). Although the demise of ideology as a determinant of social values and practices has been widely celebrated, more recent reports suggest that the celebrations may themselves be ideological in character. My use of the term is intended to retain the place of ideology in consciousness, and indeed perhaps to ensure the permanence of that place, without pejorative commitment.

Ideology is part of the deep structure of self-consciousness. By self-consciousness I understand that capacity of human beings to conceive themselves in relation to other humans, to human structures and institutions, and to the nonhuman or natural environment, and to act in the light of these conceived relationships. Exhibited in these thoughts and activities is a conception of the self-as-human. This conception need not be, and typically is not, actually expressed in self-consciousness. Rather, it must be inferred from a person's actual thoughts and activities, insofar as they concern himself, his fellows, his society, and his world, as that underlying structure of ideas which affords their most economical foundation. This conception of self-as-human is thus a theoretical construct that we attribute to the ground of self-consciousness to explain its content, the surface of overt thought and action. This theoretical construct is what I refer to as ideology. . . .

The articulation of an ideology, like the articulation of any deep structure, cannot be expected to be an easy task. Many recent studies, especially in moral philosophy but also in political philosophy, have tended to ignore it. They have focused on the language or the logic of morals and politics and on practical, moral, and political reasoning, but frequently they have examined only the surface structure, the ideas we consciously express about ourselves. John Rawls' *A Theory of Justice* is a pioneering work in many respects, but in none more important than in its awareness of the significance of deep structure, although Rawls seems to suggest that this structure is invariant for human beings and not relative only to our own society. And it is most noteworthy that in articulating this deep structure, he is led to develop, once again in the history of our political thought, the theory of the social contract.

The theory of the social contract has been advanced in more and less embracing forms. Thomas Hobbes and John Locke are classic exponents of these contrasting approaches. Since my concern is primarily with the Hobbist variant, I shall begin with a brief sketch of its alternative.

Locke supposes that a certain group of men, namely landed proprietors, those who have successfully appropriated or inherited real property or estate, contract together for mutual protection and well-being. Their contract brings civil government into existence, but civil government is not, in Locke's view, the only or the primary ground for social relationships among human beings. Locke's landed proprietors are heads of households, and their household relationships—of man with wife, father with child, and master with servant—are prior to and indeed fall outside of the contractual relationship which gives rise to political society. Furthermore, although here Locke is less explicit, it seems evident that landed proprietors enter into relationships of sociability, one with another, which are neither conditions nor consequences of the contract among them. And their relations one with another, and with other human beings, explicitly fall under the divine law of nature, which regulates conduct outside political society, in the state of nature, as well as conduct within it.

Hobbes' theory affords an altogether larger scope to contractual relations. Indeed, for Hobbes, relations among human beings are of two kinds only: relations of hostility, which obtain in and constitute the state of nature, and relations of contract, which obtain in and constitute the state of society. In the state of nature, every man has the right to do whatever he will in order to preserve and benefit himself; the result is the state of war "where every man is Enemy to every man." To bring this self-defeating condition to an end, every man is supposed to contract with his fellows to establish a commonwealth under a single and all-powerful sovereign. Only within a commonwealth is any sociability possible. The family is itself a miniature commonwealth; the father, or sometimes the mother, is sovereign, and the children are supposed to contract with their parent to obey in return for being allowed to live, in the way in which the vanquished in war contracts with the victor. And this latter contract, of vanquished with victor, which establishes sovereignty by acquisition, is explicitly stated by Hobbes to constitute the relation between servant and master. The contractual relationship among men, in establishing political society, is thus the model on which all other human relationships are interpreted.

It is Hobbes' radical contractarianism which I am attributing to our ideology. To make this attribution is to hold that our thoughts and activities, insofar as they concern ourselves and our relationships, are best understood by supposing that we treat all of these relationships as if they were contractual. Only the relation of hostility is excluded from the scope of contract, and only it is natural to man. All other human relationships are treated as essentially similar in character, and all are conventional, the product of human agreement.

The theory of the social contract, as part of our ideology, is not concerned with the objective character of social institutions and relationships. It is not a piece of speculative, but purportedly actual, history or sociology. Contractarians do not suppose, either explicitly or implicitly, that human society originated in a contract, or is now maintained by contract. They do not suppose that children contract with their parents. To suppose that the theory of the social contract must be intended to explain the origin of actual societies is to confuse deep structure with surface structure; our contractual conception of human relationships may ground an explanation which makes no appeal to contract.

The theory itself concerns the rationale of relationships among persons, and between society and its members, rather than the cause of those relationships. The justification of rights and duties, institutions and practices, is to be found by regarding them as if they were contractual, and showing the rationality of this hypothetical contractual base. Of course, a theory of rationale does have an explanatory function. Were the theory true, then fully self-conscious beings whose social environment was entirely the product of their deliberate choice would only relate contractually one to another. For such beings the theory of the social contract, and indeed our entire ideology, would not be a theoretical construct, but rather the conscious basis of their social thought and practice. As part of our ideology, then, the contract theory rationalizes social relationships by providing an ideal, non-actual explanation of their existence.

In attributing this ideology to us, I am not defending it. I am not claiming that society is to be understood, or ought to be understood, as if it were contractual. It may well be absurd so to understand society. What I am doing is claiming that our thoughts and actions are to be understood as if we supposed that all social relationships were to be rationalized in contractual terms. Note that "as if" plays a dual role in my account: our conscious thoughts, and overt actions, are to be explained *as if* we held the theory of the social contract, that is, the theory that all social relationships are to be understood *as if* they were contractual.

I should not want to argue that radical contractarianism of a Hobbist kind has unequivocally dominated our thoughts and practices. Rather, I believe this to be the final form of the contractarian conception of society, the form towards which it develops as an ideology, gradually increasing its influence on our thoughts, and leading us to abandon earlier ideas of human relationships as natural or supernatural rather than as conventional. I believe, although I cannot fully defend this belief here, that our society is moving towards a more Hobbist position. Evidence for this may be found in political life, for example in the "social contract" proposals of the British government under former Prime Minister Harold Wilson. But the most significant recent evidence is found in the extension of contractarian thought to family and domestic life. We may cite the arguments and practices of those who seek to divest the marriage contract of its religious and moral overtones, to treat it as the ordinary contract which, they argue, it really is. We may cite those who suppose that housework should be paid for, or that childraising is but one occupation among many possible vocations, and that those who do it, too, should be remunerated. And we may cite the words of a Montreal girl on the "jock circuit" (the circuit of those who offer nonprofessional diversion to professional athletes): "In a way, it's a sort of business arrangement—but then, aren't all man-woman relationships?"

On reflection, we may disavow contractarianism. We may insist that there is more to human relationships than the conventions which result from agreement. The contractarian can admit this, as long as he holds that these other features of human relationships are nonessential, a sentimental residue from the past, or an emotional patina which affords a more pleasing aura to an otherwise bare artifice. But the contractarian can also maintain that we delude ourselves, and that indeed our ideology induces us to preach what we do not practice. The practice of contractarianism may indeed be most effective if it is explicitly denied. The surface structure induced by the ideology may have a content incompatible with it. . . .

To conceive all social relationships as contractual is to suppose that men, with their particular human characteristics, are prior to society. The contract theory expresses this priority in temporal terms, giving us the picture of men in a state of nature entering society of on the basis of a contract. But, as I have pointed out, the language of the theory is the language of ideal explanation; the men in the state of nature are not ourselves. The theory does not require that actual human individuals are temporally prior to their society; here, as elsewhere, temporal priority is a metaphor for conceptual priority.

What contractarianism does require is, first of all, that individual human beings not only can, but must, be understood apart from society. The fundamental characteristics of men are not products of their social existence. Rather, in affording the motivations that underlie human activity in the state of nature and that are expressed in natural hostility, they constitute the conditions of man's social existence. Thus man is social because he is human, and not human because he is social. In particular, self-consciousness and language must be taken as conditions, not products, of society.

But more than this is implicit in contractarianism. It would be compatible with the claim that the individual is prior to society, to suppose nonetheless that human sociability is itself a natural and fundamental characteristic of individuals, which expresses itself directly in social relations among human beings. And this is denied by contract theory in its insistence upon the essentially conventional character of society. Men who were naturally sociable would not need to contract together in order to form society, and would not rationalize society in contractarian terms. Although contract might be the foundation of government, as in Locke, society would not be a purely artificial creation. Contract as the foundation of all society is required only by men who are not inherently sociable.

Furthermore, radical contractarianism is incompatible with the view that men undergo fundamental change in becoming members of society. Men's reasons for contracting one with another are supposed to arise out of their presocial needs in the state of nature. If contractarian ideology is to be effective in rationalizing social relationships, then these needs must be represented, not as only presocial, but as permanent, so that the reasons for entering the contract will also be reasons for maintaining the society created thereby. Society is thus conceived as a mere instrument for men whose fundamental motivation is presocial, nonsocial, and fixed. If men are, in fact, socialized beings, so that human nature is in part a social product, then contractarian ideology must conceal this, representing social needs as if they were the product of presocial nature. Rousseau may use the device, and even the title, of the social contract, but the theory which he formulates tends to subvert contractarian ideology, in its overt distinction of social man from natural man.

Although the contractarian cannot represent man as a social being, he need not deny, as Hobbes may seem to, that human beings as we know them, within society, do display sociable characteristics. The contractarian need but insist that man is sociable only because he creates society; human sociability is the product, and not the condition, of social existence. And as the product of what is itself conventional, this sociability is but an accidental attribute of human nature, an overlay on a fundamentally and permanently nonsocial character, possessing a merely conventional existence.

The correlate of the claim that man is nonsocial by nature is, of course, the claim that society is not, and cannot be, an end in itself. Man's social existence is not self-justifying . . .

To conceive all social relationships as contractual is to deny that reason either determines or presupposes an order, a rational order, within which men are related prior to any agreement among themselves. This severely constrains the contractarian conception of rationality; I shall argue that it requires that rationality be conceived as related instrumentally to the satisfaction of individual interests.

Hobbes offers a useful way of formulating the problem of relating rationality to the theory of the social contract. "That is done by *right*, which is not done against reason," Hobbes claims, so that "we ought to judge those actions only *wrong*, which are repugnant to right reason. . . . But that *wrong* which is done, we say it is done against some law. Therefore *true reason* is a certain *law*." Reason, in other words, determines a framework of rights and laws, within which all men find themselves. But surely these rights and laws must determine relationships among men, which, being grounded in reason alone, are natural rather than conventional. If this were so, then radical contractarianism would have to be abandoned in favor of the Lockean theory that contract supplements and completes man's natural social relationships. Hobbes does not accept any such relationships; how then does he accommodate reason?

Hobbes keeps his conception of rationality consistent with his contractarianism by treating reason as both individualistic and instrumental. He speaks of "that Reason, which dictateth to every man his own good," and says that "all the voluntary actions of men tend to the benefit of themselves; and those actions are most Reasonable, that conduce most to their ends." Given this conception of rationality; he is able to argue that every man has an unlimited, permissive right or liberty to do all things, so that each may do as he sees fit in order to preserve and benefit himself. The laws, to which every man is naturally subject, are but "Theorems concerning what conduceth to the conservation and defence of themselves." Hence reason does not in itself determine a system of rights and laws which relate men one to another in any way other than the natural relation of hostility. The "rational" order corresponding to the unlimited right of nature is the condition of war of every man with every man.

Contrast Hobbes' conception of reason with views which suppose rational standards transcending individual interests. The Stoic holds that all men, as rational, are capable of apprehending the laws of nature, in terms of which all are related as members of a cosmopolis transcending more limited, conventional societies. The medieval Christian supposes that all men, as rational, are capable of apprehending the divinely ordained laws of nature, in terms of which all are related directly to God, and indirectly to their fellows. The Kantian supposes that all men, as rational, are directly related one to another as members of a Kingdom of Ends in which each must treat his fellows, not merely as means, but as ends in themselves. In each case there is an order—the Stoic cosmopolis, the Christian Kingdom of God, the Kantian Kingdom of Ends—which is constituted either by or in accordance with reason, to which all men belong, and within which all are related. This relationship is prior to human agreement, depending solely on man's rationality. It may of course be the basis of further, contractual relationships, but these are only of secondary importance.

Each of these positions may be brought into verbal agreement with Hobbes' claim that "those actions are most Reasonable, that conduce most to their ends," but only by equivocating on "ends." Where Hobbes speaks of the ends subjectively given by men's passions, the Stoic, Christian, or Kantian speaks of the ends objectively given by Nature, God, or Reason itself. Such objective ends constitute a natural order within which all men are related, and so each of these views is incompatible with radical contractarianism.

To specify the contractarian conception of rationality more precisely I shall relate it to the view of human activity developed in the preceding section. A person is a rational agent if and only if he acts to fulfill his (subjective) ends as far as possible. If it be agreed, as I have argued, that the contractarian ideology involves the conception of human activity as appropriative, then a person is a rational agent if and only if he acts to appropriate as much as possible. As much what? Here, our ideology exhibits a historical development. What is to be appropriated is first thought of as real property, land or estate. The distinction between land and other forms of property is then denied, and what is to be appropriated becomes the universal measure of property, money. Finally, in a triumph of abstraction, money as a particular object is replaced by the purely formal notion of utility, an object conveniently divested of all content. The rational man is, as Samuel Gompers succinctly recognized, simply the man who seeks *more*. . . .

I have suggested that the ideology of radical contractarianism is manifesting itself increasingly in our overt consciousness. And this consciousness is spreading more and more widely. In itself, the ideology embraces everyone, so that, as more and more people attain self-awareness, they do so in the terms provided by the deep structure of our thought—in the terms, then, of contractarianism.

The likely end of the current fad for liberation movements, whatever the ostensible aim of these movements, will be to extend contractarian self-awareness to new areas of human activity and new groups of human beings. Radical feminists will go the way of radical trade unionists; women will join the system rather than overthrow it. But as all persons come to consider all human relationships to be contractual, they will not achieve the happy state of ideally rational appropriators, or even the cohesive unity of the male bourgeoisie. The absorptive capacity of the system is being overstrained, so that the effect of extending contractarian ideology is and will continue to be to corrode all of those bonds which in the real world have been the underpinning of the market. Bereft of its framework, the bargaining order will collapse into competitive chaos.

Love and patriotism are myths to the contractarian. But these myths, and not reason, have been the real support for the enduring coercive order, enabling it to enlist fear and thus assure the survival of the state. And the contractarian state, rational to the constrained maximizer but effective only because of its basis in these myths, has maintained the bargaining order of the market. Remove this basis by bringing all human beings to awareness of themselves as appropriators, and the practical incoherence of contractarian ideology manifests itself in the inability of conscious contractarians to maintain the coercive basis of their social relationships. Thus the triumph of radical contractarianism leads to the destruction, rather than the rationalization, of our society, for what real men and women who believe the ideology need to keep them from the war of all against all is not reason, but the Hobbist sovereign, and he is not available.

The ideology of radical contractarianism is, of course, but one among many possible ways of structuring our thought about man, society, and reason. We may see that this way of thinking is, from a practical point of view, bankrupt, and indeed that it will destroy us if we remain its adherents. But other ways of thinking, however possible they may be, are not produced to order. Faced with the falling of the dusk, the owl of Minerva spreads its wings—and takes flight.

Annette Baier, "Against Social Contract Understandings of Justice," from "Trust and Antitrust" (1986)

Like Gauthier in the previous reading, Baier is concerned to understand the pre-suppositions of the dominant contractarian model of justice. But her concern goes beyond describing those presuppositions; she is concerned to make clear the distorting effects of contractarian thinking. Baier focuses on the phenomenon of trust—one's "accepted vulnerability to another's possible but not expected ill will (or lack of good will) toward one." Trust is pervasive, but in its sources, rationale, and the relationships to which it gives rise it differs radically from the "cool, distanced" relationships resulting from contracts between independent adults. (At least part of the cause of philosophers' overlooking the importance of trust arises from the fact that most historically prominent philosophers have been unmarried men, with little experience in dealing with intimate relationships of dependence.) And, what's more, it is only within an environment in which trust flourishes that contractual relationships can have any place at all. Indeed, an account of justice resting on agreements among free and equal beings ignores the deep need for guidance in dealing with those that are quite obviously not equal to normal adult humans but still possessing moral standing: children, animals, the sick, the disabled.

Moral philosophers have always been interested in cooperation between people, and so it is surprising that they have not said more than they have about trust. It seems fairly obvious that any form of cooperative activity, including the division of labor, requires the cooperators to trust one another to do their bit, or at the very least to trust the overseer with his whip to do his bit, where coercion is relied on. One would expect contractarians to investigate the forms of trust and distrust parties to a contract exhibit. Utilitarians too should be concerned with the contribution to the general happiness of various climates of trust, so be concerned to understand the nature, roots, and varieties of trust. One might also have expected those with a moral theory of the virtues to have looked at trustworthiness, or at willingness to give trust. But when we turn to the great moral philosophers, in our tradition, what we find can scarcely be said to be even a sketch of a moral theory of trust. At most we get a few hints of directions in which we might go. . . .

Trust, the phenomenon we are so familiar with that we scarcely notice its presence and its variety, is shown by us and responded to by us not only with intimates but with strangers, and even with declared enemies. We trust our enemies not to fire at us when we lay down our arms and put out a white flag. In Britain burglars and police used to trust each other not to carry deadly weapons. We often trust total strangers, such as those from whom we ask directions in foreign cities, to direct rather than misdirect us, or to tell us so if they do not know what we want to know; and we think we should do the same for those who ask the same help from us. Of course we are often disappointed, rebuffed, let down, or betrayed when we exhibit such trust in others, and we are often exploited when we show the wanted trustworthiness. We do in fact, wisely or stupidly, virtuously or viciously, show trust in a great variety of forms, and manifest a great variety of versions of trustworthiness, both with intimates and with strangers. We trust those we encounter in lonely library stacks to be searching for books, not victims. We sometimes let ourselves fall asleep on trains or planes, trusting neighboring strangers not to take advantage of our defenselessness. We put our bodily safety into the hands of pilots, drivers, doctors, with scarcely any sense of recklessness. We used not to suspect that the food we buy might be deliberately poisoned, and we used to trust our children to day-care centers.

We may still have no choice but to buy food and to leave our children in day-care centers, but now we do it with suspicion and anxiety. Trust is always an invitation not only to confidence tricksters but also to terrorists, who discern its most easily destroyed and socially vital forms. Criminals, not moral philosophers, have been the experts at discerning different forms of trust. Most of us notice a given form of trust most easily after its sudden demise or severe injury. We inhabit a climate of trust as we inhabit an atmosphere and notice it as we notice air, only when it becomes scarce or polluted.

We may have no choice but to continue to rely on the local shop for food, even after some of the food on its shelves has been found to have been poisoned with intent. We can still rely where we no longer trust. What is the difference between trusting others and merely relying on them? It seems to be reliance on their good will toward one, as distinct from their dependable habits, or only on their dependably exhibited fear, anger, or other motives compatible with ill will toward one, or on motives not directed on one at all. We may rely on our fellows' fear of the newly appointed security guards in shops to deter them from injecting poison into the food on the shelves, once we have ceased to trust them. We may rely on the shopkeeper's concern for his profits to motivate him to take effective precautions against poisoners and also trust him to *want* his customers not to be harmed by his products, at least as long as this want can be satisfied without frustrating his wish to increase his profits. Trust is often mixed with other species of reliance on persons. Trust which is reliance on another's good will, perhaps minimal good will, contrasts with the forms of reliance on others' reactions and attitudes which are shown by the comedian, the advertiser, the blackmailer, the kidnapper-extortioner, and the terrorist, who all depend on particular attitudes and reactions of others for the success of their actions. We all depend on one anothers' psychology in countless ways, but this is not yet to trust them. The trusting can be betrayed, or at least let down, and not just disappointed. Kant's neighbors who counted on his regular habits as a clock for their own less automatically regular ones might be disappointed with him if he slept in one day, but not let down by him, let alone had their trust betrayed. When I trust another, I depend on her good will toward me. I need not either acknowledge this reliance nor believe that she has either invited or acknowledged such trust since there is such a thing as unconscious trust, as unwanted trust, as forced receipt of trust, and as trust which the trusted is unaware of. (Plausible conditions for proper trust will be that it survives consciousness, by both parties, and that the trusted has had some opportunity to signify acceptance or rejection, to warn the trusting if their trust is unacceptable.)

Where one depends on another's good will, one is necessarily vulnerable to the limits of that good will. One leaves others an opportunity to harm one when one trusts, and also shows one's confidence that they will not take it. Reasonable trust will require good grounds for such confidence in another's good will, or at least the absence of good grounds for expecting their ill will or indifference. Trust then, on this first approximation, is accepted vulnerability to another's possible but not expected ill will (or lack of good will) toward one. . . .

The great moral theorists in our tradition not only are all men, they are mostly men who had minimal adult dealings with (and so were then minimally influenced by) women. With a few significant exceptions (Hume, Hegel, J. S. Mill, Sidgwick, maybe Bradley) they are a collection of gays, clerics, misogynists, and puritan bachelors. It should not surprise us, then, that particularly in the modern period they managed to relegate to the mental background the web of trust tying most moral agents to one another, and to focus their philosophical attention so single-mindedly on cool, distanced relations between more or less free and equal adult strangers, say, the members of an all male club, with membership rules and rules for dealing with rule breakers and where the form of cooperation was restricted to ensuring that each member could read his *Times* in peace and have no one step on his gouty toes. Explicitly assumed or recognized obligations toward others with the same obligations and the same power to see justice done to rule breakers then are seen as the moral norm.

Relations between equals and nonintimates will *be* the moral norm for adult males whose dealings with others are mainly business or restrained social dealings with similarly placed males. But for lovers, husbands, fathers, the ill, the very young, and the elderly, other relationships with their moral potential and perils will loom larger. For Hume, who had several strong-willed and manipulative women to cooperate or contend with in his adult life, for Mill, who had Harriet Taylor on his hands, for Hegel, whose domestic life was of normal complication, the rights and duties of equals to equals in a civil society which recognized only a male electorate could only be *part* of the moral story. They could not ignore the virtues and vices of family relationships, male-female relationships, master-slave, and employer-employee relationships as easily as could Hobbes, Butler, Bentham, or Kant. Nor could they as easily adopt the usual compensatory strategies of the moral philosophers who confine their attention to the rights and duties of free and equal adults to one another—the strategy of claiming, if pressed, that these rights are the *core* of all moral relationships and maybe also claiming that any other relationships, engendering additional or different rights and duties, come about only by an exercise of one of the core rights, the right to promise. Philosophers who remember what it was like to be a dependent child, or know what it is like to be a parent, or to have a dependent parent, an old or handicapped relative, friend, or neighbor will find it implausible to treat such relations as simply cases of comembership in a kingdom of ends, in the given temporary conditions of one-sided dependence.

To the extent that these claims are correct (and I am aware that they need more defense than I have given them here) it becomes fairly easy to see one likely explanation of the neglect in Western moral philosophy of the full range of sorts of trust. Both before the rise of a society which needed contract as a commercial device, and after it, women were counted on to serve their men, to raise their children to fill the roles they were expected to fill and not deceive their men about the paternity of these children. What men counted on one another for, in work and war, presupposed this background domestic trust, trust in women not merely not to poison their men (Nietzsche derides them for learning less than they might have in the kitchen), but to turn out sons who could trust and be trusted in traditional men's roles and daughters who would reduplicate their own capacities for trust and trustworthiness. Since the women's role did not include the writing of moral treatises, any thoughts they had about trust, based on their experience of it, did not get into our tradition (or did Diotima teach Socrates something about trust as well as love?). And the more powerful men, including those who did write the moral treatises, were in the morally awkward position of being, collectively, oppressors of women, exploiters of women's capacity for trustworthiness in unequal, nonvoluntary, and non-contract-based relationships. Understandably, they did not focus their attention on forms of trust and demands for trustworthiness which it takes a Nietzsche to recognize without shame. Humankind can bear only so much reality.

The recent research of Carol Gilligan has shown us how intelligent and reflective twentieth-century women see morality, and how different their picture of it is from that of men, particularly the men who eagerly assent to the claims of currently orthodox contractarian-Kantian moral theories. Women cannot now, any more than they could when oppressed, ignore that part of morality and those forms of trust which cannot easily be forced into the liberal and particularly the contractarian mold. Men may but women cannot see morality as essentially a matter of keeping to the minimal moral traffic rules, designed to restrict close encounters between autonomous persons to self-chosen ones. Such a conception presupposes both an equality of power and a natural separateness from others, which is alien to women's experience of life and morality. For those most of whose daily dealings are with the less powerful or the more powerful, a moral code designed for those equal in power will be at best nonfunctional, at worst an offensive pretense of equality as a substitute for its actuality. But equality is not even a desirable ideal in all relationships— children not only are not but should not be equal in power to adults, and we need a morality to guide us in our dealings with those who either cannot or should not achieve equality of power (animals, the ill, the dying, children while still young) with those with whom they have unavoidable and often intimate relationships.

Modern moral philosophy has concentrated on the morality of fairly cool relationships between those who are deemed to be roughly equal in power to determine the rules and to instigate sanctions against rule breakers. It is not surprising, then, that the main form of trust that any attention has been given to is trust in governments, and in parties to voluntary agreements to do what they have agreed to do. As much as possible is absorbed into the latter category, so that we suppose that paying for what one takes from a shop, doing what one is employed to do, returning what one has borrowed, supporting one's spouse, are all cases of being faithful to binding voluntary agreements, to contracts of some sort. (For Hume, none of these would count as duties arising from contract or promise.) Yet if I think of the trust I show, say, in the plumber who comes from the municipal drainage authority when I report that my drains are clogged, it is not plausibly seen as trust that he will fulfill his contractual obligations to me or to his employer. When I trust him to do whatever is necessary and safe to clear my drains, I take his expertise and his lack of ill will for granted. Should he plant explosives to satisfy some unsuspected private or social grudge against me, what I might try to sue him for (if I escaped alive) would not be damages for breach of contract. His wrong, if wrong it were, is not breach of contract, and the trust he would have disappointed would not have been that particular form of trust.

Contract enables us to make explicit just what we count on another person to do, in return for what, and should they not do just that, what damages can be extracted from them.

The beauty of promise and contract is its explicitness. But we can only make explicit provisions for such contingencies as we imagine arising. Until I become a victim of a terrorist plumber I am unlikely, even if I should insist on a contract before giving plumbers access to my drains, to extract a solemn agreement that they not blow me up. Nor am I likely to specify the alternative means they *may* use to clear my drains, since if I knew enough to compile such a list I would myself have to be a competent plumber. Any such detailed instructions must come from their plumbing superiors; I know nothing or little about it when I confidently welcome the plumber into the bowels of my basement. I trust him to do a nonsubversive plumbing job, as he counts on me to do a nonsubversive teaching job, should he send his son to my course in the history of ethics. Neither of us relies on a contract with the other, and neither of us need know of any contract (or much about its contents) the other may have with a third coordinating party.

It does not, then, seem at all plausible, once we think about actual moral relations in all their sad or splendid variety, to model all of them on one rather special one, the relation between promisor to promisee. We count on all sorts of people for all sorts of vital things, without any contracts, explicit or implicit, with them or with any third coordinating party. For these cases of trust in people to do their job conscientiously and not to take the opportunity to do us harm once we put things we value into their hands are different from trust in people to keep their promises in part because of the very indefiniteness of what we are counting on them to do or not to do. The subtlety and point of promising is to declare precisely *what* we count on another to do, and as the case of Shylock and Bassanio shows, that very definiteness is a limitation as well as a functional excellence of an explicit agreement.

Another functional excellence of contracts, which is closely connected with the expressness that makes breach easily established and damages or penalty decidable with a show of reasonable justice, is the *security* they offer the trusting party. They make it possible not merely for us to trust at will but to trust with minimal vulnerability. They are a device for trusting others enough for mutually profitable future-involving exchanges without taking the risks trusters usually do take. They are designed for cooperation between mutually suspicious risk-averse strangers, and the vulnerability they involve is at the other extreme from that incurred by trusting infants. Contracts distribute and redistribute risk so as to minimize it for both parties, but trusting those more powerful persons who purport to love one increases one's risks while increasing the good one can hope to secure. Trust in fellow contracters is a limit case of trust, in which fewer risks are taken, for the sake of lesser goods.

Promises do, nevertheless, involve some real trust in the other party's good will and proper use of discretionary powers. Hume said that "to perform promises is requisite to beget trust and confidence in the common offices of life." But performing promises is not the only performance requisite for that. Shylock did not welsh on an agreement, but he was nevertheless not a trustworthy party to an agreement. For to insist on the letter of an agreement, ignoring the vague but generally understood unwritten background conditions and exceptions, is to fail to show that discretion and goodwill which a trustworthy person has. To be someone to be trusted with a promise, as well as to be trusted as a promisor, one must be able to use discretion not as to when the promise has been kept but, rather, as to when to insist that the promise be kept, or to instigate penalty for breach of promise, when to keep and when not to keep one's promise. I would feel morally let down if someone who had promised to help me move house arrived announcing, "I had to leave my mother, suddenly taken ill, to look after herself in order to be here, but I couldn't break my promise to you." From such persons I would accept no further promises, since they would have shown themselves untrustworthy in the always crucial respect of judgment and willingness to use their discretionary powers. Promises *are* morally interesting, and one's performance as party to a promise is a good indicator of one's moral character, but not for the reasons contractarians suppose.

The domination of contemporary moral philosophy by the so-called Prisoner's Dilemma problem displays most clearly this obsession with moral relations between minimally trusting, minimally trustworthy adults who are equally powerful. Just as the only trust Hobbist man shows is trust in promises, provided there is assurance of punishment for promise breakers, so is this the only sort of trust nontheological modern moral philosophers have given much attention at all to, as if once we have weaned ourselves from the degenerate form of absolute and unreciprocated trust in God, all our capacity for trust is to be channelled into the equally degenerate form of formal voluntary and reciprocated trust restricted to equals. But we collectively cannot bring off such a limitation of trust to minimal and secured trust, and we can deceive ourselves that we do only if we avert our philosophical gaze from the ordinary forms of trust I have been pointing to. It was not really that, after Hobbes, people *did* barricade their bodies as well as their possessions against all others before daring to sleep. Some continued to doze off on stagecoaches, to go abroad unarmed, to give credit in business deals, to count on others turning up on time for appointments, to trust parents, children, friends, and lovers not to rob or assault them when welcomed into intimacy with them. And the usual array of vicious forms of such trust, trustworthiness, and demands for them, continued to flourish. Slaves continued to be trusted to cook for slaveowners; women, with or without marriage vows, continued to be trusted with the property of their men, trusted not to deceive them about the paternity of their children, and trusted to bring up their sons as patriarchs, their daughters as suitable wives or mistresses for patriarchs. Life went on, but the moral philosophers, or at least those we regard as the great ones, chose to attend only to a few of the moral relations normal life exhibited. Once Filmer [author of *Patriarcha,* which explained political authority as an inheritance from Adam] was disposed of, they concentrated primarily *not* on any of the relations between those of unequal power—parent to child, husband to wife, adult to aged parent, slaveowner to slave, official to citizen, employer to employee—but on relations between roughly equal parties or between people in those respects in which they could be seen as equals.

Such relationships of mutual respect are, of course, of great moral importance. Hobbes, Locke, Rousseau, Hume, Kant, Sidgwick, Rawls, all have helped us to see more clearly how we stand in relation to anonymous others, like ourselves in need, in power, and in capacity. One need not minimize the importance of such work in moral philosophy in order to question its completeness. But a complete moral philosophy would tell us how and why we should act and feel toward others in relationships of shifting and varying power asymmetry and shifting and varying intimacy. It seems to me that we philosophers have left that task largely to priests and revolutionaries, the self-proclaimed experts on the proper attitude of the powerless to the powerful. But these relationships of inequality—some of them, such as parent-child, of unavoidable inequality—make up much of our lives, and they, as much as our relations to our equals, determine the state of moral health or corruption in which we are content to live. I think it is high time we look at the morality and immorality of relations between the powerful and the less powerful, especially at those in which there is trust between them.

Part Three:
Justice and Society

What is the *social role* of justice, its place and function in society? Is its function, as Hobbes insisted, to guarantee security and safety? Is it, as John Locke insisted, primarily to safeguard our property? Or is it rather to maximize the public good? How is that good to be determined, and how is it to be distributed? (But, after all, isn't that just the central question of the nature of justice itself?) Does the idea of justice presuppose, as so much of our modern rhetoric and ideology insists, that everyone is to be treated equally? Does this mean that everyone is in fact equal? This would seem to fly in the face of the most obvious common sense. People are different, and some of their differences are relevant to questions of social justice. True, they are all human beings. (Is justice limited to our dealings with human beings?) And isn't the question of justice precisely to what extent and for what reasons we should distinguish between people—in terms of their needs, their abilities, their contributions, their individual rights? Does equality mean that everyone must be treated similarly? But this would, of course, be the height of injustice: to give two students the same grade despite the fact that one studied and the other did not; to give two employees the same raise although one produced great results and the other sent the company into bankruptcy; to give two criminals the same sentence although one robbed the bank with a sawed-off shotgun and the other took two newspapers for the price of one. Perhaps equality means only that we should not arbitrarily discriminate, that we should treat like cases alike and be consistent in our judgments. But isn't this a demand simply of logic rather than one of justice? Isn't the key question here what are considerations of justice; the special concerns of our central economic (and social?) institution, the free market; and the always problematic concept of equality, which for many thinkers remains the crucial if not the sole criterion for most questions of basic justice? The central tension that emerges in the readings here is that between equality and rights. The right to own private property, for example, has often been blamed for the grotesque inequalities of wealth in modern society (by Rousseau, for example, and also by Karl Marx and his followers). So, too, the free market, which begins by presupposing the right to private property, has as one of its most obvious consequences that its distributive results depend on commercial insight and intelligence, ingenuity and inventiveness, being in the right place at the right time, and in other ways just having plain good luck. Not surprisingly, people who have been raised and educated in the wiles of the market or in the professions that support and participate in the market (e.g., law) do quite well in such a society; those who are deprived of any such education and experience or never get the opportunity to enter into the market may be doomed to a life of poverty and deprivation. But it is this uncomfortable observation that leads defenders of the market to insist all the more on the importance of equality, for without equal opportunity to enter into it and compete, the market can hardly be free and is therefore unfair as well. In other words, the idea of a free market both presupposes the necessity of equality of opportunity and accepts the inevitable inequalities that result from the various exchanges and people's very different abilities and fortunes. And yet, it can be and often has been argued that the free market, even with its inevitable inequalities, ensures prosperity for all, even those who are least advantaged.

This claim, that the free market maximizes mutual good, is quite different from the claim that the market rests upon a natural right to own private property. First of all, it is an empirical claim, and one can (at least in principle) actually test and check to see whether a market society is or is not as prosperous as, say, a socialist society. But how does one measure such prosperity? In the days before Adam Smith—in the economic philosophy of mercantilism—the wealth of a nation was measured by the amount of money in the royal treasury. After Adam Smith and his radical revision of the idea of "the wealth of nations," the prosperity of a people was to be measured by the comfort of the individual citizens. But how do we do this? It is one thing to speak in an abstract way of the "utility" of this or that social program—or, indeed, of the "utility" of justice itself—but something else to speak about the precise measure of the amount and distribution of that utility. Do we, as John Stuart Mill suggests, count "each person as one and as no more than one" and then aim at the greatest overall good, conceived as the sum of the goods of individuals? Does this then mean that we should tolerate the most extreme inequality if the total sum is maximized? Or are we to distribute the goods of society as evenly and as equally as possible? How much of a sacrifice in overall prosperity should we be willing to tolerate for the sake of equality? And what happens to the freedom of the market, and how do we go about redistributing the goods of society while at the same time respecting rights to private property? Indeed, what happens to the very idea of rights, once the utilitarian concern for overall aggregate goodness comes to dominate?

The readings that follow represent both classic defenses and classic objections to private property and the free market, as well as Mill's classic defense of justice as a mode of social utility. The question of equality weaves its way through virtually all of the readings, and so, too, the matter of rights—in particular, property rights—looms in them as well. But we have ended this part of the book with a selection that tries not to solve these puzzles but to throw them into cross-cultural perspective. Both the idea of equality and that of rights are central to our society, but there are other societies in which such ideas are not the central focus with respect to the social role of justice.

The Declaration of Independence and the Amendments to the Constitution of the United States of America

The Declaration of Independence (1776) is perhaps the single most famous example of social contract theory at work in practical politics. It states outright that governments receive "their just powers from the consent of the governed." It holds that when a government fails to perform its duties, "it is the Right of the People to alter or to abolish it" and even "their duty to throw off such Government, and to provide new Guards for their future security." That is, of course, just what this bold and elegant document does. The Declaration is also the source of our best-known statement about natural rights, indicating a considerable eclecticism on the part of Thomas Jefferson and the other authors of the document (see, for example, Garry Wills, *Inventing America*, 1978). But the statement itself is a remarkable tour de force: "*We hold these truths to be self-evident*"—blocking any route to philosophical disagreement and indicating what would now be called a "nonnegotiable set of demands"—"*that all men are created equal*"—as if this had been a matter of routine recognition all through the ages—"*that they are endowed by their Creator with certain inalienable Rights*"—again, marking out an area of practical concern that is absolutely unconditional and nonnegotiable—"*that among these are Life, Liberty, and the pursuit of Happiness.*" The Declaration has a Lockean ring, particularly in its reference to natural rights, but it omits mention of the central Lockean right of private property. According to historical accounts (e.g., Carl Becker in *The Declaration of Independence*), that phrase was originally a part of the opening paragraph, but it was deleted and replaced with the more innocuous and egalitarian "pursuit of happiness." What is unmistakable and virtually definitive of our outlook as a nation, however, is the uncompromising stand on the primacy of individual rights. This is no mere declaration of national sovereignty or cultural autonomy. It does not indicate just another rupture in government or disastrous disagreement in policy. It is stated, through and through, that it is first of all the break of a naturally free people from a government that is despotic, and it is primarily the multiple violation of the rights of representation and fair treatment that justifies the breach.

The Constitution was ratified in 1787. It was and is a remarkable document, an ingenious balancing act between competing political forces and philosophies and intended, above all, to prevent just that sort of concentration of unrepresentative authority that had led to the revolution and the break from the English. But the careful tripartite structuring of the government and the cautious balancing of state and federal power did not satisfactorily answer one of the driving concerns of the revolution, the protection of individual rights. Accordingly, again after much debate and heated argument, ten amendments to the completed Constitution were proposed and adopted. These ten amendments, collectively "The Bill of Rights," spelled out and guaranteed against the incursions of federal power (some of) the specific natural rights suggested in the Declaration of Independence. (Amendment IX insists on the incompleteness of the list.) Again, the right to property as such is not itself the subject of any of the amendments, but it is clearly presupposed in them. So, too, it has been argued that the right of privacy itself, though not spelled out as such in any of the amendments, is presupposed and guaranteed by virtually all of them. The precise meaning of these amendments has been the subject of terrific popular, legislative, and judicial debate. But beneath these debates it is all too easy for Americans to miss the remarkable fact—so evident in contrast to civilized countries that do not have any such formal document (e.g., Australia)—that we do take personal rights to be the very bedrock of our political culture, the ultimate justification for having a government in the first place and an absolute limit on government interference.

The Bill of Rights went into effect on December 15, 1791. Since then, the moral and political development of the United States has resulted in the proposal and adoption of over a dozen further amendments. Some of these have to do with the specific workings of the government (e.g., Amendment XXII, which limits a president to two elected terms in office), but others, like the Bill of Rights itself, are profound moral statements about what we as a people take to be basic rights. The most morally important of these, no doubt, are the belated recognition that slavery has no place in a society of free individuals and the guarantee of equal protection of the laws to all citizens. These amendments are included below, along with the proposed "Equal Rights Amendment," which was proposed in 1972 but never ratified.

From the Declaration of Independence

When in the Course of human events, it becomes necessary for one people to dissolve the political bonds which have connected them with another, and to assume among the powers of the earth, the separate and equal station to which the Laws of Nature and of Nature's God entitle them, a decent respect to the opinions of mankind requires that they should declare the causes which impel them to the separation.—We hold these truths to be self-evident, that all men are created equal, that they are endowed by their Creator with certain inalienable Rights, that among these are Life, Liberty and the pursuit of Happiness.—That to secure these rights, Governments are instituted among Men, deriving their just powers from the consent of the governed.—That whenever any Form of Government becomes destructive of these ends, it is the Right of the People to alter or to abolish it, and to institute new Government, laying its foundation on such principles and organizing its powers in such form, as to them shall seem most likely to effect their Safety and Happiness. Prudence, indeed, will dictate that Governments long established should not be changed for light and transient causes; and accordingly all experience hath shown, that mankind are more disposed to suffer, while evils are sufferable, than to right themselves by abolishing the forms to which they are accustomed. But when a long train of abuses and usurpations, pursuing invariably the same Object evinces a design to reduce them under absolute Despotism, it is their right, it is their duty, to throw off such Government, and to provide new Guards for their future security.— . . .

A Prince, whose character is thus marked by every act which may define a Tyrant, is unfit to be the ruler of a free people. Nor have We been wanting in attentions to our British brethren. We have warned them from time to time of attempts by their legislature to extend an unwarrantable jurisdiction over us. We have reminded them of the circumstances of our emigration and settlement here. We have appealed to their native justice and magnanimity, and we have conjured them by the ties of our common kindred to disavow these usurpations, which would inevitably interrupt our connections and correspondence. They too have been deaf to the voice of justice and of consanguinity. We must, therefore, acquiesce in the necessity, which denounces our Separation, and hold them, as we hold the rest of mankind, Enemies in War, in Peace Friends.—

We, Therefore, the Representatives of the United States of America, in General Congress, Assembled, appealing to the Supreme Judge of the world for the rectitude of our intentions, do, in the Name, and by Authority of the good People of these Colonies, solemnly publish and declare, That these United Colonies are, and of Right ought to be Free and Independent States; that they are Absolved from all Allegiance to the British Crown, and that all political connection between them and the State of Great Britain, is and ought to be totally dissolved; and that as Free and Independent States, they have full Power to levy War, conclude Peace, contract Alliances, establish Commerce, and to do all other Acts and Things which Independent States may of right do.—And for the support of this Declaration, with a firm reliance on the protection of Divine Providence, we mutually pledge to each other our Lives, our Fortunes and our sacred Honor.

Amendments to the Constitution

Articles in addition to, and Amendment of the Constitution of the United States of America, proposed by Congress, and ratified by the Legislatures of the several States, pursuant to the fifth Article of the original Constitution.

Amendment I

Congress shall make no law respecting an establishment of religion, or prohibiting the free exercise thereof; or abridging the freedom of speech, or of the press; or the right of the people peaceably to assemble, and to petition the Government for a redress of grievances.

Amendment II

A well regulated Militia, being necessary to the security of a free State, the right of the people to keep and bear Arms, shall not be infringed.

Amendment III

No Soldier shall, in time of peace be quartered in any house, without the consent of the Owner, nor in time of war, but in a manner to be prescribed by law.

Amendment IV

The right of the people to be secure in their persons, houses, papers, and effects, against unreasonable searches and seizures, shall not be violated, and no Warrants shall issue, but upon probable cause, supported by Oath or affirmation, and particularly describing the place to be searched, and the persons or things to be seized.

Amendment V

No person shall be held to answer for a capital, or otherwise infamous crime, unless on a presentment or indictment of a Grand Jury, except in cases arising in the land or naval forces, or in the Militia, when in actual service in time of War or public danger; nor shall any person be subject for the same offence to be twice put in jeopardy of life or limb; nor shall be compelled in any criminal case to be a witness against himself, nor be deprived of life, liberty, or property, without due process of law; nor shall private property be taken for public use, without just compensation.

Amendment VI

In all criminal prosecutions, the accused shall enjoy the right to a speedy and public trial, by an impartial jury of the State and district wherein the crime shall have been committed, which district shall have been previously ascertained by law, and to be informed of the nature and cause of the accusation; to be confronted with the witnesses against him; to have compulsory process for obtaining witnesses in his favor, and to have the Assistance of Counsel for his defence.

Amendment VII

In Suits at common law, where the value in controversy shall exceed twenty dollars, the right of trial by jury shall be preserved, and no fact tried by a jury, shall be otherwise re-examined in any Court of the United States, than according to the rules of the common law.

Amendment VIII

Excessive bail shall not be required, or excessive fines imposed, nor cruel and unusual punishments inflicted.

Amendment IX

The enumeration in the Constitution, of certain rights, shall not be construed to deny or disparage others retained by the people.

Amendment X

The powers not delegated to the United States by the Constitution, nor prohibited by it to the States, are reserved to the States respectively, or to the people.

Amendment XIII

Neither slavery nor involuntary servitude, except as a punishment for crime whereof the party shall have been duly convicted, shall exist within the United States, or any place subject to their jurisdiction.

Amendment XIV

All persons born or naturalized in the United States, and subject to the jurisdiction thereof, are citizens of the United States and of the State wherein they reside. No State shall make or enforce any law which shall abridge the privileges or immunities of citizens of the United States; nor shall any State deprive any person of life, liberty, or property, without due process of law; nor deny to any person within its jurisdiction the equal protection of the laws.

Amendment XV

The right of citizens of the United States to vote shall not be denied or abridged by the United States or by any State on account of race, color, or previous condition of servitude.

Amendment XIX

The right of citizens of the United States to vote shall not be denied or abridged by the United States or by any State on account of sex.

Equal Rights for Women

Equality of rights under the law shall not be denied or abridged by the United States or by any State on account of sex.

John Locke, "Of Property," from the *Second Treatise on Government* (1690)

That private property is to be counted as a natural right, as appealing and obvious as the idea sounds to us, was something of a revolutionary idea in itself, what Otto von Gierke calls "a landmark in the history of thought." The idea that the earth belongs to humans as a gift of God seemed obvious enough in the era of Locke (1632–1704), but that we should have the right, as individuals, to possess bits and pieces of the whole he took to be something of a problem. He begins modestly and persuasively enough: everyone has an essential and in an obvious sense "inalienable" piece of property in his or her own body. But Locke moves quickly to the subsequent claim that whatever one does or makes with this body is also one's own and whatever objects one "mixes one's labor with" are also one's own. Since labor is "the unquestionable property of the laborer," whatever one produces through one's labor is also one's own property. This essential argument has a proviso, and that is "where there is enough and as good left in common for others"—by itself enough to halt many developers and latter-day robber barons who would leave in the wake of their labor nature destroyed and communities harmed. Locke also makes clear that greed and gluttony are not justified or excused by the notion that property is a natural right: "Nothing was made by God for man to spoil or destroy," he says, and indeed the whole argument is ultimately framed within the understanding that, by taking one's own, one does not thereby injure anyone else. (For a contemporary attempt to defend a Lockean view of property, see the selection by Robert Nozick in Part Five.)

Of Property

25.   Whether we consider natural reason, which tells us that men, being once born, have a right to their preservation, and consequently to meat and drink and such other things as nature affords for their subsistence; or revelation, which gives us an account of those grants God made of the world to Adam, and to Noah and his sons; it is very clear that God, as King David says (Psalm cxv. 16), "has given the earth to the children of men," given it to mankind in common. But this being supposed, it seems to some a very great difficulty how any one should ever come to have a property in anything. I will not content myself to answer that if it be difficult to make out property upon a supposition that God gave the world to Adam and his posterity in common, it is impossible that any man but one universal monarch should have any property upon a supposition that God gave the world to Adam and his heirs in succession, exclusive of all the rest of his posterity. But I shall endeavor to show how men might come to have a property in several parts of that which God gave to mankind in common, and that without any express compact of all the commoners.

26.   God, who has given the world to men in common, has also given them reason to make use of it to the best advantage of life and convenience. The earth and all that is therein is given to men for the support and comfort of their being. And though all the fruits it naturally produces and beasts it feeds belong to mankind in common, as they are produced by the spontaneous hand of nature; and nobody has originally a private dominion exclusive of the rest of mankind in any of them, as they are thus in their natural state; yet, being given for the use of men, there must of necessity be a means to appropriate them some way or other before they can be of any use or at all beneficial to any particular man. The fruit or venison which nourishes the wild Indian, who knows no enclosure and is still a tenant in common, must be his, and so his, i.e., a part of him, that another can no longer have any right to it before it can do him any good for the support of his life.

27.   Though the earth and all inferior creatures be common to all men, yet every man has a property in his own person; this nobody has any right to but himself. The labor of his body and the work of his hands, we may say, are properly his. Whatsoever then he removes out of the state that nature has provided and left it in, he has mixed his labor with, and joined to it something that is his own, and thereby makes it his property. It being by him removed from the common state nature has placed it in, it has by this labor something

annexed to it that excludes the common right of other men. For this labor being the unquestionable property of the laborer, no man but he can have a right to what that is once joined to, at least where there is enough and as good left in common for others.

28.   He that is nourished by the acorns he picked up under an oak, or the apples he gathered from the trees in the wood, has certainly appropriated them to himself. Nobody can deny but the nourishment is his. I ask, then, When did they begin to be his? When he digested or when he ate or when he boiled or when he brought them home? Or when he picked them up? And it is plain, if the first gathering made them not his, nothing else could. That labor put a distinction between them and common; that added something to them more than nature, the common mother of all, had done; and so they became his private right. And will anyone say he had no right to those acorns or apples he thus appropriated because he had not the consent of all mankind to make them his? Was it a robbery thus to assume to himself what belonged to all in common? If such a consent as that was necessary, man had starved, notwithstanding the plenty God had given him. We see in commons, which remain so by compact, that it is the taking any part of what is common and removing it out of the state nature leaves it in which begins the property, without which the common is of no use. And the taking of this or that part does not depend on the express consent of all the commoners. Thus the grass my horse has bit, the turfs my servant has cut, and the ore I have digged in any place where I have a right to them in common with others, become my property without the assignation or consent of anybody. The labor that was mine, removing them out of that common state they were in, has fixed my property in them.

29.   By making an explicit consent of every commoner necessary to any one's appropriating to himself any part of what is given in common, children or servants could not cut the meat which their father or master had provided for them in common without assigning to every one his peculiar part. Though the water running in the fountain be every one's, yet who can doubt but that in the pitcher is his only who drew it out? His labor has taken it out of the hands of nature where it was common and belonged equally to all her children, and has thereby appropriated it to himself.

30.   Thus this law of reason makes the deer that Indian's who has killed it; it is allowed to be his goods who has bestowed his labor upon it, though before it was the common right of every one. And amongst those who are counted the civilized part of mankind, who have made and multiplied positive laws to determine property, this original law of nature, for the beginning of property in what was before common, still takes place; and by virtue thereof what fish any one catches in the ocean, that great and still remaining common of mankind, or what ambergris any one takes up here, is, by the labor that removes it out of that common state nature left it in, made his property who takes that pains about it. And even amongst us, the hare that anyone is hunting is thought his who pursues her during the chase; for, being a beast that is still looked upon as common and no man's private possession, whoever has employed so much labor about any of that kind as to find and pursue her has thereby removed her from the state of nature wherein she was common, and has begun a property.

31.   It will perhaps be objected to this that "if gathering the acorns, or other fruits of the earth, etc., makes a right to them, then any one may engross as much as he will." To which I answer: not so. The same law of nature that does by this means give us property does also bound that property, too. "God has given us all things richly" (1 Tim. vi. 17), is the voice of reason confirmed by inspiration. But how far has he given it us? To enjoy. As much as any one can make use of to any advantage of life before it spoils, so much he may

by his labor fix a property in; whatever is beyond this is more than his share and belongs to others. Nothing was made by God for man to spoil or destroy. And thus considering the plenty of natural provisions there was a long time in the world, and the few spenders, and to how small a part of that provision the industry of one man could extend itself and engross it to the prejudice of others, especially keeping within the bounds set by reason of what might serve for his use, there could be then little room for quarrels or contentions about property so established.

32.   But the chief matter of property being now not the fruits of the earth and the beasts that subsist on it, but the earth itself, as that which takes in and carries with it all the rest, I think it is plain that property in that, too, is acquired as the former. As much land as a man tills, plants, improves, cultivates, and can use the product of, so much is his property. He by his labor does, as it were, enclose it from the common. Nor will it invalidate his right to say everybody else has an equal title to it, and therefore he cannot appropriate, he cannot enclose, without the consent of all his fellow commoners—all mankind. God, when he gave the world in common to all mankind, commanded man also to labor, and the penury of his condition required it of him. God and his reason commanded him to subdue the earth, i.e., improve it for the benefit of life, and therein lay out something upon it that was his own, his labor. He that in obedience to this command of God subdued, tilled, and sowed any part of it, thereby annexed to it something that was his property, which another had no title to, nor could without injury take from him.

33.   Nor was this appropriation of any parcel of land by improving it any prejudice to any other man, since there was still enough and as good left, and more than the yet unprovided could use. So that, in effect, there was never the less left for others because of his enclosure for himself; for he that leaves as much as another can make use of does as good as take nothing at all. Nobody could think himself injured by the drinking of another man, though he took a good draught, who had a whole river of the same water left him to quench his thirst; and the case of land and water, where there is enough for both, is perfectly the same.

David Hume, "The Circumstances of Justice and the Rules of Property," from *An Enquiry Concerning the Principles of Morals* (1751) and *A Treatise of Human Nature* (1739)

David Hume (1711–1776) was a Scotsman, gone south to London to fulfill an ambition he described as "literary fame." Though steeped in the Scottish enlightenment, he was anxious to make a name for himself in English letters, and his philosophy is a curious mix of Scots "common sense" and English conservatism, plus, of course, his own unique blend of paganism and scepticism. In Hume's writings in social philosophy, this paganism and scepticism appear in his rejection of the idea that rules of justice are laws laid down by God or written into the nature of things for the human intellect to discover. Rather, the rules of justice—among which are rules concerning private property—have their validity only from their conduciveness to the public good. He argues for this claim by showing, first, that under certain conditions—those in which justice would not conduce to the public good—justice would not be considered a virtue, and secondly, by illustrating how the formulation and observance of the rules of private property result in a stability that promotes the public interest.

From *An Enquiry Concerning the Principles of Morals*

That Justice is useful to society, and consequently that *part* of its merit, at least, must arise from that consideration, it would be a superfluous undertaking to prove. That public utility is the *sole* origin of justice, and that reflections on the beneficial consequences of this virtue are the *sole* foundation of its merit; this proposition, being more curious and important, will better deserve our examination and enquiry.

Let us suppose that nature has bestowed on the human race such profuse *abundance* of all *external* conveniencies, that, without any uncertainty in the event, without any care or industry on our part, every individual finds himself fully provided with whatever his most voracious appetites can want, or luxurious imagination wish or desire. His natural beauty, we shall suppose, surpasses all acquired ornaments; the perpetual clemency of the seasons renders useless all clothes or covering; the raw herbage affords him the most delicious fare; the clear fountain, the richest beverage. No laborious occupation required: no tillage: no navigation. Music, poetry, and contemplation form his sole business: conversation, mirth, and friendship his sole amusement.

It seems evident that, in such a happy state, every other social virtue would flourish, and receive tenfold increase; but the cautious, jealous virtue of justice would never once have been dreamed of. For what purpose make a partition of goods, where every one has already more than enough? Why give rise to property, where there cannot possibly be any injury? Why call this object *mine,* when upon the seizing of it by another, I need but stretch out my hand to possess myself to what is equally valuable? Justice, in that case, being totally useless, would be an idle ceremonial, and could never possible have place in the catalogue of virtues.

We see, even in the present necessitous condition of mankind, that, wherever any benefit is bestowed by nature in an unlimited abundance, we leave it always in common among the whole human race, and make no subdivisions of right and property. Water and air, though the most necessary of all objects, are not challenged as the property of individuals; nor can any man commit injustice by the most lavish use and enjoyment of these blessings. In fertile extensive countries, with few inhabitants, land is regarded on the same footing. And no topic is so much insisted on by those, who defend the liberty of the seas, as the unexhausted use of them in navigation. Were the advantages, procured by navigation, as inexhaustible, these reasoners had never had any adversaries to refute; nor had any claims ever been advanced of a separate, exclusive dominion over the ocean.

It may happen, in some countries, at some periods, that there be established a property in water, none in land; if the latter be in greater abundance than can be used by the inhabitants, and the former be found, with difficulty, and in very small quantities.

Again; suppose, that, though the necessities of human race continue the same as at present, yet the mind is so enlarged, and so replete with friendship and generosity, that every man has the utmost tenderness for every man, and feels no more concern for his own interest than for that of his fellows; it seems evident, that the use of justice would, in this case, be suspended by such an extensive benevolence, nor would the divisions and barriers of property and obligation have ever been thought of. Why should I bind another, by a deed or promise, to do me any good office, when I know that he is already prompted, by the strongest inclination, to seek my happiness, and would, of himself, perform the desired service; except the hurt, he thereby receives, be greater than the benefit accruing to me? in which case, he knows, that, from my innate humanity and friendship, I should be the first to oppose myself to his imprudent generosity. Why raise land-marks between my neighbour's field and mine, when my heart has made no division between our interests; but shares all his joys and sorrows with the same force and vivacity as if originally my own? Every man, upon this supposition, being a second self to another, would trust all his interests to the discretion of every man; without jealousy, without partition, without distinction. And the whole human race would form only one family; where all would lie in common, and be used freely, without regard to property; but cautiously too, with as entire regard to the necessities of each individual, as if our own interests were most intimately concerned.

In the present disposition of the human heart, it would, perhaps, be difficult to find complete instances of such enlarged affections; but still we may observe, that the case of families approaches towards it; and the stronger the mutual benevolence is among the individuals, the nearer it approaches; till all distinction of property be, in a great measure, lost and confounded among them. Between married persons, the cement of friendship is by the laws supposed so strong as to abolish all division of possessions; and has often, in reality, the force ascribed to it. And it is observable, that, during the ardour of new enthusiasms, when every principle is inflamed into extravagance, the community of goods has frequently been attempted; and nothing but experience of its inconveniencies, from the returning or disguised selfishness of men, could make the imprudent fanatics adopt anew the ideas of justice and of separate property. So true is it, that this virtue derives its existence entirely from its necessary *use* to the intercourse and social state of mankind.

To make this truth more evident, let us reverse the foregoing suppositions; and carrying everything to the opposite extreme, consider what would be the effect of these new situations. Suppose a society to fall into such want of all common necessaries, that the utmost frugality and industry cannot preserve the greater number from perishing, and the whole from extreme misery; it will readily, I believe, be admitted, that the strict laws of justice are suspended, in such a pressing emergence, and give place to the stronger motives of necessity and self-preservation. Is it any crime, after a shipwreck, to seize whatever means or instrument of safety one can lay hold of, without regard to former limitations of property? Or if a city besieged were perishing with hunger; can we imagine, that men will see any means of preservation before them, and lose their lives, from a scrupulous regard to what, in other situations, would be the rules of equity and justice? The use and tendency of that virtue is to procure happiness and security, by preserving order in society: but where the society is ready to perish from extreme necessity, no greater evil can be dreaded from violence and injustice; and every man may now provide for himself by all the means, which prudence can dictate, or humanity permit. The public, even in less urgent necessities, opens granaries, without the consent of proprietors; as justly supposing, that the authority of magistracy may, consistent with equity, extend so far: but were any number of men to assemble, without the tie of laws or civil jurisdiction; would an equal partition of bread in a famine, though effected by power and even violence, be regarded as criminal or injurious?

Suppose likewise, that it should be a virtuous man's fate to fall into the society of ruffians, remote from the protection of laws and government; what conduct must he embrace in that melancholy situation? He sees such a desperate rapaciousness prevail; such a disregard to equity, such contempt of order, such stupid blindness to future consequences, as must immediately have the most tragical conclusion, and must terminate in destruction to the greater number, and in a total dissolution of society to the rest. He, meanwhile, can have no other expedient than to arm himself, to whomever the sword he seizes, or the buckler, may belong: To make provision of all means of defence and security: And his particular regard to justice being no longer of use to his own safety or that of others, he must consult the dictates of self-preservation alone, without concern for those who no longer merit his care and attention.

When any man, even in political society, renders himself by his crimes, obnoxious to the public, he is punished by the laws in his goods and person; that is, the ordinary rules of justice are, with regard to him, suspended for a moment, and it becomes equitable to inflict on him, for the *benefit* of society, what otherwise he could not suffer without wrong or injury.

The rage and violence of public war; what is it but a suspension of justice among the warring parties, who perceive, that this virtue is now no longer of any *use* or advantage to them? The laws of war, which then succeed to those of equity and justice, are rules calculated for the *advantage* and *utility* of that particular state, in which men are now placed. And were a civilized nation engaged with barbarians, who observed no rules even of war, the former must also suspend their observance of them, where they no longer serve to any purpose; and must render every action or encounter as bloody and pernicious as possible to the first aggressors.

Thus, the rules of equity or justice depend entirely on the particular state and condition in which men are placed, and owe their origin and existence to that utility, which results to the public from their strict and regular observance. Reverse, in any considerable circumstance, the condition of men: Produce extreme abundance or extreme necessity: Implant in the human breast perfect moderation and humanity, or perfect rapaciousness and malice: By rendering justice totally *useless,* you thereby totally destroy its essence, and suspend its obligation upon mankind. . . .

It must, indeed, be confessed, that nature is so liberal to mankind, that, were all her presents equally divided among the species, and improved by art and industry, every individual would enjoy all the necessaries, and even most of the comforts of life; nor would ever be liable to any ills, but such as might accidentally arise from the sickly frame and constitution of his body. It must also be confessed, that, wherever we depart from this equality, we rob the poor of more satisfaction than we add to the rich, and that the slight gratification of a frivolous vanity, in one individual, frequently costs more than bread to many families, and even provinces. It may appear withal, that the rule of equality, as it would be highly *useful,* is not altogether *impracticable;* but has taken place, at least in an imperfect degree, in some republics; particularly that of Sparta; where it was attended, it is said, with the most beneficial consequences. Not to mention that the Agrarian laws, so frequently claimed in Rome, and carried into execution in many Greek cities, proceeded, all of them, from a general idea of the utility of this principle.

But historians, and even common sense, may inform us, that, however specious these ideas of *perfect* equality may seem, they are really, at bottom, *impracticable;* and were they not so, would be extremely *pernicious* to human society. Render possessions ever so equal, men's different degrees of art, care, and industry will immediately break that equality. Or if you check these virtues, you reduce society to the most extreme indigence; and instead of preventing want and beggary in a few, render it unavoidable to the whole community. The most rigorous inquisition too is requisite to watch every inequality on its first appearance; and the most severe jurisdiction, to punish and redress it. But besides, that so much authority must soon degenerate into tyranny, and be exerted with great partialities; who can possibly be possessed of it, in such a situation as is here supposed? Perfect equality of possessions, destroying all subordination, weakens extremely the authority of magistracy, and must reduce all power nearly to a level, as well as property.

We may conclude, therefore, that, in order to establish laws for the regulation of property, we must be acquainted with the nature and situation of man; must reject appearances, which may be false, though specious; and must search for those rules, which are, on the whole, most *useful* and *beneficial.* Vulgar sense and slight experience are sufficient for this purpose; where men give not way to too selfish avidity, or too extensive enthusiasm.

Who sees not, for instance, that whatever is produced or improved by a man's art or industry ought, for ever, to be secured to him, in order to give encouragement to such *useful* habits and accomplishments? That the property ought also to descend to children and relations, for the same *useful* purpose? That it may be alienated by consent, in order to beget that commerce and intercourse, which is so *beneficial* to human society? And that all contracts and promises ought carefully to be fulfilled, in order to secure mutual trust and confidence, by which the general *interest* of mankind is so much promoted?

Examine the writers on the laws of nature; and you will always find, that, whatever principles they set out with, they are sure to terminate here at last, and to assign, as the ultimate reason for every role which they establish, the convenience and necessities of mankind. . . .

From *A Treatise of Human Nature*

No one can doubt that the convention for the distinction of property and for the stability of possession is of all circumstances the most necessary to the establishment of human society, and that after the agreement for the fixing and observing of this rule there remains little or nothing to be done towards settling a perfect harmony and concord. All the other passions, beside this of interest, are either easily restrained, or are not of such pernicious consequence when indulged. *Vanity* is rather to be esteemed a social passion and a bond of union among men. *Pity* and *love* are to be considered in the same light. And as to *envy* and *revenge*, though pernicious, they operate only by intervals, and are directed against particular persons whom we consider as our superiors or enemies. This avidity alone of acquiring goods and possessions for ourselves and our nearest friends is insatiable, perpetual, universal, and directly destructive of society. There scarce is any one who is not actuated by it; and there is no one who has not reason to fear from it, when it acts without any restraint and gives way to its first and most natural movements. So that, upon the whole, we are to esteem the difficulties in the establishment of society to be greater or less, according to those we encounter in regulating and restraining this passion.

It is certain that no affection of the human mind has both a sufficient force and a proper direction to counterbalance the love of gain, and render men fit members of society by making them abstain from the possessions of others. Benevolence to strangers is too weak for this purpose; and as to the other passions, they rather inflame this avidity, when we observe that the larger our possessions are, the more ability we have of gratifying all our appetites. There is no passion, therefore, capable of controlling the interested affection but the very affection itself, by an alteration of its direction. Now, this alteration must necessarily take place upon the least reflection; since it is evident that the passion is much better satisfied by its restraint than by its liberty, and that, in preserving society, we make much greater advances in the acquiring possessions than in the solitary and forlorn condition which must follow upon violence and an universal licence. The question, therefore, concerning the wickedness or goodness of human nature enters not in the least into that other question concerning the origin of society; nor is there anything to be considered but the degrees of men's sagacity or folly. For whether the passion of self-interest be esteemed vicious or virtuous, it is all a case, since itself alone restrains it; so that if it be virtuous, men become social by their virtue; if vicious, their vice has the same effect. . . .

Here then is a proposition which, I think, may be regarded as certain, *that it is only from the selfishness and confined generosity of man, along with the scanty provision nature has made for his wants that justice derives its origin.* If we look backward we shall find that this proposition bestows an additional force on some of those observations which we have already made on this subject.

First, we may conclude from it that a regard to public interest, or a strong extensive benevolence, is not our first and original motive for the observation of the rules of justice, since it is allowed that if men were endowed with such a benevolence, these rules would never have been dreamed of.

Secondly, we may conclude from the same principle that the sense of justice is not founded on reason, or on the discovery of certain connections and relations of ideas which are eternal, immutable, and universally obligatory. For since it is confessed that such an alteration as that above mentioned, in the temper and circumstances of mankind, would entirely alter our duties and obligations, it is necessary upon the common system *that the sense of virtue is derived from reason,* to show the change which this must produce in the relations and ideas. But it is evident that the only cause why the extensive generosity of man and the perfect abundance of everything would destroy the very idea of justice is because they render it useless; and that, on the other hand, his confined benevolence and his necessitous condition give rise to that virtue only by making it requisite to the public interest and to that of every individual. It was therefore a concern for our own and the public interest which made us establish the laws of justice; and nothing can be more certain than that it is not any relation of ideas which gives us this concern, but our impressions and sentiments, without which everything in nature is perfectly indifferent to us, and can never in the least affect us. The sense of justice, therefore, is not founded on our ideas but on our impressions.

Thirdly, we may further confirm the foregoing proposition *that those impressions, which give rise to this sense of justice, are not natural to the mind of man, but arise from artifice and human conventions.* For since any considerable alienation of temper and circumstances destroys equally justice and injustice, and since such an alteration has an effect only by changing our own and the public interest, it follows that the first establishment of the rules of justice depends on these different interests. But if men pursued the public interest naturally, and with a hearty affection, they would have never dreamed of restraining each other by these rules; and if they pursued their own interest, without any precaution, they would run headlong into every kind of injustice and violence. These rules, therefore, are artificial and seek their end in an oblique and indirect manner; nor is the interest which gives rise to them of a kind that could be pursued by the natural and inartificial passions of men.

To make this more evident, consider that, though the rules of justice are established merely by interest, their connection with interest is somewhat singular, and is different from what may be observed on other occasions. A single act of justice is frequently contrary to *public interest;* and were it to stand alone, without being followed by other acts, may in itself be very prejudicial to society. When a man of merit, of a beneficent disposition, restores a great fortune to a miser or a seditious bigot, he has acted justly and laudably; but the public is a real sufferer. Nor is every single act of justice, considered apart, more conducive to private interest than to public; and it is easily conceived how a man may impoverish himself by a single instance of integrity, and have reason to wish that, with regard to that single act, the laws of justice were for a moment suspended in the universe. But however single acts of justice may be contrary either to public or private interest, it is certain that the whole plan or scheme is highly conductive, or indeed absolutely requisite, both to the support of society and the well-being of every individual. It is impossible to separate the good from the ill. Property must be stable, and must be fixed by general rules.

Adam Smith, "Justice as a Moral Sentiment," from *A Theory of the Moral Sentiments* (1759), and "The Virtues of the Free Market," from *The Wealth of Nations* (1776)

Economists and defenders of the free market should no longer be surprised by this, but Adam Smith (1723–1790) wrote *two* great books of philosophy, not only that bible of capitalism, *The Wealth of Nations*. The other, which preceded it, was *A Theory of the Moral Sentiments*, and it was a book that argued that self-interest (greed, or the profit motive, depending on one's views of the market) was *not* the motive that moved modern civilization. Smith never doubted the existence or the power of self-interest, but he always insisted that it was balanced in us by a number of *moral sentiments*, especially sympathy for our fellow humans. In sympathy, we in some sense share or at least "feel for" the sufferings of others, and such feelings hold in check our temptations to hurt others as well. Foremost among those prohibitive feelings that prevent us from doing harm to others is the feeling of *justice*, which Smith, here going against his Edinburgh friend Hume, takes to be a "natural" and not merely "artificial" sentiment. Furthermore, Smith, like Hume, takes one of the primary motives of our behavior to be the *approval of others*, thus blending and (to stubborn egoists) confusing motives of self-interest and altruism. Thus justice has threefold support: the force of the sentiment itself, a sense of sympathy, which renders us incapable of being indifferent to the sufferings of others, and the near unanimous approval of our fellow citizens. (Thrasymachus, presumably, is not among them.) But justice, above all, is ultimately *useful,* and this is what justifies it; in this Smith wholly agrees with his friend Hume. Smith distinguishes between what he calls "beneficence" (wanting to do good) and justice, insisting that both are desirable but only the latter is essential, for while a society can survive (but not happily) without citizens who are helpful and generous with one another, it could not survive at all in the presence of general mutual harm.

In *The Wealth of Nations,* Smith famously argues for the virtues of the free market system. That system presupposes, first of all, the institution of private property, for what could one buy or sell (and what would one bother to produce) if the right of ownership were not assumed at the outset? But the institution of private property and the workings of the free market virtually ensure some great inequalities between the few rich and the relatively many poor, and the inevitable enmity between them, according to Smith (as well as Hume), demands the existence of civil government. But it is not the right to private property that justifies the market itself, according to Smith, and here he differs from some of his more illustrious philosophical followers (e.g., Robert Nozick). Smith's defense of the market is ultimately utilitarian, based on the straightforward empirical argument that the market alone will ensure greater prosperity for all citizens. But it should be said that Smith did not have much to say about the very poor, those who do not benefit from any rise in prosperity, and it should also be said that Smith never thought that the market could similarly take care of all social problems or that the government should be "minimal" and limited to the protection of property and other individual rights. To the contrary, the strong sense of community defended in *A Theory of the Moral Sentiments* is presupposed throughout *The Wealth of Nations,* and there can be no sense of justice based on prosperity alone.

From *A Theory of the Moral Sentiments*

There is, however, another virtue, of which the observance is not left to the freedom of our own wills, which may be extorted by force, and of which the violation exposes to resentment, and consequently to punishment. This virtue is justice: the violation of justice is injury: it does real and positive hurt to some particular persons, from motives which are naturally disapproved of. It is, therefore, the proper object of resentment, and of punishment, which is the natural consequence of resentment. As mankind go along with, and approve of the violence employed to avenge the hurt which is done by injustice, so they much more go along with, and approve of, that which is employed to prevent and beat off the injury, and to restrain the offender from hurting his neighbours. The person himself who mediates an injustice is sensible of this, and feels that force may, with the utmost propriety, be made use of, both by the person whom he is about to injure, and by others, either to obstruct the execution of his crime, or to punish him when he has executed it. And upon this is founded that remarkable distinction between justice and all the other social virtues, which has of late been particularly insisted upon by an author of very great and original genius, that we feel ourselves to be under a strict obligation to act according to justice, than agreeably to friendship, charity, or generosity; that the practise of these last mentioned virtues seems to be left in some measure to our own choice, but that, somehow or other, we feel ourselves to be in a peculiar manner tied, bound, and obligated to the observation of justice. We feel, that is to say, that force may, with the utmost propriety, and with the approbation of all mankind, be made use of to constrain us to observe the rules of the one, but not to follow the precepts of the other. . . .

Of the Sense of Justice, of Remorse, and of the Consciousness of Merit

There can be no proper motive for hurting our neighbour, there can be no incitement to do evil to another, which mankind will go along with, except just indignation for evil which that other has done to us. To disturb his happiness merely because it stands in the way of our own, to take from him what is of real use to him merely because it may be of equal or of more use to us, or to indulge, in this manner, at the expence of other people, the natural preference which every man has for his own happiness above that of other people, is what no impartial spectator can go along with. Every man is, no doubt, by nature, first and principally recommended to his own care; and as he is fitter to take care of himself than of any other person, it is fit and right that it should be so. Every man, therefore, is much more deeply interested in whatever immediately concerns himself, than in what concerns any other man: and to hear, perhaps, of the death of another person, with whom we have no particular connection, will give us less concern, will spoil our stomach, or break our rest much less than a very insignificant disaster which has befallen ourselves.

But though the ruin of our neighbour may affect us much less than a very small misfortune of our own, we must not ruin him to prevent that small misfortune, nor even to prevent our own ruin. We must, here, as in all other cases, view ourselves not so much according to that light in which we may naturally appear to ourselves, as according to that in which we naturally appear to others. Though every man may, according to the proverb, be the whole world to himself, to the rest of mankind he is a most insignificant part of it. Though his own happiness may be of more importance to him than that of all the world besides, to every other person it is of no more consequence than that of any other man. Though it may be true, therefore, that every individual, in his own breast, naturally prefers himself to all mankind, yet he dares not look mankind in the face, and avow that he acts according to this principle. He feels that in this preference they can never go along with him, and that how natural soever it may be to him, it must always appear excessive and extravagant to them.

When he views himself in the light in which he is conscious that others will view him, he sees that to them he is but one of the multitude in no respect better than any other in it. If he would act so as that the impartial spectator may enter into the principles of his conduct, which is what of all things he has the greatest desire to do, he must, upon this, as upon all other occasions, humble the arrogance of his self-love, and bring it down to something which other men can go along with. They will indulge it so far as to allow him to be more anxious about, and to pursue with more earnest assiduity, his own happiness than that of any other person. Thus far, whenever they place themselves in his situation, they will readily go along with him. In the race for wealth, and honours, and preferments, he may run as hard as he can, and strain every nerve and every muscle, in order to outstrip all his competitors. But if he should justle, or throw down any of them, the indulgence of the spectators is entirely at an end. It is a violation of fair play, which they cannot admit of. This man is to them, in every respect, as good as he: they do not enter into that self-love by which he prefers himself so much to this other, and cannot go along with the motive from which he hurt him. They readily, therefore, sympathize with the natural resentment of the injured, and the offender becomes the object of their hatred and indignation. He is sensible that he becomes so, and feels that those sentiments are ready to burst out from all sides against him.

As the greater and more irreparable the evil that is done, the resentment of the sufferer runs naturally the higher; so does likewise the sympathetic indignation of the spectator, as well as the sense of guilt in the agent. Death is the greatest evil which one man can inflict upon another, and excites the highest degree of resentment in those who are immediately connected with the slain. Murder, therefore, is the most atrocious of all crimes which affect individuals only, in the sight both of mankind, and of the person who has committed it. To be deprived of that which we are possessed of, is a greater evil than to be disappointed of what we have only the expectation. Breach of property, therefore, theft and robbery, which take from us what we are possessed of, are greater crimes than breach of contract, which only disappoints us of what we expected. The most sacred laws of justice, therefore, those whose violation seems to call loudest for vengeance and punishment, are the laws which guard the life and person of our neighbour; the next are those which guard his property and possessions, and last of all come those which guard what are called his personal rights, or what is due to him from the promises of others.

The violator of the more sacred laws of justice can never reflect on the sentiments which mankind must entertain with regard to him, without feeling all the agonies of shame, and horror, and consternation. When his passion is gratified, and he begins coolly to reflect on his past conduct, he can enter into none of the motives which influenced it. They appear now as detestable to him as they did always to other people. By sympathizing with the hatred and abhorrence which other men must entertain for him, he becomes in some measure the object of his own hatred and abhorrence. The situation of the person, who suffered by his injustice, now calls upon his pity. He is grieved at the thought of it; regrets the unhappy effects of his own conduct, and feels at the same time that they have rendered him the proper object of the resentment and indignation of mankind, and of what is the natural consequence of resentment, vengeance and punishment. The thought of this perpetually haunts him, and fills him with terror and amazement. He dares no longer look society in the face, but imagines himself as it were rejected, and thrown out from the affections of all mankind. He cannot hope for the consolation of sympathy in this his greatest and most dreadful distress. The remembrance of his crimes has shut out all fellow-feeling with him from the hearts of his fellow-creatures. The sentiments which they entertain with regard to him, are the very thing which he is most afraid of. Every thing seems hostile, and he would be glad to fly to some inhospitable desert, where he might never more behold the face of a human creature, nor read in the countenance of mankind the condemnation of his crimes.

But solitude is still more dreadful than society. His own thoughts can present him with nothing but what is black, unfortunate, and disastrous, the melancholy forebodings of incomprehensible misery and ruin. The horror of solitude drives him back into society, and he comes again into the presence of mankind, astonished to appear before them, loaded with shame and distracted with fear, in order to supplicate some little protection from the countenance of those very judges, who he knows have already all unanimously condemned him. Such is the nature of that sentiment, which is properly called remorse; of all the sentiments which can enter the human breast the most dreadful. It is made up of shame from the sense of the impropriety of past conduct; of grief for the effects of it; of pity for those who suffer by it; and of the dread and terror of punishment from the consciousness of the justly provoked resentment of all rational creatures.

The opposite behaviour naturally inspires the opposite sentiment. The man who, not from frivolous fancy, but from proper motive, has performed a generous action, when he looks forward to those whom he has served, feels himself to be the natural object of their love and gratitude, and, by sympathy with them, of the esteem and approbation of all mankind. And when he looks backward to the motive from which he acted, and surveys it in the light in which the indifferent spectator will survey it, he still continues to enter into it, and applauds himself by sympathy with the approbation of this supposed impartial judge. In both these points of view his own conduct appears to him every way agreeable. His mind, at the thought of it, is filled with cheerfulness, serenity, and composure. He is in friendship and harmony with all mankind, and looks upon his fellow creatures with confidence and benevolent satisfaction, secure that he has rendered himself worthy of their most favourable regards. In the combination of all these sentiments consists the consciousness of merit, or of deserved reward.

Of the Utility of this Constitution of Nature

It is thus that man, who can subsist only in society, was fitted by nature to that situation for which he was made. All the members of human society stand in need of each others' assistance, and are likewise exposed to mutual injuries. Where necessary assistance is reciprocally afforded from love, from gratitude, from friendship, and esteem, the society flourishes and is happy. All the different members of it are bound together by the agreeable bands of love and affection, and are, as it were, drawn to one common centre of mutual good offices.

But though the necessary assistance should not be afforded from such generous and disinterested motives, though among the different members of the society there should be no mutual love and affection, the society, though less happy and agreeable, will not necessarily be dissolved. Society may subsist among different men, as among different merchants, from a sense of its utility, without any mutual love or affection; and though no man in it should owe any obligation, or be bound in gratitude to any other, it may still be upheld by a mercenary exchange of good offices according to an agreed valuation.

Society, however, cannot subsist among those who are at all times ready to hurt and injure one another. The moment that injury begins, the moment that mutual resentment and animosity take place, all the bonds of it are broke asunder, and the different members of which it consisted are, as it were, dissipated and scattered abroad by the violence and opposition of their discordant affections. If there is any society among robbers and murderers, they must at least, according to the trite observation, abstain from robbing and murdering one another. Beneficence, therefore, is less essential to the existence of society than justice. Society may subsist, though not in the most comfortable state, without beneficence; but the prevalence of injustice must utterly destroy it. . . .

Among nations of hunters, as there is scarce any property, or at least none that exceeds the value of two or three days labour; so there is seldom any established magistrate or any regular administration of justice. Men who have no property can injure one another only in their persons or reputations. But when one man kills, wounds, beats, or defame another, though he to whom the injury is done suffers, he who does it receives no benefit. It is otherwise with the injuries to property. The benefit of the person who does the injury is often equal to the loss of him who suffers it. Envy, malice, or resentment, are the only passions which can prompt one man to injure another in his person or reputation. But the greater part of men are not very frequently under the influence of those passions; and the very worst men are so only occasionally. As their gratification too, how agreeable soever it may be to certain characters, is not attended with any real or permanent advantage, it is in the greater part of men commonly restrained by prudential considerations. Men may live together in society with some tolerable degree of security, though there is no civil magistrate to protect them from the injustice of those passions. But avarice and ambition in the rich, in the poor the hatred of labour and the love of present ease and enjoyment, are the passions which prompt to invade property, passions much more steady in their operation, and much more universal in their influence.

Wherever there is great property, there is great inequality. For one very rich man, there must be at least five hundred poor, and the affluence of the few supposes the indigence of the many. The affluence of the rich excites the indignation of the poor, who are often both driven by want, and prompted by envy, to invade his possessions. It is only under the shelter of the civil magistrate that the owner of that valuable property, which is acquired by the labour of many years, or perhaps of many successive generations, can sleep a single night in security. He is at all times surrounded by unknown enemies, whom, though he never provoked, he can never appease, and from whose injustice he can be protected only by the powerful arm of the civil magistrate continually held up to chastise it. The acquisition of valuable and extensive property, therefore, necessarily requires the establishment of civil government. Where there is no property, or at least none that exceeds the value of two or three days labour, civil government is not so necessary.

From *The Wealth of Nations*

It is the great multiplication of the productions of all the different arts, in consequence of the division of labour, which occasions, in a well-governed society, that universal opulence which extends itself to the lowest ranks of the people. Every workman has a great quantity of his own work to dispose of beyond what he himself has occasion for; and every other workman being exactly in the same situation, he is enabled to exchange a great quantity of his own goods for a great quantity, or, what comes to the same thing, for the price of a great quantity of theirs. He supplies them abundantly with what they have occasion for, and a general plenty diffuses itself through all the different ranks of the society.

Observe the accommodation of the most common artificer or day-labourer in a civilised and thriving country, and you will perceive that the number of people of whose industry a part, though but a small part, has been employed in procuring him this accommodation, exceeds all computation. The woollen coat, for example, which covers the day-labourer, as coarse and rough as it may appear, is the produce of the joint labour of a great multitude of workmen. The shepherd, the sorter of the wool, the wool-comber or carder, the dyer, the scribbler, the spinner, the weaver, the fuller, the dresser, with many others, must all join their different arts in order to complete even this homely production. How many merchants and carriers, besides, must have been employed in transporting the materials from some of those workmen to others who often live in a very distant part of the country! How much commerce and navigation in particular, how many shipbuilders, sailors, sailmakers, ropemakers, must have been employed in order to bring together the different drugs made use of by the dyer, which often come from the remotest corners of the world! What a variety of labour too is necessary in order to produce the tools of the meanest of those workmen! To say nothing of such complicated machines as the ship of the sailor, the mill of the fuller, or even the loom of the weaver, let us consider only what a variety of labour is requisite in order to form that very simple machine, the shears with which the shepherd clips the wool. The miner, the builder of the furnace for smelting the ore, the feller of the timber, the burner of the charcoal to be made use of in the smelting house, the brickmaker, the bricklayer, the workmen who attend the furnace, the millwright, the forger, the smith, must all of them join their different arts in order to produce them.

Were we to examine, in the same manner, all the different parts of his dress and household furniture, the coarse linen shirt which he wears next his skin, the shoes which cover his feet, the bed which he lies on, and all the different parts which compose it, the kitchen grate at which he prepares his victuals, the coals which he makes use of for that purpose, dug from the bowels of the earth, and brought to him perhaps by a long sea and a long land carriage, all the other utensils of his kitchen, all the furniture of his table, the knives and forks, the earthen or pewter plates upon which he serves up and divides his victuals, the different hands employed in preparing his bread and his beer, the glass window which lets in the heat and the light, and keeps out the wind and the rain, with all the knowledge and art requisite for preparing that beautiful and happy invention, without which these northern parts of the world could scarce have afforded a very comfortable habitation, together with the tools of all the different workmen employed in producing those different conveniences; if we examine, I say, all these things, and consider what a variety of labour is employed about each of them, we shall be sensible that without the assistance and cooperation of many thousands, the very meanest person in a civilised country could not be provided, even according to, what we very falsely imagine, the easy and simple manner in which he is commonly accommodated. Compared, indeed, with the more extravagant luxury of the great, his accommodation must no doubt appear extremely simple and easy; and yet it may be true, perhaps, that the accommodation of an European prince does not always so much exceed that of an industrious and frugal peasant, as the accommodation of the latter exceeds that of many an African king, the absolute master of the lives and liberties of ten thousand naked savages.

This division of labour, from which so many advantages are derived, is not originally the effect of any human wisdom, which foresees and intends that general opulence to which it gives occasion. It is the necessary, though very slow and gradual consequence of a certain propensity in human nature which has in view no such extensive utility; the propensity to truck, barter, and exchange one thing for another.

Whether this propensity be one of those original principles in human nature, of which no further account can be given; or whether, as seems more probable, it be the necessary consequence of the faculties of reason and speech, it belongs not to our present subject to enquire. It is common to all men, and to be found in no other race of animals, which seem to know neither this nor any other species of contracts. Two greyhounds, in running down the same hare, have sometimes the appearance of acting in some sort of concert. Each turns her towards his companion, or endeavours to intercept her when his companion turns her towards himself.

This, however, is not the effect of any contract, but of the accidental concurrence of their passions in the same object at that particular time. Nobody ever saw a dog make a fair and deliberate exchange of one bone for another with another dog. Nobody ever saw one animal by its gestures and natural cries signify to another, this is mine, that yours; I am willing to give this for that. When an animal wants to obtain something either of a man or of another animal, it has no other means of persuasion but to gain the favour of those whose service it requires. A puppy fawns upon its dam, and a spaniel endeavours by a thousand attractions to engage the attention of its master who is at dinner, when it wants to be fed by him. Man sometimes uses the same arts with his brethren, and when he has no other means of engaging them to act according to his inclinations, endeavours by every servile and fawning attention to obtain their good will. He has not time, however, to do this upon every occasion. In civilised society he stands at all times in need of the cooperation and assistance of great multitudes, while his whole life is scarce sufficient to gain the friendship of a few persons.

In almost every other race of animals each individual, when it is grown up to maturity, is entirely independent, and in its natural state has occasion for the assistance of no other living creature. But man has almost constant occasion for the help of his brethren, and it is in vain for him to expect it from their benevolence only. He will be more likely to prevail if he can interest their self-love in his favour, and show them that it is for their own advantage to do for him what he requires of them. Whoever offers to another a bargain of any kind, proposes to do this. Give me that which I want, and you shall have this which you want, is the meaning of every such offer; and it is in this manner that we obtain from one another the far greater part of those good offices which we stand in need of. It is not from the benevolence of the butcher, the brewer, or the baker, that we expect our dinner, but from their regard to their own interest. We address ourselves, not to their humanity but to their self-love, and never talk to them of our own necessities but of their advantages. Nobody but a beggar chooses to depend chiefly upon the benevolence of his fellow-citizens. Even a beggar does not depend upon it entirely. The charity of well-disposed people, indeed, supplies him with the whole fund of his subsistence. But though this principle ultimately provides him with all the necessaries of life which he has occasion for, it neither does nor can provide him with them as he has occasion for them. The greater part of his occasional wants are supplied in the same manner as those of other people, by treaty, by barter, and by purchase. With the money which one man gives him he purchases food. The old clothes which another bestows upon him he exchanges for other old clothes which suit him better, or for lodging, or for food, or for money, with which he can buy either food, clothes, or lodging, as he has occasion. . . .

And thus the certainty of being able to exchange all that surplus part of the produce of his own labour, which is over and above his own consumption, for such parts of the produce of other men's labour as he may have occasion for, encourages every man to apply himself to a particular occupation, and to cultivate and bring to perfection whatever talent or genius he may possess for that particular species of business.

The difference of natural talents in different men is, in reality, much less than we are aware of, and the very different genius which appears to distinguish men of different professions, when grown up to maturity, is not upon many occasions so much the cause, as the effect of the division of labour. The difference between the most dissimilar characters, between a philosopher and a common street porter, for example, seems to arise not so much from nature, as from habit, custom, and education. When they came into the world, and for the first six or eight years of their existence, they were, perhaps, very much alike, and neither their parents nor play-fellows could perceive and remarkable difference. About that age, or soon after, they come to be employed in very different occupations. The difference of talents comes then to be taken notice of, and widens by degrees, till at last the vanity of the philosopher is willing to acknowledge scarce any resemblance. But without the disposition to truck, barter, and exchange, every man must have procured to himself every necessary and convenience of life which he wanted. All must have had the same duties to perform, and the same work to do, and there could have been no such difference of employment as could alone give occasion to any great difference of talents.

As it is this disposition which forms that difference of talents, so remarkable among men of different professions, so it is this same disposition which renders that difference useful. Many tribes of animals acknowledged to be all of the same species, derive from nature a much more remarkable distinction of genius, than what, antecedent to custom and education, appears to take place among men. By nature a philosopher is not in genius and disposition half so different from a street porter, as a mastiff is from a greyhound, or a greyhound from a spaniel, or this last from a shepherd's dog. Those different tribes of animals, however, though all of the same species, are of scarce any use to one another. The strength of the mastiff is not, in the least, supported either by the swiftness of the greyhound, or by the sagacity of the spaniel, or by the docility of the shepherd's dog. The effects of those different geniuses and talents, for want of the power or disposition to barter and exchange, cannot be brought into a common stock, and do not in the least contribute to the better accommodation and convenience of the species. Each animal is still obliged to support and defend itself, separately and independently, and derives no sort of advantage from that variety of talents with which nature has distinguished its fellows. Among men, on the contrary, the most dissimilar geniuses are of use to one another; the different produces of their respective talents, by the general disposition to truck, barter, and exchange, being brought, as it were, into a common stock, where every man may purchase whatever part of the produce of other men's talents he has occasion for.

Is this improvement in the circumstances of the lower ranks of the people to be regarded as an advantage or as an inconvenience to the society? The answer seems at first sight abundantly plain. Servants, labourers, and workmen of different kinds, make up the far greater part of every great political society. But what improves the circumstances of the greater part can never be regarded as an inconvenience to the whole. No society can surely be flourishing and happy, of which the far greater part of the members are poor and miserable. It is but equity, besides, that they who feed, clothe, and lodge the whole body of the people, should have such a share of the produce of their own labour as to be themselves tolerably well fed, clothed, and lodged.

. . . the annual revenue of every society is always precisely equal to the exchangeable value of the whole annual produce of its industry, or rather is precisely the same thing with that exchangeable value. As every individual, therefore, endeavours as much as he can both to employ his capital in the support of domestic industry, and so to direct that industry that its produce may be of the greatest value; every individual necessarily labours to render the annual revenue of the society as great as he can. He generally, indeed, neither intends to promote the public interest, nor knows how much he is promoting it. By preferring the support of domestic to that of foreign industry, he intends only his own security and by directing that industry in such a manner as its produce may be of the greatest value, he intends only his own gain, and he is in this, as in many other cases, led by an invisible hand to promote an end which was no part of his intention. Nor is it always the worse for the society that it was no part of it. By pursuing his own interest he frequently promotes that of the society more effectually than when he really intends to promote it. I have never known much good done by those who affected to trade for the public good. It is an affectation, indeed, not very common among merchants, and very few words need be employed in dissuading them from it.

Immanuel Kant, "Rightful Ownership," from *The Philosophy of Law* (1797)

Immanuel Kant (1724–1804) utterly rejected the utility-minded and sentiment-based ethics of his illustrious predecessors Hume and Smith, and for him the notion of "justice" or "rights"—including the right to private property, or "possession"—required a firm *rational* basis. Kant distinguishes between merely "sensible" possession of an object—that is, one's physically possessing it—and the more philosophically significant notion of "intelligible" possession, which means that one has a *right* to the thing in question even when he or she is not using it, and it is not in his or her physical possession at all. Kant argues that ownership is not something external to one's self or "will" but rather essential to it. The violation of a person's property, in other words, is not just a cause of inconvenience but a violation of the person's freedom, that is, his or her most basic sense of self. In developing this view, Kant asks a typically Kantian question, "How is possession possible?" He distinguishes, as he does in other works, between an "analytic" (or trivially true) and a "synthetic" proposition, where the latter (but not the former) provides us with some substantial information about the subject in question, in this case the idea that one can rightfully possess or own an object not physically in his or her possession. That is, according to Kant, a matter of *necessity* and not merely empirical. Property law thus protects what is already acknowledged by a law of a more basic kind, and one can see in Kant some affinity to Locke, except that Locke's "natural" right to property becomes a strictly "rational" (or "de jure") right for Kant, part of the definition of one's self as well as (as in Locke) the definition of the object in question.

Anything is *"Mine" by Right*, or is rightfully Mine, when I am so connected with it, that if any other Person should make use of it without my consent, he would do me a lesion or injury. The subjective condition of the use of anything is *Possession* of it.

An *external* thing, however, as such could only be mine, if I may assume it to be possible that I can be wronged by the use which another might make of it *when it is not actually in my possession.* Hence it would be a contradiction to have anything External as one's own, were not the conception of Possession capable of two different meanings, as *sensible* Possession that is perceivable by the senses, and *rational* Possession that is perceivable only by the Intellect. By the former is to be understood a *physical* Possession, and by the latter, a purely *juridical* Possession of the same object.

The description of an Object as *"external* to me" may signify either that it is merely "different and distinct from me as a Subject," or that it is also "a thing placed *outside* of me, and to be found elsewhere in space or time." Taken in the first sense, the term Possession signifies "rational Possession," and, in the second sense, it must mean "Empirical Possession." A rational or *intelligible* Possession, if such be possible, is Possession *viewed apart from physical holding or detention (detentio).* . . .

It is possible to have any external object of my Will as Mine. In other words, a Maxim to this effect—were it to become law—that any object on which the Will can be exerted must remain objectively in itself *without an owner,* as "res nullius," is contrary to the Principle of Right.

For an object of any act of my Will, is something that it would be *physically* within my power to use. Now, suppose there were things that *by right* should absolutely not be in our power, or, in other words, that it would be wrong or inconsistent with the freedom of all, according to universal Law, to make use of them. On this supposition, Freedom would so far be depriving itself of the use of its voluntary activity, in thus putting *useable* objects out of all possibility of *use.* In practical relations, this would be to annihilate them, by making them *res nullius,* notwithstanding the fact that acts of Will in relation to such things would formally harmonize, in the actual use of them, with the external freedom of all according to universal Laws. . . .

Any one who would assert the Right to a thing as his, must be in possession of it as an object. Were he not its actual possessor or owner, he could not be wronged or injured by the use which another might make of it without his consent. For, should anything external to him, and in no way connected with him by Right, affect this object, it could not affect himself as a Subject, nor do him any wrong, unless he stood in a relation of Ownership to it. . . .

Definitions are *nominal* or *real*. A nominal Definition is sufficient merely to *distinguish* the object defined from all other objects, and it springs out of a complete and definite *exposition* of its conception. A real Definition further suffices for a *Deduction* of the conception defined, so as to furnish a knowledge of the reality of the object.—The *nominal Definition* of the external "Mine" would thus be: "The external Mine is anything outside of myself, such that any hindrance of my use of it at will, would be doing me an injury or wrong as an infringement of that Freedom of mine which may coexist with the freedom of all others according to a universal Law." The *real Definition* of this conception may be put thus: "The external Mine is anything outside of myself, such that any prevention of my use of it would be a wrong, *although I may not be in possession of it* so as to be actually holding it as an object."—I must be in some kind of possession of an external object, if the object is to be regarded as *mine;* for, otherwise, any one interfering with this object would not, in doing so, affect me; nor, consequently, would he thereby do me any wrong. Hence, a *rational Possession (possession noumenon)* must be assumed as possible, if there is to be rightly an external "Mine and Thine." Empirical Possession is thus only phenomenal possession of holding (detention) of the object in the sphere of sensible *appearance (possessio phenomenon)*. . . .

The question, "How is an *external Mine and Thine* possible?" resolves itself into this other question, "How is a *merely juridical* or *rational* Possession possible?" . . .

All Propositions of Right—as juridical propositions—are Propositions a priori, for they are practical Laws of Reason. But the juridical Proposition a priori respecting *empirical Possession is analytical;* for it says nothing more than what follows by the principle of Contradiction, from the conception of such possession; namely, that if I am the holder of a thing in the way of being physically connected with it, any one interfering with it without my consent—as, for instance, in wrenching an apple out of my hand—affects and detracts from my freedom as that which is internally Mine; and consequently the maxim of his action is in direct contradiction to the Axiom of Right. The proposition expressing the principle of an empirical rightful Possession, does not therefore go beyond the Right of a Person in reference to himself.

On the other hand, the Proposition expressing the possibility of the Possession of a thing external to me, after abstraction of all the conditions of empirical possession in space and time—consequently presenting the assumption of the possibility of a *Possessio Noumenon*—goes beyond these limiting conditions; and because this Proposition asserts a possession even without physical holding, as necessary to the conception of the external Mine and Thine, it is *synthetical*. And thus it becomes a problem for Reason to show how such a Proposition, extending its range beyond the conception of empirical possession, is possible a priori.

In this manner, for instance, the act of taking possession of a particular portion of the soil, is a mode exercising the private free-will without being an act of *usurpation*. The possessor founds upon the innate Right of *common possession* of the surface of the earth, and upon the universal Will corresponding a priori to it, which allows a *private Possession* of the soil; because what are mere things would be otherwise made in themselves and by a Law, into inappropriable objects. Thus a first appropriator acquires originally by primary possession a particular portion of the ground; and by Right (*jure*) he resists every other person who would hinder him in the private use of it, although while the "state of Nature" continues, this cannot be done by juridical means (*de jure*), because a public Law does not yet exist. . . .

Simple physical Possession, or holding of the soil, involves already certain relations of Right to the thing, although it is certainly not sufficient to enable me to regard it as Mine. Relative to others, so far as they know, it appears as a first possession in harmony with the law of external freedom; and, at the same time, it is embraced in the universal original possession which contains a priori the fundamental principle of the possibility of a private possession. Hence to disturb the first occupier or holder of a portion of the soil in his use of it, is a lesion or wrong done to him. The first taking of Possession has therefore a Title of Right in its favour, which is simply the principle of the original common possession; and the saying that "It is well for those who are in possession," when one is not bound to authenticate his possession, is a principle of Natural Right that establishes the juridical act of taking possession, as a ground of acquisition upon which every first possessor may found. . . .

Now it is just an abstraction from physical possession of the object of my free-will in the sphere of sense, that the Practical Reason wills that a rational possession of it shall be thought, according to intellectual conceptions which are not empirical, but contain a priori the conditions of rational possession. Hence it is in this fact, that we found the ground of the validity of such a rational conception of possession (*possessio noumenon*) as the principle of a universally valid *Legislation*. For such a Legislation is implied and contained in the expression, "This external object is *mine*," because an Obligation is thereby imposed upon all others in respect of it, who would otherwise not have been obliged to abstain from the use of this object.

The mode, then, of having something External to myself as Mine, consists in a specially juridical connection of the Will of the Subject with that object, independently of the empirical relations to it in Space and Time, and in accordance with the conception of a rational possession.

G. W. F. Hegel, "Justice, Property, and Law," from *The Philosophy of Right* (1821)

G. W. F. Hegel (1770–1831) published his *Philosophy of Right* less than fifteen years after the *Phenomenology of Spirit* but a virtual millennium later in terms of social and political change. The earlier book had been composed during the exhilarating days of Napoleon's greatest successes and the promise of liberal reform throughout Europe. The later book was written during "the Reaction," when conservative forces clamped down on all liberal and revolutionary ideas and sentiments, and Hegel, now a distinguished professor in Berlin, had given up his sense of a new and better world. He now tries to come to grips with what is already there, announces that "the rational is actual and the actual is rational," and attacks those social philosophies that would try to imagine a merely ideal society. Philosophy should not tell the world what it ought to be; it is enough to understand it. (One can and should contrast this book, which the young Karl Marx knew well, with Marx's own declaration, years later, that "philosophers have only tried to understand the world, . . . the point, however, is to change it.")

In *The Philosophy of Right*, Hegel attempts to lay out a very different picture of society and justice from the ones we find in the British philosophers. Hegel found the British emphasis on "utility" simply vulgar. The British emphasis on the individual nd the neglect of community he found utterly wrongheaded, and Hegel, more than most, defended a conception of society as primary, and "right"—not rights— as first of all a function of the whole—or what he opaquely calls "free infinite personality"—rather than of the individual. Hegel's writing here is notoriously difficult, but the theme is easily stated. What we call the individual is the product of a certain way of thinking, not immediate at all but mediated by society. The ultimate will is not the individual will but what Rousseau called the "general will," or "universal will," which has "all particular individuality absorbed within it." Free will, accordingly, is not a metaphysical feature of an individual but a larger notion, inseparable from a society and its history. And Hegel consequently distinguishes what Kant calls "morality"—a function of purely individual autonomy—and "ethical life," or "*Sittlichkeit*," which he takes to be the primary "natural" unit of social life and (though he does not use any term other than *Rechts*, or *right*) justice.

Ethical life or Sittlichkeit begins (as in Rousseau) with the family and one's primal sense of belonging, in existing first of all as a family member and not as an individual. This limited and clearly natural unit becomes incorporated into the larger notion of civil society, conceived as an association of "self-subsistent" members

From Hegel's *Philosophy of Right*, translated by T. M. Knox and published by Oxford University Press, 1942. Reprinted by permission of Oxford University Press.

who see themselves as associated only because of their individual needs and protected by an "external organization" (think of Nozick's "protective associations").
But this is no true community, although the very notion of the individual in such an
association is, of course, ultimately dependent on the association itself, for the
members do not recognize themselves collectively as a community. Here, essentially, is Hegel's charge against the British conception of the state as an external
force created by individuals to protect their self-interests. Such a conception gets
things backward. What is needed is an explicit and formal recognition of the community as a community, and this is the function of a constitution, which renders the
community a state. The constitution, for Hegel, does not "set up" the state but rather
recognizes the legitimacy of what has been there all along. We should also note that
"the state" here refers not to the government but to the entire community, as for-
malized by the constitution.

Hegel goes into some detail about the nature of property and its role in society. But we can anticipate that Hegel's discussion will have an antiutilitarian twist
to it and will not take the concept of individual rights as primary. Property, for
Hegel, is not just a matter of "mixing one's labor" with nature but rather of expressing oneself in nature. The difference might seem slight but it is culturally and historically enormous. Property for Hegel is not a right but rather an expression of one's
very self, and accordingly, it need not be an individual self. Hegel's sense of property is much more qualified than that found in British philosophy. We might note
that he discusses at some length the notion of alienation of property, a concept that
would have enormous importance two decades later in the writings of the young
Karl Marx. What Hegel means by this, however, is simply the fact that one can give
away or sell the products of one's labor, and it is because we can do this that the
institution of contracts becomes essential to the concept of private property. But
Hegel also makes the point that, while one can give away or sell the products of
one's labor, one cannot give away or sell the source of that labor, one's self (one's
talents, etc.). I can do this for a period of time, of course—if (e.g.) I work for someone for wages—but if I were to so alienate all of myself, I would make myself into
another's property and thereby cease to be a person. For Marx, of course, this is just
the problem, that a wage system that ruthlessly exploits the needs of workers
reduces them to the subhuman and makes virtual slaves of them.

* * *

. . . the truth about Right, Ethics, and the state is as old as its public recognition and formulation in the law of the land, in the morality of everyday life, and in religion. What more
does this truth require—since the thinking mind is not content to possess it in this ready
fashion? It requires to be grasped in thought as well; the content which is already rational
in principle must win the *form* of rationality and so appear well-founded to untrammelled
thinking. Such thinking does not remain stationary at the given, whether the given be
upheld by the external positive authority of the state or the *consensus hominum,* or by the
authority of inward feeling and emotion and by the "witness of the spirit" which directly
concurs with it. On the contrary, thought which is free starts out from itself and thereupon
claims to know itself as united in its innermost being with the truth. . . .

It is just this placing of philosophy in the actual world which meets with misunder-
standings, and so I revert to what I have said before, namely that, since philosophy is the

exploration of the rational, it is for that very reason the apprehension of the present and the actual, not the erection of a beyond, supposed to exist, God knows where, or rather which exists, and we can perfectly well say where, namely in the error of a one-sided, empty, ratiocination. In the course of this book, I have remarked that even Plato's *Republic*, which passes proverbially as an empty ideal, is in essence nothing but an interpretation of the nature of Greek ethical life. Plato was conscious that there was breaking into that life in his own time a deeper principle which could appear in it directly only as a longing still unsatisfied, and so only as something corruptive. To combat it, he needs must have sought aid from that very longing itself. But this aid had to come from on High and all that Plato could do was to seek it in the first place in a particular external form of that same Greek ethical life. By that means he thought to master this corruptive invader, and thereby he did fatal injury to the deeper impulse which underlay it, namely free infinite personality. Still, his genius is proved by the fact that the principle on which the distinctive character of his Idea of the state turns is precisely the pivot on which the impending world revolution turned at that time.

What is rational is actual and what is actual is rational. On this conviction the plain man like the philosopher takes his stand, and from it philosophy starts in its study of the universe of mind as well as the universe of nature. If reflection, feeling, or whatever form subjective consciousness may take, looks upon the present as something vacuous and looks beyond it with the eyes of superior wisdom, it finds itself in a vacuum, and because it is actual only in the present, it is itself mere vacuity. If on the other hand the Idea passes for "only an Idea," for something represented in an opinion, philosophy rejects such a view and shows that nothing is actual except the Idea. Once that is granted, the great thing is to apprehend in the show of the temporal and transient the substance which is immanent and the eternal which is present. . . .

. . . To comprehend what is, this is the task of philosophy, because what is, is reason. Whatever happens, every individual is a child of his time; so philosophy too is its own time apprehended in thoughts. It is just as absurd to fancy that a philosophy can transcend its contemporary world as it is to fancy that an individual can overleap his own age. . . .

One word more about giving instruction as to what the world ought to be. Philosophy in any case always comes on the scene too late to give it. As the thought of the world, it appears only when actuality is already there cut and dried after its process of formation has been completed. The teaching of the concept, which is also history's inescapable lesson, is that it is only when actuality is mature that the ideal first appears over against the real and that the ideal apprehends this same real world in its substance and builds it up for itself into the shape of an intellectual realm. When philosophy paints its grey in grey, then has a shape of life grown old. By philosophy's grey in grey it cannot be rejuvenated but only understood. The owl of Minerva spreads its wings only with the falling of the dusk. . . .

1.   The subject-matter of the philosophical science of right is the Idea of right, i.e., the concept of right together with the actualization of that concept. . . .

3.   Right is positive in general (*a*) when it has the *form* of being valid in a particular state, and this legal authority is the guiding principle for the knowledge of right in this positive form, i.e. for the science of positive law. (*b*) Right in this positive form acquires a positive element in its *content*

  (α) through the particular national character of a people, its stage of historical development, and the whole complex of relations connected with the necessities of nature;

  (β) because a system of positive law must necessarily involve the application of the universal concept to particular, externally given, characteristics of objects and cases. This application lies outside speculative thought and the development of the concept, and is the subsumption by the Understanding [of the particular under the universal];

(γ) through the finally detailed provisions requisite for actually pronouncing judgement in court.

If inclination, caprice, and the sentiments of the heart are set up in opposition to positive right and the laws, philosophy at least cannot recognize authorities of that sort.—That force and tyranny may be an element in law is accidental to law and has nothing to do with its nature. . . .

Natural law, or law from the philosophical point of view, is distinct from positive law; but to pervert their difference into an opposition and a contradiction would be a gross misunderstanding. . . .

4.   The basis of right is, in general, mind; its precise place and point of origin is the will. The will is free, so that freedom is both the substance of right and its goal, while the system of right is the realm of freedom made actual, the world of mind brought forth out of itself like a second nature. . . .

5.   The will contains (α) the element of pure indeterminacy or that pure reflection of the ego into itself which involves the dissipation of every restriction and every content either immediately presented by nature, by needs, desires, and impulses, or given and determined by any means whatever. This is the unrestricted infinity of absolute abstraction or universality, the pure thought of oneself. . . .

33.   In correspondence with the stages in the development of the Idea of the absolutely free will, the will is

> A. immediate; its concept therefore is abstract, namely personality, and its embodiment is an immediate external thing—the sphere of *Abstract* or *Formal Right;*
> B. reflected from its external embodiment into itself—it is then characterized as subjective individuality in opposition to the universal. The universal here is characterized as something inward, the good, and also as something outward, a world presented to the will; both these sides of the Idea are here mediated only by each other. This is the Idea in its division or in its existence as particular; and here we have the right of the subjective will in relation to the right of the world and the right of the Idea, though only the Idea implicit—the sphere of *Morality;*
> C. the unity and truth of both these abstract moments—the Idea of the good not only apprehended in thought but so realized both in the will reflected into itself and in the external world that freedom exists as substance, as actuality and necessity, no less than as subjective will; this is the Idea in its absolutely universal existence—*Ethical Life.*
> But on the same principle the ethical substance is
> (a) natural mind, the *Family;*
> (b) on its division and appearance, *Civil Society;*
> (c) the *State* as freedom, freedom universal and objective even in the free self-subsistence of the particular will. This actual and organic mind (α) of a single nation (β) reveals and actualizes itself through the inter-relation of the particular national minds until (γ) in the process of world-history it reveals and actualizes itself as the universal world-mind whose right is supreme.

"Morality" and "ethical life," which perhaps usually pass current as synonyms, are taken here in essentially different senses. Yet even commonplace thinking seems to be distinguishing them; Kant generally prefers to use the world "morality" and, since the principles of action in his philosophy are always limited to this conception, they make the standpoint of ethical life completely impossible, in fact they explicitly nullify and spurn it.

41.   A person must translate his freedom into an external sphere in order to exist as Idea. Personality is the first, still wholly abstract, determination of the absolute and infinite will, and therefore this sphere distinct from the person, the sphere capable of embodying his freedom, is likewise determined as what is immediately different and separable from him.

42.   What is immediately different from free mind is that which, both for mind and in itself, is the external pure and simple, a thing, something not free, not personal, without rights. . . .

43.   As the concept in its *immediacy,* and so as in essence a unit, a person has a *natural* existence partly within himself and partly of such a kind that he is related to it as to an external world.—It is only these things in their immediacy as things, not what they are capable of becoming through the mediation of the will, i.e. things with determinate characteristics, which are in question here where the topic under discussion is personality, itself at this point still in its most elementary immediacy.

Mental aptitudes, erudition, artistic skill, even things ecclesiastical (like sermons, masses, prayers, consecration of votive objects), inventions, and so forth, become subjects of a contract, brought on to a parity, through being bought and sold, with things recognized as things. It may be asked whether the artist, scholar, &c., is from the legal point of view in possession of his art, erudition, ability to preach a sermon, sing a mass, &c., that is, whether such attainments are "things." We may hesitate to call such abilities, attainments, aptitudes, &c., "things," for while possession of these may be the subject of business dealings and contracts, as if they were things, there is also something inward and mental about it, and for this reason the Understanding may be in perplexity about how to describe such possession in legal terms, because its field of vision is as limited to the dilemma that this is "either a thing or not a thing" as to the dilemma "either finite or infinite." Attainments, erudition, talents, and so forth are, of course, owned by free mind and are something internal and not external to it, but even so, by expressing them it may embody them in something external and alienate them (see below), and in this way they are put into the category of "things." Therefore they are not immediate at the start but only acquire this character through the mediation of mind which reduces its inner possessions to immediacy and externality.

It was an unjustifiable and unethical proviso of Roman law that children were from their father's point of view "things." Hence he was legally the owner of his children, although, of course, he still also stood to them in the ethical relation of love (though this relation must have been much weakened by the injustice of his legal position). Here, then, the two qualities "being a thing" and "not being a thing" were united, though quite wrongly.

In the sphere of abstract light, we are concerned only with the person as person, and therefore with the particular (which is indispensable if the person's freedom is to have scope and reality) only in so far as it is something separable from the person and immediately different from him, no matter whether this separability constitutes the essential nature of the particular, or whether the particular receives it only through the mediation of the subjective will. Hence in this sphere we are concerned with mental aptitudes, erudition, &c., only in so far as they are possessions in a legal sense; we have not to treat here the possession of our body and mind which we can achieve through education, study, habit, &c., and which exists as an *inward* property of mind. But it is not until we come to deal with alienation that we need begin to speak of the *transition* of such mental property into the external world where it falls under the category of property in the legal sense.

44.   A person has as his substantive end the right of putting his will into any and every thing and thereby making it his, because it has no such end in itself and derives its destiny and soul from his will. This is the absolute right of appropriation which man has over all "things." . . .

45.   To have power over a thing *ab extra* constitutes possession. The particular aspect of the matter, the fact that I make something my own as a result of my natural need, impulse, and caprice, is the particular interest satisfied by possession. But I as free will am an object to myself in what I possess and thereby also for the first time am an actual will, and this is the aspect which constitutes the category of *property,* the true and right factor in possession.

If emphasis is placed on my needs, then the possession of property appears as a means to their satisfaction, but the true position is that, from the standpoint of freedom, property is the first embodiment of freedom and so is in itself a substantive end.

46.   Since my will, as the will of a person, and so as a single will, becomes objective to me in property, property acquires the character of private property, and common property of such a nature that it may be owned by separate persons acquires the character of an inherently dissoluble partnership in which the retention of my share is explicitly a matter of my arbitrary preference. . . .

53.   Property has its modifications determined in the course of the will's relation to the thing. This relation is

(A) *taking possession* of the thing directly (here it is in the thing *qua* something positive that the will has its embodiment);

(B) *use* (the thing is negative in contrast with the will and so it is in the thing as something to be negated that the will has its embodiment);

(C) *alienation,* the reflection of the will back from the thing into itself.

54.   We take possession of a thing (α) by directly grasping it physically, (β) by forming it, and (φ) by merely marking it as ours. . . .

59.   By being taken into possession, the thing acquires the predicate "mine" and my will is related to it positively. Within this identity, the thing is equally established as something negative, and my will in this situation is a particular will, i.e. need, inclination, and so forth. Yet my need, as the particular aspect of a single will, is the positive element which finds satisfaction, and the thing, as something negative in itself, exists only for my need and is at its service.—The use of the thing is my need being externally realized through the change, destruction, and consumption of the thing. The thing thereby stands revealed as naturally self-less and so fulfils its destiny. . . .

63.   A thing in use is a single thing determined quantitatively and qualitatively and related to a specific need. But its specific utility, being quantitatively determinate, is at the same time comparable with [the specific utility of] other things of like utility. Similarly, the specific need which it satisfies is at the same time need in general and thus is comparable on its particular side with other needs, while the thing in virtue of the same considerations is comparable with things meeting other needs. This, the thing's universality, whose simple determinate character arises from the particularity of the thing, so that it is *eo ipso* abstracted from the thing's specific quality, is the thing's *value,* wherein its genuine substantiality becomes determinate and an object of consciousness. As full owner of the thing, I am *eo ipso* owner of its value as well as of its use. . . .

65.   The reason I can alienate my property is that it is mine only in so far as I put my will into it. Hence I may abandon as a *res nullius* anything that I have or yield it to the will of another and so into his possession, provided always that the thing in question is a thing external by nature.

66.   Therefore those goods, or rather substantive characteristics, which constitute my own private personality and the universal essence of my self-consciousness are inalienable and my right to them is imprescriptible. Such characteristics are my personality as such, my universal freedom of will, my ethical life, my religion. . . .

67.   Single products of my particular physical and mental skill and of my power to act I can alienate to someone else and I can give him the use of my abilities for a restricted period, because, on the strength of this restriction, my abilities acquire an external relation to the totality and universality of my being. By alienating the whole of my time, as crystallized in my work, and everything I produced, I would be making into another's property the substance of my being, my universal activity and actuality, my personality. . . .

68.   What is peculiarly mine in a product of my mind may, owing to the method whereby it is expressed, turn at once into something external like a "thing" which *eo ipso* may then be produced by other people. The result is that by taking possession of a thing of this kind, its new owner may make his own the thoughts communicated in it or the mechanical invention which it contains, and it is ability to do this which sometimes (i.e. in the case of books) constitutes the value of these things and the only purpose of possessing them. But besides this, the new owner at the same time comes into possession of the universal methods of so expressing himself and producing numerous other things of the same sort. . . .

71.   Existence as determinate being is in essence being for another. One aspect of property is that it is an existent as an external thing, and in this respect property exists for other external things and is connected with their necessity and contingency. But it is also an existent as an embodiment of the will, and from this point of view the "other" for which it exists can only be the will of another person. This relation of will to will is the true and proper ground in which freedom is existent.—The sphere of contract is made up of this mediation whereby I hold property not merely by means of a thing and my subjective will, but by means of another person's will as well and so hold it in virtue of my participation in a common will.

Reason makes it just as necessary for men to enter into contractual relationships—gift, exchange, trade, &c.—as to possess property. While all they are conscious of is that they are led to make contracts by need in general, by benevolence, advantage, &c., the fact remains that they are led to do this by reason implicit within them, i.e. by the Idea of the real existence of free personality, "real" here meaning "present in the will alone."

Contract presupposes that the parties entering it recognize each other as persons and property owners. It is a relationship at the level of mind objective, and so contains and presupposes from the start the moment of recognition.

72.   Contract brings into existence the property whose external side, its side as an existent, is no longer a mere "thing" but contains the moment of a will (and consequently the will of a second person also). Contract is the process in which there is revealed and mediated the contradiction that I am and remain the independent owner of something from which I exclude the will of another only in so far as in identifying my will with the will of another I cease to be an owner. . . .

74.   This contractual relationship, therefore, is the means whereby one identical will can persist within the absolute difference between independent property owners. It implies that each, in accordance with the common will of both, ceases to be an owner and

yet is and remains one. It is the mediation of the will to give up a property, a single property, and the will to take up another, i.e. another belonging to someone else; and this mediation takes place when the two wills are associated in an identity in the sense that one of
them comes to its decision only in the presence of the other. . . .

76.   Contract is *formal* when the double consent whereby the common will is
brought into existence is apportioned between the two contracting parties so that one of
them has the negative moment—the alienation of a thing—and the other the positive
moment—the appropriation of the thing. Such a contract is *gift*. But contract may be called
real when each of the two contracting wills is the sum of these mediating moments and
therefore in such a contract becomes a property owner and remains so. This is a contract of
exchange. . . .

142.   Ethical life is the Idea of freedom in that on the one hand it is the good
become alive—the good endowed in self-consciousness with knowing and willing and
actualized by self-conscious action—while on the other hand self-consciousness has in the
ethical realm its absolute foundation and the end which actuates its effort. Thus ethical life
is the concept of freedom developed into the existing world and the nature of self-consciousness. . . .

144.   The objective ethical order, which comes on the scene in place of good in the
abstract, is substance made concrete by subjectivity as infinite form. Hence it posits within
itself distinctions whose specific character is thereby determined by the concept, and which
endow the ethical order with a stable content independently necessary and subsistent in
exaltation above subjective opinion and caprice. These distinctions are absolutely valid
laws and institutions.

145.   It is the fact that the ethical order is the system of these specific determinations of the Idea which constitutes its rationality. Hence the ethical order is freedom or the
absolute will as what is objective, a circle of necessity whose moments are the ethical powers which regulate the life of individuals. To these powers individuals are related as accidents to substance, and it is in individuals that these powers are represented, have the shape
of appearance, and become actualized. . . .

151.   But when individuals are simply identified with the actual order, ethical life
(*das Sittliche*) appears as their general mode of conduct, i.e. as custom (*Sitte*), while the
habitual practice of ethical living appears as a second nature which, put in the place of the
initial, purely natural will, is the soul of custom permeating it through and through, the significance and the actuality of its existence. It is mind living and present as a world, and the
substance of mind thus exists now for the first time as mind.

152.   In this way the ethical substantial order has attained its right, and its right its
validity. That is to say, the self-will of the individual has vanished together with his private
conscience which had claimed independence and opposed itself to the ethical substance.
For, when his character is ethical, he recognizes as the end which moves him to act the universal which is itself unmoved but is disclosed in its specific determinations as rationality
actualized. He knows that his own dignity and the whole stability of his particular ends are
grounded in this same universal, and it is therein that he actually attains these. Subjectivity
is itself the absolute form and existent actuality of the substantial order, and the distinction
between subject on the one hand and substance on the other, as the object, end, and controlling power of the subject, is the same as, and has vanished directly along with, the distinction between them in form. . . .

153.   The right of individuals to be subjectively destined to freedom is fulfilled
when they belong to an actual ethical order, because their conviction of their freedom finds

its truth in such an objective order, and it is in an ethical order that they are actually in possession of their own essence or their own inner universality. . . .

154.   The right of individuals to their *particular* satisfaction is also contained in the ethical substantial order, since particularity is the outward appearance of the ethical order—a mode in which that order is existent.

155.   Hence in this identity of the universal will with the particular will, right and duty coalesce, and by being in the ethical order a man has rights in so far as he has duties, and duties in so far as he has rights. In the sphere of abstract right, I have the right and another has the corresponding duty. In the moral sphere, the right of my private judgment and will, as well as of my happiness, has not, but only ought to have, coalesced with duties and become objective.

156.   The ethical substance, as containing independent self-consciousness united with its concept, is the actual mind of a family and a nation.

157.   The concept of this Idea has being only as mind, as something knowing itself and actual, because it is the objectification of itself, the movement running through the form of its moments. It is therefore

(A) ethical mind in its natural or immediate phase—the *Family*. This substantiality loses its unity, passes over into division, and into the phase of relation, i.e. into

(B) *Civil Society*—an association of members as self-subsistent individuals in a universality which, because of their self-subsistence, is only abstract. Their association is brought about by their needs, by the legal system—the means to security of person and property—and by an external organization for attaining their particular and common interests. This external stage

(C) is brought back to and welded into unity in the *Constitution of the State* which is the end and actuality of both the substantial universal order and the public life devoted thereto. . . .

158.   The family, as the immediate substantiality of mind, is specifically characterized by love, which is mind's feeling of its own unity. Hence in a family, one's frame of mind is to have self-consciousness of one's individuality within this unity as the absolute essence of oneself, with the result that one is in it not as an independent person but as a member.

159.   The right which the individual enjoys on the strength of the family unity and which is in the first place simply the individual's life within this unity, takes on the *form* of right (as the abstract moment of determinate individuality) only when the family begins to dissolve. At that point those who should be family-members both in their inclination and in actuality begin to be self-subsistent persons, and whereas they formerly constituted one specific moment within the whole, they now receive their share separately and so only in an external fashion by way of money, food, educational expenses, and the like.

160.   The family is completed in these three phases:

(a) *Marriage,* the form assumed by the concept of the family in its immediate phase;

(b) *Family Property and Capital* (the external embodiment of the concept) and attention to these;

(c) *The Education of Children and the Dissolution of the Family.* . . .

181.   The family disintegrates (both essentially, through the working of the principle of personality, and also in the course of nature) into a plurality of families, each of which conducts itself as in principle a self-subsistent concrete person and therefore as externally related to its neighbours. In other words, the moments bound together in the unity of the family, since the family is the ethical Idea still in its concept, must be released

from the concept to self-subsistent objective reality. This is the stage of difference. This gives us, to use abstract language in the first place, the determination of particularity which is related to universality but in such a way that universality is its basic principle, though still only an inward principle; for that reason, the universal merely shows in the particular as its form. Hence this relation of reflection prima facie portrays the disappearance of ethical life or, since this life as the essence necessarily shows itself, this relation constitutes the world of ethical appearance—civil society. . . .

182.   The concrete person who is himself the subject of his particular aims, is, as a totality of wants and a mixture of caprice and physical necessity, one principle of civil society. But the particular person is essentially so related to other particular persons that each establishes himself and finds satisfaction by means of the others, and at the same time purely and simply by means of the form of universality, the second principle here.

183.   In the course of the actual attainment of selfish ends—an attainment conditioned in this way by universality—there is formed a system of complete interdependence, wherein the livelihood, happiness, and legal status of one man is interwoven with the livelihood, happiness, and rights of all. On this system, individual happiness, &c., depend, and only in this connected system are they actualized and secured. This system may be prima facie regarded as the external state, the state based on need, the state as the Understanding envisages it. . . .

188.   Civil society contains three moments:

(A) The mediation of need and one-man's satisfaction through his work and the satisfaction of the needs of all others—the *System of Needs*.

(B) The actuality of the universal principle of freedom therein contained—the protection of property through the *Administration of Justice*.

(C) Provision against contingencies still lurking in systems (A) and (B), and care for particular interests as a common interest, by means of the *Police* and the *Corporation*. . . .

199.   When men are thus dependent on one another and reciprocally related to one another in their work and the satisfaction of their needs, subjective self-seeking turns into a contribution to the satisfaction of the needs of everyone else. That is to say, by a dialectical advance, subjective self-seeking turns into the mediation of the particular through the universal, with the result that each man in earning, producing, and enjoying on his own account is *eo ipso* producing and earning for the enjoyment of everyone else. The compulsion which brings this about is rooted in the complex interdependence of each on all, and it now presents itself to each as the universal permanent capital which gives each the opportunity, by the exercise of his education and skill, to draw a share from it and so be assured of his livelihood, while what he thus earns by means of his work maintains and increases the general capital.

200.   A particular man's resources, or in other words his opportunity of sharing in the general resources, are conditioned, however, partly by his own unearned principal (his capital), and partly by his skill; this in turn is itself dependent not only on his capital, but also on accidental circumstances whose multiplicity introduces differences in the development of natural, bodily, and mental characteristics, which were already in themselves dissimilar. In this sphere of particularity, these differences are conspicuous in every direction and on every level, and, together with the arbitrariness and accident which this sphere contains as well, they have as their inevitable consequence disparities of individual resources and ability. . . .

201.   The infinitely complex, criss-cross, movements of reciprocal production and exchange, and the equally infinite multiplicity of means therein employed, become crystallized, owing to the universality inherent in their content, and distinguished into general groups. As a result, the entire complex is built up into particular systems of needs, means, and types of work relative to these needs, modes of satisfaction and of theoretical and practical education, i.e. into systems, to one or other of which individuals are assigned—in other words, into class-divisions. . . .

208.   As the private particularity of knowing and willing, the principle of this system of needs contains absolute universality, the universality of freedom, only abstractly and therefore as the right of property. At this point, however, this right is no longer merely implicit but has attained its recognized actuality as the protection of property through the administration of justice.

209.   The relatedness arising from the reciprocal bearing on one another of needs and work to satisfy these is first of all reflected into itself as infinite personality, as abstract right. But it is this very sphere of relatedness—a sphere of education—which gives abstract right the determinate existence of being something universally recognized, known, and willed, and having a validity and an objective actuality mediated by this known and willed character.

It is part of education, of thinking as the consciousness of the single in the form of universality, that the ego comes to be apprehended as a universal person in which all are identical. A man counts as a man in virtue of his manhood alone, not because he is a Jew, Catholic, Protestant, German, Italian, &c. This is an assertion which thinking ratifies and to be conscious of it is of infinite importance. It is defective only when it is crystallized, e.g. as a cosmopolitanism in opposition to the concrete life of the state.

210.   The objective actuality of the right consists, first, in its existence for consciousness, in its being known in some way or other; secondly, in its possessing the power which the actual possesses, in its being valid, and so also in its becoming known as universally valid. . . .

211.   The principle of rightness becomes the law (*Gesetz*) when, in its objective existence, it is posited (*gesetzt*), i.e. when thinking makes it determinate for consciousness and makes it known as what is right and valid; and in acquiring this determinate character, the right becomes positive law in general. . . .

In becoming law, what is right acquires for the first time not only the form proper to its universality, but also its true determinacy. Hence making a law is not to be represented as merely the expression of a rule of behaviour valid for everyone, though that is one moment in legislation; the more important moment, the inner essence of the matter, is knowledge of the content of the law in its determinate universality.

Since it is only animals which have their law as instinct, while it is man alone who has law as custom, even systems of customary law contain the moment of being thoughts and being known. Their difference from positive law consists solely in this, that they are known only in a subjective and accidental way, with the result that in themselves they are less determinate and the universality of thought is less clear in them. (And apart from this, knowledge of a system of law either in general or in its details, is the accidental possession of a few.) The supposition that it is customary law, on the strength of its character as custom, which possesses the privilege of having become part of life is a delusion, since the valid laws of a nation do not cease to be its customs by being written and codified—and besides, it is as a rule precisely those versed in the deadest of topics and the deadest of thoughts who talk nowadays of "life" and of "becoming part of life." When a nation begins to acquire even a little culture, its customary law must soon come to be collected and put together. Such a collection is a legal code, but one which, as a mere collection, is markedly formless, indeterminate, and fragmentary. The main difference between it and a code properly so-called is that in the latter the principles of jurisprudence in their universality, and so in their determinacy, have been apprehended in terms of thought and expressed. English national law or municipal law is contained, as is well known, in statutes (written laws) and in so-called "unwritten" laws. This unwritten law, however, is as good as written, and knowledge of it may, and indeed must, be acquired simply by reading the numerous quartos which it fills. The monstrous confusion, however, which prevails both in English law and its administration is graphically portrayed by those acquainted with the matter. In particular, they comment on the fact that, since this unwritten law is contained in court verdicts and judgements, the judges are continually legislators. The authority of precedent is binding on them, since their predecessors have done nothing but give expression to the unwritten law; and yet they are just as much exempt from its authority, because they are themselves repositories of the unwritten law and so have the right to criticize previous judgements and pronounce whether they accorded with the unwritten law or not. . . .

No greater insult could be offered to a civilized people or to its lawyers than to deny them ability to codify their law; for such ability cannot be that of constructing a legal system with a novel content, but only that of apprehending, i.e. grasping in thought, the content of existing laws in its determinate universality and then applying them to particular cases. . . .

219.   By taking the form of law, right steps into a determinate mode of being. It is then something on its own account, and in contrast with particular willing and opining of the right, it is self-subsistent and has to vindicate itself as something universal. This is achieved by recognizing it and making it actual in a particular case without the subjective feeling of private interest; and this is the business of a public authority—the court of justice.

John Stuart Mill, "Social Justice and Utility," from *Utilitarianism* (1861)

John Stuart Mill (1806–1873) was aware that one of the strongest objections to his theory of utilitarianism—the view that right actions (dispositions, policies, institutions) are those that produce the greatest amount of happiness overall—was the charge that the principle of utility took no account of rights and justice. Hume, of course, had argued a full century before that the sole justification for justice was public utility, and Adam Smith had offered a similar argument after him, but the point was not yet convincing. (Nor is it still, considering the repetition of many of the same charges by such philosophers as John Rawls.) Mill begins by shifting the burden, questioning whether the ideal of justice would make any sense or have any appeal at all if it were not also expedient, and much of Mill's argument (following a much more belligerent argument of a similar sort by Jeremy Bentham many years earlier) consists in undermining the appearance of justice as a clear and immediately intelligible ideal. He runs through the notion of rights, in particular, and distinguishes legal and moral rights and the idea of desert. He briefly discusses punishment and makes the point (wholly consistent with his own utilitarian insistence on equality) that justice requires impartiality. He then discusses equality as such, pointing out that "so many diverse applications" of the term "justice" ought surely to be an "embarrassment." Mill tries to soothe this embarrassment by pointing out the etymology of the word, meaning law in various languages, and concluding that what the word really expresses, in all its various usages, is the recognition that some things ought and some things ought not to be done, coupled with the desire that there should be some enforcement or sanction for the latter, whether by actual law or not. The result of this argument is to make the point that justice is not a particular ideal that can therefore be contrasted with utility, but rather a very general moral concern that can be easily reconciled (if not identified) with social utility.

So, too, Mill considers rights as independent ideals embodied in persons and argues that a right should rather be considered as a claim that a person can legitimately make on society. Why should society acknowledge or defend my rights? Mill's answer, predictably, is for the reason of general utility. The opposition to this answer, Mill argues, results only from a natural thirst for retaliation or revenge, an appetite that cannot be squared with a desire for the security and well-being of all. Needless to say, Mill has virtually the whole of modern thought on his side here as well as the particular history of utilitarianism, which began (in part) as an attack on the barbarity of the penal system and an insistence on effective deterrence rather than retribution and revenge. But clearly the sort of insistence that goes into the juxtaposition of justice and utility does not turn on the much more limited notion of retribution alone. And whether the long-term effects of justice are indeed conducive to general utility (a claim far more often asserted with a few loose and intuitive examples rather than rigorously argued), it is clear that particular acts of *injustice*, especially if undetected, may substantially improve public utility while particular acts of justice may well not.

In all ages of speculation one of the strongest obstacles to the reception of the doctrine that utility or happiness is the criterion of right and wrong has been drawn from the idea of justice. The powerful sentiment and apparently clear perception which that word recalls with a rapidity and certainty resembling an instinct have seemed to the majority of thinkers to point to an inherent quality in things; to show that the just must have an existence in nature as something absolute, generically distinct from every variety of the expedient and, in idea, opposed to it, though (as is commonly acknowledged) never, in the long run, disjoined from it in fact.

In the case of this, as of our other moral sentiments, there is no necessary connection between the question of its origin and that of its binding force. That a feeling is bestowed on us by nature does not necessarily legitimate all its promptings. The feeling of justice might be a peculiar instinct, and might yet require, like our other instincts, to be controlled and enlightened by a higher reason. If we have intellectual instincts leading us to act in a particular way, as well as animal instincts that prompt us to act in a particular way, there is no necessity that the former should be more infallible in their sphere than the latter in theirs; it may as well happen that wrong judgments are occasionally suggested by those, as wrong actions by these. But though it is one thing to believe that we have natural feelings of justice, and another to acknowledge them as an ultimate criterion of conduct, these two opinions are very closely connected in point of fact. Mankind are always predisposed to believe that any subjective feeling, not otherwise accounted for, is a revelation of some objective reality. Our present object is to determine whether the reality to which the feeling of justice corresponds is one which needs any such special revelation, whether the justice or injustice of an action is a thing intrinsically peculiar and distinct from all its other qualities or only a combination of certain of those qualities presented under a peculiar aspect. For the purpose of this inquiry it is practically important to consider whether the feeling itself, of justice and injustice, is *sui generis* like our sensations of color and taste or a derivative feeling formed by a combination of others. And this it is the more essential to examine, as people are in general willing enough to allow that objectively the dictates of justice coincide with a part of the field of general expediency; but inasmuch as the subjective mental feeling of justice is different from that which commonly attaches to simple expediency, and, except in the extreme cases of the latter, is far more imperative in its demands, people find it difficult to see in justice only a particular kind or branch of general utility, and think that its superior binding force requires a totally different origin.

To throw light upon this question, it is necessary to attempt to ascertain what is the distinguishing character of justice, or of injustice; what is the quality, or whether there is any quality, attributed in common to all modes of conduct designated as unjust (for justice, like many other moral attributes, is best defined by its opposite), and distinguishing them from such modes of conduct as are disapproved, but without having that particular epithet of disapprobation applied to them. If in everything which men are accustomed to characterize as just or unjust some one common attribute or collection of attributes is always present, we may judge whether this particular attribute or combination of attributes would be capable of gathering round it a sentiment of that peculiar character and intensity of virtue of the general laws of our emotional constitution, or whether the sentiment is inexplicable and requires to be regarded as a special provision of nature. If we find the former to be the case, we shall, in resolving this question, have resolved also the main problem; if the latter, we shall have to seek for some other mode of investigating it:

To find the common attributes of a variety of objects, it is necessary to begin by surveying the objects themselves in the concrete. Let us therefore advert successively to the various modes of action and arrangements of human affairs which are classed, by universal or widely spread opinion, as just or as unjust. The things well known to excite the sentiments associated with those names are of a very multifarious character. I shall pass them rapidly in review, without studying any particular arrangement.

In the first place, it is mostly considered unjust to deprive anyone of his personal liberty, his property, or any other thing which belongs to him by law. Here, therefore, is one instance of the application of the terms "just" and "unjust" in a perfectly definite sense, namely, that it is just to respect, unjust to violate, the *legal rights* of anyone. But this judgment admits of several exceptions, arising from the other forms in which the notions of justice and injustice present themselves. For example, the person who suffers the deprivation may (as the phrase is) have *forfeited* the rights which he is so deprived of—a case to which we shall return presently. But also—

Secondly, the legal rights of which he is deprived may be rights which *ought* not to have belonged to him; in other words, the law which confers on him these rights may be a bad law. When it is so or when (which is the same thing for our purpose) it is supposed to be so, opinions will differ as to the justice or injustice of infringing it. Some maintain that no law, however bad, ought to be disobeyed by an individual citizen; that his opposition to it, if shown at all, should only be shown in endeavoring to get it altered by competent authority. This opinion (which condemns many of the most illustrious benefactors of mankind, and would often protect pernicious institutions against the only weapons which, in the state of things existing at the time, have any chance of succeeding against them) is defended by those who hold it on grounds of expediency, principally on that of the importance to the common interest of mankind, of maintaining inviolate the sentiment of submission to law. Other persons, again, hold the directly contrary opinion that any law, judged to be bad, may blamelessly be disobeyed, even though it be not judged to be unjust but only expedient, while others would confine the license of disobedience to the case of unjust laws; but, again, some say that all laws which are inexpedient are unjust, since every law imposes some restriction on the natural liberty of mankind, which restriction is an injustice unless legitimated by tending to their good. Among these diversities of opinion it seems to be universally admitted that there may be unjust laws, and that law, consequently, is not the ultimate criterion of justice, but may give to one person a benefit, or impose on another an evil, which justice condemns. When, however, a law is thought to be unjust, it seems always to be regarded as being so in the same way in which a breach of law is unjust, namely, by infringing somebody's right, which, as it cannot in this case be a legal right, receives a different appellation and is called a moral right. We may say, therefore, that a second case of injustice consists in taking or withholding from any person that to which he has a *moral right.*

Thirdly, it is universally considered just that each person should obtain that (whether good or evil) which he *deserves,* and unjust that he should obtain a good or be made to undergo an evil which he does not deserve. This is, perhaps, the clearest and most emphatic form in which the idea of justice is conceived by the general mind. As it involves the notion of desert, the question arises what constitutes desert? Speaking in a general way, a person is understood to deserve good if he does right, evil if he does wrong; and in a more particular sense, to deserve good from those to whom he does or has done good, and evil from those to whom he does or has done evil. The precept of returning good for evil has never been regarded as a case of the fulfillment of justice, but as one in which the claims of justice are waived, in obedience to other considerations.

Fourthly, it is confessedly unjust to *break* faith with anyone: to violate an engagement, either express or implied, or disappoint expectations raised by our own conduct, at least if we have raised those expectations knowingly and voluntarily. Like the other obligations of justice already spoken of, this one is not regarded as absolute, but as capable of being overruled by a stronger obligation of justice on the other side, or by such conduct on the part of the person concerned as is deemed to absolve us from our obligation to him and to constitute a *forfeiture* of the benefit which he has been led to expect.

Fifthly, it is, by universal admission, inconsistent with justice to be *partial*—to show favor or preference to one person over another in matters to which favor and preference do not properly apply. Impartiality, however, does not seem to be regarded as a duty in itself, but rather as instrumental to some other duty; for it is admitted that favor and preference are not always censurable, and, indeed, the cases in which they are condemned are rather the exception than the rule. A person would be more likely to be blamed than applauded for giving his family or friends no superiority in good offices over strangers when he could do so without violating any other duty; and no one thinks it unjust to seek one person in preference to to another as a friend, connection, or companion. Impartiality where rights are concerned is of course obligatory, but this is involved in the more general obligation of giving to everyone his right. A tribunal, for example, must be impartial because it is bound to award, without regard to any other consideration, a disputed object to the one of two parties who has the right to it. There are other cases in which impartiality means being solely influenced by desert, as with those who, in the capacity of judges, preceptors, or parents, administer reward and punishment as such. There are cases, again, in which it means being solely influenced by consideration for the public interest, as in making a selection among candidates for a government employment. Impartiality, in short, as an obligation of justice, may be said to mean being exclusively influenced by the considerations which it is supposed ought to influence the particular case in hand, and resisting solicitation of any motives which prompt to conduct different from what those considerations would dictate.

Nearly allied to the idea of impartiality is that of *equality,* which often enters as a component part both into the conception of justice and into the practice of it, and, in the eyes of many persons, constitutes its essence. But in this, still more than in any other case, the notion of justice varies in different persons, and always conforms in its variations to their notion of utility. Each person maintains that equality is the dictate of justice, except where he thinks that expediency requires inequality. The justice of giving equal protection to the rights of all is maintained by those who support the most outrageous inequality in the rights themselves. Even in slave countries it is theoretically admitted that the rights of the slave, such as they are, ought to be as sacred as those of the master, and that a tribunal which fails to enforce them with equal strictness is wanting in justice; while, at the same time, institutions which leave to the slave scarcely any rights to enforce are not deemed unjust because they are not deemed inexpedient. Those who think that utility requires distinctions of rank do not consider it unjust that riches and social privileges should be unequally dispensed; but those who think this inequality inexpedient think it unjust also. Whoever thinks that government is necessary sees no injustice in as much inequality as is constituted by giving to the magistrate powers not granted to other people. Even among those who hold leveling doctrines, there are differences of opinion about expediency. Some communists consider it unjust that the produce of labor of the community should be shared on any other principle than that of exact equality; others think it just that those should receive most whose wants are greatest; while others hold that those who work harder, or who produce more, or whose services are more valuable to the community, may justly claim a larger quota in the division of the produce. And the sense of natural justice may be plausibly appealed to in behalf of every one of these opinions.

Among so many diverse applications of the term "justice," which yet is not regarded as ambiguous, it is a matter of some difficulty to seize the mental link which holds them together, and on which the moral sentiment adhering to the term essentially depends. Perhaps, in this embarrassment, some help may be derived from the history of the word, as indicated by its etymology.

In most if not in all languages, the etymology of the word which corresponds to "just" points distinctly to an origin connected with the ordinances of law. *Justum* is a form of *jussum*, that which has been ordered. *Dikaion* comes directly from *dike*, a suit at law. *Recht*, from which came *right* and *righteous*, is synonymous with law. The courts of justice, the administration of justice, are the courts and the administration of law. *La justice*, in French, is the established term for judicature. I am not committing the fallacy, imputed with some show of truth to Horne Tooke, of assuming that a word must still continue to mean what it originally meant. Etymology is slight evidence of what the idea now signified is, but the very best evidence of how it sprang up. There can, I think, be no doubt that the *idée mère*, the primitive element, in the formation of the notion of justice was conformity to law. It constituted the entire idea among the Hebrews, up to the birth of Christianity; as might be expected in the case of a people whose laws attempted to embrace all subjects on which precepts were required, and who believed those laws to be a direct emanation from the Supreme Being. But other nations, and in particular the Greeks and Romans, who knew that their laws had been made originally, and still continued to be made, by men, were not afraid to admit that those men might make bad laws; might do, by law, the same things, and from the same motives, which if done by individuals without the sanction of law would be called unjust. And hence the sentiment of injustice came to be attached, not to all violations of law, but only to violations of such laws as *ought* to exist, including such as ought to exist but do not, and to laws themselves if supposed to be contrary to what ought to be law. In this manner the idea of law and of its injunctions was still predominant in the notion of justice, even when the laws actually in force ceased to be accepted as the standard of it.

It is true that mankind consider the idea of justice and its obligations as applicable to many things which neither are, nor is it desired that they should be, regulated by law. Nobody desires that laws should interfere with the whole detail of private life; yet everyone allows that in all daily conduct a person may and does show himself to be either just or unjust. But even here, the idea of the breach of what ought to be law still lingers in a modified shape. It would always give us pleasure, and chime in with our feelings of fitness, that acts which we deem unjust should be punished, though we do not always think it expedient that this should be done by the tribunals. We forego that gratification on account of incidental inconveniences. We should be glad to see just conduct enforced and injustice repressed, even in the minutest details, if we were not, with reason, afraid of trusting the magistrate with so unlimited an amount of power over individuals. When we think that a person is bound in justice to do a thing, it is an ordinary form of language to say that he ought to be compelled to do it. We should be gratified to see the obligation enforced by anybody who had the power. If we see that its enforcement by law would be inexpedient, we lament the impossibility, we consider the impunity given to injustice as an evil, and strive to make amends for it by bringing a strong expression of our own and the public disapprobation to bear upon the offender. Thus the idea of legal constraint is still the generating idea of the notion of justice, though undergoing several transformations before that notion as it exists in an advanced state of society becomes complete. . . .

I have, throughout, treated the idea of a *right* residing in the injured person and violated by the injury, not as a separate element in the composition of the idea and sentiment, but as one of the forms in which the other two elements clothe themselves. These elements are a hurt to some assignable person or persons, on the one hand, and a demand for punishment, on the other. An examination of our own minds, I think, will show that these two things include all that we mean when we speak of violation of a right. When we call anything a person's right, we mean that he has a valid claim on society to protect him in the possession of it, either by the force of law or by that of education and opinion. If he has what we consider a sufficient claim, on whatever account, to have something guaranteed to him by society, we say that he has a right to it. If we desire to prove that anything does not belong to him by right, we think this done as soon as it is admitted that society ought not to take measures for securing it to him, but should leave him to chance or to his own exertions. Thus a person is said to have a right to what he can earn in fair professional competition, because society ought not to allow any other person to hinder him from endeavoring to earn in that manner as much as he can. But he has not a right to three hundred a year, though he may happen to be earning it; because society is not called on to provide that he shall earn that sum. On the contrary, if he owns ten thousand pounds three-per-cent stock, he *has* a right to three hundred a year because society has come under an obligation to provide him with an income of that amount.

To have a right, then, is, I conceive, to have something which society ought to defend me in the possession of. If the objector goes on to ask why it ought, I can give him no other reason than general utility. If that expression does not seem to convey a sufficient feeling of the strength of the obligation, nor to account for the peculiar energy of the feeling, it is because there goes to the composition of the sentiment, not a rational only but also an animal element—the thirst for retaliation; and this thirst derives its intensity, as well as its moral justification, from the extraordinarily important and impressive kind of utility which is concerned. The interest involved is that of security, to everyone's feelings the most vital of all interests. All other earthly benefits are needed by one person, not needed by another; and many of them can, if necessary, be cheerfully foregone or replaced by something else; but security no human being can possibly do without; on it we depend for all our immunity from evil and for the whole value of all and every good, beyond the passing moment, since nothing but the gratification of the instant could be of any worth to us if we could be deprived of everything the next instant by whoever was momentarily stronger than ourselves. Now this most indispensable of all necessaries, after physical nutriment, cannot be had unless the machinery for providing it is kept unintermittedly in active play. Our notion, therefore, of the claim we have on our fellow creatures to join in making safe for us the very groundwork of our existence gathers feelings around it so much more intense than those concerned in any of the more common cases of utility that the difference in degree (as is often the case in psychology) becomes a real difference in kind. The claim assumes that character of absoluteness, that apparent infinity and incommensurability with all other considerations which constitute the distinction between the feeling of right and wrong and that of ordinary expediency and inexpediency. The feelings concerned are so powerful, and we count so positively on finding a responsive feeling in others (all being alike interested) that *ought* and *should* grow into *must*, and recognized indispensability becomes a moral necessity, analogous to physical, and often not inferior to it in binding force.

If the preceding analysis, or something resembling it, be not the correct account of the notion of justice—if justice be totally independent of utility, and be a standard per se, which the mind can recognize by simple introspection of itself—it is hard to understand why that internal oracle is so ambiguous, and why so many things appear either just or unjust, according to the light in which they are regarded. . . .

Most of the maxims of justice current in the world, and commonly appealed to in its transactions, are simply instrumental to carrying into effect the principles of justice which we have now spoken of. That a person is only responsible for what he has done voluntarily, or could voluntarily have avoided, that it is unjust to condemn any person unheard; that the punishment ought to be proportioned to the offense, and the like, are maxims intended to prevent the just principle of evil for evil from being perverted to the infliction of evil without that justification. The greater part of these common maxims have come into use from the practice of courts of justice, which have been naturally led to a more complete recognition and elaboration than was likely to suggest itself to others, of the rules necessary to enable them to fulfill their double function—of inflicting punishment when due, and of awarding to each person his right.

That first of judicial virtues, impartiality, is an obligation of justice, partly for the reason last mentioned, as being a necessary condition of the fulfillment of other obligations of justice. But this is not the only source of the exalted rank, among human obligations, of those maxims of equality and impartiality, which, both in popular estimation and in that of the most enlightened, are included among the precepts of justice. In one point of view, they may be considered as corollaries from the principles already laid down. If it is a duty to do to each according to his deserts, returning good for good, as well as repressing evil by evil, it necessarily follows that we should treat all equally well (when no higher duty forbids) who have deserved equally well of *us*, and that society should treat all equally well who have deserved equally well of *it*, that is, who have deserved equally well absolutely. This is the highest abstract standard of social and distributive justice, toward which all institutions and the efforts of all virtuous citizens should be made in the utmost possible degree to converge. But this great moral duty rests upon a still deeper foundation, being a direct emanation from the first principle of morals, and not a mere logical corollary from secondary or derivative doctrines. It is involved in the very meaning of utility, or the greatest happiness principle. That principle is a mere form of words without rational signification unless one person's happiness, supposed equal in degree (with the proper allowance made for kind), is counted for exactly as much as another's. Those conditions being supplied, Bentham's dictum, "everybody to count for one, nobody for more than one," might be written under the principle of utility as an explanatory commentary. The equal claim of everybody to happiness, in the estimation of the moralist and of the legislator, involves an equal claim to all the means of happiness except in so far as the inevitable conditions of human life and the general interest in which that of every individual is included set limits to the maxim; and those limits ought to be strictly construed. As every other maxim of justice, so this is by no means applied or held applicable universally; on the contrary, as I have already remarked, it bends to every person's ideas of social expediency. But in whatever case it is seemed applicable at all, it is held to be the dictate of justice. All persons are deemed to have a *right* to equality of treatment, except when some recognized social expediency requires the reverse. And hence all social inequalities which have ceased to be considered expedient assume the character, not of simple inexpediency, but of injustice, and appear so tyrannical that people are apt to wonder how they ever could have been tolerated—forgetful that they themselves, perhaps, tolerate other inequalities under an equally mistaken notion of expediency, the correction of which would make that which they approve seem quite as monstrous as what they have at last learned to condemn. The entire history of social improvement has been a series of transitions by which one custom or institution after another, from being a supposed primary necessity of social existence, has passed into the rank of a universally stigmatized injustice and tyranny. So it has been with the distinctions of slaves and freemen, nobles and serfs, patricians and plebeians; and so it will be, and in part already is, with the aristocracies of color, race, and sex.

It appears from what has been said that justice is a name for certain moral requirements which, regarded collectively, stand higher in the scale of social utility, and are therefore of more paramount obligation, than any others, though particular cases may occur in which some other social duty is so important as to overrule any one of the general maxims of justice. Thus, to save a life, it may not only be allowable, but a duty, to steal or take by force the necessary food or medicine, or to kidnap and compel to officiate the only qualified medical practitioner. In such cases, as we do not call anything justice which is not a virtue, we usually say, not that justice must give way to some other moral principle, but that what is just in ordinary cases is, by reason of that principle, not just in the particular case. By this useful accommodation of language, the character of indefeasibility attributed to justice is kept up, and we are saved from the necessity of maintaining that there can be laudable injustice.

Friedrich Engels, "Against Arm-Chair Justice," from *Anti-Dühring* (1878), and Karl Marx, "From Each According to His Ability, To Each According to His Needs," from *A Critique of the Gotha Programme* (1875)

Friedrich Engels (1820–1895) met Karl Marx (1818–1883) in the 1840s, when the latter was in virtual exile from his German homeland. The two became lifelong friends. Engels was the well-to-do son of a Manchester industrialist, but he spent much of his life formulating and defending the principles of communism and attacks on capitalism, and he supported his financially much worse off colleague for much of his life.

It may seem remarkable that, in the voluminous collected works of Marx and Engels—two philosophers who would have seemed more than any others to be obsessed with questions of justice—they virtually never discussed the question of justice as such. The short excerpt from Engels's polemic *Anti-Dühring* gives us an

From *Anti-Dühring*, from *Karl Marx–Frederick Engels*, Vol. 25. Reprinted by the permission of International Publishers, and *Critique of the Gotha Programme*, ed. C.P. Durr. Reprinted by the permission of International Publishers.

important clue why. They considered the concepts of "justice" and "injustice" to be but abstract philosophical ideals, useless for the purpose of actually changing the world and making it more just. Moreover, one can easily surmise that these two radical thinkers suspected that the terms *justice* and *injustice* had been thoroughly co-opted by the very system they opposed. A vocabulary that had been so taken over by discussions of "merit" and "rights" would have no place in the new philosophy—the basis of which is offered by Marx in the second selection—of "from each according to his abilities, to each according to his needs."

Against Arm-Chair Justice

If for the impending overthrow of the present mode of distribution of the products of labour, with its crying contrasts of want and luxury, starvation and surfeit, we had no better guarantee than the consciousness that this mode of distribution is unjust, and that justice must eventually triumph, we should be in a pretty bad way, and we might have a long time to wait. The mystics of the Middle Ages who dreamed of the coming millennium were already conscious of the injustice of class antagonisms. On the threshold of modern history, three hundred and fifty years ago, Thomas Münzer proclaimed it to the world. In the English and the French bourgeois revolutions the same call resounded—and died away. And if today the same call for the abolition of class antagonisms and class distinctions, which up to 1830 had left the working and suffering classes cold, if today this call is re-echoed a millionfold, if it takes hold of one country after another in the same order and in the same degree of intensity that modern industry develops in each country, if in one generation it has gained a strength that enables it to defy all the forces combined against it and to be confident of victory in the near future—what is the reason for this? The reason is that modern large-scale industry has called into being on the one hand a proletariat, a class which for the first time in history can demand the abolition, not of this or that particular class organisation, or of this or that particular class privilege, but of classes themselves, and which is in such a position that it must carry through this demand on pain of sinking to the level of the Chinese coolie. On the other hand this same large-scale industry has brought into being, in the bourgeoisie, a class which has the monopoly of all the instruments of production and means of subsistence, but which in each speculative boom period and in each crash that follows it proves that it has become incapable of any longer controlling the productive forces, which have grown beyond its power; a class under whose leadership society is racing to ruin like a locomotive whose jammed safety-valve the driver is too weak to open. In other words, the reason is that both the productive forces created by the modern capitalist mode of production and the system of distribution of goods established by it have come into crying contradiction with that mode of production itself, and in fact to such a degree that, if the whole of modern society is not to perish, a revolution in the mode of production and distribution must take place, a revolution which will put an end to all class distinctions. On this tangible, material fact, which is impressing itself in a more or less clear form, but with insuperable necessity, on the minds of the exploited proletarians—on this fact, and not on the conceptions of justice and injustice held by any armchair philosopher, is modern socialism's confidence in victory founded.

From Each According to His Ability, to Each According to His Needs

1. Labour is the source of all wealth and all culture *and since* useful labour is only possible in society and through society, the proceeds of labour belong undiminished with equal right to all members of society.

First Part of the Paragraph: "Labour is the source of all wealth and all culture."

Labour is *not the source* of all wealth. *Nature* is just as much the source of use values (and it is surely of such that material wealth consists!) as is labour, which itself is only the manifestation of a natural force, human labour power. That phrase is to be found in all children's primers and is correct in so far as it is *implied* that labour proceeds with the appropriate subjects and instruments. But a socialist programme cannot allow such bourgeois phrases to cause the *conditions* to be ignored that alone give them meaning. And in so far as man from the beginning behaves towards nature, the primary source of all instruments and subjects of labour, as her owner, treats her as belonging to him, his labour becomes the source of use values, therefore also of wealth. The bourgeois have very good grounds for fancifully ascribing *supernatural creative power* to labour, since it follows precisely from the fact that labour depends on nature, that the man who possesses no other property than his labour power must, in all conditions of society and culture, be the slave of other men who have made themselves the owners of the material conditions of labour. He can only work with their permission, and hence only live with their permission.

Let us now leave the sentence as it stands, or rather limps. What would one have expected as conclusion? Obviously this:

> Since labour is the source of all wealth, in society also no one can appropriate wealth except as the product of labour. Therefore, if he himself does not work, he lives by the labour of others and also acquires his culture at the expense of the labour of others.

Instead of this, by means of the words "*and since*" a second proposition is added in order to draw a conclusion from this and not from the first one.

Second Part of the Paragraph: "Useful labour is only possible in society and through society."

According to the first proposition, labour was the source of all wealth and all culture, therefore also no society is possible without labour. Now we learn, conversely, that no "useful" labour is possible without society.

One could just as well have said that only in society can useless and even generally harmful labour become a branch of gainful occupation, that only in society can one live by being idle, etc., etc.;—in short one could just as well have copied the whole of Rousseau.

And what is "useful" labour? Surely only labour which produces the intended useful effect. A savage—and man was a savage after he had ceased to be an ape—who has killed an animal with a stone, who collects fruits, etc., performs "useful" labour.

Thirdly: The Conclusion: "And since useful labour is only possible in society and through society—the proceeds of labour belong undiminished with equal right to all members of society."

A fine conclusion! If useful labour is only possible in society and through society, the proceeds of labour belong to society—and only so much therefrom accrues to the individual worker as is not required to maintain the "condition" of labour, society.

In fact, also, this proposition has at all times been made use of by the champions of the *prevailing state of society.* First come the claims of the government and everything connected with it, since it is the social organ for the maintenance of the social order; then come the claims of the various kinds of private property, for the various kinds of private property are the foundations of society, etc. One sees that such hollow phrases can be twisted and turned as desired.

The first and second parts of the paragraph have some intelligible connection only in the following wording: "Labour only becomes the source of wealth and culture as social labour," or, what is the same thing, "in and through society."

This proposition is incontestably correct, for although isolated labour (its material conditions presupposed) can also create use values, it can create neither wealth nor culture.

But equally incontestable is this other proposition: "In proportion as labour develops socially, and becomes thereby a source of wealth and culture, poverty and neglect develop among the workers, and wealth and culture among the non-workers."

This is the law of all history hitherto. What, therefore, had to be done here, instead of making general phrases about "labour" and "society," was to prove concretely how in present capitalist society the material, etc., conditions have at last been created which will enable and compel the workers to lift this social curse.

In fact, however, the whole paragraph, incorrect in style and content, is only there in order to inscribe the Lassallean catch-word of the "undiminished proceeds of labour" as a slogan at the top of the party banner. I shall return to the "proceeds of labour," "equal right," etc., later on, since the same thing recurs in a somewhat different form.

> 2. In present-day society, the instruments of labour are the monopoly of the capitalist class; the resulting dependence of the working class is the cause of misery and servitude in all its forms.

This sentence, borrowed from the Statutes of the International, is incorrect in this "improved" edition.

In present-day society the instruments of labour are the monopoly of the landowners (the monopoly of property in land is even the basis of the monopoly of capital) *and* the capitalists. In the passage in question, the Statutes of the International do not mention by name either the one or the other class of monopolists. They speak of the "*monopoly of the means of labour, that is the sources of life.*" The addition, "*sources of life*" makes it sufficiently clear that land is included in the instruments of labour.

The correction was introduced because Lassalle, for reasons now generally known, attacked *only* the capitalist class and not the landowners. In England, the capitalist is usually not even the owner of the land on which his factory stands.

> 3. The emancipation of labour demands the promotion of the instruments of labour to the common property of society, and the co-operative regulation of the total labour with equitable distribution of the proceeds of labour.

"Promotion of the instruments of labour to the common property" ought obviously to read, their "conversion into the common property," but this only in passing.

What are the "proceeds of labour"? The product of labour or its value? And in the latter case, is it the total value of the product or only that part of the value which labour has newly added to the value of the means of production consumed?

The "proceeds of labour" is a loose notion which Lassalle has put in the place of definite economic conceptions.

What is "equitable distribution"?

Do not the bourgeois assert that the present-day distribution is "equitable"? And is it not, in fact, the only "equitable" distribution on the basis of the present-day mode of pro-duction? Are economic relations regulated by legal conceptions or do not, on the contrary, legal relations arise from economic ones? Have not also the socialist sectarians the most varied notions about "equitable" distribution?

To understand what idea is meant in this connection by the phrase "equitable distri-bution," we must take the first paragraph and this one together. The latter implies a society wherein "the instruments of labour are common property, and the total labour is co-opera-tively regulated," and from the first paragraph we learn that "the proceeds of labour belong undiminished with equal right to all members of society."

"To all members of society"? To those who do not work as well? What remains then of the "undiminished proceeds of labour"? Only to those members of society who work? What remains then of the "equal right" of all members of society?

But "all members of society" and "equal right" are obviously mere phrases. The ker-nel consists in this, that in this communist society every worker must receive the "undi-minished" Lassallean "proceeds of labour."

Let us take first of all the words "proceeds of labour" in the sense of the product of labour, then the co-operative proceeds of labour are the *total social product.*

From this is then to be deducted:

First, cover for replacement of the means of production used up.

Secondly, additional portion for expansion of production.

Thirdly, reserve or insurance fund to provide against mis-adventures, disturbances through natural events, etc.

These deductions from the "undiminished proceeds of labour" are an economic neces-sity and their magnitude is to be determined by available means and forces, and partly by calculation of probabilities, but they are in no way calculable by equity.

There remains the other part of the total product, destined to serve as means of con-sumption.

Before this is divided among the individuals, there has to be deducted from it:

First, the general costs of administration not belonging to production.

This part will, from the outset, be very considerably restricted in comparison with present-day society and it diminishes in proportion as the new society develops.

Secondly, that which is destined for the communal satisfaction of needs, such as schools, health services, etc.

From the outset this part is considerably increased in comparison with present-day society and it increases in proportion as the new society develops.

Thirdly, funds for those unable to work, etc., in short, what is included under so-called official poor relief today.

Only now do we come to the "distribution" which the programme, under Lassallean influence, alone has in view in its narrow fashion, namely that part of the means of con-sumption which is divided among the individual producers of the co-operative society.

The "undiminished proceeds of labour" have already quietly become converted into the "diminished" proceeds, although what the producer is deprived of in his capacity as a private individual benefits him directly or indirectly in his capacity as a member of society.

Just as the phrase "undiminished proceeds of labour" has disappeared, so now does the phrase "proceeds of labour" disappear altogether.

Within the co-operative society based on common ownership of the means of produc-tion, the producers do not exchange their products; just as little does the labour employed on the products appear here *as the value* of these products, as a material quality possessed by them, since now, in contrast to capitalist society, individual labour no longer exists in an indirect fashion but directly as a component part of the total labour. The phrase "proceeds of labour," objectionable even today on account of its ambiguity, thus loses all meaning.

What we have to deal with here is a communist society, not as it has *developed* on its own foundations, but, on the contrary, as it *emerges* from capitalist society; which is thus in every respect, economically, morally and intellectually, still stamped with the birth-marks of the old society from whose womb it emerges. Accordingly the individual producer receives back from society—after the deductions have been made—exactly what he gives to it. What he has given to it is his individual amount of labour. For example, the social working day consists of the sum of the individual labour hours; the individual labour time of the individual producer is the part of the social labour day contributed by him, his share in it. He receives a certificate from society that he has furnished such and such an amount of labour (after deducting his labour for the common fund), and with this certificate he draws from the social stock of means of consumption as much as the same amount of labour costs. The same amount of labour which he has given to society in one form, he receives back in another.

Here obviously the same principle prevails as that which regulates the exchange of commodities, as far as this is exchange of equal values. Content and form are changed, because under the altered circumstances no one can give anything except his labour, and because, on the other hand, nothing can pass into the ownership of individuals except individual means of consumption. But, as far as the distribution of the latter among the individual producers is concerned, the same principle prevails as in the exchange of commodity-equivalents, so much labour in one form is exchanged for an equal amount of labour in another form.

Hence, *equal right* here is still in principle—*bourgeois right*, although principle and practice are no longer in conflict, while the exchange of equivalents in commodity exchange only exists on the *average* and not in the individual case.

In spite of this advance, this *equal right* is still stigmatised by a bourgeois limitation. The right of the producers is *proportional* to the labour they supply; the equality consists in the fact that measurement is made with an *equal standard*, labour.

But one man is superior to another physically or mentally and so supplies more labour in the same time, or can labour for a longer time; and labour, to serve as a measure, must be defined by its duration or intensity, otherwise it ceases to be a standard of measurement. This *equal* right is an unequal right for unequal labour. It recognises no class differences, because everyone is only a worker like everyone else; but it tacitly recognises unequal individual endowment and thus productive capacity as natural privileges. *It is therefore a right of inequality in its content, like every right.* Right by its very nature can only consist in the application of an equal standard; but unequal individuals (and they would not be different individuals if they were not unequal) are only measurable by an equal standard in so far as they are brought under an equal point of view, are taken from one *definite* side only, e.g., in the present case are regarded *only as workers,* and nothing more seen in them, everything else being ignored. Further, one worker is married, another not; one has more children than another and so on and so forth. Thus with an equal output, and hence an equal share in the social consumption fund, one will in fact receive more than another, one will be richer than another, and so on. To avoid all these defects, right, instead of being equal, would have to be unequal.

But these defects are inevitable in the first phase of communist society as it is when it has just emerged after prolonged birth pangs from capitalist society. Right can never be higher than the economic structure of society and the cultural development thereby determined.

In a higher phase of communist society, after the enslaving subordination of individuals under division of labour, and therewith also the antithesis between mental and physical labour, has vanished; after labour, from a mere means of life, has itself become the prime necessity of life; after the productive forces have also increased with the all-round development of the individual, and all the springs of co-operative wealth flow more abundantly—only then can the narrow horizon of bourgeois right be fully left behind and society inscribe on its banners: from each according to his ability, to each according to his needs!

Friedrich von Hayek, "Against 'Social Justice,'" from *The Mirage of Social Justice* (1978)

Friedrich von Hayek (1899–1992) was long one of the foremost defenders of the laissez-faire market system and a harsh critic of all schemes—however well intended—to interfere with the market and to impose on it some predesigned pattern of distribution, including (especially) attempts to distribute wealth more evenly and equally and efforts to ensure that the market in fact rewards merit. Social justice, he tells us, is an illusion at best, and in some hands it is an idea that greatly endangers our personal freedoms. The central argument is that any effort to predetermine distribution patterns, no matter what the criteria, necessarily involves placing power in the hands of a central authority—presumably the government—and thus takes it away from individual citizens. The attempt to distribute the goods of society more equally, for example, requires taking wealth away from some, who presumably would not like to part with it and perhaps would not do so of their own free will. Thus their liberty is violated and the power required by government to take

From *Law, Legislation, and Liberty,* Vol. 2, *The Mirage of Social Justice* by F. A. von Hayek, published by the University of Chicago Press. Copyright © 1978 by F. A. von Hayek and reprinted by permission of the publisher and the author.

it away from them "must progressively approach nearer and nearer to a totalitarian system." What is less recognized, however, is the fact that the free market, whatever its other virtues, does not dependably reward merit—whether hard work or talent or successful results—and is as much a matter of luck as it is of effort or desert. We are predictably and naturally upset, von Hayek admits, when we see virtue (particularly our own) go unrewarded, but the cost of correcting such disappointments is, once again, unwarranted and dangerous meddling in the market. Who is to say who deserves what, and what authority are we willing to entrust with such judgments? "Society has simply become the new deity to which we complain and clamor for redress if it does not fulfill the expectations it has created," but there is, von Hayek insists, no one to blame. It is this wholesale dismissal of responsibility, perhaps, that has aroused such indignation in response. E. F. Schumacher, in partial retort, has called the free market system "the institutionalization of irresponsibility." And why, it may be asked, should the market itself be more trustworthy, with no one in control (that is, assuming that it is in fact truly "free"), than some selected commission of judges, or duly elected representatives? But von Hayek argues, persuasively for many, that justice cannot be conceived in terms of anything like results or rewards, and the uncertainty of the economic game is an essential part of the practice. At best, we can try to make the rules themselves as fair as possible and take some trouble to make sure that people don't cheat, but even then, a "level playing field" (as some say now) cannot guarantee that everyone will have an even starting point, and von Hayek argues—as most conservatives who otherwise share his sense of the market do not—against equal opportunity as just another version of the same government interference, ultimately unlimited in its scope and eventually, he warns, nothing less than a nightmare.

The Conquest of Public Imagination by "Social Justice"

The appeal to "social justice" has nevertheless by now become the most widely used and most effective argument in political discussion. Almost every claim for government action on behalf of particular groups is advanced in its name, and if it can be made to appear that a certain measure is demanded by "social justice," opposition to it will rapidly weaken. People may dispute whether or not the particular measure is required by "social justice." But that this is the standard which ought to guide political action, and that the expression has a definite meaning, is hardly ever questioned. In consequence, there are today probably no political movements or politicians who do not readily appeal to "social justice" in support of the particular measures which they advocate.

It also can scarcely be denied that the demand for "social justice" has already in a great measure transformed the social order and is continuing to transform it in a direction which those who called for it never foresaw. Though the phrase has undoubtedly helped occasionally to make the law more equal for all, whether the demand for justice in distribution has in any sense made society juster or reduced discontent must remain doubtful.

The expression of course described from the beginning the aspirations which were at the heart of socialism. Although classical socialism has usually been defined by its demand for the socialization of the means of production, this was for it chiefly a means thought to be essential in order to bring about a "just" distribution of wealth; and since socialists have later discovered that this redistribution could in a great measure, and against less resistance, be brought about by taxation (and government services financed by it), and have in practice often shelved their earlier demands, the realization of "social justice" has become their chief promise. It might indeed be said that the main difference between the order of society at which classical liberalism aimed and the sort of society into which it is now being transformed is that the former was governed by principles of just individual conduct while the new society is to satisfy the demands for "social justice"—or, in other words, that the former demanded just action by the individuals while the latter more and more places the duty of justice on authorities with power to command people what to do. . . .

I believe that "social justice" will ultimately be recognized as a will-o'-the-wisp which has lured men to abandon many of the values which in the past have inspired the development of civilization—an attempt to satisfy a craving inherited from the traditions of the small group but which is meaningless in the Great Society of free men. Unfortunately, this vague desire which has become one of the strongest bonds spurring people of good will to action, not only is bound to be disappointed. This would be sad enough. But, like most attempts to pursue an unattainable goal, the striving for it will also produce highly undesirable consequences, and in particular lead to the destruction of the indispensable environment in which the traditional moral values alone can flourish, namely personal freedom. . . .

. . . It is now necessary clearly to distinguish between two wholly different problems which the demand for "social justice" raises in a market order.

The first is whether within an economic order based on the market the concept of "social justice" has any meaning or content whatever.

The second is whether it is possible to preserve a market order while imposing upon it (in the name of "social justice" or any other pretext) some pattern of remuneration based on the assessment of the performance or the needs of different individuals or groups by an authority possessing the power to enforce it.

The answer to each of these questions is a clear no.

Yet it is the general belief in the validity of the concept of "social justice" which drives all contemporary societies into greater and greater efforts of the second kind and which has a peculiar self-accelerating tendency: the more dependent the position of the individuals or groups is seen to become on the actions of government, the more they will insist that the governments aim at some recognizable scheme of distributive justice; and the more governments try to realize some preconceived pattern of desirable distribution, the more they must subject the position of the different individuals and groups to their control. So long as the belief in "social justice" governs political action, this process must progressively approach nearer and nearer to a totalitarian system. . . .

The first insight which should shake this certainty is that we experience the same feelings also with respect to differences in human fates for which clearly no human agency is responsible and which it would therefore clearly be absurd to call injustice. Yet we do cry out against the injustice when a succession of calamities befalls one family while another steadily prospers, when a meritorious effort is frustrated by some unforeseeable accident, and particularly if of many people whose endeavours seem equally great, some succeed brilliantly while others utterly fail. It is certainly tragic to see the failure of the most meritorious efforts of parents to bring up their children, of young men to build a career, or of an explorer or scientist pursuing a brilliant idea. And we will protest against such a fate although we do not know anyone who is to blame for it, or any way in which such disappointments can be prevented.

It is no different with regard to the general feeling of injustice about the distribution of material goods in a society of free men. Though we are in this case less ready to admit it, our complaints about the outcome of the market as unjust do not really assert that somebody has been unjust; and there is no answer to the question of *who* has been unjust. Society has simply become the new deity to which we complain and clamour for redress if it does not fulfil the expectations it has created. There is no individual and no cooperating group of people against which the sufferer would have a just complaint, and there are no conceivable rules of just individual conduct which would at the same time secure a functioning order and prevent such disappointments.

The only blame implicit in those complaints is that we tolerate a system in which each is allowed to choose his occupation and therefore nobody can have the power and the duty to see that the results correspond to our wishes. For in such a system in which each is allowed to use his knowledge for his own purposes the concept of "social justice" is necessarily empty and meaningless, because in it nobody's will can determine the relative incomes of the different people, or prevent that they be partly dependent on accident. "Social justice" can be given a meaning only in a directed or "command" economy (such as an army) in which the individuals are ordered what to do; and any particular conception of "social justice" could be realized only in such a centrally directed system. It presupposes that people are guided by specific directions and not by rules of just individual conduct. Indeed, no system of rules of just individual conduct, and therefore no free action of the individuals, could produce results satisfying any principle of distributive justice.

The Rationale of the Economic Game in Which Only the Conduct of the Players but Not the Result Can Be Just

We have seen earlier that justice is an attribute of human conduct which we have learnt to exact because a certain kind of conduct is required to secure the formation and maintenance of a beneficial order of actions. The attribute of justice may thus be predicated about the intended results of human action but not about circumstances which have not deliberately been brought about by men. Justice requires that in the "treatment" of another person or persons, i.e. in the intentional actions affecting the well-being of other persons, certain uniform rules of conduct be observed. It clearly has no application to the manner in which the impersonal process of the market allocates command over goods and services to particular people: this can be neither just nor unjust, because the results are not intended or foreseen, and depend on a multitude of circumstances not known in their totality to anybody. The conduct of the individuals in that process may well be just or unjust; but since their wholly just actions will have consequences for others which were neither intended nor foreseen, these effects do not thereby become just or unjust.

The fact is simply that we consent to retain, and agree to enforce, uniform rules for a procedure which has greatly improved the chances of all to have their wants satisfied, but at the price of all individuals and groups incurring the risk of unmerited failure. With the acceptance of this procedure the recompense of different groups and individuals becomes exempt from deliberate control. It is the only procedure yet discovered in which information widely dispersed among millions of men can be effectively utilized for the benefit of all—and used by assuring to all an individual liberty desirable for itself on ethical grounds. It is a procedure which of course has never been "designed" but which we have learnt gradually to improve after we had discovered how it increased the efficiency of men in the groups who had evolved it.

It is a procedure which, as Adam Smith (and apparently before him the ancient Stoics) understood, in all important respects (except that normally it is not pursued solely as a diversion) is wholly analogous to a game, namely a game partly of skill and partly of chance. It proceeds, like all games, according to rules guiding the actions of individual participants whose aims, skills, and knowledge are different, with the consequence that the outcome will be unpredictable and that there will regularly be winners and losers. And while, as in a game, we are right in insisting that it be fair and that nobody cheat, it would be nonsensical to demand that the results for the different players be just. They will of necessity be determined partly by skill and partly by luck. Some of the circumstances which make the services of a person more or less valuable to his fellows, or which may make it desirable that he change the direction of his efforts, are not of human design or foreseeable by men. . . .

The long and the short of it all is that men can be allowed to decide what work to do only if the remuneration they can expect to get for it corresponds to the value their services have to those of their fellows who receive them; and that *these values which their services will have to their fellows will often have no relations to their individual merits or needs.* Reward for merit earned and indication of what a person should do, both in his own and in his fellows' interest, are different things. It is not good intentions or needs but doing what in fact most benefits others, irrespective of motive, which will secure the best reward. Among those who try to climb Mount Everest or to reach the Moon, we also honour not those who made the greatest efforts, but those who got there first.

The Alleged Necessity of a Belief in the Justice of Rewards

It has been argued persuasively that people will tolerate major inequalities of the material positions only if they believe that the different individuals get on the whole what they deserve, that they did in fact support the market order only because (and so long as) they thought that the differences of remuneration corresponded roughly to differences of merit, and that in consequence the maintenance of a free society presupposes the belief that some sort of "social justice" is being done. The market order, however, does not in fact owe its origin to such beliefs, or was originally justified in this manner. This order could develop, after its earlier beginnings had decayed during the middle ages and to some extent been destroyed by the restrictions imposed by authority, when a thousand years of vain efforts to discover substantively just prices or wages were abandoned and the late schoolmen recognized them to be empty formulae and taught instead that the prices determined by just conduct of the parties in the market, i.e. the competitive prices arrived at without fraud, monopoly and violence, was all that justice required. It was from this tradition that John Locke and his contemporaries derived the classical liberal conception of justice for which, as has been rightly said, it was only "the way in which competition was carried on, not its results," that could be just or unjust.

It is unquestionably true that, particularly among those who were very successful in the market order, a belief in a much stronger moral justification of individual success developed, and that, long after the basic principles of such an order had been fully elaborated and approved by catholic moral philosophers, it had in the Anglo-Saxon world received strong support from Calvinist teaching. It certainly is important in the market order (or free enterprise society, misleadingly called "capitalism") that the individuals believe that their well-being depends primarily on their own efforts and decisions. Indeed, few circumstances will do more to make a person energetic and efficient than the belief that it depends chiefly on him whether he will reach the goals he has set himself. For this reason this belief is often encouraged by education and governing opinion—it seems to me, generally much to the benefit of most of the members of the society in which it prevails, who will owe many important material and moral improvements to persons guided by it. But it leads no doubt also to an exaggerated confidence in the truth of this generalization which to those who regard themselves (and perhaps are) equally able but have failed must appear as a bitter irony and severe provocation.

It is probably a misfortune that, especially in the USA, popular writers like Samuel Smiles and Horatio Alger, and later the sociologist W. G. Sumner, have defended free enterprise on the ground that it regularly rewards the deserving, and it bodes ill for the future of the market order that this seems to have become the only defence of it which is understood by the general public. That it has largely become the basis of the self-esteem of the businessman often gives him an air of self-righteousness which does not make him more popular.

It is therefore a real dilemma to what extent we ought to encourage in the young the belief that when they really try they will succeed, or should rather emphasize that inevitably some unworthy will succeed and some worthy fail—whether we ought to allow the views of those groups to prevail with whom the over-confidence in the appropriate reward of the able and industrious is strong and who in consequence will do much that benefits the rest, and whether without such partly erroneous beliefs the large numbers will tolerate actual differences in rewards which will be based only partly on achievement and partly on mere chance. . . .

"Social Justice" and Equality

The most common attempts to give meaning to the concept of "social justice" resort to egalitarian considerations and argue that every departure from equality of material benefits enjoyed has to be justified by some recognizable common interest which these differences serve. This is based on a specious analogy with the situation in which some human agency has to distribute rewards, in which case indeed justice would require that these rewards be determined in accordance with some recognizable rule of general applicability. But earnings in a market system, though people tend to regard them as rewards, do not serve such a function. Their rationale (if one may use this term for a role which was not designed but developed because it assisted human endeavour without people understanding how), is rather to indicate to people what they ought to do if the order is to be maintained on which they all rely. The prices which must be paid in a market economy for different kinds of labour and other factors of production if individual efforts are to match, although they will be affected by effort, diligence, skill, need, etc., cannot conform to any one of these magnitudes; and considerations of justice just do not make sense with respect to the determination of a magnitude which does not depend on anyone's will or desire, but on circumstances which nobody knows in their totality. . . .

The postulate of material equality would be a natural starting point only if it were a necessary circumstance that the shares of the different individuals or groups were in such a manner determined by deliberate human decision. In a society in which this were an unquestioned fact, justice would indeed demand that the allocation of the means for the satisfaction of human needs were effected according to some uniform principle such as merit or need (or some combination of these), and that, where the principle adopted did not justify a difference, the shares of the different individuals should be equal. The prevalent demand for material equality is probably often based on the belief that the existing inequalities are the effect of somebody's decision—a belief which would be wholly mistaken in a genuine market order and has still only very limited validity in the highly interventionist "mixed" economy existing in most countries today. This now prevalent form of economic order has in fact attained its character largely as a result of governmental measures aiming at what was thought to be required by "social justice."

When the choice, however, is between a genuine market order, which does not and cannot achieve a distribution corresponding to any standard of material justice, and a system in which a government uses its powers to put some such standard into effect, the question is not whether government ought to exercise, justly or unjustly, powers it must exercise in any case, but whether government should possess and exercise additional powers which can be used to determine the shares of the different members of society. The demand for "social justice," in other words, does not merely require government to observe some principle of action according to uniform rules in those actions which it must perform in any case, but demands that it undertake additional activities, and thereby assume new responsibilities—tasks which are not necessary for maintaining law and order and providing for certain collective needs which the market could not satisfy.

The great problem is whether this new demand for equality does not conflict with the equality of the rules of conduct which government must enforce on all in a free society. There is, of course, a great difference between government treating all citizens according to the same rules in all the activities it undertakes for other purposes, and government doing what is required in order to place the different citizens in equal (or less unequal) material positions. Indeed, there may arise a sharp conflict between these two aims. Since people will differ in many attributes which government cannot alter, to secure for them the same material position would require that government treat them very differently. Indeed, to assure the same material position to people who differ greatly in strength, intelligence, skill, knowledge and perseverance as well as in their physical and social environment, government would clearly have to treat them very differently to compensate for those disadvantages and deficiencies it could not directly alter. Strict equality of those benefits which government could provide for all, on the other hand, would clearly lead to the inequality of the material positions.

This, however, is not the only and not even the chief reason why a government aiming to secure for its citizens equal material positions (or any determined pattern of material welfare) would have to treat them very unequally. It would have to do so because under such a system it would have to undertake to tell people what to do. Once the rewards the individual can expect are no longer an appropriate indication of how to direct their efforts to where they are most needed, because these rewards correspond not to the value which their services have for their fellows, but to the moral merit or desert the persons are deemed to have earned, they lose the guiding function they have in the market order and would have to be replaced by the commands of the directing authority. A central planning office would, however, have to decide on the tasks to be allotted to the different groups or individuals wholly cn grounds of expediency or efficiency and, in order to achieve its ends, would have to impose upon them very different duties and burdens. The individuals might be treated according to uniform rules so far as their rewards were concerned, but certainly not with respect to the different kinds of work they would have to be made to do. In assigning people to their individual tasks, the central planning authority would have to be guided by considerations of efficiency and expediency and not by principles of justice or equality. No less than in the market order would the individuals in the common interest have to submit to great inequality—only these inequalities would be determined not by the interaction of individual skills in an impersonal process, but by the uncontradictable decision of authority.

As is becoming clear in ever increasing fields of welfare policy, an authority instructed to achieve particular results for the individuals must be given essentially arbitrary powers to make the individuals do what seems necessary to achieve the required result. Full equality for most cannot but mean the equal submission of the great masses under the command of some élite who manages their affairs. While an equality of rights under a limited government is possible and an essential condition of individual freedom, a claim for equality of material position can be met only by a government with totalitarian powers.

"Equality of Opportunity"

It is of course not to be denied that in the existing market order not only the results but also the initial chances of different individuals are often very different; they are affected by circumstances of their physical and social environment which are beyond their control but in many particular respects might be altered by some governmental action. The demand for equality of opportunity or equal starting conditions (*Startgerechtigkeit*) appeals to, and has been supported by, many who in general favour the free market order. So far as this refers to such facilities and opportunities as are of necessity affected by governmental decisions (such as appointments to public office and the like), the demand was indeed one of the central points of classical liberalism, usually expressed by the French phrase "la carrière ouverte aux talents." There is also much to be said in favour of the government providing on an equal basis the means for the schooling of minors who are not yet fully responsible citizens, even though there are grave doubts whether we ought to allow government to administer them.

But all this would still be very far from creating real equality of opportunity, even for persons possessing the same abilities. To achieve this government would have to control the whole physical and human environment of all persons, and have to endeavour to provide at least equivalent chances for each; and the more government succeeded in these endeavours, the stronger would become the legitimate demand that, on the same principle, any still remaining handicaps must be removed—or compensated for by putting extra burden on the still relatively favoured. This would have to go on until government literally controlled every circumstance which could affect any person's well-being. Attractive as the phrase of equality of opportunity at first sounds, once the idea is extended beyond the facilities which for other reasons have to be provided by government, it becomes a wholly illusory ideal, and any attempt concretely to realize it apt to produce a nightmare.

Bernard Williams, "Equality," from "The Idea of Equality" (1976)

Bernard Williams (1929–) has often argued against modern moralists in favor of the ancient conceptions of virtue defended by Plato and Aristotle. But on the subject of equality he sides with the moderns and against the ancients, defending the often confused insistence that all humans are equal in a way that is neither trivial nor absurd. He begins by distinguishing an obviously false factual claim (all people are in fact equal in their various abilities and endowments) and a more political principle that insists that people ought to be *treated* in the same way. He rejects the saving but inadequate interpretation of the former, which turns into "all men are men," and he acknowledges that substantial qualifications are due the latter, for instance, the recognition that differences as well as similarities are essential considerations for the nature of treatment, whether reward or punishment. He suggests, however, that "all men are men" is not actually as trivial as it looks, and carries with it some important insights regarding the nature of equality. He also takes Kant's insistence on both our universal moral capacities and our (related) status as "ends in themselves" to insist that this, too, is some ground for our considerations of equality. But the bulk of Williams's argument concerns the important qualification that being treated as equals presupposes the recognition that it is in different and often unequal circumstances that we expect to be so treated, and the factual differences between us result in unequal opportunities that make equal treatment difficult and perplexing. In the preceding selection, von Hayek flatly claims that equal opportunity is illusory and impossible. What Williams attempts to give us in some indication of how it can be meaningful and, with considerable conceptual as well as political effort, possible.

The idea of equality is used in political discussion both in statements of fact, or what purport to be statements of fact—that men *are* equal—and in statements of political principles or aims—that men *should be* equal, as at present they are not. The two can be, and often are, combined: the aim is then described as that of securing a state of affairs in which men are treated as the equal beings which they in fact already are, but are not already treated as being. In both these uses, the idea of equality notoriously encounters the same difficulty: that on one kind of interpretation the statements in which it figures are much too strong, and on another kind much too weak, and it is hard to find a satisfactory interpretation that lies between the two.

To take first the supposed statement of fact: it has only too often been pointed out that to say that all men are equal in all those characteristics in respect of which it makes sense to say that men are equal or unequal, is a patent falsehood; and even if some more restricted selection is made of these characteristics, the statement does not look much better. Faced with this obvious objection, the defender of the claim that all men are equal is likely to offer a weaker interpretation. It is not, he may say, in their skill, intelligence, strength, or virtue that men are equal, but merely in their being men: it is their common humanity that constitutes their equality. On this interpretation, we should not seek for some special characteristics in respect of which men are equal, but merely remind ourselves that they are all men. Now to this it might be objected that being men is not a respect in which men can strictly speaking be said to be *equal;* but, leaving that aside, there is the more immediate objection that if all that the statement does is to remind us that men are men, it does not do very much, and in particular does less than its proponents in political argument have wanted it to do. What looked like a paradox has turned into a platitude.

I shall suggest in a moment that even in this weak form the statement is not so vacuous as this objection makes it seem; but it must be admitted that when the statement of equality ceases to claim more than is warranted, it rather rapidly reaches the point where it claims less than is interesting. A similar discomfiture tends to overcome the practical maxim of equality. It cannot be the aim of this maxim that all men should be treated alike in all circumstances, or even that they should be treated alike as much as possible. Granted that, however, there is no obvious stopping point before the interpretation which makes the maxim claim only that men should be treated alike in similar circumstances; and since "circumstances" here must clearly include reference to what a man is, as well as to his purely external situation, this comes very much to saying that for every difference in the way men are treated, some general reason or principle of differentiation must be given. This may well be an important principle; some indeed have seen in it, or in something very like it, an essential element of morality itself. But it can hardly be enough to constitute the principle that was advanced in the name of *equality.* It would be in accordance with this principle, for example, to treat black men differently from others just because they were black, or poor men differently just because they were poor, and this cannot accord with anyone's idea of equality.

In what follows I shall try to advance a number of considerations that can help to save the political notion of equality from these extremes of absurdity and of triviality. These considerations are in fact often employed in political argument, but are usually bundled together into an unanalysed notion of equality in a manner confusing to the advocates, and encouraging to the enemies, of that ideal. These considerations will not enable us to define a distinct third interpretation of the statements which use the notion of equality; it is rather that they enable us, starting with the weak interpretations, to build up something that in practice can have something of the solidity aspired to by the strong interpretations. In this discussion, it will not be necessary all the time to treat separately the supposedly factual application of the notion of equality, and its application in the maxim of action. Though it is sometimes important to distinguish them, and there are clear grounds for doing so, similar considerations often apply to both. The two go significantly together: on the one hand, the point of the supposedly factual assertion is to back up social ideals and programmes of political action; on the other hand—a rather less obvious point, perhaps—those political proposals have their force because they are regarded not as gratuitously egalitarian, aiming at equal treatment for reasons, for instance, of simplicity or tidiness, but as affirming an equality which is believed in some sense already to exist, and to be obscured or neglected by actual social arrangements.

1.   *Common humanity.* The factual statement of men's equality was seen, when pressed, to retreat in the direction of merely asserting the equality of men as men; and this was thought to be trivial. It is certainly insufficient, but not, after all, trivial. That all men are human is, if a tautology, a useful one, serving as a reminder that those who belong anatomically to the species *homo sapiens,* and can speak a language, use tools, live in societies, can interbreed despite racial differences, etc., are also alike in certain other respects more likely to be forgotten. These respects are notably the capacity to feel pain, both from immediate physical causes and from various situations represented in perception and in thought; and the capacity to feel affection for others, and the consequences of this, connected with the frustration of this affection, loss of its objects, etc. The assertion that men are alike in the possession of these characteristics is, while indisputable and (it may be) even necessarily true, not trivial. For it is certain that there are political and social arrangements that systematically neglect these characteristics in the case of some groups of men, while being fully aware of them in the case of others; that is to say, they treat certain men as though they did not possess these characteristics, and neglect moral claims that arise from these characteristics and which would be admitted to arise from them. . . .

I have discussed this point in connexion with very obvious human characteristics of feeling pain and desiring affection. There are, however, other and less easily definable characteristics universal to humanity, which may all the more be neglected in political and social arrangements. For instance, there seems to be a characteristic which might be called "a desire for self-respect"; this phrase is perhaps not too happy, in suggesting a particular culturally-limited, bourgeois value, but I mean by it a certain human desire to be identified with what one is doing, to be able to realise purposes of one's own, and not to be the instrument of another's will unless one has willingly accepted such a rôle. This is a very inadequate and in some ways rather empty specification of a human desire; to a better specification, both philosophical reflexion and the evidences of psychology and anthropology would be relevant. Such investigations enable us to understand more deeply, in respect of the desire I have gestured towards and of similar characteristics, what it is to be human; and of what it is to be human, the apparently trivial statement of men's equality as men can serve as a reminder.

2.   *Moral capacities.* So far we have considered respects in which men can be counted as all alike, which respects are, in a sense, negative: they concern the capacity to suffer, and certain needs that men have, and these involve men in moral relations as the recipients of certain kinds of treatment. It has certainly been a part, however, of the thought of those who asserted that men were equal, that there were more positive respects in which men were alike; that they were equal in certain things that they could do or achieve, as well as in things that they needed and could suffer. In respect of a whole range of abilities, from weight-lifting to the calculus, the assertion is, as was noted at the beginning, not plausible, and has not often been supposed to be. It has been held, however, that there are certain other abilities, both less open to empirical test and more essential in moral connexions, for which it is true that men are equal. These are certain sorts of moral ability or capacity, the capacity for virtue or achievement of the highest kind of moral worth. . . .

That men should be regarded from the human point of view, and not merely [as "miners," or "inventors," or "agricultural labourers," or "junior executives"] is part of the content that might be attached to Kant's celebrated injunction "treat each man as an end in himself, and never as a means only." But I do not think that this is all that should be seen in this injunction, or all that is concerned in the notion of "respect." What is involved in the examples just given could be explained by saying that each man is owed an effort at identification: that he should not be regarded as the surface to which a certain label can be applied, but one should try to see the world (including the label) from his point of view. This injunction will be based on, though not of course fully explained by, the notion that men are conscious beings who necessarily have intentions and purposes and see what they are doing in a certain light. But there seem to be further injunctions connected with the Kantian maxim, and with the notion of "respect," that go beyond these considerations. There are forms of exploiting men or degrading them which would be thought to be excluded by these notions, but which cannot be excluded merely by considering how the exploited or degraded men see the situation. For it is precisely a mark of extreme exploitation or degradation that those who suffer it do *not* see themselves differently from the way they are seen by the exploiters; either they do not see themselves as anything at all, or they acquiesce passively in the rôle for which they have been cast. Here we evidently need something more than the precept that one should respect and try to understand another man's consciousness of his own activities; it is also that one may not suppress or destroy that consciousness. . . .

    3.   *Equality in unequal circumstances.* The notion of equality is invoked not only in connexions where men are claimed in some sense all to be equal, but in connexions where they are agreed to be unequal, and the question arises of the distribution of, or access to, certain goods to which their inequalities are relevant. It may be objected that the notion of equality is in fact misapplied in these connexions, and that the appropriate ideas are those of fairness or justice, in the sense of what Aristotle called "distributive justice," where (as Aristotle argued) there is no question of regarding or treating everyone as equal, but solely a question of distributing certain goods in proportion to men's recognised inequalities.

    I think it is reasonable to say against this objection that there is some foothold for the notion of equality even in these cases. It is useful here to make a rough distinction between two different types of inequality, inequality of *need* and inequality of *merit,* with a corresponding distinction between goods—on the one hand, goods demanded by the need, and on the other, goods that can be earned by the merit. In the case of needs, such as the need for medical treatment in case of illness, it can be presumed for practical purposes that the persons who have the need actually desire the goods in question, and so the question can indeed be regarded as one of distribution in a simple sense, the satisfaction of an existing desire. In the case of merit, such as for instance the possession of abilities to profit from a university education, there is not the same presumption that everyone who has the merit has the desire for the goods in question, though it may, of course, be the case. Moreover, the good of a university education may be legitimately, even if hopelessly, desired by those who do not possess the merit; while medical treatment or unemployment benefit are either not desired, or not legitimately desired, by those who are not ill or unemployed, i.e. do not have the appropriate need. Hence the distribution of goods in accordance with merit has a competitive aspect lacking in the case of distribution according to need. For these reasons, it is appropriate to speak, in the case of merit, not only of the distribution of the good, but of the distribution of the opportunity of achieving the good. But this, unlike the good itself, can be said to be distributed equally to everybody, and so one does encounter a notion of *general* equality, much vaunted in our society today, the notion of equality of opportunity. . . .

    [Suppose that we understand] the notion of equality of opportunity in the normal political sense of equality of opportunity for *everyone in society* to secure certain goods. This notion is introduced into political discussion when there is question of the access to certain goods which, first, even if they are not desired by everyone in society, are desired by large numbers of people in all sections of society (either for themselves, or, as in the case of education, for their children), or would be desired by people in all sections of society if they knew about the goods in question and thought it possible for them to attain them; second, are goods which people may be said to earn or achieve; and third, are goods which not all the people who desire them can have. This third condition covers at least three different cases, however, which it is worth distinguishing. Some desired goods, like positions of prestige, management, etc., are *by their very nature* limited: whenever there are some people who are in command or prestigious positions, there are necessarily others who are not. Other goods are *contingently* limited, in the sense that there are certain conditions of access to them which in fact not everyone satisfies, but there is no intrinsic limit to the numbers who might gain access to it by satisfying the conditions: university education is usually regarded in this light nowadays, as something which requires certain conditions of admission to it which in fact not everyone satisfies, but which an indefinite proportion of people might satisfy. Third, there are goods which are *fortuitously* limited, in the sense that although everyone or large numbers of people satisfy the conditions of access to them, there is just not enough of them to go round; so some more stringent conditions or system of rationing have to be imposed, to govern access in an imperfect situation. A good can, of course, be both contingently and fortuitously limited at once: when, due to shortage of supply, not even the people who are qualified to have it, limited in numbers though they are, can in every case have it. It is particularly worth distinguishing those kinds of limitation, as there can be significant differences of view about the way in which a certain good is limited. While most would now agree that high education is contingently limited, a Platonic view would regard it as necessarily limited.

Now the notion of equality of opportunity might be said to be the notion that a limited good shall in fact be allocated on grounds which do not a priori exclude any section of those that desire it. But this formulation is not really very clear. For suppose grammar school education (a good perhaps contingently, and certainly fortuitously, limited) is allocated on grounds of ability as tested at the age of 11; this would normally be advanced as an example of equality of opportunity, as opposed to a system of allocation on grounds of parents' wealth. But does not the criterion of ability exclude a priori a certain section of people, viz. those that are not able—just as the other excludes a priori those who are not wealthy? Here it will obviously be said that this was not what was meant by a priori exclusion: the present argument just equates this with exclusion of anybody, i.e. with the mere existence of some condition that has to be satisfied. What then is a priori exclusion? It must mean exclusion on grounds *other* than those appropriate or rational for the good in question. But this still will not do as it stands. For it would follow from this that so long as those allocating grammar school education on grounds of wealth thought that such grounds were appropriate or rational (as they might in one of the ways discussed above in connexion with private schools), they could sincerely describe their system as one of equality of opportunity— which is absurd.

Hence it seems that the notion of equality of opportunity is more complex than it first appeared. It requires not merely that there should be no exclusion from access on grounds other than those appropriate or rational for the good in question, but that the grounds considered appropriate for the good should themselves be such that people from all sections of society have an equal chance of satisfying them. What now is a "section of society"? Clearly we cannot include under this term sections of the populace identified just by the characteristics which figure in the grounds for allocating the good—since, once more, any grounds at all must exclude some section of the populace. But what about sections identified by characteristics which are *correlated* with the grounds of exclusion? There are important difficulties here: to illustrate this, it may help first to take an imaginary example.

Suppose that in a certain society great prestige is attached to membership of a warrior class, the duties of which require great physical strength. This class has in the past been recruited from certain wealthy families only; but egalitarian reformers achieve a change in the rules, by which warriors are recruited from all sections of the society, on the results of a suitable competition. The effect of this, however, is that the wealthy families still provide virtually all the warriors, because the rest of the populace is so under-nourished by reason of poverty that their physical strength is inferior to that of the wealthy and well nourished. The reformers protest that equality of opportunity has not really been achieved; the wealthy reply that in fact it has, and that the poor now have the opportunity of becoming warriors—it is just bad luck that their characteristics are such that they do not pass the test. "We are not," they might say, "excluding anyone *for* being poor; we exclude people for being weak, and it is unfortunate that those who are poor are also weak."

This answer would seem to most people feeble, and even cynical. This is for reasons similar to those discussed before in connexion with equality before the law; that the supposed equality of opportunity is quite empty—indeed, one may say that it does not really exist—unless it is made more effective than this. For one knows that it could be made more effective; one knows that there is a causal connexion between being poor and being under-nourished, and between being undernourished and being physically weak. One supposes further that something could be done—subject to whatever economic conditions obtain in the imagined society—to alter the distribution of wealth. All this being so, the appeal by the wealthy to the "bad luck" of the poor must appear as disingenuous.

It seems then that a system of allocation will fall short of equality of opportunity if the allocation of the good in question in fact works out unequally or disproportionately between different sections of society, if the unsuccessful sections are under a disadvantage which could be removed by further reform or social action. This was very clear in the imaginary example that was given, because the causal connexions involved are simple and well known. In actual fact, however, the situations of this type that arise are more complicated, and it is easier to overlook the causal connexions involved. This is particularly so in the case of educational selection, where such slippery concepts as "intellectual ability" are involved. It is a known fact that the system of selection for grammar schools by the "11+" examination favours children in direct proportion to their social class, the children of professional homes having proportionately greater success than those from working-class homes. We have every reason to suppose that these results are the product, in good part, of environmental factors; and we further know that imaginative social reform, both of the primary educational system and of living conditions, would favourably affect those environmental factors. In these circumstances, this system of educational selection falls short of equality of opportunity.

This line of thought points to a connexion between the idea of equality of opportunity, and the idea of equality of persons, which is stronger than might at first be suspected. We have seen that one is not really offering equality of opportunity to Smith and Jones if one contents oneself with applying the same criteria to Smith and Jones at, say, the age of 11; what one is doing there is to apply the same criteria to Smith as affected by favourable conditions and to Jones as affected by unfavourable but curable conditions. Here there is a necessary pressure to equal up the conditions: to give Smith and Jones equality of opportunity involves regarding their conditions, where curable, as themselves part of what is done to

Smith and Jones, and not part of Smith and Jones themselves. Their identity, for these purposes, does not include their curable environment, which is itself unequal and a contributor of inequality. This abstraction of persons in themselves from unequal environments is a way, if not of regarding them as equal, at least of moving recognisably in that direction; and is itself involved in equality of opportunity. . . .

If the idea of equality ranges as widely as I have suggested, this type of conflict is bound to arise with it. It is an idea which, on the one hand, is invoked in connexion with the distribution of certain goods, some at least of which are bound to confer on their possessors some preferred status or prestige. On the other hand, the idea of equality of respect is one which urges us to give less consideration to those structures in which people enjoy status or prestige, and to consider people independently of those goods, on the distribution of which equality of opportunity precisely focuses our, and their, attention. There is perhaps nothing formally incompatible in these two applications of the idea of equality: one might hope for a society in which there existed both a fair, rational, and appropriate distribution of these goods, and no contempt, condescension, or lack of human communication between persons who were more and less successful recipients of the distribution. Yet in actual fact, there are deep psychological and social obstacles to the realisation of this hope; as things are, the competitiveness and considerations of prestige that surround the first application of equality certainly militate against the second. How far this situation is inevitable, and how far in an economically developed and dynamic society, in which certain skills and talents are necessarily at a premium, the obstacles to a wider realisation of equality might be overcome, I do not think that we know: these are in good part questions of psychology and sociology, to which we do not have the answers.

When one is faced with the spectacle of the various elements of the idea of equality pulling in these different directions, there is a strong temptation, if one does not abandon the idea altogether, to abandon some of its elements: to claim, for instance, that equality of opportunity is the only ideal that is at all practicable, and equality of respect a vague and perhaps nostalgic illusion; or, alternatively, that equality of respect is genuine equality, and equality of opportunity an inegalitarian betrayal of the ideal—all the more so if it were thoroughly pursued, as now it is not. To succumb to either of these simplifying formulae would, I think, be a mistake. Certainly, a highly rational and efficient application of the ideas of equal opportunity, unmitigated by the other considerations, could lead to a quite inhuman society (if it worked—which, granted a well-known desire of parents to secure a position for their children at least as good as their own, is unlikely). On the other hand, an ideal of equality of respect that made no contact with such things as the economic needs of society for certain skills, and human desire for some sorts of prestige, would be condemned to a futile Utopianism, and to having no rational effect on the distribution of goods, position, and power that would inevitably proceed. If, moreover, as I have suggested, it is not really known how far, by new forms of social structure and of education, these conflicting claims might be reconciled, it is all the more obvious that we should not throw one set of claims out of the window; but should rather seek, in each situation, the best way of eating and having as much cake as possible. It is an uncomfortable situation, but the discomfort is just that of genuine political thought. It is no greater with equality than it is with liberty, or any other noble and substantial political ideal.

David Miller, "On Three Types of Justice," from *Social Justice* (1976)

So far, we have discussed the concept of justice only with reference to a particular kind of society—modern, industrialized, market societies with long histories, a keen sense of progress, and perhaps a problematic sense of community and human relationships. It is in such a context that our conceptions of justice bounce back and forth between the notion of individual rights and concerns for public utility, between the concern for private property and larger social considerations. It is in this context, too, that the freedom of the market and the authority of the state come into such apparent conflict, and the rights and desert of the successful rub uncomfortably against the needs of the poor. But if justice can take on such various faces even within our society, how many more appearances must it make if we expand our vision to consider societies very different from our own. For example, the search for the notion of justice (or a rough equivalent) in current-day Japan would be extremely difficult, not because of some mere translation problem, but because the cultural and contextual differences would be so great that our usual concerns, summarized in terms of "merit" and "rights," for instance, would find no comparable social structures. And yet, philosophers since Plato have often talked as if the idea of justice as expressed in their own language represented a universal concept, the same the world over (although some societies approximate it much more than others, of course). To undermine this impression, we have excerpted the skeleton of a much more global argument by David Miller (1903–), drawn from his book *Social Justice*, in which he argues that there are three very different sorts of contexts in which concepts of justice develop, and these concepts are in turn very different indeed. Our central concept of property rights, for example, is all but missing in other conceptions of justice, and the idea that a person may be meaningfully said to "own" goods that he or she is not actively using and that others desperately need is an idea that some other cultures quite happily live without.

In my inquiry up to this point I have tried to explicate the familiar idea of social justice, first by separating its three distinct, conflicting elements, and then by showing how each element corresponds to a different way of viewing society, represented in my analysis by the political theories of Hume, Spencer, and Kropotkin. Each of these images of society (the stable order, the competitive market, the solidaristic community) plays a part in the think-

From *Social Justice* by David Miller, published by Oxford University Press, 1976, and reprinted by permission of the publisher.

ing of our contemporaries. Any given person will adhere most closely to one image in particular, and to the corresponding conception of justice. Rather than explore the reasons for these individual differences, however, I want to ask whether ideas of justice do not vary systematically from one social context to the next. Some writers have suggested that men everywhere share a common sense of justice, which can be expressed as a general principle that incorporates more specific conceptions of justice. Although this may hold of the most basic notions of justice (such as the golden rule: treat others as you would like them to treat you under similar circumstances), I shall try to show that substantive ideas of social justice—the principles used to assess the distribution of benefits and burdens among the members of society—take radically different forms in different types of society. To do this, I shall start by comparing the social ideas characteristic of three such types. The types will be referred to as primitive societies, hierarchical societies, and market societies. Our own society will later be presented as a modified form of market society.

This classification is not meant to be an exhaustive social typology: many societies do not belong to any of the three categories. The purpose of the classification is rather to enable us to form a better understanding of the social ideas of market societies by looking at the corresponding ideas of societies with very different structures. In describing each type of society, I shall pick out its most distinctive features, without suggesting that these features will be wholly absent in the other types. Thus primitive societies will display, to a small degree, traits which are characteristic of market societies, and so on. The types are distinguished by the relative prominence or insignificance of features which will be found in societies of every kind.

Let me now outline the three social types to be used in the analysis, before discussing briefly the kind of explanation of social ideas which is to be attempted. Primitive societies, first of all, are small-scale societies in which the basic nexus between man and man is kinship. Men in these societies gain subsistence by hunting and gathering, tending flocks, or simple agriculture. The division of labour is not extensive, and there is no strong, well-defined system of political authority; if such authority exists at all, it will be vested in the village headman or council of elders. Contract, although it may occur occasionally, is not an important feature of these societies.

In hierarchical societies, men are arranged vertically in social strata, each stratum having a definite rank in the hierarchy. There is a strong, though not universal, tendency for economic dominance, social prestige, and political power to combine in the hands of the group at the top of the hierarchy. Each person is assigned to a stratum largely on the basis of his birth, since social mobility is low or non-existent. Stratum membership confers traditionally established rights and obligations, and largely determines the type of work which the individual will perform. Contract is again not an important feature of these societies.

I shall confine my discussion to a particular sub-type of hierarchical society, namely feudal society. In this sub-type the social mobility of individuals is slight rather than non-existent; a man is not tightly bound within the stratum of his birth (whereas in caste society, for example, there is no individual social mobility and each stratum forms a self-contained social unit with its own rules and authority structure).

Market societies, finally, are typically large, economically developed societies, in which the basic nexus between man and man is contract. The division of labour is extensive, and each man is formally free to decide upon his occupation, to enter into whatever associations he wishes, and generally to choose his place in society. The central institution of these societies is the economic market in which commodities (including human labour) are bought and sold. Kinship is of small importance and authority is largely the creature of contract.

How can this typology be used to explain variations in men's ideas of justice? The fundamental assumption made here is that a man's sense of justice is strongly affected by the nature of the relationships which he enjoys with other men. The social structure of a particular society generates a certain type of interpersonal relationship, which in turn gives rise to a particular way of assessing and evaluating other men, and of judging how benefits and burdens should be distributed. My aim is to show that there is an intelligible connection between the nature of a man's relationship with other men and his conception of justice. The argument, in other words, takes this form: given that a person's relationships with others are predominantly of this type, it is *rational* or *appropriate* for him to adopt the following conception of justice. . . . Such an argument appeals to common notions of rationality and appropriateness; the existence of such notions is an assumption which cannot here be justified. Furthermore, my general methodology—the view that explanation takes the form, first, of demonstrating a correlation between social structures and certain ideas, and, second, of showing an intelligible connection between the two elements—is taken for granted.

Primitive Societies

There is one rather obvious sense in which men in primitive societies do not have our concept of social justice. Whether we place the emphasis on the principle of desert or on the principle of need, we have in either case an understanding of social justice as an ideal which stands in contrast to the existing state of affairs; typically, as I have argued throughout Part II, our ideals of social justice form parts of wider views of society which, to a greater or lesser extent, go beyond society as it now is. Such world-views are not to be found in primitive societies. Primitive men do not conceive of the possibility of transforming society so that it comes to match up to a social ideal. If, therefore, we are to find a concept of social justice in these societies, we must look, not for an abstract ideal, but for an idea which is expressed in actual social practices. We should turn our attention, for instance, to the way in which primitive societies allocate parcels of land to their members, or to the manner in which tribesmen share out the spoils of a hunting expedition. Of course, we must examine not only the physical distribution of goods, but the principles which lie behind this distribution, in so far as we can discover what they are.

My thesis, however, will be that primitive societies do not practise social justice as we understand it. Their treatment of individuals and their manner of distributing benefits are guided by principles which do not correspond to the principles of social justice found in modern societies. There are points of resemblance, but the divergences are more striking. To show this, I shall focus my attention on those elements of social organization which are common to the great majority of primitive societies. These societies show wide variation in certain respects, but it would be impossible here to give adequate attention to individual differences.

It was commonly held by nineteenth-century investigators of tribal societies that these societies practised communism. No distinction, they said, was made between one man's property and his neighbour's, and each took from the common pool whatever items he needed. (This view was especially strongly maintained by L. H. Morgan, who passed it on to Marx and Engels.) Modern anthropological opinion, however, agrees in regarding this as a serious error. The earlier investigators, failing to find property rights which were the exact analogues of those in market societies, concluded that common ownership must prevail. In fact, private ownership is the norm in primitive societies, but the rights of ownership are different from, and generally more restricted than, the corresponding rights in a society such as our own. At the very least, primitive men own their clothes, items for their personal use, their tools, and weapons. It is also usual for them to own their cattle, their crops, and whatever they have produced, gathered, or killed by their own labour. The ownership of land is a rather more complicated matter: with hunters and gatherers, and with primitive pastoralists, the lands generally belong to the tribe as a whole, private ownership having little point in these cases. With agriculturalists, however, private ownership of farming and gardening land is again the norm, though as we shall see the *sense* in which the land is privately owned must be properly understood.

When we speak of a person owning something, our standard meaning is that he has an absolute and exclusive right to the enjoyment of that thing. His right excludes any other person having an equivalent right to the same object, and he is permitted to use the object as he likes within the law, to sell it to whom he pleases, and to destroy it if he wishes. Primitive ownership is rarely of this kind. A man who possesses a personal ornament may be obliged to pass it on to a kinsman at some definite time in the future. A hunter returning with a catch may be under an obligation to distribute some portion of that catch to other persons specified or unspecified. Thus in Samoa "fishermen on returning to the shore have to give a portion of their catch to anyone they meet in the lagoon or on the shore . . . ," and similar practices are to be found elsewhere, for example among several of the Eskimo peoples. The ways in which primitive rights of property in land differ from their equivalents in modern society deserve fuller examination. . . .

These limitations which primitive people place on rights of ownership furnish us with important clues about their social thinking. We have seen that the strict protection of individual rights which is demanded by our own conception of social justice reflects the view that justice concerns the proper treatment which is due to each individual, irrespective of general social utility. In this perspective, the just act and the socially useful act may on occasion diverge. By contrast, primitive men naturally think of the welfare of the group and subordinate the welfare of particular persons to that general end. While it may be going too far to say with Maine that the subject of rights and duties in primitive societies is the group, not the individual, it is certainly true that rights are granted in these societies when it serves the common interest to do so, and they are limited or rescinded on the same basis. This thinking underlies the restrictions on property rights which we have observed, and is particularly well illustrated by the borrowing of canoes permitted by the people of Tikopia. Of a similar practice which existed among the Chuckchi Eskimos, an observer writes:

> It is contrary to the sense of justice of the natives to allow a good boat to lie idle on shore, when near by are hunters in need of one.

I should say of this practice rather that it shows the *weakness* of the Eskimos' sense of justice, and their willingness to allow considerations of common interest to override individual claims. The same tendency can be seen in primitive thinking on questions of distribution: when John Ladd asked a Navaho Indian how he would distribute 500 sheep among his fellows, his informant replied that they should be given to those best able to look after them. . . .

The two most fundamental relationships in feudal society were that between lord and vassal, and that between lord and serf. Each took the general form of a contract between superior and inferior, in which the inferior party offered to perform certain specified services for the other in return for protection and the opportunity to make a living. In the case of vassalage, the contract was made between two men who were nominally free (the obligations of a vassal did not pass directly to his descendants), the vassal swearing in general to be his lord's "man" and in particular to give military service of a stated nature and extent; the lord offering protection and a fief, which generally consisted of a landed estate sufficient to support the vassal. As for serfdom, the contract here was largely tacit since the serf's status was passed on to his descendants without a renewal of the agreement, but the relationship was again a reciprocal one, the serf performing tasks of many kinds for his lord in return for protection and the right to till a share of the estate. The relationship was regulated by the "custom of the manor." The difference between these two contracts should not be overstressed since in practice vassalage tended to become heritable, the son of the previous vassal routinely swearing homage to the lord. We may therefore conclude that feudal society was built upon contracts between man and man which differed from the "free contracts" of market societies in being contracts of allegiance (rather than contracts between equals) whose terms were governed by custom (rather than being chosen by the parties) and which were in practice largely heritable.

An immediate consequence of the feudal relationships was that, as in primitive societies, property rights were divided among a number of men of different status. Apart from a residue of free peasant proprietors (known as "allodialists"), each piece of land was owned by a number of men, from the tenant who actually worked the land, through the lord to whom he owed service, to the lord of that lord, and so on. Each man had a distinct set of rights over the land, the exercise of which was governed by custom.

Feudal law was likewise fragmented. Each man was subject to the rules of law prevailing in his locality, and little attempt was made to create a uniform legal system. Since a man carried his law with him, there was truth in the remark attributed to the Archbishop of Lyons, that when five men were gathered together it was no surprise if each of them obeyed a different law. Feudal law was also fragmented in another sense: men of different status in the hierachy were tried by different courts for committing the same crime, and were liable to receive different penalties as well. Manorial lords administered the law among their tenants, while they themselves were judged by a group of their peers.

Within the law, custom was dominant. We may conveniently consider this under two aspects. First, as far as the content of the law was concerned, custom took precedence over deliberately enacted law. If two laws were found to be in contradiction, the older of the two was thought to possess superior validity. In fact, the feudal period exhibited a decided preference for unwritten custom, which, as Bloch points out, was by no means irrational since unwritten law could undergo subtle changes to meet new social needs more easily than could codified law. Second, in deciding particular cases, established practice was almost always the clinching factor. Thus if the right to work a piece of land was in dispute between two men, the one who could prove that he (or his ancestors) had ploughed the field in earlier years was certain to succeed in his suit.

Against this background we may understand the conception of justice in medieval Christianity. Justice was seen as an important social virtue, and was thought primarily to consist in the observance or enforcement of the law. In terms of our own analysis, justice was interpreted as the protection of a man's legal rights, these rights deriving by custom from his position in the social hierarchy. We have seen that the law in feudal society was fragmented, and this conception of justice therefore contained no notion of the equal treatment of all men: it was thought rather, as one writer has put it, that "law and justice have as their true purpose the harmonious preservation of the social status quo in the interest of common peace and order."

Although justice was predominantly identified in the minds of medieval Christian writers with the protection of legally established rights, secondary recognition was given to the claims of need. Here the doctrine that by natural law all property was originally held in common became of practical importance. Because God had in the beginning given the earth to all men to enjoy in common, it followed, first, that no one had a right to take for himself more than he needed, and, second, that a man had only a right to take that of which he made good use. A distinction was drawn between necessities and superfluities, at a level which depended upon a man's station in life. As Tierney puts it, "medieval canonists took it for granted that different styles of living were appropriate to the different grades in the hierarchy"; superfluities were the goods which a man possessed over and above this accepted standard of living. It was a matter of justice that superfluous goods should be given to those in need, whereas if a man gave away his own necessities to another this was an act of charity or mercy. Aquinas took this doctrine a step further when he argued that a man in need was entitled to avail himself of another man's property;

> It is not theft, properly speaking, to take secretly and use another's property in a case of extreme need; because that which he takes for the support of his life becomes his own property by reason of that need.

What is the connection between the feudal conception of justice and the conditions of life in feudal society? Let us begin by noting that the supply of food and other basic goods was more certain in feudal societies than in most primitive societies. Although poor by comparison to modern market societies, they generally afforded the peasantry a subsistence income and of course allowed privileged groups—the nobility and the clergy—to live off the surplus created by the peasants. In considering primitive societies, I argued that an overriding concern for economic survival militated against the development of a sense of justice; the main preoccupation of feudal society, however, was less economic survival than the preservation of order—what men feared was that society would disintegrate into a congeries of warring platoons, as indeed it did from time to time. To preserve order in the absence of a sovereign power, it was above all necessary that customary rights and obligations should be respected; in such a context it becomes intelligible that justice should become an important value, and that it should be interpreted in a conservative sense, to refer to the protection of established rights. We have repeatedly stressed that in feudal society the function of justice was to stabilize the social hierarchy in the interests of order.

We may turn now to the social relationships characteristic of feudalism. How did men holding different positions in the hierarchy encounter one another? First, it was clear that each man had a single dominant role, determined mainly by the type of work he performed, and these sole differences were made perfectly manifest in differences of dress, speech, etc. Second, there was at the same time sufficient geographical and social mobility to make it clear that the various estates were not occupied by men of different "breeds": there was a sense of common humanity and an appreciation that the separation of men into estates was conventional, although of course absolutely necessary. Third, the relationship between superior and inferior was a personal one. The serf was not subordinated to the nobility as a collective group but tied to one particular lord, and equally the vassal swore homage either to a single lord or (through a corruption of the institution) to a small number of lords. Writers on feudalism have observed that the system worked best when this personal relationship was preserved through sustained contact between master and man. Now if we take these three points together, what moral ideas are likely to emerge from such a system of relationships? First, the strength of role divisions is such that more emphasis will be laid on maintaining the various roles than on giving each person his due as an individual. Justice will be thought to consist primarily in treating a man according to his station rather than according to his particular personal qualities. In other words, (as I shall argue later) justice as desert can only emerge as a value when the market has rendered role divisions much more fluid, so that we encounter other men as individuals rather than as the occupants of fixed roles. So long as role distinctions remain strong, the appropriate way of understanding justice is as the protection of a man's rights which derive from his social position.

We have also seen, however, that in feudal society the occupants of different roles were linked to one another by ties of personal dependence. Relationships of this type naturally created a sense of mutual obligation rather than a sense of mutual indifference. Although there was no question of the lord acknowledging the serf as his equal, he did recognize that they were connected by a personal bond, and that he therefore had a responsibility for the serf's welfare (no doubt in practice such responsibilities were often evaded, but we are here considering the moral responses appropriate to feudal society). This is the basis of the recognition given to the claims of need in the feudal conception of justice. A condition of need gave a man a just claim on the resources of those placed in privileged positions, and especially of course on the master to whom he was personally tied. We should again note the contrast with market society where impersonal market relationships predominate, and men are likely to encounter one another as strangers.

At the beginning of this chapter, I introduced the social typology which I was about to use with the observation that each type of society—primitive, feudal, and market—was distinguished by the prominence of certain features within it, while features characteristic of the other types would be present to a lesser degree. It is particularly important to bear this in mind when discussing market society. I shall describe the early capitalist systems of Western Europe and America as "market societies," while acknowledging that in real terms these systems superimposed "nonmarket" social structures and relationships upon market ones. What are the distinctive social relationships which make up a market society? Its social structure is created out of a series of contracts and exchanges between otherwise free and equal individuals. By contrast to their situation in primitive society, men in market society are not bound by obligations of kinship and traditional status. By contrast to feudalism, they have no fixed place in a hierarchy, and owe no allegiance to any superior. Under a market system, men are equal before the law. They are free to choose their occupations, to join whatever associations they wish, to buy and sell in the market, to make contracts without restriction, to gain wealth and prestige. Any social and economic inequalities arise from these activities. Most of what each man produces is exchanged in the market, rather than consumed directly; this implies a fairly extensive division of labour and a system of mutual interdependence centred on the market.

If we compare this market model with the actual conditions of Western capitalism (at any point in its development) we shall see that, although market relations have always been predominant, they have been combined with other elements of social structure, especially with the existence of vertical class divisions. Capitalist societies are not pure market societies, firstly because they typically contain an aristocratic class whose social position is inherited rather than achieved through production and exchange; and secondly, because they contain a working class whose situation is only partly a market one. The worker enters into market relationships with his employer (he freely exchanges his services for a wage) and with the tradesmen from whom he buys his goods, but his relationship with his fellow workers is not basically a market one. It is rather one of mutual assistance and mutual support for security, and for protection against a common opponent—the employer. Trade unions, the chief institutional form through which this class solidarity has been expressed, have rightly been recognized by theorists of the market as incompatible with a pure market system, rather as the communal compact of medieval burgesses was seen by feudal thinkers as alien to that system. We shall later examine what effect its ambiguous position—half in and half out of the market—has had on the social ideas of the working class.

The fact that in the real world market relations only exist in conjunction with vertical class divisions has the unfortunate consequence that we cannot find a homogeneous market society with an appropriate set of shared social ideas. But it may be possible to overcome this difficulty to a certain degree by finding within market societies a group of people for whom market relations are particularly salient. During the earlier period of capitalism, particularly in Britain and the U.S.A., the middle class appear to form such a group. I include among the middle class capitalists, merchants, shopkeepers, and (more arguably) independent artisans and farmers. These men worked for themselves, and their success depended upon their ability to produce and sell in the market. They inherited no fixed position in society, yet the social structure was sufficiently open for them to rise in the world according to their ability and good fortune, at least until they reached the very top of the social scale.

As market relationships became more prominent, and as the middle class began to exert more social influence, a new theory, which we may refer to as individualism, was developed. This theory abandoned any notion of a natural hierarchy in society, and began instead with the idea that men were born free and equal, possessing sets of rights which derived from their inherent natural capacities. Society was seen as the product of the contracts and associations into which these free individuals had entered for their own advantage. The social order was not a constraint on human ambitions, rather whatever order society possessed was the result of human wants and interests, and ideally at least should be readily modifiable if those wants and interests changed. A man's duty was no longer to remain within his station, but instead to take on whatever tasks, and reap whatever rewards, his abilities would allow him. In religious thought, this meant that the doctrine of the "calling" was transformed from a recipe for economic traditionalism into the demand that each man should seek out the calling most suited to his capacities. The parable of the talents was cited to show that God had granted each man abilities in order that he should put them to the best use possible, and gain his just reward in the process.

An integral part of individualism was a conception of justice as the requital of desert. This criterion is stressed to the exclusion both of the protection of rights and of the fulfilment of needs. Of course, in individualist theory the rights of property are inviolable, and contracts must be enforced, but the ultimate ground for these views is either utilitarian or else resides in the conception of justice referred to. Individualism has no time for rights as such, when these are neither socially useful nor necessary to ensure that desert gets its proper reward; it would not, for instance, acknowledge that the rights traditionally attached to a particular social position were in any way worthy of respect. Anything that a man may justly claim he must earn by exercising his capacities in a socially useful way, in which case the institutions of property, contract, and exchange will ensure that he gets a fair return.

Why should individualism, and the theory of justice as the reward of merit that goes with it, have been produced by market society, and especially by the group in that society for whom market relations were particularly salient? One answer is that individualism is simply a correct description of market society; and that the market really does reward people according to their deserts. But this is manifestly too crude an answer, and neither of the claims contained in it is very plausible. We shall do better to look for an intelligible link between the social position of the group we have singled out for examination and the ideas of justice to which it adhered. The relevant features of the social position of the middle-class entrepreneur or tradesman are as follows: first, the lack of a fixed social status such as would be provided by a hierarchical society, but instead the opportunity to make one's way in the world by one's efforts; second, the absence of a traditional set of rights and obligations—whether to kinsmen, etc., as in primitive society, or to superiors and/or inferiors as in hierarchical society; third, social and geographical mobility, with the consequence that many of one's social encounters are with strangers; fourth, the prominence of market relations themselves—particularly the exchange of goods and services, and free entry into contract.

The fourth of these features is perhaps the most important. The intellectual results of the exchange relationship have been classically analysed by Marx and Bouglé. Both see the market as essentially egalitarian in its implications; it undermines hierarchical social and legal relations because market power is solely a function of the amount of exchange value (goods or money) that a person possesses. From the point of view of the market traditional social distinctions are irrelevant, and there is a contradiction between the equality of the market place and, say, the social inequality of a system of estates. As market relations become more dominant, egalitarian demands are made—for equal human rights, equality before the law, political equality, etc. But this egalitarianism stops short of economic equality in the strong sense, for the market requires equality in the exchange of values rather than the equal treatment of individuals. Its principle of operation is that each man should receive back the exact equivalent in value of what he brings to the market; however, the amount brought to the market will depend upon the productive powers of the individual, which differ of course from person to person. What the market achieves is a distribution according to desert (where desert is measured by the creation of exchange value) rather than economic equality. Bouglé is correct when, in setting out the "egalitarian ideas" which characterize modern (late nineteenth-century) society, he gives the principle "to each according to his works" as the criterion of economic distribution, and rejects the principle of equal distribution which he believes to enjoy little favour with his contemporaries.

We can thus see how the experience of the market leads people to adopt a conception of justice as the requital of desert. The paradigmatic exchange relationship takes place between two people who are strangers to one another, who owe neither deference nor services to each other, and whose knowledge is limited to the relative values of the goods or services to be exchanged. This relationship allows no foothold either to the notion of protecting rights or to the notion of satisfying needs. Established rights are irrelevant because neither person stands in any fixed role relationship towards the other, there are no standing obligations, and so on. Needs are irrelevant because each party to the exchange is bent solely on making the most favourable bargain possible, and in any case has no knowledge of the needs of the other party. On the other hand, although an exchange relationship does not have as its *direct* object the requital of desert, it does *indirectly* bring about this result provided that desert is defined in such a way that a person's deserts are embodied in the commodity which he brings to the exchange. At the very least, the definition of justice as desert is the only substantive conception which is consistent with the type of interpersonal relationship characteristic of the market.

The argument of the last chapter, reduced to its simplest terms, is that our concept of social justice has grown out of the specific arrangements of market society, and that while other types of society may embody concepts which are in certain respects analogous to ours, they do not have any single concept with the same range of uses. Furthermore, some of the conflicts which are inherent in our concept can be understood by reference to its historical development under the impact of social change—for instance, the rather uncertain place occupied by the idea of need in our thinking about justice may be explained by reference to the changes in social thought accompanying the transition from free market to organized capitalism. Now if this argument is to be fully successful, it should eventually give a complete sociological account of the structure of the concept which was originally revealed by philosophical analysis. If the philosophical and sociological parts of this inquiry are compared, however, it will be seen that one of the three constituent elements of our concept of justice—the principle of rights—has been omitted from the sociological account of market society; and the reasons for this omission must now be explained.

From our point of view the cardinal feature of market societies, not shared by primitive or hierarchical societies, is that their members characteristically evaluate the social distribution of benefits by reference to certain ideal standards of distribution—namely criteria of desert and need. This is above all what we have in mind when we talk about the idea of social justice. The point I was concerned to make was that although other kinds of society clearly have fixed rules of distribution, etc., they do not have an idea of social justice in the sense just explained. Having said this, and having looked at various differences between market and other societies which may serve to explain it, we may now go on to say that the general criteria of social justice can only be implemented by establishing fixed institutions and rules, and thus by conferring certain positive rights upon individuals. Because such implementation is always imperfect, there must arise the conflicts between established rights and deserts or needs which we analysed in chapter one. Once a right has been established, it gains its own intrinsic value because individuals come to govern their actions by reference to it, and so any interference with rights will affect the security and freedom of action of some people. But in market societies rights are open to criticism as they are not in, say, feudal societies. The question of whether an individual ought to have the rights that he does may always be raised, and if a given distribution of rights is seen to be sufficiently unjust (by a desert or need criterion) we may decide to alter it. Thus what is distinctive about the social thinking of market societies is their assessment of existing rights by ideal standards of social justice, and it is these ideal standards which stand most in need of sociological explanation. This accounts for the direction of the argument in the last chapter.

Finally, we should note that actual market societies still contain some remnants of "feudal" thinking, in which rights are accepted even though they have no foundation in one of the ideal standards of justice. For instance, a few people will be found to accept the notion of a "natural aristocracy"—of a class of people with an inherited right to govern their inferiors. This should serve to remind us that our social classification was a classification of ideal types, and that real societies will always contain elements drawn from each type; thus market societies contain some hierarchical elements, and so forth.

Part Four: Justice and Punishment

Punishment is, perhaps, the original meaning of justice and it is, no doubt, one of its most enduring aspects. Whether a society is free market or socialist, whether it is a free-wheeling democracy or a ruthless dictatorship, whether it systematically respects or routinely violates human rights, there are always those who break the law and violate whatever there is of a public trust, and they must be punished. They must, we think, but why? What reasons do we have for punishing offenders? What gives us, or the state acting in the name of the people, the right to deprive citizens of their wealth, their freedom, or their very lives?

What is at issue here is the rationale for *retribution*—as opposed to, say, *revenge*. No matter how much the behaviors of these may resemble each other—and it is clear that they can, as illustrated in the description of the Sardinian code of vengeance in the selection that begins this section—retribution and revenge are distinct notions. Robert Nozick suggests a number of distinctions between the two: retribution is impersonal, revenge personal; retribution is always for a wrong, revenge sometimes merely for a slight; retribution is intrinsically limited in its severity by the offense, revenge is not; and so forth. But conceptual analysis, cogent as it may be, is not justification: even if we agree that an infliction of some kind of loss on an agent is justified because of some wrong that agent has committed, we still know nothing about *why* it is justifiable intentionally to inflict such harm on someone. After all, to punish, to inflict retribution, seems on its face to be a bad thing: it involves the causing of suffering, the depriving of wealth, or liberty, or citizenship, or even life. Yet there is supposed to be something about the conditions under which this deprivation takes place that makes it permissible, even mandatory, for the state to cause this kind of suffering.

One prominent account of how punishment is justified appeals to a natural idea: The only reason to allow or to cause what is otherwise bad is that we can thereby bring about a greater good than we otherwise could provide. When I have a toothache, I suffer the dentist's drill in order to bring about the compensating greater good of relief. So, too, we might think that while punishment is considered on its own a bad thing, it can be a good thing if punishing brings about a greater good than not punishing would. One school of thought on the justification of punishment appealed to this principle as a master rule for all moral and political reasoning: it is, as we saw in the discussion of John Stuart Mill's view in Part Three, the *principle of utility*, which holds that in every moral decision the relevant standard in making the decision is the amount of good that will be brought about: one should always act so as to bring about the greatest good among the alternative possibilities. Punishing, then, falls under the governance of this principle as well: what justifies punishing, the intentional infliction of harm upon wrongdoers, is the good that can be brought about thereby. Society benefits both from the example set by punishing a criminal (thus discouraging others from performing similar criminal acts) and from the effects of the act of punishing on the criminal himself or herself. The selection from Jeremy Bentham's work is a clear example of this view: Bentham accounts for the need to punish in terms of its utility, and ultimately determines the amount of punishment to be inflicted by a cost-benefit analysis of suffering inflicted versus social gains achieved. The most serious objection to the utilitarian account of punishment has been that it seems that the utilitarian view would sanction punishing the innocent in some cases, if such punishment could bring about greater good. (If, for example, there were danger that the state would be seen as ineffective, thus encouraging more wrongdoing, there might be justification for framing some innocent people in order to give evidence for the state's capacity to catch and convict offenders.) In the selection from John Rawls—himself no utilitarian—Rawls argues that this objection to the utilitarian view can be answered, and that the way it can be answered actually bolsters the overall plausibility of the utilitarian theory of punishment.

The classic alternative to the utilitarian position on punishment has been a view called "retributivism": those guilty of crimes should be punished because they deserve to be punished; their wrongdoing both makes it permissible to punish them and gives the state good reasons to do so. While the utilitarians determine the amount of punishment that is appropriate by appeal to maximizing standards—what punishment would secure the best results overall?—the retributivists tend to rely upon *proportion* as the standard: the punishment inflicted should be proportionate to the severity of the offense. The theory of punishment offered by Immanuel Kant is perhaps the most famous example of unvarnished retributivism: the rationale for punishing someone is only that he or she has committed a crime; the crime should be punished according to the principle of equality (the severity of the punishment must somehow "equal" the severity of the crime); and the duty to punish is so weighty that even if a civil society decided to dissolve itself it must execute the last murderer in prison before it does so, so that "bloodguiltiness may not remain on the people." Later retributivists have toned down the stringency of this duty to punish, and have suggested that even if we can make little sense of the notion of punishment equaling the crime we can still provide alternative retributivist interpretations of the notion of proportionality (e.g., more severe punishments should be given to more severe crimes, less severe punishments to less severe crimes). But we might still wonder about the fundamental principle of the retributivist view, the brute claim that crime merits punishment. How, the utilitarian critic might ask, are you to explain the truth of this principle to one who rejects it, or is uncertain about it? (For, after all, the utilitarian thinks that punishment is just one of many issues decided by a broader principle, the principle of utility.) Michael Moore, a contemporary retributivist, takes up this challenge. The substance of his defense is that many of us affirm claims similar to the retributivist principle, so that the retributivist principle coheres well with many other principles that we already accept. And, further, we can get some evidence for the retributivist view by our attitudes toward ourselves when we recognize that we have done wrong: we tend to see ourselves as worthy of punishment. Why, Moore asks, would you see yourself as worthy of punishment, yet fail to extend this judgment to others whom you recognize to be guilty of wrongdoing?

Retributivism and utilitarianism have dominated the debate over the justifiability of punishment. But there are other powerful views that have emerged, representatives of which we have included in this section: Hegel's view that punishment is somehow self-chosen, that the wrongdoer invites his or her own punishment; Nietzsche's view that punishment is merely the expression of resentment; and Hampton's account of punishment as not merely a deterrent against future crime but as an educating device, something that exhibits the wrongfulness of a crime to the offender. And Robert Solomon, coming back to the distinction between retribution and revenge with which the section opens, calls into question the depth of the divide between these notions, wondering whether revenge is to be dismissed so quickly after all.

We conclude Part Four with a number of readings focusing on the death penalty, a punishment unique in its irreversibility and irrevocability. The death penalty continues to enjoy a great deal of popular support in the United States, despite its wide prohibition in European countries. But the current empirical data on the capacity of the death penalty to serve as an effective deterrent is far from clear: There is no conclusive evidence that the presence of the death penalty, or its removal, has any effect on the number of violent crimes committed. This seems to be a case, then, in which the particular theory of punishment that we affirm might make a clear practical difference in our stance on the justification of capital punishment. But matters turn out to be not so clear cut: In *Gregg* v. *Georgia,* the 1976 case reaffirming the constitutional validity of the death penalty, the majority appealed both to considerations of retribution and deterrence in arguing for the validity of the death penalty, while the minority dismissed retribution as a justification on the basis of its being mere vengeance and dismissed deterrence as a justification on account of the inconclusiveness of the data. Hugo Bedau, a longtime opponent of the death penalty, argues against the death penalty both as an ineffective deterrent and as unnecessary for achieving adequate retribution. And Ernest van den Haag has suggested that even if the data are inconclusive, it would be better to err in favor of potential innocent victims of crime rather than in favor of convicted murderers. The relevance of the data, the interpretation of proportionality between crime and punishment, the relative weights of retribution and deterrence—all of these must enter into an account of the justifiability of punishment by death. But we should not lose sight of the act itself, what the state undertakes to do when it punishes someone capitally. In the selection that concludes this section, Albert Camus asks us to focus on this act, and to consider whether to be in the business of execution makes the state horrible in ways that even the worst of individual wrongdoers is not.

Pietro Marongiu and Graeme Newman, "Patterns of Vengeance," from *Vengeance* (1987)

In *Vengeance,* Pietro Marongiu (1946–) and Graeme Newman (1939–) describe a variety of traditional cultural practices concerning revenge. The idea that vengeance is a primitive emotion or even an instinct neglects the enormous amount of cultural stimulation, support, and structure—and even a semblance of legitimacy—that vengeance receives from particular social rules and expectations. In many parts of the world, retaliation and vengeance—not legal retribution—are built into the social system of justice. Vengeance is a personal, familial, or tribal matter, not an impersonal function of the state. In the following excerpt, the authors describe the Sardinian code of vengeance.

―――――

The Sardinian Code of Vengeance

Su sambene no est abba. (Blood is not water)
— A Sardinian saying.

In Sardinia, the presence of a long established code of vengeance that displays a high degree of formalization and seems, to this day, to regulate the mechanism of the feuds as well as individual vengeance, has been analyzed by Antonio Pigliaru. It has been interpreted as an expression of the wider discrepancy between cultural models of the inner areas of the island and that of Italian society in general. This hypothesis was stated some years ago in the now classic book by Wolfgang and Ferracuti, *The Subculture of Violence.*

Because of its unique history and culture, a particular lifestyle has been maintained in the inner areas of Sardinia that serves to regulate and control violent behavior. The state, traditionally viewed by the inhabitants as a source of "foreign" domination, was always immersed in conflict with the local inhabitants. Historically, in fact, this authority has been sporadic and essentially remote. This condition of conflict, linked to the permanent social organization of extended families and clans that were also in conflict with each other for control of territory and goods, has produced, over the centuries, a climate of isolation and antagonism towards external forces of change. It is not then surprising that the Sardinian pastoral society has developed a system of defining and controlling conflict by avoiding any

From *Vengeance* by Pietro Marongiu and Graeme Newman and published by Rowman & Littlefield, Publishers, Inc. Reprinted by permission of the publisher.

recourse to a third party—i.e., the state. We can see that this is an attempt to maintain social order without resorting to the obedience model.

The antagonism between the two models of reciprocity and obedience that we have proposed to explain the phenomenon of vengeance is also clear if we consider this customary code, and in general, the conflict between a pastoral subculture and the wider Italian culture. The culture of vengeance that underlies this code is also responsible, at least in part, for the mechanism of identification and support of bandit figures that are opposed to the pressing external cultural forces. In this context, the code seems to express the need of the pastoral society to exercise a limitation and control on the destructive mechanism of vengeful exchange. In order to do this, the code must be able to define offensive and vengeful action in terms of crimes and punishments. It must be able to establish "objective" limitations to vengeful behavior beyond the definitions of offense given by each party or faction.

The Offenses

According to the code of vengeance, "one determinate action is offensive when the event from which depends the existence of such offense is foreseen in order to damage dignity and honor." Property damage in itself is not an offense, and is not sufficient cause for vengeance unless it were done with specific intent to offend the honor of the clan or individual. In this case the offensive will is determined by the basis of objective circumstances or subjective circumstances such as the intensity of malice and condition of the offender, or the relation between the offender and the offended.

In addition, the code of vengeance considers other kinds of offenses of different degrees of gravity. The most serious offense is murder. Other offenses are bearing false witness and spying. The code states clearly that the collective or individual responsibility is the constitutive element of the offense itself. In fact, according to "article 5" of the code, the responsibility for the offensive action is individual or collective according to whether the offense follows the action of a single person or that of a group that is operating as a group. The group is organized according to family structure, and is not responsible for the offenses when they are produced by a single member of the group. Only when the group expresses clear and active solidarity in favor of the culprit, is collective responsibility seen as part of the offense.

Antonio Pigliaru has observed that intentionality is the essential element of the offenses because vengeance, at this stage in its development (i.e. focused on the original offender, rather than unfocused like that of Achilles), must be intentional in order to be directed to the proper source of offense.

Therefore, the offenses can be extinguished only when the "victim/offender" recognizes his responsibility, and takes on himself the charge to repay the "debt" that is "requested" by the offended person, or, when the offender acts in a situation in which he has no other choice (e.g. where he is forced by violence), in which case the author of the violence is responsible for the offense. Once it is stated that the offense is an act set up in order to damage the honor of the other, we must determine exactly what it means to damage the dignity and honor of another.

Pigliaru says that the intent of the offender is either to annihilate or return to a position of weakness the other person or family by hitting them at their weakest point. For example, the use of arson makes clear that there is no material gain from the offense, but ensures that the other faction is placed at a loss. The intent to injure the other party is therefore clear. It is to upset the reciprocity and balance of power between the two factions by taking advantage of the weakness of the other, trying to impose authority with violence, and annihilate the enemy by violent means. The offense is, in this way, similar to, and derivative of, the primitive feeling that we identified at the beginning of this book, of being arbitrarily subjected to a tyrannical power against which one seems powerless to act.

The Punishment

Article 1 of the vengeance code states that vengeance is obligatory. The offenses MUST be avenged. Once the collective or individual responsibility for the offense has been proven, the law of vengeance obliges all persons concerned to take revenge. Obviously, the primary responsibility for implementing vengeance is with the offended person or group. In the Sardinian code, vengeance consists essentially of an offense that is given in response to that which was received. This offense should, in its classic form, match the precipitating offense in kind, but may nevertheless return more damage than was received. The vengeful act should be proportional, but progressive.

We have observed that this tendency of vengeful exchange leads, within the limits of progressive graduation, to the extreme form of retaliation, which is blood vengeance, i.e. murder as revenge. The extreme difficulty in reaching a peaceful resolution to the conflict is most evident when, in blood vengeance, one is required to avenge a previous homicide. Predictably, bloody offenses are the only ones for which the code provides no "statute of limitations." Murders are never forgotten. In this way, the limitless "market" for vengeance is perpetuated. The punishment of blood vengeance is inflicted not only for homicides, but also for crimes "against honor," such as breaking a promise of marriage, spying, and bearing false witness.

The progressive tendency of vengeful exchange is clear; the offense that has acted as vengeance in itself constitutes a new offense which should be avenged. Blood vengeance in particular is a capital offense, even though it is given in order to avenge a preceding blood offense. In this instance we see the classic basis of what outsiders are inclined to call "chaos." It is a society in which there is no way to distinguish between crimes and punishments. They are, in fact, interchangeable, equally justifiable, equally criminal.

In recognizing the two elements of proportionality and responsibility (personal and collective) in vengeance, the code seems to be an evolution in comparison with the old conception of vengeance in which the retaliation was automatically and mechanically inflicted on all the members of the offender group. However, the maturation of vengeance is not quite as advanced as it was in Hamlet. That is to say, the societal and cultural form of vengeance is not as "primitive" a form of social control as it seems at first glance. Rather, it seems to be halfway between the primitive and the civilized. On the one hand, it does provide the basic distinctions that most established legal codes provide, such as the analysis of intent, the distinction of individual and collective responsibility; but on the other hand the mechanism of control is unable to go the full way of pronouncing which of the acts is criminal and which is not. To attain this, we need a "civilized" society in which a third party— the state—is able to transcend the opposing factions and pronounce which acts are criminal and which are not. It is apparent in feuding societies that the opposing factions will even join together in order to oppose a third party, almost invariably perceived as foreign and representative of an illegitimate order.

The pastoral society of Sardinia, in its warlike attitude, represents an interesting example, rare in western society, of the problems related to the regulation of social conflict, especially the maintenance of a permanent but unstable "equilibrium," without resort to an external principle authority. According to the Sardinian code, more than what could be done, must be done. The necessity to reap vengeance is also more than a private duty. Rather, it is a public duty in the sense that it must be performed on behalf of a code that is adhered to by both factions. The community is served by each side carrying out its duty to avenge. The avenger will even consider revenge as a necessary and unavoidable destiny from which there is no escape. The existence of rigid and immovable rules is typical of any traditional society. The wonder of vengeance is that, in this context, it provides the moral basis for the social order. Vengeance reveals itself as a kind of violence that eradicates the moral damage that was the consequence of another act of violence—a violence that cancels out each previous act, yet recreates iself. It is just as Marx analyzed capital. It works wonders, creating new commodities, which in turn, through social exchange, recreate capital.

Robert Nozick,"Retribution and Revenge," from *Philosophical Explanations* (1981)

In discussions of the moral justification for inflicting punishment, almost every author distinguishes between revenge on one hand and retribution on the other. Both involve some sort of infliction of harm on one for some past offense he or she has committed, but retribution is supposed to have rational support and be essential to justice, while revenge or vengeance, we are told, is just an emotion, an instinct, and not worthy of the honorable name of "justice." In the following excerpt, Robert Nozick (1938–) marks a variety of distinctions, including not only the emotionality of revenge in contrast to the possible impersonality and coolness of retribution, but also the insistence that retribution is always done for a wrong and not merely for a personal harm or offense, and that retribution requires strict limits to punishment while revenge "by its nature need set no limits, although the revenger may limit what he inflicts for external reasons." Nozick allows that punishment is often done for mixed motives, but he ultimately defends only retribution, on the grounds that it "sends a message" to the criminal (and to others, too), and ends by asking the question why, for this purpose, punishment is ultimately necessary at all. (For a theory of retribution similar to Nozick's, see the excerpt by Jean Hampton later in Part Four.)

The view that people deserve punishment for their wrongful acts, independently of the deterrent effect of such punishment, strikes some people as a primitive view, expressive only of the thirst for revenge. Before pursuing the underlying rationale of retribution, punishment inflicted as deserved for a past wrong, we should consider some ways in which retribution differs from revenge.

>   1. Retribution is done for a wrong, while revenge may be done for an injury or harm or slight and need not be for a wrong.
>   2. Retribution sets an internal limit to the amount of the punishment, according to the seriousness of the wrong, whereas revenge internally need set no limit to what is inflicted. Revenge by its nature need set no limits, although the revenger may limit what he inflicts for external reasons.
>   3. Revenge is personal: "this is because of what you did to my———" (self, father, group, and so on). Whereas the agent of retribution need have no special or personal tie to the victim of the wrong for which he exacts retribution.

Do not say he exacts the penalty because of the injury done to his own moral code; that overextends the notion of personal tie. Steps sometimes are taken to exclude the personal tie from intruding in a process of retribution and clouding the nature of what is happening by blurring the distinctness of retribution from revenge. Thus, under a system of capital punishment, if the sister of the official executioner is murdered and the killer is apprehended, someone else will be substituted to perform that execution.

This third point has two aspects: revenge can be desired only by someone with a personal tie (others can desire that some such person inflict revenge, but their desire is not a desire for revenge), and it can be inflicted only by (the agent of) someone with a personal tie. (Revenge may involve differing notions of linkage: (a) because of what you did to my———; (b) because of what you did to me. If someone kills your father, under linkage *a* you kill him while under *b* you kill his father.) Retribution, on the other hand, may be desired or inflicted by people without such a tie. This personal factor also enters into the revenger's desire, noted below, that his connection to the victim for whom revenge is being exacted be known to the recipient of revenge.

>   4. Revenge involves a particular emotional tone, pleasure in the suffering of another, while retribution either need involve no emotional tone, or involves another one, namely, pleasure at justice being done. Therefore, the thirster after revenge often will want to experience (see, be present at) the situation in which the revengee is suffering, whereas with retribution there is no special point in witnessing its infliction.

This connects with the previous point about the personal tie; one purpose of revenge may be to produce a psychological effect in the person who seeks revenge (that particular emotional tone, for example), while retribution has no such personal purpose.

>   5. There need be no generality in revenge. Not only is the revenger not committed to revenging any similar act done to anyone; he is not committed to avenging all done to himself. Whether he seeks vengeance, or thinks it appropriate to do so, will depend upon how he feels at the time about the act of injury. Whereas the imposer of retribution, inflicting deserved punishment for a wrong, is committed to (the existence of some) general principles (prima facie) mandating punishment in other similar circumstances. Furthermore, if possible these general standards will be made known and clear in the process of retribution; even those who act in retribution against the guilty agents of a torturing dictatorship, keeping their own identities secret, will make the principles known.

In drawing these contrasts between retribution and revenge, I do not deny that there can be mixed cases, or that people can be moved by mixed motives, partially a desire for retribution, partially a desire for revenge, or that a stated desire can mask another one that is operative. Usually, it is charged that those favoring retribution really crave revenge; but this will be especially implausible in the absence of a special tie to the victim. (The charge never is made in the other direction, that some who call for revenge really are seeking retribution but are embarrassed at appearing moralistic.) The charge itself, though, recognizes the distinction, even as it seeks to blur it. That retribution can be distinguished from revenge and is, on its surface at least, less primitive neither shows that, nor explains why, retribution is justified. Nor does it explain why retribution and revenge so often have been confused.

Retribution and revenge share a common structure: a penalty is inflicted for a reason (a wrong or injury) with the desire that the other person know why this is occurring and know that he was intended to know. (In the comic books of my youth, the villain seeking revenge always was thwarted by his desire that the hero not merely die but realize why he was dying and at whose hand, in prolonged agony—this gave the hero extended opportunity to escape.) I shall spell out that common structure as it is exemplified by retribution; this must be modified in accordance with the contrasts we have listed to obtain an account of revenge. . . .

"Poetic justice" involves the wrongdoer's undergoing a consequence that approximately could be visited upon him in retribution but which was not produced in that way, usually owing to the failure of one of the first two conditions of retribution. A system of karma, whereby the moral quality of acts produces effects automatically in (this or) another lifetime, is not a system of poetic justice. It is crucial to poetic justice that the (penalty) effect is not a result of the moral quality of the act, even though it appropriately would fit that moral quality. Thus, although very many poetically just things could occur, there could not be a system of poetic justice. The generality a system involves (supporting subjunctives about what would occur) could stem only from the (appropriate) effects being due to the moral quality of the acts, qua moral quality, and so the justice done would not be merely "poetic."

The conditions demarcating retribution explain what otherwise appears to be a ludicrous phenomenon. If someone sentenced to death falls perilously ill or is accidentally injured or attempts suicide the day before the scheduled execution, then the execution is postponed and measures are taken to bring the condemned person back to health so that he then can be executed. Although due-process reasons might be conjured up for this, I believe the reason is that his punishment is to involve something's being visited upon him by others because of the wrongness of his act. His death by natural causes or by his own hand would avoid this, so measures are taken to restore him for punishment. . . .

. . . Retributive punishment is an act of communicative behavior. Revenge also fits this communicative structure, though with a somewhat different message; this provides an explanation of why the two are so often confused.

What is the message of retributive punishment, and why is it communicated in that especially forceful and unwelcome way? The (Gricean) message is: this is how wrong what you did was. . . .

. . . In the case of retributive matching punishment where, to the extent feasible, the penalty inflicted on the wrongdoer is the same as the wrong or harm he did, perhaps the message then is: this is (precisely) the wrong you did. But if our intention is to mean his act was that (magnitude of) wrong, why don't we just say so and spare him the penalty? (Don't say we first must get his attention.) What justifies us in inflicting upon him so unwelcome a mode of communication?

We may view different "theories" of punishment as focusing upon different aspects of communication: the sender of a message, the recipient of this message, the transmission itself. Some have pointed out that punishment has an expressive function, wherein the sender condemns the crime. More frequently, the literature focuses upon the recipient. Under this rubric, we might see punishment as an attempt to demonstrate to the wrongdoer that his act was wrong, not only to mean the act is wrong but to *show* him its wrongness. Some retributive theorists see the showing as having a further goal: the moral improvement of the offender. Punishment is supposed to achieve this goal by bringing home to the offender the nature of what he has done, from which he is to realize its wrongness. Since these theorists see the central purpose of punishment in its further consequences, they have been termed teleological retributivists. . . .

The (Gricean) message of teleological retributive punishment is delivered in a way so that the delivery is evidence that or shows that it is true. (Compare a telegram that says "you have just received a telegram.") Receiving the message (sent that way), "this is how wrong what you did was," is supposed to convince one that it is true; the message, via its sending, is to be self-supporting.

Jeremy Bentham, "A Utilitarian Theory of Punishment," from *Introduction to the Principles of Morals and Legislation* (1789)

The reflections—or better, prescriptions—offered by Jeremy Bentham (1748–1832) concerning the justification and application of punishment are merely one instance of his wide-ranging effort to reform legal practice through appeal to rational principles. The principle that Bentham puts forward as the master rule, the rule to which anyone must appeal in advocating one policy, procedure, or statute over another, is the *principle of utility*: that actions, rules, and institutions are justified only to the extent that they bring about the greater overall good, where by "good" Bentham means pleasure and the absence of pain. By this standard, punishment, being by definition an intentional infliction of something unpleasant (or the intentional deprivation of something pleasant), is immediately suspect. But that does not mean that punishment is *never* justified: rather, the infliction of pain in punishment can be justified, but only if the evil inherent in punishment is capable of bringing about a sufficiently large countervailing good. In the excerpt that follows, Bentham spells out as precisely as he can the conditions under which the state can and should inflict legal punishment.

———

Of the Principle of Utility

I.   Nature has placed mankind under the governance of two sovereign masters, *pain* and *pleasure*. It is for them alone to point out what we ought to do, as well as to determine what we shall do. On the one hand the standard of right and wrong, on the other the chain of causes and effects, are fastened to their throne. They govern us in all we do, in all we say, in all we think: every effort we can make to throw off our subjection, will serve but to demonstrate and confirm it. In words a man may pretend to abjure their empire: but in reality he will remain subject to it all the while. The *principle of utility* recognises this subjection, and assumes it for the foundation of that system, the object of which is to rear the fabric of felicity by the hands of reason and of law. Systems which attempt to question it, deal in sounds instead of sense, in caprice instead of reason, in darkness instead of light.

But enough of metaphor and declamation: it is not by such means that moral science is to be improved.

II.   The principle of utility is the foundation of the present work: it will be proper therefore at the outset to give an explicit and determinate account of what is meant by it. By the principle of utility is meant that principle which approves or disapproves of every action whatsoever, according to the tendency which it appears to have to augment or diminish the happiness of the party whose interest is in question: or, what is the same thing in other words, to promote or to oppose that happiness. I say of every action whatsoever; and therefore not only of every action of a private individual, but of every measure of government.

III.   By utility is meant that property in any object, whereby it tends to produce benefit, advantage, pleasure, good, or happiness, (all this in the present case comes to the same thing) or (what comes again to the same thing) to prevent the happening of mischief, pain, evil, or unhappiness to the party whose interest is considered: if that party be the community in general, then the happiness of the community: if a particular individual, then the happiness of that individual.

IV.   The interest of the community is one of the most general expressions that can occur in the phraseology of morals: no wonder that the meaning of it is often lost. When it has a meaning, it is this. The community is a fictitious *body,* composed of the individual persons who are considered as constituting as it were its *members.* The interest of the community then is, what?—the sum of the interests of the several members who compose it.

V.   It is in vain to talk of the interest of the community, without understanding what is the interest of the individual. A thing is said to promote the interest, or to be *for* the interest, of an individual, when it tends to add to the sum total of his pleasures: or, what comes to the same thing, to diminish the sum total of his pains.

VI.   An action then may be said to be conformable to the principle of utility, or, for shortness sake, to utility, (meaning with respect to the community at large) when the tendency it has to augment the happiness of the community is greater than any it has to diminish it.

VII.   A measure of government (which is but a particular kind of action, performed by a particular person or persons) may be said to be conformable to or dictated by the principle of utility, when in like manner the tendency which it has to augment the happiness of the community is greater than any which it has to diminish it. . . .

Cases Unmeet for Punishment

§ 1.   General View of Cases Unmeet for Punishment

I.   The general object which all laws have, or ought to have, in common, is to augment the total happiness of the community; and therefore, in the first place, to exclude, as far as may be, every thing that tends to subtract from that happiness: in other words, to exclude mischief.

II.   But all punishment is mischief: all punishment in itself is evil. Upon the principle of utility, if it ought at all to be admitted, it ought only to be admitted in as far as it promises to exclude some greater evil.

III.   It is plain, therefore, that in the following cases punishment ought not to be inflicted.

1. Where it is *groundless:* where there is no mischief for it to prevent; being mischievous upon the whole.

2. Where it must be *inefficacious:* where it cannot act so as to prevent the mischief.

3. Where it is *unprofitable,* or too *expensive:* where the mischief it would produce would be greater than what it prevented.

4. Where it is *needless:* where the mischief may be prevented, or cease of itself, without it: that is, at a cheaper rate.

§ 2.   Cases in Which Punishment Is Groundless

These are,

IV.   1. Where there has never been any mischief: where no mischief has been produced to any body by the act in question. Of this number are those in which the act was such as might, on some occasions, be mischievous or disagreeable, but the person whose interest it concerns gave his *consent* to the performance of it. This consent, provided it be free, and fairly obtained, is the best proof that can be produced, that, to the person who gives it, no mischief, at least no immediate mischief, upon the whole, is done. For no man can be so good a judge as the man himself, what it is gives him pleasure or displeasure.

V.   2. Where the mischief was *outweighed:* although a mischief was produced by that act, yet the same act was necessary to the production of a benefit which was of greater value than the mischief. This may be the case with any thing that is done in the way of precaution against instant calamity, as also with any thing that is done in the exercise of the several sorts of powers necessary to be established in every community, to wit, domestic, judicial, military, and supreme.

VI.   3. Where there is a certainty of an adequate compensation: and that in all cases where the offence can be committed. This supposes two things: 1. That the offence is such as admits of an adequate compensation: 2. That such a compensation is sure to be forthcoming. Of these suppositions, the latter will be found to be a merely ideal one: a supposition that cannot, in the universality here given to it, be verified by fact. It cannot, therefore, in practice, be numbered amongst the grounds of absolute impunity. It may, however, be admitted as a ground for an abatement of that punishment, which other considerations, standing by themselves, would seem to dictate.

§ 3.   Cases in Which Punishment Must be Inefficacious

These are,

VII.   1. Where the penal provision is *not established* until after the act is done. Such are the cases, 1. Of an ex-post-facto law; where the legislator himself appoints not a punishment till after the act is done. 2. Of a sentence beyond the law; where the judge, of his own authority, appoints a punishment which the legislator had not appointed.

VIII.   2. Where the penal provision, though established, is *not conveyed* to the notice of the person on whom it seems intended that it should operate. Such is the case where the law has omitted to employ any of the expedients which are necessary, to make sure that every person whatsoever, who is within the reach of the law, be apprized of all the cases whatsoever, in which (being in the station of life he is in) he can be subjected to the penalties of the law.

IX.   3. Where the penal provision, though it were conveyed to a man's notice, *could produce no effect* on him, with respect to the preventing him from engaging in any act of the *sort* in question. Such is the case, 1. In extreme *infancy;* where a man has not yet attained that state or disposition of mind in which the prospect of evils so distant as those which are held forth by the law, has the effect of influencing his conduct. 2. In *insanity;* where the person, if he has attained to that disposition, has since been deprived of it through the influence of some permanent though unseen cause. 3. In *intoxication;* where he has been deprived of it by the transient influence of a visible cause: such as the use of wine, or opium, or other drugs, that act in this manner on the nervous system: which condition is indeed neither more nor less than a temporary insanity produced by an assignable cause.

X.   4. Where the penal provision (although, being conveyed to the party's notice, it might very well prevent his engaging in acts of the sort in question, provided he knew that it related to those acts) could not have this effect, with regard to the *individual* act he is about to engage in: to wit, because he knows not that it is of the number of those to which the penal provision relates. This may happen, 1. In the case of *unintentionality;* where he intends not to engage, and thereby knows not that he is about to engage, in the *act* in which eventually he is about to engage. 2. In the case of *unconsciousness;* where, although he may know that he is about to engage in the *act* itself, yet, from not knowing all the material *circumstances* attending it, he knows not of the *tendency* it has to produce that mischief, in contemplation of which it has been made penal in most instances. 3. In the case of *missupposal;* where, although he may know of the tendency the act has to produce that degree of mischief, he supposes it, though mistakenly, to be attended with some circumstance, or set of circumstances, which, if it had been attended with, it would either not have been productive of that mischief, or have been productive of such a greater degree of good, as has determined the legislator in such a case not to make it penal.

XI.   5. Where, though the penal clause might exercise a full and prevailing influence, were it to act alone, yet by the *predominant* influence of some opposite cause upon the will, it must necessarily be ineffectual; because the evil which he sets himself about to undergo, in the case of his *not* engaging in the act, is so great, that the evil denounced by the penal clause, in case of his engaging in it, cannot appear greater. This may happen, 1. In the case of *physical danger;* where the evil is such as appears likely to be brought about by the unassisted powers of *nature.* 2. In the case of a *threatened mischief;* where it is such as appears likely to be brought about through the intentional and conscious agency of *man*.

XII.   6. Where (though the penal clause may exert a full and prevailing influence over the *will* of the party) yet his *physical faculties* (owing to the predominant influence of some physical cause) are not in a condition to follow the determination of the will: insomuch that the act is absolutely *involuntary*. Such is the case of physical *compulsion or restraint*, by whatever means brought about; where the man's hand, for instance, is pushed against some object which his will disposes him *not* to touch; or tied down from touching some object which his will disposes him to touch.

§ 4.   Cases Where Punishment Is Unprofitable

These are,

XIII.   1. Where, on the one hand, the nature of the offence, on the other hand, that of the punishment, are, *in the ordinary state of things*, such, that when compared together, the evil of the latter will turn out to be greater than that of the former.

XIV.   Now the evil of the punishment divides itself into four branches, by which so many different sets of persons are affected. 1. The evil of *coercion* or *restraint:* or the pain which it gives a man not to be able to do the act, whatever it be, which by the apprehension of the punishment he is deterred from doing. This is felt by those by whom the law is *observed*. 2. The evil of *apprehension:* or the pain which a man, who has exposed himself to punishment, feels at the thoughts of undergoing it. This is felt by those by whom the law has been *broken,* and who feel themselves in *danger* of its being executed upon them. 3. The evil of *sufferance:* or the pain which a man feels, in virtue of the punishment itself, from the time when he begins to undergo it. This is felt by those by whom the law is broken, and upon whom it comes actually to be executed. 4. The pain of sympathy, and the other *derivative* evils resulting to the persons who are in *connection* with the several classes of original sufferers just mentioned. Now of these four lots of evil, the first will be greater or less, according to the nature of the act from which the party is restrained: the second and third according to the nature of the punishment which stands annexed to that offence.

XV.   On the other hand, as to the evil of the offence, this will also, of course, be greater or less, according to the nature of each offence. The proportion between the one evil and the other will therefore be different in the case of each particular offence. The cases, therefore, where punishment is unprofitable on this ground, can by no other means be discovered, than by an examinations of each particular offence; which is what will be the business of the body of the work.

XVI.   2. Where, although in the *ordinary state* of things, the evil resulting from the punishment is not greater than the benefit which is likely to result from the force with which it operates, during the same space of time, towards the excluding the evil of the offence, yet it may have been rendered so by the influence of some *occasional circumstances*. In the number of these circumstances may be, 1. The multitude of delinquents at a particular juncture; being such as would increase, beyond the ordinary measure, the *quantum* of the second and third lots, and thereby also of a part of the fourth lot, in the evil of the punishment. 2. The extraordinary value of the services of some one delinquent; in the case where the effect of the punishment would be to deprive the community of the benefit of those services. 3. The displeasure of the *people;* that is, of an indefinite number of the members of the *same* community, in cases where (owing to the influence of some occasional incident) they happen to conceive, that the offence or the offender ought not to be punished at all, or at least ought not to be punished in the way in question. 4. The displeasure of *foreign powers;* that is, of the governing body, or a considerable number of the members of some *foreign* community or communities, with which the community in question is connected.

§ 5.   *Cases Where Punishment Is Needless*

These are,

XVII.   1. Where the purpose of putting an end to the practice may be attained as effectually at a cheaper rate: by instruction, for instance, as well as by terror: by informing the understanding, as well as by exercising an immediate influence on the will. This seems to be the case with respect to all those offences which consist in the disseminating pernicious principles in matters of *duty;* of whatever kind the duty be; whether political, or moral, or religious. And this, whether such principles be disseminated *under,* or even *without,* a sincere persuasion of their being beneficial. I say, even *without:* for though in such a case it is not instruction that can prevent the writer from endeavouring to inculcate his principles, yet it may the readers from adopting them: without which, his endeavouring to inculcate them will do no harm. In such a case, the sovereign will commonly have little need to take an active part: if it be the interest of *one* individual to inculcate principles that are pernicious, it will as surely be the interest of *other* individuals to expose them. But if the sovereign must needs take a part in the controversy, the pen is the proper weapon to combat error with, not the sword.

Of the Proportion Between Punishments and Offences

I.   We have seen that the general object of all laws is to prevent mischief; that is to say, when it is worth while; but that, where there are no other means of doing this than punishment, there are four cases in which it is *not* worth while.

II.   When it *is* worth while, there are four subordinate designs or objects, which, in the course of his endeavours to compass, as far as may be, that one general object, a legislator, whose views are governed by the principle of utility, comes naturally to propose to himself.

III.   1. His first, most extensive, and most eligible object, is to prevent, in as far as it is possible, and worth while, all sorts of offences whatsoever: in other words, so to manage, that no offence whatsoever may be committed.

IV.   2. But if a man must needs commit an offence of some kind or other, the next object is to induce him to commit an offence *less* mischievous, *rather* than one *more* mischievous: in other words, to choose always the *least* mischievous, of two offences that will either of them suit his purpose.

V.   3. When a man has resolved upon a particular offence, the next object is to dispose him to do *no more* mischief than is *necessary* to his purpose: in other words, to do as little mischief as is consistent with the benefit he has in view.

VI.   4. The last object is, whatever the mischief be, which it is proposed to prevent, to prevent it at as *cheap* a rate as possible.

Immanuel Kant, "A Retributivist Theory of Punishment," from *The Philosophy of Law* (1797)

The moral philosophy of Immanuel Kant (1724–1804) centers on the all-important notions of "duty" and "obligation"—an ethics of "right" or "law" (*Recht*) and not merely of human goods and interests. He juxtaposed his philosophy against the various ethics of moral sentiment and of the public good that dominated the British moral philosophy of the period. Against the moral sentiment theories of Hume, Smith, and others, Kant insisted that what is right must be a matter of universal, timeless, a priori principle, not of a possibly transitory sentimentality or of any mere set of feelings. Against the utilitarianism of Bentham and others, Kant argued that mere utility could not explain the uncompromising character of justice, much less account for those instances in which justice is demonstrably opposed to public utility. Kant's concern with punishment, in particular, is simply as a requirement of justice: he offers no theory of public utility or deterrence, no therapeutic view about rehabilitation and reform. He warns of "woe to him who creeps through the serpent windings of Utilitarianism," for the justification of punishment is not through its consequences, whether for the criminal or for the community as a whole. Kant gives the example of a criminal condemned to death who is offered the alternative of participating in a dangerous medical experiment. Kant repudiates such a bargain with scorn, for "Justice would cease to be justice, if it were bartered away for any consideration whatever."

What, then, is the nature and justification of punishment? For Kant, it is straightforward retribution, and nothing but retribution. As Nozick notes in a previous selection, retribution is different from vengeance, which is a passion (though hardly a moral sentiment) and personal, insofar as retribution is dictated by reason and is applied by the law of the court. The principle according to which retribution operates is "the principle of equality," that is, that the punishment inflicted should be the equivalent of the nature and severity of the crime. "All other standards," Kant says, "are wavering and uncertain." Thus, the principle of retribution, like that of retaliation, insists on matching "like with like." The punishment must not only *fit* the crime, but be *equal to* the crime. In many cases, however, this equivalence is far from obvious—for example, in measuring the equality of pain endured by a rich man and a poor man paying a fine, or the humiliation suffered by a person of high social status as opposed to one of lower status. The one crime in which equivalence is not at all in question, however, is murder. There is no equality between taking the life of another and any penalty less than death. But note that, in addition to his insistence on equivalence, Kant also employs what we might call the "erasure" metaphor—a punishment in some sense erases (which is not to say "reverses" or "undoes") the crime. It is in this context that Kant makes his infamous demand that, even if society were to be dissolved, it would be necessary to execute the last murderer in prison, "that bloodguiltiness may not remain upon the people."

Kant has especially hard words to say about the kindlier moral sentiments applied to the problem of punishment. Against Beccaria's 1764 defense of "the passionate sentimentality of a humane feeling" (against capital punishment), Kant replies that his arguments are wholesale sophistry and "a perversion of right." In reply to Beccaria's argument, that it is impossible that people should agree (in the original "social contract") to their own punishment, Kant insists that a criminal does not will punishment, but rather chooses to do some punishable action. But this distinction yields a rather large conclusion, that the rationality of punishment demands a distinct tribunal of public justice separate from the people over whom it rules. Not only is a crime a violation of the law rather than a mere offense against a person, but judgment against crimes must be made by the law and not by any person or group of persons.

Judicial or Juridical Punishment (*pœna forensis*) is to be distinguished from Natural Punishment (*pœna naturalis*), in which Crime as Vice punishes itself, and does not as such come within the cognizance of the Legislator. Juridical Punishment can never be administered merely as a means for promoting another Good either with regard to the Criminal himself or to Civil Society, but must in all cases be imposed only because the individual on whom it is inflicted *has committed a Crime*. For one man ought never to be dealt with merely as a means subservient to the purpose of another, nor be mixed up with the subjects of Real Right. Against such treatment his Inborn Personality has a Right to protect him, even although he may be condemned to lose his Civil Personality. He must first be found guilty and *punishable*, before there can be any thought of drawing from his Punishment any benefit for himself or his fellow-citizens. The Penal Law is a Categorical Imperative; and woe to him who creeps through the serpent-windings of Utilitarianism to discover some advantage that may discharge him from the Justice of Punishment, or even from the due measure of it, according to the Pharisaic maxim: "It is better that *one* man should die than that the whole people should perish." For if Justice and Righteousness perish, human life would no longer have any value in the world.—What, then, is to be said of such a proposal as to keep a Criminal alive who has been condemned to death, on his being given to understand that if he agreed to certain dangerous experiments being performed upon him, he would be allowed to survive if he came happily through them? It is argued that Physicians might thus obtain new information that would be of value to the Commonweal. But a Court of Justice would repudiate with scorn any proposal of this kind if made to it by the Medical Faculty; for Justice would cease to be Justice, if it were bartered away for any consideration whatever.

But what is the mode and measure of Punishment which Public Justice takes as its Principle and Standard? It is just the Principle of Equality, by which the pointer of the Scale of Justice is made to incline no more to the one side than the other. It may be rendered by saying that the undeserved evil which any one commits on another, is to be regarded as perpetrated on himself. Hence it may be said: "If you slander another, you slander yourself; if you steal from another, you steal from yourself; if you strike another, you strike yourself;

if you kill another, you kill yourself." This is the Right of Retaliation (*jus talionis*); and properly understood, it is the only Principle which in regulating a Public Court, as distinguished from mere private judgment, can definitely assign both the quality and the quantity of a just penalty. All other standards are wavering and uncertain; and on account of other considerations involved in them, they contain no principle conformable to the sentence of pure and strict Justice. It may appear, however, that difference of social status would not admit the application of the Principle of Retaliation, which is that of "Like with Like." But although the application may not in all cases be possible according to the letter, yet as regards the effect it may always be attained in practice, by due regard being given to the disposition and sentiment of the parties in the higher social sphere. Thus a pecuniary penalty on account of a verbal injury, may have no direct proportion to the injustice of slander; for one who is wealthy may be able to indulge himself in this offence for his own gratification. Yet the attack committed on the honour of the party aggrieved may have its equivalent in the pain inflicted upon the pride of the aggressor, especially if he is condemned by the judgment of the Court, not only to retract and apologize, but to submit to some meaner ordeal, as kissing the hand of the injured person. In like manner, if a man of the highest rank has violently assaulted an innocent citizen of the lower orders, he may be condemned not only to apologize but to undergo a solitary and painful imprisonment, whereby, in addition to the discomfort endured, the vanity of the offender would be painfully affected, and the very shame of his position would constitute an adequate Retaliation after the principle of "Like with Like." But how then would we render the statement: "If you *steal* from another, you steal from yourself"? In this way, that whoever steals anything makes the property of all insecure; he therefore robs himself of all security in property, according to the Right of Retaliation. Such a one has nothing, and can acquire nothing, but he has the Will to live; and this is only possible by others supporting him. But as the State should not do this gratuitously, he must for this purpose yield his powers to the State to be used in penal labour; and thus he falls for a time, or it may be for life, into a condition of slavery.—But whoever has committed Murder, must *die*. There is, in this case, no juridical substitute or surrogate, that can be given or taken for the satisfaction of Justice. There is no *Likeness* or proportion between Life, however painful, and Death; and therefore there is no Equality between the crime of Murder and the retaliation of it but what is judicially accomplished by the execution of the Criminal. His death, however, must be kept free from all maltreatment that would make the humanity suffering in his Person loathsome or abominable. Even if a Civil Society resolved to dissolve itself with the consent of all its members—as might be supposed in the case of a People inhabiting an island resolving to separate and scatter themselves throughout the whole world—the last Murderer lying in the prison ought to be executed before the resolution was carried out. This ought to be done in order that every one may realize the desert of his deeds, and that bloodguiltiness may not remain upon the people; for otherwise they might all be regarded as participators in the murder as a public violation of Justice.

The Equalization of Punishment with Crime, is therefore only possible by the cognition of the Judge extending even to the penalty of Death, according to the Right of Retaliation. This is manifest from the fact that it is only thus that a Sentence can be pronounced over all criminals proportionate to their internal *wickedness;* as may be seen by considering the case when the punishment of Death has to be inflicted, not on account of a murder, but on account of a political crime that can only be punished capitally. . . .

Against these doctrines, the Marquis Beccaria has given forth a different view. Moved by the compassionate sentimentality of a humane feeling, he has asserted that all Capital

Punishment is wrong in itself and unjust. He has put forward this view on the ground that the penalty of death could not be contained in the original Civil Contract; for, in that case, every one of the People would have had to consent to lose his life if he murdered any of his fellow-citizens. But, it is argued, such a consent is impossible, because no one can thus dispose of his own life.—All this is mere sophistry and perversion of Right. No one undergoes Punishment because he has willed to be punished, but because he has willed *a punishable Action;* for it is in fact no Punishment when any one experiences what he wills, and it is impossible for any one to *will* to be punished. To say, "I *will* to be punished, if I murder any one," can mean nothing more than, "I submit myself along with all the other citizens to the Laws", and if there are any Criminals among the People, these Laws will include Penal Laws. The individual who, as a Co-legislator, enacts *Penal Law,* cannot possibly be the same Person who, as a Subject, is punished according to the Law; for, *quâ* Criminal, he cannot possibly be regarded as having a voice in the Legislation, the Legislator being rationally viewed as just and holy. If any one, then, enact a Penal Law against himself as a Criminal, it must be the pure juridically law-giving Reason (*homo noumenon*), which subjects him as one capable of crime, and consequently as another Person (*homo phenomenon*), along with all the others in the Civil Union, to this Penal Law. In other words, it is not the People taken distributively, but the Tribunal of public Justice, as distinct from the Criminal, that prescribes Capital Punishment; and it is not to be viewed as if the Social Contract contained the Promise of all the individuals to allow themselves to be punished, thus disposing of themselves and their lives. For if the Right to punish must be grounded upon a promise of the wrongdoer, whereby he is to be regarded as being willing to be punished, it ought also to be left to him to find himself deserving of the Punishment; and the Criminal would thus be his own Judge. The chief error of this sophistry consists in regarding the judgment of the Criminal himself, necessarily determined by his Reason, that he is under obligation to undergo the loss of his life, as a judgment that must be grounded on a resolution of his *Will* to take it away himself; and thus the execution of the Right in question is represented as united in one and the same person with the adjudication of the Right.

G. W. F. Hegel, "Punishment as Self-Chosen," from *The Philosophy of Right* (1821)

G. W. F. Hegel (1770–1831) begins by distinguishing between mere harm and a violation of society itself, which threatens its stability and strength. At the same time, however, the power of society makes the crime of any particular offender all the less dangerous, and this allows for considerable discretion and the possibility of mercy. Like Kant, Hegel distinguishes injury to society from injury to an individual, and it is the former, not the latter, that requires punishment. (The "subjectively infinite" is the individual, the "universal thing" is society.) Again following Kant, Hegel accepts the idea of retribution and "measurement," in terms of both quantity and quality (how great an injury? what kind of injury?), but the danger to society is the primary concern. This is why, Hegel explains, punishment often does not fit the crime, for the seriousness of the injury to the person may have little relationship to the threat to society. Hegel further insists that there is no across-the-board notion of balance or fit: "a penal code is the child of its age and the state of civil society at the time." Again, it is the sanctity of the particular society that is the main concern, not the interests of the various citizens or even the public good, and not, as in Kant, a universal principle of reason as such.

Hegel (in general) has much more appreciation for the passions than Kant did, and so he gives recognition to the significance of revenge, but without defending or trying to justify it as such. Revenge, he tells us, is implicit retribution, "implicit right." The motive is the same, but retribution takes on the "objective" form of the law and recognizes itself as not merely personal but as a function of "the injured universal"— the threatened society. Revenge as such is not justified, but when taken up by society and made "universal"—that is, public, objective, a matter of law—it is "the satisfaction of justice" itself. Hegel, too, uses the image of crime as "annulled" by the punishment (the "erasure" metaphor). Law is thus "restored." Hegel curiously suggests that punishment also allows for "the reconciliation of the criminal with himself," as if the benefits of punishment accrued not only to society, but also to the criminal. Taken by itself, this might seem to be a perverse view. But one of Hegel's great virtues is what we might call his "holistic" thinking about these issues. Punishment, for him, does not simply serve retribution, or deterrence, or rehabilitation, but rather encompasses all of these together. There may be no explicit mention of deterrence or social utility, but these are hardly excluded from consideration. There is no particular celebration of reason or even "right" as such, but these are certainly the aus-

From Hegel's *Philosophy of Right*, translated by T. M. Knox and published by Oxford University Press, 1942. Reprinted by permission of Oxford University Press.

pices under which punishment is justified. And, as in Kant (and before him, Rousseau), Hegel insists that punishment is ultimately not the imposition of society upon the individual so much as the individual imposing the law on himself, facing up to the consequences of his own freely chosen action.

If crime and its annulment (which later will acquire the specific character of punishment) are treated as if they were unqualified evils, it must, of course, seem quite unreasonable to will an evil merely because "another evil is there already." To give punishment this superficial character of an evil is, amongst the various theories of punishment, the fundamental presupposition of those which regard it as a preventive, a deterrent, a threat, as reformative, & c., and what on these theories is supposed to result from punishment is characterized equally superficially as a good. But it is not merely a question of an evil or of this, that, or the other good; the precise point at issue is wrong and the righting of it. If you adopt that superficial attitude to punishment, you brush aside the objective treatment of the righting of wrong, which is the primary and fundamental attitude in considering crime; and the natural consequence is that you take as essential the moral attitude, i.e. the subjective aspect of crime, intermingled with trivial psychological ideas of stimuli, impulses too strong for reason, and psychological factors coercing and working on our ideas (as if freedom were not equally capable of thrusting an idea aside and reducing it to something fortuitous!). The various considerations which are relevant to punishment as a phenomenon and to the bearing it has on the particular consciousness, and which concern its effects (deterrent, reformative, &c.) on the imagination, are an essential topic for examination in their place, especially in connexion with modes of punishment, but all these considerations presuppose as their foundation the fact that punishment is inherently and actually just. In discussing this matter the only important things are, first, that crime is to be annulled, not because it is the producing of an evil, but because it is an infringement of the right as right, and secondly, the question of what that positive existence is which crime possesses and which must be annulled; it is this existence which is the real evil to be removed, and the essential point is the question of where it lies. So long as the concepts here at issue are not clearly apprehended, confusion must continue to reign in the theory of punishment.

100.   The injury [the penalty] which falls on the criminal is not merely *implicitly* just—as just, it is *eo ipso* his implicit will, an embodiment of his freedom, his right; on the contrary, it is also a right *established* within the criminal himself, i.e. in his objectively embodied will, in his action. The reason for this is that his action is the action of a rational being and this implies that it is something universal and that by doing it the criminal has laid down a law which he has explicitly recognized in his action and under which in consequence he should be brought as under his right. . . .

218.   Since property and personality have legal recognition and validity in civil society, wrongdoing now becomes an infringement, not merely of what is subjectively infinite, but of the universal thing which is existent with inherent stability and strength. Hence a new attitude arises: the action is seen as a danger to society and thereby the magnitude of the wrongdoing is increased. On the other hand, however, the fact that society has become strong and sure of itself diminishes the external importance of the injury and so leads to a mitigation of its punishment.

The fact that an injury to one member of society is an injury to all others does not alter the conception of wrongdoing, but it does alter it in respect of its outward existence as an injury done, an injury which now affects the mind and consciousness of civil society as a whole, not merely the external embodiment of the person directly injured. In heroic times, as we see in the tragedy of the ancients, the citizens did not feel themselves injured by wrongs which members of the royal houses did to one another.

Implicitly, crime is an infinite injury; but as an existent fact it must be measured in quantity and quality; and since its field of existence here has the essential character of affecting an idea and consciousness of the validity of the laws, its danger to civil society is a determinant of the magnitude of a crime, or even *one* of its qualitative characteristics.

Now this quality of magnitude varies with the state of civil society; and this is the justification for sometimes attaching the penalty of death to a theft of a few pence or a turnip, and at other times a light penalty to a theft of a hundred or more times that amount. If we consider its danger to society, this seems at first sight to aggravate the crime; but in fact it is just this which has been the prime cause of the mitigation of its punishment. A penal code, then, is primarily the child of its age and the state of civil society at the time. . . .

220.   When the right against crime has the form of revenge, it is only right implicit, not right in the form of right, i.e. no *act* of revenge is justified. Instead of the injured party, the injured *universal* now comes on the scene, and this has its proper actuality in the court of law. It takes over the pursuit and the avenging of crime, and this pursuit consequently ceases to be the subjective and contingent retribution of revenge and is transformed into the genuine reconciliation of right with itself, i.e. into punishment. Objectively, this is the reconciliation of the law with itself; by the annulment of the crime, the law is restored and its authority is thereby actualized. Subjectively, it is the reconciliation of the criminal with himself, i.e. with the law known by him as his own and as valid for him and his protection; when this law is executed upon him, he himself finds in this process the satisfaction of justice and nothing save his own act.

Friedrich Nietzsche, "Punishment and *Ressentiment,*" from *On the Genealogy of Morals* (1887)

The "genealogy of morals" offered by Friedrich Nietzsche (1844–1900) is a combination of history and social psychology with an eye to developing an explanation—not a justification—of our current conceptions of morality and justice. His polemical but now infamous view is that much of what we call morality—or what he calls alternatively "herd" or "slave" morality—is in fact the ingenious expression of that vicious emotion that we know as *ressentiment.* Morality, in short, is not what it seems: it is not a system of categorical imperatives, or directives to maximize utility; rather, it is a grand strategy, motivated by what Nietzsche calls "the will to power," whose aim is to elevate and protect the weak and mediocre against the strong and noble. Predictably, Nietzsche also attacks the increasingly popular philosophies of democracy and socialism, and many of the standard demands of modern justice, notably the emphasis on equality and fairness, fall prey to his displeasure as well. Nietzsche has rightly been cited as the most thoroughgoing critic of morality, and he has been recognized (e.g., by Alasdair MacIntyre in *After Virtue*) as the diagnostician of what ails us in both contemporary morals and moral philosophy. But what is too rarely appreciated is that Nietzsche's campaign of destruction has an affirmative side, a positive view of morals. This is, perhaps, nowhere so evident as in his discussion of justice in the *Genealogy*. Rather than dismiss justice as one more manifestation of slave morality, as we might expect him to do, Nietzsche defends justice as a high, noble ideal. It is, in a sense, the virtue of mercy—"forgiving and forgetting"—but not from a position of weakness but from strength. The idea is that one should be so self-sufficient and satisfied with one's life that one just doesn't worry about the petty injuries inflicted by others. The noble person does not reject revenge or retribution as wrong, but as unnecessary, as beneath his or her dignity.

As for the nature and origins of punishment, Nietzsche's account is no less striking. The urge to punish is, at least in part, the expression of resentment, but this is very different from justice. Justice is "a strong power seeking a means of putting an end to the senseless raging of *ressentiment* among the weaker powers . . . — partly by taking the object of *ressentiment* out of the hands of revenge, partly by substituting for revenge the struggle against the enemies of peace and order, partly by devising and . . . imposing settlements . . . but finally the institution of *law*."

From On the Genealogy of Morals (1887) by Friedrich Nietzsche, translated by Walter Kaufmann and R. J. Hollingdale. Copyright © 1967 by Random House. Inc. Reprinted by permission of the publisher.

Nietzsche ultimately comes down to an extremely positivistic conception of justice, but not, he hastens to add, as "sovereign and universal," as means of preventing struggle or treating everyone as equals. That, he suggests, is not justice, but a kind of despair, a dissolute principle that is "hostile to life."

————————

As its power increases, a community ceases to take the individual's transgressions so seriously, because they can no longer be considered as dangerous and destructive to the whole as they were formerly: the malefactor is no longer "set beyond the pale of peace" and thrust out; universal anger may not be vented upon him as unrestrainedly as before—on the contrary, the whole from now on carefully defends the malefactor against this anger, especially that of those he has directly harmed, and takes him under its protection. A compromise with the anger of those directly injured by the criminal; an effort to localize the affair and to prevent it from causing any further, let alone a general, disturbance; attempts to discover equivalents and to settle the whole matter (*compositio*); above all, the increasingly definite will to treat every crime as in some sense *dischargeable*, and thus at least to a certain extent to *isolate* the criminal and his deed from one another—these traits become more and more clearly visible as the penal law evolves. As the power and self-confidence of a community increase, the penal law always becomes more moderate; every weakening or imperiling of the former brings with it a restoration of the harsher forms of the latter. The "creditor" always becomes more humane to the extent that he has grown richer; finally, how much injury he can endure without suffering from it becomes the actual *measure* of his wealth. It is not unthinkable that a society might attain such a *consciousness of power* that it could allow itself the noblest luxury possible to it—letting those who harm it go *unpunished*. "What are my parasites to me?" it might say. "May they live and prosper: I am strong enough for that!"

The justice which began with, "everything is dischargeable, everything must be discharged," ends by winking and letting those incapable of discharging their debt go free: it ends, as does every good thing on earth, by *overcoming itself.* This self-overcoming of justice: one knows the beautiful name it has given itself—*mercy;* it goes without saying that *mercy* remains the privilege of the most powerful man, or better, his—beyond the law. . . .

Here a word in repudiation of attempts that have lately been made to seek the origin of justice in quite a different sphere—namely in that of *ressentiment.* To the psychologists first of all, presuming they would like to study *resentiment* close up for once, I would say: this plant blooms best today among anarchists and anti-Semites—where it has always bloomed, in hidden places, like the violet, though with a different odor. And as like must always produce like, it causes us no surprise to see a repetition in such circles of attempts often made before . . . to sanctify *revenge* under the name of *justice*—as if justice were at bottom merely a further development of the feeling of being aggrieved—and to rehabilitate not only revenge but all *reactive* affects in general. To the latter as such I would be the last to raise any objection: in respect to the entire biological problem (in relation to which the value of these affects has hitherto been underrrated) it even seems to me to constitute a *service.* All I draw attention to is the circumstance that it is the spirit of *ressentiment* itself out of which this new nuance of scientific fairness (for the benefit of hatred, envy, jealousy, mistrust, rancor, and revenge) proceeds. For this "scientific fairness" immediately ceases and gives way to accents of deadly enmity and prejudice once it is a question of dealing with another group of affects, affects that, it seems to me, are of even greater biological value than those reactive affects and consequently deserve even more to be *scientifically* evaluated and esteemed: namely, the truly *active* affects, such as lust for power, avarice, and the like.

So much against this tendency in general: as for Dühring's specific proposition that the home of justice is to be sought in the sphere of the reactive feelings, one is obliged for truth's sake to counter it with a blunt antithesis: the *last* sphere to be conquered by the spirit of justice is the sphere of the reactive feelings! When it really happens that the just man remains just even toward those who have harmed him (and not merely cold, temperate, remote, indifferent: being just is always a *positive* attitude), when the exalted, clear objectivity, as penetrating as it is mild, of the eye of justice and *judging* is not dimmed even under the assault of personal injury, derision, and calumny, this is a piece of perfection and supreme mastery on earth—something it would be prudent not to expect or to *believe* in too readily. On the average, a small dose of aggression, malice, or insinuation certainly suffices to drive the blood into the eyes—and fairness out of the eyes—of even the most upright people. The active, aggressive, arrogant man is still a hundred steps closer to justice than the reactive man; for he has absolutely no need to take a false and prejudiced view of the object before him in the way the reactive man does and is bound to do. For that reason the aggressive man, as the stronger, nobler, more courageous, has in fact also had at all times a *freer* eye, a *better* conscience on his side: conversely, one can see who has the invention of the "bad conscience" on his conscience—the man of *ressentiment!*

Finally, one only has to look at history: in which sphere has the entire administration of law hitherto been at home—also the need for law? In the sphere of reactive men, perhaps? By no means: rather in that of the active, strong, spontaneous, aggressive. From a historical point of view, law represents on earth—let it be said to the dismay of the above-named agitator (who himself once confessed: "the doctrine of revenge is the red thread of justice that runs through all my work and efforts")—the struggle *against* the reactive feelings, the war conducted against them on the part of the active and aggressive powers who employed some of their strength to impose measure and bounds upon the excesses of the reactive pathos and to compel it to come to terms. Wherever justice is practiced and maintained one sees a stronger power seeking a means of putting an end to the senseless raging of *ressentiment* among the weaker powers that stand under it (whether they be groups or individuals)—partly by taking the object of *ressentiment* out of the hands of revenge, partly by substituting for revenge the struggle against the enemies of peace and order, partly by devising and in some cases imposing settlements, partly by elevating certain equivalents for injuries into norms to which from then on *ressentiment* is once and for all directed. The most decisive act, however, that the supreme power performs and accomplishes against the predominance of grudges and rancor—it always takes this action as soon as it is in any way strong enough to do so—is the institution of *law,* the imperative declaration of what in general counts as permitted, as just, in its eyes, and what counts as forbidden, as unjust: once it has instituted the law, it treats violence and capricious acts on the part of individuals or entire groups as offenses against the law, as rebellion against the supreme power itself, and thus leads the feelings of its subjects away from the direct injury caused by such offenses; and in the long run it thus attains the reverse of that which is desired by all revenge that is fastened exclusively the viewpoint of the person injured: from now on the eye is trained to an ever more *impersonal* evaluation of the deed, and this applies even to the eye of the injured person himself (although last of all, as remarked above).

"Just" and "unjust" exist, accordingly, only after the institution of the law (and *not,* as Dühring would have it, after the perpetration of the injury). To speak of just or unjust *in itself* is quite senseless; *in itself,* of course, no injury, assault, exploitation, destruction can be "unjust," since life operates *essentially*, that is in its basic functions, through injury, assault, exploitation, destruction and simply cannot be thought of at all without this character. One must indeed grant something even more unpalatable: that, from the highest biological stand-point, legal conditions can never be other than *exceptional conditions,* since they constitute a partial restriction of the will of life, which is bent upon power, and are subordinate to its total goal as a single means: namely, as a means of creating *greater* units of power. A legal order thought of as sovereign and universal, not as a means in the struggle between power-complexes but as a means of *preventing* all struggle in general—perhaps after the communistic cliché of Dühring, that every will must consider every other will its equal—would be a principle *hostile to life,* an agent of the dissolution and destruction of man, an attempt to assassinate the future of man, a sign of weariness, a secret path to nothingness.—

> . . . Let us eliminate the concept of *sin* from the world—and let us soon dispatch the concept of *punishment* after it! May these exiled monsters live somewhere else henceforth and not among men—if they insist on living and will not perish of disgust with themselves! . . .
>
> *Dawn,* section 202

> *That man be delivered from revenge,* that is for me the bridge to the highest hope . . .
> *Zarathustra* II, "On the Tarantulas"

John Rawls,"A Defense of the Utilitarian View," from "Two Concepts of Rules" (1955)

John Rawls (1921–), as is clear from excerpts from his work that appear in Parts Two and Five, does not himself affirm a utilitarian conception of social justice. But in the following excerpt Rawls is concerned to defend the utilitarian account of punishment from a commonly raised objection to it. Utilitarianism, it might be argued, is necessarily at odds with justice, for given its appeal to the principle of utility as the final decider of moral and political questions, surely occasions could arise that would justify the inflicting of punishment on the innocent. Suppose, for example, that the only way to prevent rioting is to frame and punish an innocent person, a

From the *Philosophical Review* 64 (1955). Copyright © 1955 Cornell University. Reprinted by permission of the publisher.

scapegoat. Would not, then, the utilitarian account of punishment endorse punishing in this case? Rawls argues that the best utilitarian view of punishment could avoid this result: we need to ask what practice of punishing the principle of utility would endorse, where a practice of punishing includes the rules that we use to decide whether a person should be punished. Surely an alternative practice of punishing (Rawls calls it "telishment") that allowed for officials to punish the innocent when it appeared to produce greater good to do so would be terribly hazardous. Less hazardous is our own practice of punishing only the guilty, within a predetermined range of severity. While our defense of the practice of punishing is utilitarian—the point of having such a practice is to produce good consequences—the procedures of that practice fit our often retributivist intuitions.

In this paper I want to show the importance of the distinction between justifying a practice and justifying a particular action falling under it, and I want to explain the logical basis of this distinction and how it is possible to miss its significance. While the distinction has frequently been made, and is now becoming commonplace, there remains the task of explaining the tendency either to overlook it altogether, or to fail to appreciate its importance.

To show the importance of the distinction I am going to defend utilitarianism against those objections which have traditionally been made against it in connection with punishment . . . in a way which makes it a much better explication of our considered moral judgments than these traditional objections would seem to admit. Thus the importance of the distinction is shown by the way it strengthens the utilitarian view regardless of whether that view is completely defensible or not.

To explain how the significance of the distinction may be overlooked, I am going to discuss two conceptions of rules. One of these conceptions conceals the importance of distinguishing between the justification of a rule or practice and the justification of a particular action falling under it. The other conception makes it clear why this distinction must be made and what is its logical basis.

The subject of punishment, in the sense of attaching legal penalties to the violation of legal rules, has always been a troubling moral question. The trouble about it has not been that people disagree as to whether or not punishment is justifiable. Most people have held that, freed from certain abuses, it is an acceptable institution. Only a few have rejected punishment entirely, which is rather surprising when one considers all that can be said against it. The difficulty is with the justification of punishment: various arguments for it have been given by moral philosophers, but so far none of them has won any sort of general acceptance; no justification is without those who detest it. I hope to show that the use of the aforementioned distinction enables one to state the utilitarian view in a way which allows for the sound points of its critics.

For our purposes we may say that there are two justifications of punishment. What we may call the retributive view is that punishment is justified on the grounds that wrongdoing merits punishment. It is morally fitting that a person who does wrong should suffer in proportion to his wrongdoing. That a criminal should be punished follows from his guilt, and the severity of the appropriate punishment depends on the depravity of his act. The state of affairs where a wrongdoer suffers punishment is morally better than the state of affairs where he does not; and it is better irrespective of any of the consequences of punishing him.

What we may call the utilitarian view holds that on the principle that bygones are bygones and that only future consequences are material to present decisions, punishment is justifiable only by reference to the probable consequences of maintaining it as one of the devices of the social order. Wrongs committed in the past are, as such, not relevant considerations for deciding what to do. If punishment can be shown to promote effectively the interest of society it is justifiable, otherwise it is not.

I have stated these two competing views very roughly to make one feel the conflict between them: one feels the force of *both* arguments and one wonders how they can be reconciled. From my introductory remarks it is obvious that the resolution which I am going to propose is that in this case one must distinguish between justifying a practice as a system of rules to be applied and enforced, and justifying a particular–action which falls under these rules; utilitarian arguments are appropriate with regard to questions about practices, while retributive arguments fit the application of particular rules to particular cases.

We might try to get clear about this distinction by imagining how a father might answer the question of his son. Suppose the son asks, "Why was *J* put in jail yesterday?" The father answers, "Because he robbed the bank at *B*. He was duly tried and found guilty. That's why he was put in jail yesterday." But suppose the son had asked a different question, namely, "Why do people put other people in jail?" Then the father might answer, "To protect good people from bad people" or "To stop people from doing things that would make it uneasy for all of us; for otherwise we wouldn't be able to go to bed at night and sleep in peace." There are two very different questions here. One question emphasizes the proper name: it asks why *J* was punished rather than someone else, or it asks what he was punished for. The other question asks why we have the institution of punishment: why do people punish one another rather than, say, always forgiving one another?

Thus the father says in effect that a particular man is punished, rather than some other man, because he is guilty, and he is guilty because he broke the law (past tense). In his case the law looks back, the judge looks back, the jury looks back, and a penalty is visited upon him for something he did. That a man is to be punished, and what his punishment is to be, is settled by its being shown that he broke the law and that the law assigns that penalty for the violation of it.

On the other hand we have the institution of punishment itself, and recommend and accept various changes in it, because it is thought by the (ideal) legislator and by those to whom the law applies that, as a part of a system of law impartially applied from case to case arising under it, it will have the consequence, in the long run, of furthering the interests of society.

One can say, then, that the judge and the legislator stand in different positions and look in different directions: one to the past, the other to the future. The justification of what the judge does, *qua* judge, sounds like the retributive view; the justification of what the (ideal) legislator does, *qua* legislator, sounds like the utilitarian view. Thus both views have a point (this is as it should be since intelligent and sensitive persons have been on both sides of the argument); and one's initial confusion disappears once one sees that these views apply to persons holding different offices with different duties, and situated differently with respect to the system of rules that make up the criminal law.

One might say, however, that the utilitarian view is more fundamental since it applies to a more fundamental office, for the judge carries out the legislator's will so far as he can

determine it. Once the legislator decides to have laws and to assign penalties for their violation (as things are there must be both the law and the penalty) an institution is set up which
involves a retributive conception of particular cases. It is part of the concept of the criminal law as a system of rules that the application and enforcement of these rules in particular cases should be justifiable by arguments of a retributive character. The decision whether
or not to use law rather than some other mechanism of social control, and the decision as
to what laws to have and what penalties to assign, may be settled by utilitarian arguments;
but if one decides to have laws then one has decided on something whose working in particular cases is retributive in form.

The answer, then, to the confusion engendered by the two views of punishment is quite
simple: one distinguishes two offices, that of the judge and that of the legislator, and one
distinguishes their different stations with respect to the system of rules which make up the
law; and then one notes that the different sorts of considerations which would usually be
offered as reasons for what is done under the cover of these offices can be paired off with
the competing justifications of punishment. One reconciles the two views by the time-honored device of making them apply to different situations.

But can it really be this simple? Well, this answer allows for the apparent intent of each
side. Does a person who advocates the retributive view necessarily advocate, as an *institution*, legal machinery whose essential purpose is to set up and preserve a correspondence
between moral turpitude and suffering? Surely not. What retributionists have rightly
insisted upon is that no man can be punished unless he is guilty, that is, unless he has broken the law. Their fundamental criticism of the utilitarian account is that, as they interpret
it, it sanctions an innocent person's being punished (if one may call it that) for the benefit
of society.

On the other hand, utilitarians agree that punishment is to be inflicted only for the violation of law. They regard this much as understood from the concept of punishment itself.
The point of the utilitarian account concerns the institution as a system of rules: utilitarianism seeks to limit its use by declaring it justifiable only if it can be shown to foster effectively the good of society. Historically it is a protest against the indiscriminate and ineffective use of the criminal law. It seeks to dissuade us from assigning to penal institutions the
improper, if not sacrilegious, task of matching suffering with moral turpitude. Like others,
utilitarians want penal institutions designed so that, as far as humanly possible, only those
who break the law run afoul of it. They hold that no official should have discretionary
power to inflict penalties whenever he thinks it for the benefit of society; for on utilitarian
grounds an institution granting such power could not be justified.

The suggested way of reconciling the retributive and the utilitarian justifications of
punishment seems to account for what both sides have wanted to say. . . .

One disputed question is whether utilitarianism doesn't justify too much. One pictures
it as an engine of justification which, if consistently adopted, could be used to justify cruel
and arbitrary institutions. Retributionists may be supposed to concede that utilitarians
intend to reform the law and to make it more humane; that utilitarians do not *wish* to justify any such thing as punishment of the innocent; and that utilitarians may appeal to the
fact that punishment presupposes guilt in the sense that by punishment one understands an
institution attaching penalties to the infraction of legal rules, and therefore that it is logically absurd to suppose that utilitarians in justifying *punishment* might also have justified
punishment (if we may call it that) of the innocent. The real question, however, is whether
the utilitarian, in justifying punishment, hasn't used arguments which commit him to
accepting the infliction of suffering on innocent persons if it is for the good of society
(whether or not one calls this punishment). More generally, isn't the utilitarian committed

in principle to accepting many practices which he, as a morally sensitive person, wouldn't want to accept? Retributionists are inclined to hold that there is no way to stop the utilitarian principle from justifying too much except by adding to it a principle which distributes certain rights to individuals. Then the amended criterion is not the greatest benefit of society *simpliciter,* but the greatest benefit of society subject to the constraint that no one's rights may be violated. Now while I think that the classical utilitarians proposed a criterion of this more complicated sort, I do not want to argue that point here. What I want to show is that there is *another* way of preventing the utilitarian principle from justifying too much, or at least of making it much less likely to do so: namely, by stating utilitarianism in a way which accounts for the distinction between the justification of an institution and the justification of a particular action falling under it.

I begin by defining the institution of punishment as follows: a person is said to suffer punishment whenever he is legally deprived of some of the normal rights of a citizen on the ground that he has violated a rule of law, the violation having been established by trial according to the due process of law, provided that the deprivation is carried out by the recognized legal authorities of the state, that the rule of law clearly specifies both the offense and the attached penalty, that the courts construe statues strictly, and that the statute was on the books prior to the time of the offense. This definition specifies what I shall understand by punishment. The question is whether utilitarian arguments may be found to justify institutions widely different from this and such as one would find cruel and arbitrary.

This question is best answered, I think, by taking up a particular accusation. Consider the following from Carritt:

> . . . the utilitarian must hold that we are justified in inflicting pain always and only to prevent worse pain or bring about greater happiness. This, then, is all we need to consider in so-called punishment, which must be purely preventive. But if some kind of very cruel crime becomes common, and none of the criminals can be caught, it might be highly expedient, as an example, to hang an innocent man, if a charge against him could be so framed that he were universally thought guilty; indeed this would only fail to be an ideal instance of utilitarian "punishment" because the victim himself would not have been so likely as a real felon to commit such a crime in the future; in all other respects it would be perfectly deterrent and therefore felicific.

Carritt is trying to show that there are occasions when a utilitarian argument would justify taking an action which would be generally condemned; and thus that utilitarianism justifies too much. But the failure of Carritt's argument lies in the fact that he makes no distinction between the justification of the general system of rules which constitutes penal institutions and the justification of particular applications of these rules to particular cases by the various officials whose job it is to administer them. This becomes perfectly clear when one asks who the "we" are of whom Carritt speaks. Who is this who has a sort of absolute authority on particular occasions to decide that an innocent man shall be "punished" if everyone can be convinced that he is guilty? Is this person the legislator, or the judge, or the body of private citizens, or what? It is utterly crucial to know who is to decide such matters, and by what authority, for all of this must be written into the rules of the institution. Until one knows these things one doesn't know what the institution is whose justification is being challenged; and as the utilitarian principle applies to the institution one doesn't know whether it is justifiable on utilitarian grounds or not.

Once this is understood it is clear what the countermove to Carritt's argument is. One must describe more carefully what the *institution* is which his example suggests, and then ask oneself whether or not it is likely that having this institution would be for the benefit of society in the long run. One must not content oneself with the vague thought that, when it's a question of *this* case, it would be a good thing if *somebody* did something even if an innocent person were to suffer.

Try to imagine, then, an institution (which we may call "telishment") which is such that the officials set up by it have authority to arrange a trial for the condemnation of an innocent man whenever they are of the opinion that doing so would be in the best interests of society. The discretion of officials is limited, however, by the rule that they may not condemn an innocent man to undergo such an ordeal unless there is, at the time, a wave of offenses similar to that with which they charge him and telish him for. We may imagine that the officials having the discretionary authority are the judges of the higher courts in consultation with the chief of police, the minister of justice, and a committee of the legislature.

Once one realizes that one is involved in setting up an *institution,* one sees that the hazards are very great. For example, what check is there on the officials? How is one to tell whether or not their actions are authorized? How is one to limit the risks involved in allowing such systematic deception? How is one to avoid giving anything short of complete discretion to the authorities to telish anyone they like? In addition to these considerations, it is obvious that people will come to have a very different attitude towards their penal system when telishment is adjoined to it. They will be uncertain as to whether a convicted man has been punished or telished. They will wonder whether or not they should feel sorry for him. They will wonder whether the same fate won't at any time fall on them. If one pictures how such an institution would actually work, and the enormous risks involved in it, it seems clear that it would serve no useful purpose. A utilitarian justification for this institution is most unlikely.

Michael Moore, "A Defense of the Retributivist View," from "The Moral Worth of Retribution" (1987)

Michael Moore (1943–) aims to defend a retributivist account of punishment—that is, an account according to which punishment is justified by the offender's morally deserving to be punished. Unlike utilitarian theories of punishment, which appeal to a more fundamental moral principle (the principle of utility) to provide their account of the justification of punishment, on Moore's view retributivism is itself fundamental: it is simply true that wrongdoing deserves punishment. How, though, can the retributivist muster a defense of that principle against those inclined to reject retributivism? Moore's strategy is to try to show that it fits better with many of our considered judgments. Most of us believe, for example, that past acts can deserve present responses—past kindness, for example, can merit present acts of gratitude. More particularly, Moore has us imagine ourselves committing a foul act—would we not, in these cases, believe ourselves to be worthy of punishment? And if so, is it not morally condescending, a sort of rejection of others' moral adulthood and moral responsibility, not to believe them to be worthy of punishment if they were to commit the same acts?

Since I will in this chapter seek to justify the retributive theory of punishment, I will first say what such a theory is. *Retributivism* is the view that punishment is justified by the moral culpability of those who receive it. A retributivist punishes because, and only because, the offender deserves it. Retributivism thus stands in stark contrast to utilitarian views that justify punishment of past offenses by the greater good of preventing future offenses. It also contrasts sharply with rehabilitative views, according to which punishment is justified by the reforming good it does the criminal. . . .

Retributivism is a very straightforward theory of punishment: We are justified in punishing because and only because offenders deserve it. Moral culpability ("desert") is in such a view both a sufficient as well as a necessary condition of liability to punitive sanctions. Such justification gives society more than merely a right to punish culpable offenders. It does this, making it not unfair to punish them, but retributivism justifies more than this. For a retributivist, the moral culpability of an offender also gives society the *duty* to punish. Retributivism, in other words, is truly a theory of justice such that, if it is true, we have an obligation to set up institutions so that retribution is achieved.

Retributivism, so construed, joins corrective justice theories of torts, natural right theories of property, and promissory theories of contract as deontological alternatives to utilitarian justifications; in each case, the institutions of punishment, tort compensation, property, and contract are justified by the rightness or fairness of the institution in question, not by the good consequences such institution may generate. Further, for each of these theories, moral desert plays the crucial justificatory role: Tort sanctions are justified whenever the plaintiff does not deserve to suffer the harm uncompensated and the defendant by his or her conduct has created an unjust situation that merits corrective action; property rights are justified whenever one party, by his or her labor, first possession, or intrinsic ownership of his or her own body, has come by such actions or status morally to deserve such entitlements; and contractual liability is justified by the fairness of imposing it on one who deserves it (because of his or her voluntary undertaking, but subsequent and unexcused breach).

Once the deontological nature of retributivism is fully appreciated, it is often concluded that such a view cannot be justified. You either believe punishment to be inherently right, or you do not, and that is all there is to be said about it. As Hugo Bedau once put it:

> Either he [the retributivist] appeals to something else—some good end—that is accomplished by the practice of punishment, in which case he is open to the criticism that he

has a nonretributivist, consequentialist justification for the practice of punishment. Or his justification does not appeal to something else, in which case it is open to the criticism that it is circular and futile.

Such a restricted view of the justifications open to a retributivist leads theorists in one of two directions: Either they hang on to retributivism, urging that it is to be justified "logically" (i.e., non-morally) as inherent in the ideas of punishment or of law or they give up retributivism as an inherently unjustifiable view. In either case, retributivism is unfairly treated, since the first alternative trivializes it and the second eliminates it.

Bedau's dilemma is surely overstated. Retributivism is no worse off in the modes of its possible justification than any other deontological theory. In the first place, one might become (like Bedau himself, apparently) a kind of "reluctant retributivist." A reluctant retributivist is someone who is somewhat repelled by retributivism but who nonetheless believes: (1) that there should be punishment; (2) that the only theories of punishment possible are utilitarian, rehabilitative, retributive, or some mixture of these; and (3) that there are decisive objections to utilitarian and rehabilitative theories of punishment, as well as to any mixed theory that uses either of these views in any combination. Such a person . . . becomes, however reluctantly, a retributivist by default.

In the second place, positive arguments can be given for retributivism that do not appeal to some good consequences of punishing. It simply is not true that "appeals to authority apart, we can justify rules and institutions only by showing that they yield advantages" or that "to justify is to provide reasons in terms of something else accepted as valuable." Coherence theories of justification in ethics allow two nonconsequentialist possibilities here:

> 1. We might justify a principle such as retributivism by showing how it follows from some yet more general principle of justice that we think to be true.
> 2. Alternatively, we can justify a moral principle by showing that it best accounts for those of our more particular judgments that we also believe to be true.

In a perfectly coherent moral system, the retributive principle would be justified in both these ways, by being part of the best theory of our moral sentiments, considered as a whole.

The first of these deontological argument strategies is made familiar to us by arguments such as that of Herbert Morris, who urges that retributivism follows from some general ideas about reciprocal advantage in social relations. Without assessing the merits of these proposals one way or another, I wish to pursue the other strategy. I examine the more particular judgments that seem to be best accounted for in terms of a principle of punishment for just deserts.

These more particular judgments are quite familiar. I suspect that almost everyone at least has a tendency—one that he may correct as soon as he detects it himself, but at least a tendency—to judge culpable wrongdoers as deserving of punishment. Consider some examples Mike Royko has used to get the blood to the eyes of readers of his newspaper column:

> The small crowd that gathered outside the prison to protest the execution of Steven Judy softly sang "We Shall Overcome". . . .
>
> But it didn't seem quite the same hearing it sung out of concern for someone who, on finding a woman with a flat tire, raped and murdered her and drowned her three small children, then said that he hadn't been "losing any sleep" over his crimes. . . .
>
> I remember the grocer's wife. She was a plump, happy woman who enjoyed the long workday she shared with her husband in their ma-and-pa store. One evening, two

young men came in and showed guns, and the grocer gave them everything in the cash register.

For no reason, almost as an afterthought, one of the men shot the grocer in the face. The woman stood only a few feet from her husband when he was turned into a dead, bloody mess.

She was about 50 when it happened. In a few years her mind was almost gone, and she looked 80. They might as well have killed her too.

Then there was the woman I got to know after her daughter was killed by a wolf-pack gang during a motoring trip. The mother called me occasionally, but nothing that I said could ease her torment. It ended when she took her own life.

A couple of years ago I spent a long evening with the husband, sister and parents of a fine young woman who had been forced into the trunk of a car in a hospital parking lot. The degenerate who kidnapped her kept her in the trunk, like an ant in a jar, until he got tired of the game. Then he killed her.

[Reprinted by permission: Tribune Media Services]

Most people react to such atrocities with an intuitive judgment that punishment (at least of some kind and to some degree) is warranted. Many will quickly add, however, that what accounts for their intuitive judgment is the need for deterrence, or the need to incapacitate such a dangerous person, or the need to reform the person. My own view is that these addenda are just "bad reasons for what we believe on instinct anyway," to paraphrase Bradley's general view of justification in ethics.

To see whether this is so, construct a thought experiment of the kind Kant originated. Imagine that these same crimes are being done, but that there is no utilitarian or rehabilitative reason to punish. The murderer has truly found Christ, for example, so that he or she does not need to be reformed; he or she is not dangerous for the same reason; and the crime can go undetected so that general deterrence does not demand punishment (alternatively, we can pretend to punish and pay the person the money the punishment would have cost us to keep his or her mouth shut, which will also serve the ends of general deterrence). In such a situation, should the criminal still be punished? My hypothesis is that most of us still feel some inclination, no matter how tentative, to punish. That is the particular judgment I wish to examine. (For those persons—saints or moral lepers, we shall see which—who do not have even a tentative inclination to punish, I argue that the reason for affirming such inclinations are also reasons to feel such inclinations.) . . .

As previewed in the first part of this chapter, there are two justificatory routes a coherentist might use in justifying retributivism. First, because of the Nietzschean attack on the retributive urge, a retributivist might abandon the justificatory route that begins with our particular judgments about punishment in individual cases, and instead focus on how retributivism is justified because of its coherence with other, more general moral beliefs we are prepared to accept. He or she might show how there is an odd lacunae in our moral judgments about desert if the retributive principle is not accepted. That is, when passing out rewards, the desert of those whose labor produced them is (for Lockeans) both a necessary and a sufficient condition for allocating a property entitlement in them. The presence of such desert justifies giving the reward to them; the absence of such desert justifies withholding it from them. Similarly, when passing out legal duties to pay for harms caused, the culpability of he or she who caused the harm and the lack of culpability of he or she who suffers the harm, is (in standard corrective justice theories) both necessary and sufficient to justify tort liability. It is only with punishment that we have an asymmetry; namely (as even most nonretributivists will assert), that desert is a necessary condition of punishment, but not sufficient by itself to justify punishment.

Such an asymmetry does not by itself render a deontologist's social theory incoherent if he or she rejects retributivism (although it might if one isolated a general principle of just deserts common to corrective justice, property allocations, and retributive justice). My only point here is that if there were such incoherence without retributivism, the latter would be justified even if the retributive urge is unworthy of us. Nothing in the Nietzschean case against retributivism could prevent this. Still, since my approach is to justify retributivism by using our more particular judgments about punishment, I need to take seriously the Nietzschean case against those judgments.

The problem with the Nietzschean case against retributivism does not lie in its presupposition that generally there is a strong connection between virtuous emotions and true moral judgments, vices and false moral judgments. The real problem for the Nietzschean critic is to show that retributive judgments are *inevitably* motivated by the black emotions of *ressentiment.* For if the critic cannot show this, then much of the contamination of those particular judgments is lifted. It is lifted because the retributive judgment would then not arise out of the kind of moral hallucination nonvirtuous emotions typically represent; rather, the retributive judgment would be only the vehicle for the expression of the emotions of *ressentiment*—dangerous for that reason, but not lacking in epistemic import for that reason. . . .

. . . I shall make the argument in three steps: First, that the inevitability of linking *ressentiment* emotions to retributive judgments is weakened when one notes, as Nietzsche himself did, that *anti*retributive judgments are also often motivated by some of those same nonvirtuous emotions; second, that in our own individual cases we can imagine being motivated to make retributive judgments by the virtuous emotions of guilt and fellow feeling; and third, that because punishment is a social institution, unlike private vengeance, it can help us to control the emotions retributive punishment expresses by controlling the aspects of punishment that all too easily allow it to express *ressentiment.*

1.   A paraphrase of Zarathustra, of which Nietzsche no doubt would have approved, would be that we should beware all those in whom the urge to punish is either actually, or claimed to be, nonexistent. As Nietzsche does tell us:

> if you are cursed, I do not like it that you want to bless. Rather, join a little in the cursing. And if you have been done a great wrong, then quickly add five little ones: a gruesome sight is a person single-mindedly obsessed by a wrong. . . . A wrong shared is half right. . . . A little revenge is more human than no revenge.
>
> (*Zarathustra*)

Everyone gets angry when their bodily integrity or other important interests are violated by another. If they care about other human beings, they are vicariously injured when someone close to them—or distant, depending on the reach of their empathy—is wronged. It is human to feel such anger at wrongful violation, and Nietzsche's thought is that not to express the anger in some retaliation is a recipe for *ressentiment* itself.

One might of course think that retaliation is a second best solution; better not to feel the anger at all so that the choice of expressing it in action, or of repressing it into the subtle revenge of pity, is not necessary. Leaving aside whether such willing away of anger is possible, is it desirable? While it has a saintly ring to it to turn the other cheek so long as it is one's own cheek that has just been slapped, is it virtuous to feel nothing stronger than sympathy for the suffering of others at the hands of wrongdoers? Where is that compassionate concern for others that is outraged because another person could have so unnecessarily caused such suffering?

Karen Horney concluded that "[t]he vindictive person thus is egocentric . . . because he has more or less severed his emotional relations to other human beings." Yet isn't this even more often true of one who feels anger only when he himself suffers at the hands of a wrongdoer, not when others suffer? An egocentric lack of compassion for others may explain the antiretributivist, forgiving attitude as easily as it may explain the desire for vengeance.

Sometimes the compassion for victims is not absent, but gets transferred to the person who is now about to suffer; namely, the wrongdoer. Such a transfer of compassion is not justified by the relative merits of the two classes of persons, unless we are to think that there is some reason to prefer wrongdoers to victims as the appropriate objects of compassion. "Out of sight, out of mind" is the reason that suggests itself, but this psychological tendency can hardly justify forgetting those who have suffered at the hands of others. My own view is that such a transfer of concern from victim to criminal occurs in large part because of our unwillingness to face our own revulsion at what was done. It allows us to look away from the horror that another person was willing to cause.

We almost cannot bear the sight. We invent for the wrongdoers a set of excusing conditions that we would not tolerate for a moment in ourselves. When they transgress, virtuous people know how ill it lies to "excuse" themselves by pointing to their own childhood or past, their lack of parental love, their need for esteem, and other causes. Virtuous people do not use the childish "something made me do it" because they know that that denies their essential freedom in bringing about some harm. They know that they did it, chose to do it, caused though that choice surely was by factors themselves unchosen. Yet we cannot stand to apply to criminals the same standard of responsibility that we apply to ourselves because we cannot stand to acknowledge that there is such a thing as evil in the world—and, worst of all, that it is not "inhuman" but a part of creatures not so different from ourselves. Lack of anger at criminals, if it does not represent simple indifference to the sufferings of others, may represent our self-deception about the potential for evil in humanity.

Such lack of anger may also represent the same fear of criminals that can motivate retributive judgments. Nietzsche:

> There is a point in the history of society when it becomes so pathologically soft and tender that among other things it sides even with those who harm it, criminals, and does this quite seriously and honestly. Punishing somehow seems unfair to it, and it is certain that imagining "punishment" and "being supposed to punish" hurts it, arouses fear in it. "It is not enough to render him *undangerous?* Why still punish? Punishing itself is terrible." With this question, herd morality, the morality of timidity, draws its ultimate consequence. . . . The imperative of herd timidity: "We want that some day there should be *nothing anymore to be afraid of!*"

(Beyond Good and Evil)

By repressing anger at wrongful violation, we may be attempting to deny that we live in a society in which there really are fearful and awful people.

Yet again, our transfer of fellow-feeling from victim to criminal, and its accompanying elimination of anger, may represent something other than indifference or inability to face evil or our own fears. It may represent a narcissism that is itself no virtue. A criminal, after all, represents an opportunity to exercise (and display, a separate point) one's virtue. The virtue in question is compassion for someone now threatened with harm. Yet such egoistic compassion becomes something other than compassion. It becomes just what Nietzsche said it becomes, the elevation of self by pity. Remarkably, one can lose compassionate concern for another by the self-conscious egoistic caricature of compassion we distinguish as pity. In pity we do not care about the other any more for his own sake, but only insofar as he allows *us* to become, in our own and others' eyes, better. We should beware, to adopt yet another paraphrase of Nietzsche, this one by Philippa Foot, all those who find others best when they find them most in need. We should beware of them because such people lack precisely the ability to feel that compassion whose outward form they ape.

2.   Resentment, indifference to others, self-deception, fear, cowardice, and pity are not virtues. They do not perhaps add up to the witches' brew of a full batch of the *ressentiment* emotions, but to the extent they motivate antiretributive judgments, they make such judgments suspect. If one accepts, as Nietzsche did, that both retributive and antiretributive judgments are often motivated by, or at least expressions of, nonvirtuous emotions, where does that leave us? It should leave us asking whether we cannot make our judgments about punishment in such a way that they are not motivated by either set of unworthy emotions.

When we make a retributive judgment—such as that Stephen Judy deserved the death penalty for his rape-murder of a young mother and his murder of her three children—we need not be motivated by the *ressentiment* emotions. Nor is the alternative some abstract, Kantian concern for justice, derived by reason alone and unsullied by any strong emotional origin. Our concern for retributive justice might be motivated by very deep emotions that are nonetheless of a wholly virtuous nature. These are the feelings of guilt we would have if we did the kinds of acts that fill the criminal appellate reports of any state.

The psychiatrist Willard Gaylin interviewed a number of people closely connected to the brutal hammering death of Bonnie Garland by her jilted boyfriend, Richard Herrin. He asked a number of those in a Christian order that had been particularly forgiving of Richard whether they could imagine themselves performing such an act under any set of circumstances. Their answer was uniformly "Yes." All of us can at least find it conceivable that there might be circumstances under which we could perform an act like Herrin's—not exactly the same, perhaps, but something pretty horrible. All of us do share this much of our common nature with the worst of criminals. (For those with a greater we—they attitude toward criminals, the thought experiment that follows must be run with a somewhat less horrible act than Richard's.)

Then ask yourself: What would you feel like if it was you who had intentionally smashed open the skull of a 23-year-old woman with a claw hammer while she was asleep, a woman whose fatal defect was a desire to free herself from your too clinging embrace? My own response, I hope, would be that I would feel guilty unto death. I couldn't imagine any suffering that could be imposed upon me that would be unfair because it exceeded what I deserved.

Is that virtuous? Such deep feelings of guilt seem to me to be the only tolerable response of a moral being. "Virtue" is perhaps an odd word in the context of extreme culpability, but such guilt seems, at the least, very appropriate. One ought to feel so guilty one wants to die. Such sickness unto death is to my mind more virtuous than the nonguilty state to which Richard Herrin brought himself, with some help from Christian counseling about the need for self-forgiveness. After three years in prison on an eight- to twenty-five-year sentence for "heat of passion" manslaughter, Richard thought he had suffered quite enough for the killing of Bonnie:

> HERRIN: I feel the sentence was excessive.
> GAYLIN: Let's talk about that a little.
> HERRIN: Well, I feel that way now and after the first years. The judge had gone overboard. . . .
>   Considering all the factors that I feel the judge should have considered: prior history of arrest, my personality background, my capacity for a productive life in society—you know, those kinds of things—I don't think he took those into con-

sideration. He looked at the crime itself and responded to a lot of public pressure or maybe his own personal feelings, I don't know. I'm not going to accuse him of anything, but I was given the maximum sentence. This being my first arrest and considering the circumstances, I don't think I should have been given eight to twenty-five years.

GAYLIN: What do you think would have been a fair sentence?

HERRIN: Well, after a year or two in prison, I felt that was enough. . . .

GAYLIN: How would you answer the kind of person who says, for Bonnie, it's her whole life; for you it's eight years. What's eight years compared to the more years she might have had?

HERRIN: I can't deny that it's grossly unfair to Bonnie but there's nothing I can do about it. . . .

She's gone—I can't bring her back. I would rather that she had survived as a complete person, but she didn't. I'm not, again . . . I'm not saying that I shouldn't have been punished, but the punishment I feel is excessive. I feel I have five more years to go, and I feel that's just too much. There's no . . . I don't see any purpose in it. It's sad what happened, but it's even sadder to waste another life. I feel I'm being wasted in here.

GAYLIN: But what about the people who say, Look, if you got two years, then someone who robs should get only two days. You know, the idea of commensurate punishment. If it is a very serious crime it has to be a very serious punishment. Are you saying two years of prison is a very serious punishment considering what you did?

HERRIN: For me, yes.

[From W. Gaylin, *The Killing of Bonnie Garland*, pp. 325—7. Copyright © 1982 by Pip Enterprises, Inc. Reprinted by permission of Simon & Schuster, Inc.]

Compared to such shallow, easily obtained self-absolution for a horrible violation of another, a deep sense of guilt looks very virtuous indeed.

To be sure, there is an entire tradition that regards guilt as a useless passion. For one thing, it is always backward-looking rather than allowing one to get on with life. For another, it betrays an indecision that Nietzsche among others found unattractive: "The bite of conscience is indecent," Nietzsche thought (*Twilight of the Idols*), because it betrays the earlier decision about which one feels guilty. Yet Nietzsche and his followers are simply wrong here. Guilt feelings are often a virtue precisely because they do look to the past. As Herbert Morris has argued, morality itself—including the morality of good character—has to take the past seriously. The alternative, of not crying over spilt milk (or blood), is truly indecent. A moral being *feels* guilty when he or she *is* guilty of past wrongs.

The virtue of feeling guilty is not raised so that punishment can be justified by its capacity to induce guilt. That is a possible retributive theory of punishment—a kind of moral rehabilitative theory—but it is not mine. Rather, the virtue of our own imagined guilt is relevant because of the general connection between the virtue of an emotion and its epistemic import. We should trust what our imagined guilt feelings tell us; for acts like those of Richard Herrin, that if we did them we would be so guilty that some extraordinarily severe punishment would be deserved. We should trust the judgments such imagined guilt feelings spawn because nonneurotic guilt, unlike *ressentiment,* comes with good epistemic credentials.

Next, we need to be clear just what judgments it is that our guilt feelings validate in this way. First and foremost, to *feel* guilty causes the judgment that we *are* guilty, in the sense that we are morally culpable. Second, such guilt feelings typically engender the judgment that we deserve punishment. I mean this not only in the weak sense of desert—that it would not be unfair to be punished—but also and more important in the strong sense that we *ought* to be punished.

One might think that this second judgment of desert (in either its weak or its strong sense) is uncalled for by our feelings of guilt, that the judgment to which our guilt feelings lead is the judgment that we ought to repair as best we can the damage we have done. Such a view would justify corrective justice theories of punishment, but not retributive theories. Yet I think that this puts too nice a face on our guilt feelings. They do not generate only a judgment that we ought to make amends in this compensatory way. Rather—and this is what troubles many critics of guilt as an emotion—to feel guilty is to judge that we must suffer. We can see this plainly if we imagine ourselves having made provisions for Bonnie's family, comforting them in any way possible, and then feeling that our debt for killing her has been paid. It is so clear that such corrective actions do *not* satisfy guilt that to feel that they do is not to have felt guilty to begin with.

Our feelings of guilt thus generate a judgment that we deserve the suffering that is punishment. If the feelings of guilt are virtuous to possess, we have reason to believe that this last judgment is correct, generated as it is by emotions whose epistemic import is not in question.

Last, we should ask whether there is any reason not to make the same judgment about Richard Herrin's actual deserts as we are willing to make about our own hypothetical deserts. If we experience any reluctance to transfer the guilt and desert *we* would possess, had we done what Richard Herrin did, to Herrin himself, we should examine that reluctance carefully. Doesn't it come from feeling more of a person than Richard? We are probably not persons who grew up in the barrio of East Los Angeles, or who found Yale an alien and disorienting culture. In any case, we certainly have never been subject to the exact same stresses and motivations as Richard Herrin. Therefore, it may be tempting to withhold from Richard the benefit each of us gives himself or herself: the benefit of being the subjective seat of a will that, although caused, is nonetheless capable of both choice and responsibility.

Such discrimination is a temptation to be resisted, because it is no virtue. It is elitist and condescending toward others not to grant them the same responsibility and desert you grant to yourself. Admittedly, there are excuses the benefit of which others as well as yourself may avail themselves. Yet that is not the distinction invoked here. Herrin had no excuse the rest of us could not come up with in terms of various causes for our choices. To refuse to grant him the same responsibility and desert as you would grant yourself is thus an instance of what Sartre called bad faith, the treating of a free, subjective will as an object. It is a refusal to admit that the rest of humanity shares with us that which makes us most distinctively human, our capacity to will and reason—and thus to be and do evil. Far from evincing fellow feeling and the allowing of others to participate in our moral life, it excludes them as less than persons.

Rather than succumbing to this elitism masquerading as egalitarianism, we should ask ourselves what Herrin deserves by asking what *we* would deserve had we done such an act. In answering this question we should listen to our guilt feelings, feelings whose epistemic import is not in question in the same way as are those of *ressentiment*. Such guilt feelings should tell us that to do an act like Herrin's is to forfeit forever any lighthearted idea of going on as before. One should feel so awful that the idea of again leading a life unchanged from before, with the same goals and hopes and happiness, should appear revoltingly incomprehensible.

3.   It is admittedly not an easy task to separate the emotions one feels, and then in addition, discriminate which of them is the cause of one's retributive judgments. We can no

more choose which emotion it will be that causes our judgments or actions than we can choose the reason for which we act. We can choose whether to act or not and whether to judge one way or another, but we cannot make it be true that some particular reason or emotion caused our action or our judgment. We must look inward as best we can to detect, but not to will, which emotions bring about our judgments; and here there is plenty of room for error and self-deception.

When we move from our judgments about the justice of retribution in the abstract, however, to the justice of a social institution that exists to exact retribution, perhaps we can gain some greater clarity. For if we recognize the dangers retributive punishment presents for the expression of resentment, sadism, and so on, we have every reason to design our punishment institutions to minimize the opportunity for such feelings to be expressed. There is no contradiction in attempting to make a retributive punishment system humane; doing so allows penitentiaries to be faithful to their names—places for penance, not excuses for sadism, prejudice, hatred, and the like.

Even the old biblical injunction—"Vengeance is mine, saith the Lord"—has something of this insight behind it. Retributive punishment is dangerous for individual persons to carry out, dangerous to their virtue and, because of that, unclear in its justification. But implicit in the biblical injunction is a promise that retribution will be exacted. For those like myself who are not theists, that cleansing function must be performed by the state, not God. If the state can perform such a function, it removes from retributive punishment, not the guilt, as Nietzsche and Sartre have it, but the *ressentiment*.

Jean Hampton, "The Message of Punishment," from "The Moral Education Theory of Punishment" (1984)

Jean Hampton (1954–1996) agrees with the utilitarians that, broadly speaking, the rationale for punishment is that punishment is necessary to protect society against those that would disrupt social life. But Hampton notes that accepting this point does not commit one to any particular view on how punishment carries out this task. On her view, criminal laws are—at least when properly formulated—always morally charged: they either forbid (or require) what is morally wrong (or right), or they solve coordination problems by enabling citizens to reach common decisions on how to promote morally desirable ends. Punishment "backs up" these laws. But punishment is not justified by its conditioning subjects against breaking the law: we should not view the law as just like an electrified fence, which the cow avoids merely because it does not want the shock. Rather, the punishment has an educative function: it teaches subjects about the moral wrongfulness of violating the law. Punishment is thus a good for the person who is punished, for it helps him or her to recognize morally decent behavior. It is, in fact, this feature of her theory of punishment that Hampton seems to find most attractive about it: on her view, no one—not even the worst of humans—deserves ill.

There are few social practices more time-honored or more widely accepted throughout the world than the practice of punishing wrongdoers. Yet if one were to listen to philosophers discussing this practice, one would think punishment impossible to justify and difficult even to understand. However, I do not believe that one should conclude that punishment as a practice is morally unjustifiable or fundamentally irrational. Instead I want to explore the promise of another theory of punishment which incorporates certain elements of the deterrence, retributivist, and rehabilitation views, but whose justification for punishment and whose formula for determining what punishment a wrongdoer deserves are distinctive and importantly different from the reasons and formulas characterizing the traditional rival theories.

This view, which I call the moral education theory of punishment, is not new. There is good reason to believe Plato and Hegel accepted something like it, and more recently, Herbert Morris and Robert Nozick have maintained that the moral education which punishment effects is at least part of punishment's justification. I want to go further, however, and suggest that by reflecting on the educative character of punishment we can provide a full and complete justification for it. Hence my discussion of the moral education theory in this paper is meant to develop it as a complete justification of punishment and to distinguish it from its traditional rivals. . . .

Philosophers who write about punishment spend most of their time worrying about whether the *state*'s punishment of criminals is justifiable, so let us begin with that particular issue.

When does punishment by the state take place? The answer to this question seems simple: the state carries out punishment upon a person when he or she has broken a *law*. Yet the fact that the state's punishment always follows the transgression of a law is surely neither coincidental nor irrelevant to the understanding and justification of this practice. What is the nature of law? This is a thorny problem which has vexed philosophers for hundreds of years. For the purposes of this article, however, let us agree with Hart that there are (at least) two kinds of law, those which are power-conferring rules, for example, rules which specify how to make a contract or a will, and those which are "rules of obligation." We are concerned with the latter kind of rule, and philosophers and legal theorists have generally analyzed the structure of this sort of law as "orders backed by threats" made by the state.

What is the subject matter of these orders? I will contend (consistent with a positivist account of law) that the subject matter *ought* to be (although it might not always be) drawn either from ethical imperatives, of the form "don't steal," or "don't murder," or else from imperatives made necessary for moral reasons, for example, "drive on the right"—so that the safety of others on the road is insured, or "advertise your university job in the professional journals"—so that blacks and women will not be denied an opportunity to secure the job. The state makes these two kinds of commands not only to define a minimal set of duties which a human being in that community must follow in his or her dealings with others, but also to designate actions which, when followed by all members of the society, will solve various problems of conflict and coordination.

And the threat? What role does it play? In the end, this is the central question for which we must have an adequate answer if we are to construct a viable theory of punishment.

The threat, which specifies the infliction of pain if the imperative is not obeyed, gives people a nonmoral incentive, that is, the avoidance of pain, to refrain from the prohibited action. The state hopes this incentive will block a person's performance of the immoral action whenever the ethical incentive fails to do so. But insofar as the threat given in the law is designed to play this kind of "deterring" role, carrying out the threat, that is, punishing someone when he or she has broken the law, is, at least in part, a way of "making good" on the threat. The threat will only deter the disobedience of the state's orders if people believe there is a good chance the pain will be inflicted upon them after they commit the crime. But if the state punishes in order to make good on its threats, then the deterrence of future crime cannot be wholly irrelevant to the justification of punishment. And anyone, including Kant, who analyzes laws as orders backed by threats must recognize that fact.

Moreover, I believe we must accept the deterrence theorist's contention that the justification of punishment is connected with the fact that it is a necessary tool for preventing future crime and promoting the public's well-being. Consider standard justifications of the state: philosophers from Plato to Kant to Hart have argued that because a community of people cannot tolerate violent and destructive behavior in its midst, it is justified in establishing a state which will coercively interfere in people's lives for publicly announced and agreed-upon reasons so that an unacceptable level of violence and harm can be prevented. Whereas we normally think the state has to respect its citizens' choices about how to live, certain choices, for example, choices to rape, to murder, or to steal, cannot be respected by a community which is committed to preserving and pursuing the well-being of its members. So when the state annexes punishment to these damaging activities, it says that such activities are not a viable option for anyone in that community.

But to say that the state's punishment is needed to prevent crime is not to commit oneself to the deterrence justification of punishment—it all depends on what one takes prevention to entail. And, as Hegel says, if we aimed to prevent wrongdoing only by deterring its commission, we would be treating human beings in the same way that we treat dogs. Consider the kind of lesson an animal learns when, in an effort to leave a pasture, it runs up against an electrified fence. It experiences pain and is conditioned, after a series of encounters with the fence, to stay away from it and thus remain in the pasture. A human being in the same pasture will get the same message and learn the same lesson—"if you want to avoid pain, don't try to transgress the boundary marked by this fence." But, unlike the animal in the pasture, a human being will also be able to reflect on the reasons for that fence's being there, to theorize about *why* there is this barrier to his freedom.

Punishments are like electrified fences. At the very least they teach a person, via pain, that there is a "barrier" to the action she wants to do, and so, at the very least, they aim to deter. But because punishment "fences" are marking *moral* boundaries, the pain which these "fences" administer (or threaten to administer) conveys a larger message to beings who are able to reflect on the reasons for these barriers' existence: they convey that there is a barrier to these actions *because* they are morally wrong. Thus, according to the moral education theory, punishment is not intended as a way of conditioning a human being to do what society wants her to do (in the way that an animal is conditioned by an electrified fence to stay within a pasture); rather, the theory maintains that punishment is intended as a way of teaching the wrongdoer that the action she did (or wants to do) is forbidden because it is morally wrong and should not be done for that reason. The theory also regards that lesson as public, and thus as directed to the rest of society. When the state makes its criminal law and its enforcement practices known, it conveys an educative message not only to the convicted criminal but also to anyone else in the society who might be tempted to do what she did.

Comparing punishments to electrical fences helps to make clear how a certain kind of deterrent message is built into the larger moral point which punishment aims to convey. If one wants someone to understand that an offense is immoral, at the very least one has to convey to him or her that it is prohibited—that it ought not to occur. Pain is the way to convey that message. The pain says "Don't!" and gives the wrongdoer a reason for not performing the action again; an animal shocked by a fence gets the same kind of message and the same kind of incentive. But the state also wants to use the pain of punishment to get the human wrongdoer to reflect on the moral reasons for that barrier's existence, so that he will make the decision to reject the prohibited action for *moral* reasons, rather than for the self-interested reason of avoiding pain.

If those who are punished (or who watch the punishment take place) reject the moral message implicit in the punishment, at least they will learn from it that there is a barrier to the actions they committed (or are tempted to commit). Insofar as they choose to respond to their punishment (or the punishment of others) merely as a threat, it can keep them within moral boundaries in the same way that fences keep animals in a pasture. This deterrent effect of punishment is certainly welcome by the state whose role is to protect its citizens, and which has erected a "punishment barrier" to certain kinds of actions precisely because those actions will seriously harm its citizens. But on the moral education view, it is incorrect to regard simple deterrence as the aim of punishment; rather, to state it succinctly, the view maintains that punishment is justified as a way to prevent wrongdoing insofar as it can teach both wrongdoers and the public at large the moral reasons for *choosing* not to perform an offense. . . .

. . . One distinction between the moral education view and the deterrence justification of punishment is that on the moral education view, the state is not concerned to use pain coercively so as to progressively eliminate certain types of behavior; rather, it is concerned to educate its citizens morally so that they choose not to engage in this behavior. Moreover, there is another important difference between the two views. On the deterrence view, the infliction of pain on certain individuals is justified as a way of promoting a larger social end. But critics of the deterrence view have pointed out that this is just to say that it is all right to *use* certain individuals to achieve a desirable social goal. The moral education theory, however, does not sanction the use of a criminal for social purposes; on the contrary, it attempts to justify punishment as a way to benefit the person who will experience it, a way of helping him to gain moral knowledge if he chooses to listen. Of course other desirable social goals will be achieved through his punishment, goals which include the education of the larger community about the immorality of the offense, but none of these ends is to be achieved at the expense of the criminal. Instead the moral good which punishment attempts to accomplish within the wrongdoer makes it something which is done *for* him, not *to* him. . . .

Some readers might wonder how close the moral education view is to the old retribution theory. Indeed references in the literature to a view of this type frequently characterize it as a variant of retribution. Nonetheless, there are sharp and important differences between the two views . . . Suffice to say now that whereas retributivism understands punishment as performing the rather metaphysical task of "negating the wrong" and "reasserting the right," the moral education theorist argues the there is a concrete moral *goal* which punishment should be designed to accomplish, and that goal includes the benefiting of the criminal himself. The state, as it punishes the lawbreaker, is trying to promote his moral personality; it realizes that "[h]is soul is in jeopardy as his victim's is not." Thus, it punishes him as a way of communicating a moral message to him, which he can accept or not, as he chooses.

Certain retributivists have also been very attracted to the idea that punishment is a kind of speech act. For example, Robert Nozick in his book *Philosophical Explanations* has provided a nice nine-point analysis of punishment which presents it as a kind of communication and which fits the account of meaning put forward by H. P. Grice. Yet if punishment is a way of (morally) speaking with a wrongdoer, then why doesn't this show that it is fundamentally justified *as a communication,* in virtue of what it is trying to communicate, rather than, in Nozick's view, as some kind of symbolic "linkage" of the criminal with "correct values"?

Indeed, I would maintain that regarding punishment as a kind of moral communication is intuitively very natural and attractive. Consider, for example, what we say when we punish others: a father who punishes his child explains that he does so in order that the child "learn his lesson"; someone who has been physically harmed by another demands punishment "so that she will understand what she did to me"; a judge recently told a well-known user of cocaine that he was receiving a stiff sentence because his "matter-of-fact dabbling in cocaine . . . tells the whole world it is all right to use it." These kinds of remarks accompanying our punishment efforts suggest that our principal concern as we punish is to get the wrongdoer to stop doing the immoral action by communicating to her that her offense was immoral. And the last remark by the judge to the cocaine user shows that when the state punishes it is important that these communications be public, so that other members of society will hear the same moral message. Even people who seem to be seeking revenge on wrongdoers behave in ways which show that they too want to make a moral point not only to the wrongdoer, but to anyone else who will listen. The hero seeking revenge in a Western movie, for example, never simply shoots the bad guy in the back when he finds him—he always confronts the bad guy first (usually in the presence of other people) and tells him *why* he is about to die. Indeed, the movie would be unsatisfying if he didn't make that communication. And surely, the hero's desire to explain his actions is linked with his desire to convey to the bad guy and to others in society that the bad guy had "done him wrong."

Moreover, if one understands punishment as a moral message aimed at educating both the wrongdoer and the rest of society about the immorality of the offense, one has a powerful explanation (at least as powerful as the one offered by retributivism) of why victims so badly want their assailants punished. If the point of punishment is to convey to the criminal (and others) that the criminal *wronged* the victim, then punishment is implicitly recognizing the victim's plight, and honoring the moral claims of that individual. Punishment affirms as a *fact* that the victim has been wronged, and as a *fact* that he is owed a certain kind of treatment from others. Hence, on this view, it is natural for the victim to demand punishment because it is a way for the community to restore his moral status after it has been damaged by his assailant. . . .

Retributivists have a very interesting criticism of the moral education theory available to them. Granted, they might maintain, that punishment is connected with moral education, still this only provides an additional reason for punishing someone—it does not provide the fundamental justification of punishment. That fundamental justification, they would argue, is retributive: wrongdoers simply *deserve* to experience pain for the sake of the wrong they have committed. As Kant has argued, however much good one intends one's punishment to effect,

> yet it must first be justified in itself as punishment, i.e. as mere harm, so that if it stopped there, and the person punished could get no glimpse of kindness hidden behind this harshness, he must yet admit that justice was done him, and that his reward was perfectly suitable to his conduct.

Moreover, such modern retributivists as Walter Moberly have argued that it is only when the wrongdoer can assent to his punishment as already justified in virtue of his offense that the punishment can do him any good.

In a certain sense, Moberly's point is simply that a criminal will perceive his punishment as vindictive and vengeful unless he understands or accepts the fact that it is justified. But should the justification of punishment be cashed out in terms of the retributive concept of desert, given that it has been difficult for retributivists to say what they mean by the criminal's "deserving" punishment simply in virtue of his offense? Robert Nozick tries to cash out the retributive link between crime and "deserved" punishment by saying that the punishment represents a kind of "linkage" between the criminal and "right values." But why is inflicting pain on someone a way of effecting this linkage? Why isn't the infliction of a pleasurable experience for the sake of the crime just as good a way of linking the wrongdoer with these right values? And if Nozick explains the linkage of pain with crime by saying that the pain is necessary in order to communicate to the criminal that his action was wrong, he has answered the question but lost his retributive theory. Other philosophers, like Hegel, speak of punishment as a way of "annulling" or "canceling" the crime and hence "deserved" for that reason. But although Hegel's words have a nice metaphorical ring to them, it is hard to see how they can be given a literal force that will explain the retributivist concept of desert. As J. L. Mackie has written, insofar as punishment occurs after the crime, it certainly cannot cancel it—past events are not eliminated by later ones.

It is partly because retributivists have been at a loss to explain the notion of desert implicit in their theory of punishment that I have sought to propose and explore a completely nonretributivist justification of punishment. But my reasons for rejecting retributivism are deeper. The retributive position is that it is somehow morally appropriate to inflict pain for pain, to take an eye for an eye, a tooth for a tooth. But how is it ever morally appropriate to inflict one evil for the sake of another? How is the society that inflicts the second evil any different from the wrongdoer who has inflicted the first? He strikes first, they strike back; why is the second strike acceptable but the first not? Plato, in a passage quoted at the start of this article, insists that both harms are wrong; and Jesus attacks retributivism for similar reasons:

> You have learned that they were told, "Eye for eye, tooth for tooth." But what I tell you is this: Do not set yourself against the man who wrongs you. . . . You have heard that they were told "Love your neighbor, hate your enemy." But what I tell you is this: Love your enemy and pray for your persecutors; only so can you be children of your heavenly father, who makes the sun rise on good and bad alike, and sends the rain on the honest and dishonest.
>
> [Matt. 5:38–9, 43–6]

In other words, both reject retributivism because they insist that the only thing human beings "deserve" in this life is *good,* that no matter what evil a person has committed, no one is justified in doing further evil to her.

But if one accepts the idea that no one can ever deserve ill, can we hope to justify punishment? Yes, if punishment can be shown to be a good for the wrongdoer. The moral education theory makes just such an attempt to explain punishment as a good for those who experience it, as something done *for* them, not to them, something designed to achieve a goal that includes their own moral well-being. This is the justification of punishment the criminal needs to hear so that he can accept it as legitimate rather than dismiss it as vindictive. Therefore, my interest in the moral education theory is connected with my desire to justify punishment *as a good* for those who experience it, and to avoid any theoretical justification of punishment that would regard it as a deserved evil. Reflection on the punishment activities of those who truly love the people they punish, for example, the infliction of pain by a parent on a beloved but naughty child, suggests to me that punishment should not be justified as a deserved evil, but rather as an attempt, by someone who cares, to improve a wayward person.

Still, the moral education theory can incorporate a particular notion of desert which might be attractive to retributivists. Anyone who is punished according to this theory would know that his punishment is "deserved," that is, morally required, insofar as the community cannot morally tolerate the immoral lesson that his act conveys to others (for example, the message that raping a woman is all right if it gives one a feeling of self-mastery) and cannot morally allow that he receive no education about the evil of his act.

So the theory's point is this: Wrong occasions punishment not because pain deserves pain, but because evil deserves correction.

Robert C. Solomon, "Justice and the Passion for Vengeance," from *A Passion for Justice* (1989)

In the following excerpt, the author argues for the importance of vengeance. While he acknowledges the legitimacy of the distinction between retribution and "mere" revenge, he argues that much of the supposed irrationality and excess of revenge has been overstated, and the denial of its role in justice leads to a false dichotomy between impersonal justice and merely personal revenge.

"I think that the deterrent argument is simply a rationalization. The motive for
punishment is revenge—not deterrence. . . . Punishment is hate."
                                                                                A. S. NEIL

Vengeance is the original meaning of justice. The word "justice" in the Old Testament and
in Homer too virtually always refers to revenge. Throughout most of history the concept of
justice has been far more concerned with the punishment of crimes and the balancing of
wrongs than it has been with the fair distribution of goods and services. "Getting even" is
and has always been one of the most basic metaphors of our moral vocabulary, and the
frightening emotion of righteous, wrathful anger is an essential part of the emotional basis
for our sense of justice, just as much as benign compassion and sympathy. Our resentment
of injustice is a necessary precondition of our passion for justice, and the urge to retribution its essential consequence. "Don't get mad, get even"—whether or not it is prudent
advice—is conceptually confused. Getting even is just an effective way of being angry, and
getting angry, as Aristotle argued long ago, already includes the desire for vengeance.
     Like it or not, I think that we have to agree with Arthur Lelyveld when he writes,
"there is no denying the aesthetic satisfaction, the sense of poetic justice, that pleasures us
when evildoers get the comeuppance they deserve. The impulse to punish is primarily an
impulse to even the score . . . That satisfaction is heightened when it becomes possible to
measure out punishment in exact proportion to the size and shape of the wrong that has been
done." The immense pleasure, the aesthetic satisfaction points to the depth of the passion,
and the need for "proportion" already indicates the intelligence involved in this supposedly
most irrational and uncontrollable emotion. This is not to say, of course, that the motive of
revenge is therefore legitimate or the action of revenge always justified. Sometimes
vengeance is wholly called for, even obligatory, and revenge is both legitimate and justified. Sometimes it is not, notably when one is mistaken about the offender or the offense.
But to seek vengeance for a grievous wrong, to revenge oneself against evil—that seems to
lie at the very foundation of our sense of justice, indeed, of our very sense of ourselves, our
dignity and our sense of right and wrong. Even Adam Smith writes, in his *Theory of the
Moral Sentiments,* "The violation of justice is injury . . . it is, therefore, the proper object
of resentment, and of punishment, which is the natural consequence of resentment." We are
not mere observers of moral life, and the desire for vengeance seems to be an integral aspect
of our recognition of evil. But it also contains—or can be cultivated to contain—the elements of its own control, a sense of its limits, a sense of balance. Thus the Old Testament
instruction that revenge should be *limited to* "an eye for an eye, a tooth for a tooth, hand for
hand, foot for foot, burning for burning, wound for wound, stripe for stripe" ("*Lex
Talionis*"), *Exodus* 21:24—5). The New Testament demands even more restraint, the
abstention from revenge oneself and the patience to entrust it to God. Both the Old and New
Testaments (more the latter than the former) also encourage "forgiveness," but there can be
no forgiveness if there is not first the desire (and the warrant) for revenge.
     Vengeance is not just punishment, no matter how harsh. It is a matter of emotion, and
like punishment, it is always *for* some offense, not just hurting for its own sake (even if, in
some other sense, it is deserved). Vengeance, then, always has its reasons (though, to be
sure, these can be mistaken, irrelevant, out of proportion or otherwise bad reasons).
Vengeance is no longer a matter of obligation and it certainly can't claim to be rational as
such but neither is it opposed to a sense of obligation (e.g. in matters of family honor) or
rationality (insofar as rationality is to be found in every emotion, even this one). Vengeance
is the emotion of "getting even," putting the world back in balance, and this simple phrase

already embodies a whole philosophy of justice, even if (as yet) unarticulated and unjustified. Philosophers have been much too quick to attribute this sense of "balance" or "retribution" to reason, but I would want to argue that it is rather a function of emotion. Kant, of course, immediately opts for the former, dismissing the latter suggestion virtually altogether. Vengeance, he suggests, is purely subjective, wholly irrational, undependable and unjustifiable. It is wholly without measure or reason, devoid of any sense of balance or justice. But I want to suggest that vengeance just is that sense of measure of balance that Kant (and so many other philosophers) attribute to reason alone. But, of course, it is ultimately the same old dichotomy that is most at fault here, the supposed antagonism between reason on the one side and passions on the other. Where would our reasoning about punishment begin if not for our emotional sense of the need for retaliation and retribution? (We should stress here that retaliation and retribution should not be confused with reparation and mere compensation, which may in some cases "undo" the damage but in no case by themselves count as punishment.) And what would our emotion be if it were not already informed and cultivated by a keen sense of its object and its target, as well as the mores and morals of the community in which the offense in question is deserving of revenge?

Vengeance, unlike justice, is said to be "blind" (though it is worth reminding ourselves which of the two is depicted in established mythology as blind-folded). Vengeance, it is said, knows no end. It is not just that it gets out of hand; it cannot be held "in hand" in the first place. And, of course, we agree that there is danger in vengeance: It is by its very nature violent, disrupting the present order of things in an often impossible attempt to get back to a prior order which has itself been violently disrupted. Such an impossibility breeds frustration, and violence—even justified as vengeance (if, indeed, revenge is possible), and this typically leads to more violence. Too often, an act of revenge (even if legitimate) results in a new offense to be righted. And when the act is perpetrated not against the same person who did the offense but against another who is part of the same family, tribe or social group (the logic of "vendetta"), the possibilities for escalation are endless. (Ironically, much of the traditional danger of escalating vengeance has been reduced or eliminated by our very strong contemporary notion of individual (rather than collective) responsibility at the same time that the emphasis on individual responsibility has increasingly denied its attachments to vengeance.) It is because of the likelihood of escalation as well as the possibilities of mistakes on a purely personal level (what John Locke called "the inconveniences" of rights-enforcement in the state of nature) that the limitation of revenge through institutionalization becomes necessary. But it does not follow that vengeance itself is illegitimate or without measure or of no importance in considerations of punishment. To the dangers of vengeance unlimited it must be countered that if punishment no longer satisfies vengeance, if it ignores not only the rights but the emotional needs of the victims of crime, then punishment no longer serves its primary purpose, even if it were to succeed in rehabilitating the criminal and deterring other crime (which it evidently, in general, does not). The restriction of vengeance by law is entirely understandable, but, again, the wholesale denial of vengeance as a legitimate motive may be a psychological disaster.

These preliminary comments are intended to unearth a number of bad arguments against vengeance (which are often generalized into even worse bad arguments concerning "negative" and violent emotions as a unified class):

1.   *Vengeance is (as such) irrational, and, consequently, it is never legitimate.* Only a moment's reflection is necessary to realize that we all recognize (whether or not we recognize at the time) the difference between justified and unjustified revenge. Vengeance

is not just the desire to harm but the desire to harm *for a reason,* and a reason of a very particular sort. To flunk a student because he has an orange punk hairdo or because he disagreed with one's pet theory in class is not justified, but to expel him for burning down the department library is another matter. But what about the fact that sometimes, while in the "grip" of revenge, we fail to recognize or properly exercise the reason and warrant for our vengeance? But the point is the word "sometimes," for there is nothing essential to vengeance that requires such failure. In indisputably rational contexts a decision-maker mistakes a means for an end, or becomes so distracted in his pursuit of the end that he neglects or simply misses the most appropriate means. In vengeance one can also get caught up in the means or obsessed and distracted by the end, but the logic of "reasons" and appropriateness is nevertheless present as a standard. Accordingly, the question is not whether vengeance is ever legitimate but rather *when* it is legitimate, when those standards and reasons are in fact appropriate and warranted.

2.   *There is no "natural" end to it.* But, of course, there is. The idea that vengeance leads to a total loss of inhibition and control ignores the built-in and cultivated satisfactions of revenge, and seems to confuse the fact that mutually vengeful acts tend to escalate with the fact that a single act of vengeance typically has its very specific goals and, consequently, its own built-in standard of satisfaction. Vengeance is *rational.* I think that we are misled here by the conflation of vengeance, which is always particular and aimed at some particular offense (or series of offenses) and the familiar *feud,* which is an on-going form of personal, family or tribal hostility whose origins may well be forgotten. In other words, we conflate hatred (which may or may not be part of vengeance) with vengeance itself. We might note here too that one reason for the escalation of violence in vengeance, even when it seems that both sides have good reason to be vengeful, is that they may have, as Elizabeth Wolgast suggests, "different arithmetics." That is, what seems to count as "getting even" to one side is evidently an overpayment according to the other, or else the frameworks in which the "balance" is calculated are themselves very different. One of Wolgast's examples is the debt of Agamemnon to Apollo, which he "pays off" by sacrificing his daughter Iphegenia. But Iphegenia's mother, Clytemnestra, does not recognize the legitimacy of that debt; she sees only the murder of her daughter. So she murders Agamemnon, which her other children Orestes and Electra then avenge by murdering her. I do not deny that such horrible sequences are possible, but there is a reason why this particular sequence should have come down to us as a *tragedy.* It is not the ordinary course or complications of revenge, and while it is easy enough to identify conflicts of "arithmetics" in our own day (e.g. in the Middle East) I believe that it is an enormous mistake to see these as the paradigm or conceptual prototype of vengeance as such.

3.   *Vengeance is always violent.* The blood-thirsty acts of the Clint Eastwood character or the Ninja assassin may hold dramatic sway over our fantasies, but the more usual act of revenge is a negative vote in the next department meeting, a forty-five minute delay in arriving to dinner or a hurtful comment or letter, delivered with a vicious twist of phrase, perhaps, but rarely the twist of a blade, except, of course, metaphorically. One might, given the current tendency to inflate the meaning of words and numb our sensitivities to moral differences, argue that such acts do indeed constitute "violence," but this certainly drains the substance from this standard objection against vengeance. Of course, there is an important if problematic distinction that is at stake here, between actually doing harm to an offender and depriving him or her of some essential human good, like liberty, for example. It is probably true that vengeance generally aims at harm whereas the cooler claims of the law tend to prefer punishments by way of deprivation—the payment of fines, for example,

or depriving the criminal of certain privileges or freedoms (to drive a car, for example, or to use the university library), even depriving him of freedom as such—though prisons today as probably always seem to be just as much infliction of harm as deprivation. (The continuing ruckus over the death penalty is, in part, due to the fact that it is one of the few punishments today that inflicts harm—indeed the ultimate harm—rather than imposing some deprivation.) But, then, it is obvious that this important distinction will not stand too much scrutiny, and it would be hard to insist for very long that sending a man to prison is not in fact actually *harming* him. And by the same token, there is much that counts as punishment and consequently satisfies the desire for revenge which need not be violence.

4.   *It takes the law "into our own hands."* (The use of "in hand" metaphors seem to abound in such discussions.) It is worth noting that historically, punishing the perpetrator for almost any offense against an individual, from an obscene gesture to rape and murder, rested with the family, and it was considered not only inappropriate but unjustifiable intrusion into private matters for the state to step in. It is a relatively recent development— and an obviously very political move—that punishment of such crimes should have become the *exclusive* province of the state. Moral objections against vengeance and the desire for public order seem to me to have far less to do with this than the usual arrogance of the state in abrogating individual rights and its desire for control. Indeed, it is a point worth pondering that major crimes against the person are in law crimes against the state. When current criminal law reduces the victim of such crimes to a mere bystander (if, that is, the victim has survived the crime), the problem is not that in vengeance we take the law "into our own hands" but rather that without vengeance justice seems not only to be taken out of our hands but eliminated as a consideration altogether. Current concerns with punishment, even those that claim to take "retribution" seriously, seem to serve the law and sanction respect for the law (or reason) rather than the need for justice. Not that the law and respect for the law are unimportant, of course, but one should not glibly identify these with justice and dismiss the passion for vengeance as something quite different and wholly illegitimate.

"Retribution" is the pivotal term in all arguments about punishment. On the one hand, "backward-looking" retribution is juxtaposed against the "forward-looking" utilitarian concerns of deterrence and rehabilitation. That is, retribution is characterized in terms of its "undoing" a past offense; deterrence and criminal reform are concerned with preventing future offenses. Much of this dispute, I would argue, is purely academic; it is almost impossible to imagine an instance in which both responsibility for the offense and concern for the future not both are at stake. (It is to get around this practical point that Kant shocks us by insisting: "even if a civil society were to dissolve itself by common agreement of all its members, the last murderer remaining in prison must first be executed.") What gets left out of the argument, except marginally, is the all-important question of *character*—which obviously refers both to one's past behavior and one's disposition to future behavior. Punishment theorists, too, like so many theorists of justice, are too caught up in the abstractions—"punishment," "deterrence"—and too dismissive of the personal motives and character of both the criminal and those who do the punishing. Judges, of course, virtually always use "discretion"—which means, essentially, that they weight many factors, past and future, in determining punishments. Retribution, so considered, is not just "getting even" and "blind" to the future but roundly concerned with the whole question of the personalities involved in guilt and punishment.

How did our passion for retribution—our need for vengeance, come about? I think that our evolutionary speculations in Chapter 3 go a long way in answering this question. In that chapter, I was primarily concerned to account for our "natural"sympathies and our sense of fellowship with others, as opposed to the antagonistic, competitive view of the "state of nature" described by writers like Hobbes. But I hope that I was sufficiently careful not to give the impression that we are naturally "nice" in any ridiculous sense, and without retreating to the too-prevalent presumptions of self-interest I nevertheless wanted to show that there is some demonstrable advantage for groups and species—if not always for us as individuals—in the evolution of cooperation. But cooperation has two sides, the willingness to cooperate, first of all, but then the resentment and punishment of those who do not cooperate as well. (This includes the expectation that one will be punished oneself if one does not cooperate.) One cannot imagine the evolution of the cooperation without the evolution of punishment, and Robert Axelrod's now-classic "tit-for-tat" model of the former explains as well the latter. In a repetitive "prisoner's dilemma" type situation, or in any on-going situation in which one person frequently has the ability to "cheat" the other(s), an optimum strategy for discouraging such cheating is to respond, dependably, with retribution. A creature endowed only with compassion, who would "understand" the motives of the criminal in every case, would be just as much of an evolutionary failure as a creature who did nothing but watch out for his or her own advantage and cheated every time. Swift and dependable retaliation is thus in the nature of social animals as well as the lesson of game theory. Vengeance is not the antagonist to rationality but its natural manifestation. To breed a social animal with "the right to make promises," according to Nietzsche, "nature's paradoxical task," is to understand the evolution of a creature who has the natural urge to punish as well as natural sympathy and a sense of social solidarity.

Vengeance is our natural sense of retribution. Needless to say, few philosophers have acknowledged this kinship. Kant, notably, defends retribution as a rational necessity but insists that it is wholly rational and not at all emotional. Virtually all "retributivists," in fact, insist on separating retribution from vengeance. On the one hand, they insist that the notion of retribution lies right at the heart of punishment—indeed, it has often been argued that it is just another word for "punishment." On the other hand, retribution is therefore defended as a product of reason, even a matter of metaphysics—the undoing of some "corrupt" or "unnatural" state caused by crime. But even retribution has often been called "barbaric," and it remains, as R. S. Gerstein recently writes, "the most unfashionable theory in philosophical and other circles" and "frequently dismissed with contempt." So why do we punish? Why not forget about the past misdeeds—which after all cannot be undone—and move on to the future? The usual argument is this: if punishment were essentially a way of preventing future crime rather than punishment for a particular past crime, then wouldn't it be justifiable to punish a wholly innocent man just as a warning to potential law-breakers? and the obvious answer to this (usually) rhetorical question is, "no! That would be the height of injustice." And so even if retribution is "barbaric," "unfashionable" and "dismissed with contempt," it has long held the dominant position against its rival theories (which emphasize deterrence and rehabilitation respectively). Too often it is defended in a purely trivial way, as the very meaning of the word "punishment," and too often it is defended with great obscurity, in metaphysical terms that are no longer even intelligible to most people. But, without assuming that what is natural is therefore desirable, I think we can argue and argue persuasively that our natural sense of vengeance—even if it requires careful correction and containment under the auspices of reason and tradition and through the machinery of the law—already gives us good grounds for punishment, even if, within the thrall of the emotion itself, we cannot articulate those grounds.

The argument that vengeance and retribution are "backward-looking" does not, I think, hold up to scrutiny. The "tit-for-tat" strategy may be a response to a past offense but it is a *strategy* just insofar as it is a way of planning a future. Thus it is not that retributivists need deny the importance or desirability of deterring crime or changing the character or at least the behavior of criminals. It is just that such activities, no matter how well-intended or conceived, do not by themselves count as punishment. But, again, why punish? I do not think that we can answer this question without reference to that supposedly primitive passion for vengeance and its implicit strategy. The idea of "evening the score" is also a way of "teaching the offender a lesson." This phrase does, of course, capture something of deterrence and rehabilitation theories as well as the idea of "getting back" at the offender, but the key point is that this is not primarily motivated by either deterrence or rehabilitation or the rationality of retribution. As Nietzsche tells us in his *Genealogy*, "the urge to punish" comes first; the reasons and attempts at justification come later.

The rationale of retribution, the "intelligence" embodied in vengeance, is the idea that "the punishment should fit the crime." This is an idea that goes back (at least) to the Biblical "eye for an eye" injunction, but it has also been long under fire as well. Since ancient times, there has been Socrates's oft-repeated objection—that punishment is the return of evil for evil and so never legitimate, no matter how horrendous the crime. So conceived, of course, punishment is just another wrong, whether carried out as a personal act of revenge or under the cool, deliberate auspices of the state legal system. (The argument that "murder is wrong, no matter who does it" has often been used as a central argument against capital punishment.) But punishment is not the return of "evil for evil." The German philosopher Hegel argued, I think convincingly, that this is one sure way to misunderstand the nature of punishment. "Harm for harm" perhaps, but it is justified and legitimate harm in return for unjustified and illegitimate harm. The hard question is, how does one get one harm to "fit" another? What does "an eye for an eye" really mean?

It seems to be false in practice that the punishment is designed to fit the crime: Punishment also has to fit the criminal and the circumstances and serve the public good. It is, accordingly, not true that the crime and nothing but the crime justifies infliction of punishment, but what this would seem to mean is that we should enlarge our sense of "fit" to include not just the offense narrowly construed but the whole context in which the crime was committed, including, first and foremost, the character of the criminal. The likelihood of a repetition of the crime and questions of deterrence are consequences of this concern rather than its motivation. But even so expanded, the idea of balance or "fit" comes under fire. How does one calculate how many years in prison it will take to "equal" the crime of armed robbery, however we take into account the history and character of the criminal and the circumstances of the crime? In what conceivable sense does time in prison "equal" the harm inflicted by the offender on his victims or on the community? My favorite objection to the "eye for an eye" formulation was levelled against retributivism by Lord Blackstone back in the eighteenth century. He queried, "what is the equivalent harm when a two-eye'd man knocks out the eye of a one-eye'd man?" Cute, to be sure, but hardly a knock-down argument against the idea that the punishment should fit the crime. Granting the gruesomeness of the concept, we do feel that familiar if embarrassing satisfaction when a vicious criminal who has intentionally blinded his innocent victim is blinded himself in an accident. To be sure, few of us would suggest that the law itself undertake to inflict such a punishment, but the notion of "fit" is evident enough to us, if only as "poetic" justice.

Kant puts the case for retribution succinctly: "only the law of retribution (*jus talionis*) can determine exactly the kind and degree of punishment," though (he carefully adds) such a determination must be made in a court of justice and not as a private judgment. It is this sense of what Kant calls "equality" that makes punishment rational, the idea of "fitting" the crime. If a man has committed a murder, Kant argues, he must die; "there is no substitute that will satisfy the requirements of legal justice. There is no sameness of kind between death and remaining alive even under the most miserable conditions." We may not agree. But we must agree that a serious crime such as murder demands a serious punishment, while a minor crime does not. Hanging a poor man for stealing a loaf of bread now strikes us as barbaric, not because we reject the idea of retribution but because we accept it (and not just because we feel compassion for the man's plight). Hanging a man for stealing food is barbaric because it doesn't "fit." It is monstrously excessive. And that means that we do indeed use the standard of "equality" in making such judgments, and we would not understand the meaning of "punishment" without it.

Much of the language with which we describe both our passion for vengeance and the concept of retribution consists largely of an interrelated group of metaphors—notably the images of "equality," "balance" and "fit." These are too often thrown together as one, and too often treated as if they were not metaphors at all but literal truths. I want to wrap up this section by distinguishing and discussing briefly four of these:

    1.   The *"debt"* metaphor: to punish is to "repay" a wrong. There is some dispute (for example, in Nietzsche, *Genealogy,* Essay II) whether the notion of legal obligation preceded or rather grew out of this idea of a debt, but with regard to punishment, the metaphorical character of "repayment" is quite clear. The suggestion that there is an implicit contract (whether via Hobbes and Locke or Plato's *Crito*) is just to repeat the question, how the metaphor of repayment can be rationally justified. In contrast with the other metaphors, punishment does not "balance the books" nor does it "erase" the wrong in question, as repayment of a debt surely does. The "debt" metaphor, by the way, is not restricted to capitalist societies; "debt" is not the same as "consumer debt" and applies to the New Guinea custom of giving a pig for a wrongful death as well as financial liability and "punitive damages." Debt, in most societies, is a moral measure rather than a monetary arrangement.

    2.   The *"fit"* metaphor, again, is the popular idea that the punishment should "fit" the crime. (W. S. Gilbert's *Mikado:* "an object all sublime/make the punishment fit the crime.") "Eye for eye, tooth for tooth," we are told since biblical times. But as many opponents and critics of retributivism have pointed out, such punishments are administered—or even make sense—only in a very limited number of crimes, e.g. intentional murder. But even then, as Albert Camus has famously pointed out,

> For there to be equivalence, the death penalty would have to punish a criminal who had warned his victim of the date at which he would inflict a horrible death on him and who, from that moment onward, had confined him at his mercy for months. Such a monster is not encountered in private life.

Defenders of retributivism gladly weaken the demands of "fit," suggesting, for instance, that it provides only a general measure, that the crucial concept here is one of "proportion"—so that petty theft is not (as it once was) punished with the harshness of a violent crime. With this, of course, we all agree, but "proportion" too misleadingly suggests quantification where there often is none, and it too summarizes rather than solves the problem of punishment. To be sure, it is somehow "fit" to trade a life for a life (or more accurately, "a death for a death"), but is it just? And there are so many qualifications and extenuating circumstances concerning intentions, risk and appropriate caution that qualify each and every case, does the singular image of "fit" make sense? But again, we recognize the *lack* of fit: witness our horror, e.g. when Afghan tribesmen summarily execute [by beheading] the hapless tourist involved in an automobile accident, even one which [were the driver to have made an insurance claim] might have been proclaimed "faultless."

3.   The *"balance"* metaphor: punishment makes things "even" again. It is through punishment that one "gets even." In epic literature, it is by punishing the villain that one "balances the forces of good and evil." One problem is that this moral balance is often simply equated, in the crudest utilitarian fashion, with a balance of pleasure and pain, as if the application of an amount of pain to the villain which is equal to the amount of pain he or she has caused (which is not the same as the amount of pleasure gotten from his crime) balances the scales. (We should remember again the standard allegorical figure of justice, this time with her scales.) Where the crime is strictly pecuniary, it might seem that balance (like the repayment of a debt) might be literally appropriate, but this, of course, isn't so. One can pay back the amount of money stolen or otherwise taken, but this does not yet take into account the offense itself. As soon as one must pay back even an extra penny, the literalness of the "balance" again comes into question. Granted the original sum has been repaid, but now what is the "cost" or the "price" of the crime? Again, my point is not that the metaphor of "balance" isn't applicable or revealing of how we think about justice, but it underscores rather than solves our problems.

4.   The *"erasure"* metaphor: the idea that we can "annul the evil" through punishment. Vendetta cultures talk about "bloodmarks (also "blood debts") not as a sign of guilt but rather of unrevenged wrong. But the obvious question is, can we undo a crime—for instance, rape or murder, in any sense whatever? In financial crimes, again, one can "erase" the debt by paying it back, but not the crime itself. For example, how does one erase the terror one suffered in an armed robbery, even if the money were to be politely returned. ("Here you are, Miss; I'm a student at the local police academy and I wanted to experience what the criminal felt like.") Indeed, how does one measure the fear that one suffers in such crimes, even if there is no "harm done" in any of the usual senses? And yet, the idea of "annulment" looms large in the history of theories of punishment, from the ancient world (in which one quite literally made the offender disappear) to modern conceptions in Hegel and Bosanquet and others. The punishment doesn't literally eliminate the crime of course, but Bosanquet's suggestion that it eliminates it *as a precedent* has the virtue of showing us how this metaphor too, hardly intelligible when taken literally, can nonetheless be given a good intelligible interpretation that is not strictly retributivist but takes future behavior into account as well.

Retributive justice consists, first of all, of retribution. That isn't much of a claim, but it is remarkable how often it is denied by our best current legal theorists. But retributivism is wrongly presented as a theory or a set of principles when it ought to be considered, first of all, as the expression of revenge. Or, rather, retribution and revenge are one and the same. (One might, adopting a distinction from Robert Nozick, say that retribution is justified revenge, where revenge is strictly personal but retribution is not.) Of course, retribution can be turned into a theory (no one would accuse Kant of mere metaphor mongering) but retributivism, I want to argue, is primarily a set of concepts and judgments embodied in a feeling, not a theory. Perhaps it was overstated in the majority opinion in United States Supreme Court decision *Gregg* v. *Georgia* (1976):

> The instinct for retribution is part of the nature of man, and channeling that instinct in the
> administration of criminal justice serves an important purpose in promoting the stability

of a society governed by law. When people begin to believe that organized society is
unwilling or unable to impose upon criminal offenders the punishment they "deserve,"
then there are sown the seeds of anarchy—of self-help, vigilante justice, and lynch law.

But at least the emotion of vengeance was taken seriously and not merely sacrificed to the
dispassionate authority of the law. Retributive justice, however rationalized, is not as such
a purely "rational matter"—but neither is it thereby "irrational" either. Most of the arguments that have been advanced against vengeance could, with only slight modifications, be
applied to the standard notions of retributive justice as well—which is not surprising if
vengeance and retributive justice are in the end identical. But in the end, it is perhaps not
just a question of whether revenge is rational or not, but whether it is—at the bottom of our
hearts as well as off the top of our heads—an undeniable aspect of the way we react to the
world, not as an instinct but as such a basic part of our world-view and our moral sense of
ourselves that it is, in that sense, unavoidable.

I have not tried here to defend vengeance as such, but my claim is that vengeance
deserves its central place in any theory of justice and, whatever else we are to say about
punishment, the desire for revenge must enter into our deliberations along with such emotions as compassion, caring and love. Any system of legal principles that does not take such
emotions into account, which does not motivate itself on their behalf, is not—whatever else
it may be—a system of justice. But vengeance as such, I do not deny, is in any case dangerous. As the Chinese used to say (and no doubt still do) "if you seek vengeance, dig two
graves." But I think that the dangers and destructiveness of vengeance are much overblown
and its importance for a sense of one's own self-esteem and integrity ignored. Many people believe that vengeance is the primary cause of the world's troubles today, unending
feuds and vendettas that block every rational effort at resolution and peace. But in addition
to my insistence that vengeance is not the same as vendetta and feuds are not the same as
vengeance, I would argue that the passionate hostilities of the world that are fueled by
revenge are only secondary and in many cases caused or at any rate aggravated and rendered unresolvable not by passion at all so much as by supposedly rational *ideology,*
abstracting and elevating personal prejudices to the status of absolute truths and giving
vengeance a set of reasons far less negotiable than any feud or mere urge to "get even."
Vengeance, at least, has its measure. Ideology, however "reasonable," may not. Goldwater:
"Extremism in the name of liberty is no vice."

Vengefulness, no doubt, is a vice, and because vengeance is so often dangerous and
destructive it makes perfectly good sense for moralists to urge us to rise "above" the urge
to vengeance. But the argument behind this need not involve forgiveness and mercy nor
need it appeal to Nietzschean "master" morality and "self-overcoming." Neither need it be
anything so detached and saintly as "turning the other cheek." The argument is that instead
of following that often narrow path to personal retribution we would much better embrace
that expansive form of social consciousness in which we become more aware of the real
desperation of others than we are of our own (usually petty) complaints. To transcend
revenge is to become keenly aware of the suffering of others with an urgency that eclipses
the blows to our own fragile egos and gives our sense of compassion priority over the urge
to vengeance. But it is not to give up vengeance as such and, as in tit-for-tat, it is the ready
willingness to retaliate that provides stability to both the social system and one's personal
sense of integrity and control. Despite volumes of propaganda to the contrary, experience
seems to show that to see oneself as a helpless victim makes one less and not more likely
to open one's heart to others. But we do not have to be or see ourselves as victims, and it is

vengeance or at least fantasies of vengeance that make this possible. Our concept of injustice is inextricably tied up with the concept of blame and with the concept of punishment, and where the injustice is personal so is the felt need for retribution. In a world in which justice is getting ever more impersonal and statistical, vengeance retains the virtue of being personal. But so, of course, does compassion, which commands not the impersonal but a more expanded sense of the personal. Between vengeance and compassion there is no doubt which is the greater virtue, but vengeance is nevertheless necessary, and compassion for one's own offender (the object of one's revenge) is often foolish rather than noble. Justice is not forgiveness nor even forgetting but rather it is getting one's emotional priorities right, putting blame aside in the face of so much other human suffering and thereby giving up vengeance for the sake of larger and more noble emotions.

United States Supreme Court, *Gregg* v. *Georgia* (1976)

Gregg v. *Georgia* was something of a landmark in 1976, when the U.S. Supreme Court reaffirmed the constitutional validity of the death penalty. The challenge had been that the death penalty was as such "cruel and unusual punishment," thus explicitly prohibited by the Bill of Rights as applied to the states through the Fourteenth Amendment. The arguments behind this decision come from a variety of sources—from the long history of punishment in the world as in the United States, from the original intentions of the framers of the Constitution, and from current endorsements of the penalty by state legislators and juries. The Court emphasizes the importance of sensitivity to changing mores and the fact that what is considered humane and legitimate in one generation may not be so in one a century or more later. Nevertheless, the decision was that the death penalty is not as such in violation of the Constitution. The Court argued that it served the social purposes of *both* deterrence and retribution, and it quotes an important passage from the earlier case of *Furman* v. *Georgia* (1972) insisting on the importance of the "instinct for retribution." The justices admit, however, that the statistical studies concerning the effects of the death penalty on the deterrence of future crimes have been "inconclusive."

The Court's decision was not, however, unanimous; seven justices were in the majority, and two in the minority. Writing for the dissent, Justice Thurgood Marshall opposes the death penalty, as he had done earlier and continued to do until his retirement. Marshall argues that the death penalty is, by any measure, excessive, and he disagrees with the majority's view that the American people support that form of punishment. Their seeming support, he argues, is the result of a lack of information. He points out that studies show that there is "no correlation between the existence of capital punishment and lower rates of capital crime," thus undermining deterrence as a justification for the death penalty, and he argues that it "defies belief" to argue that the death penalty is necessary to prevent people from taking the law into their own hands. The extreme penalty of life imprisonment, Marshall argues, is just as strong an expression of moral outrage of the community as the penalty of death. Finally, he reiterates an argument as old as Socrates, that it is wrong to return evil for evil.

Majority Opinion

The issue in this case is whether the imposition of the sentence of death for the crime of murder under the law of Georgia violates the Eighth and Fourteenth Amendments.

I

The petitioner, Troy Gregg, was charged with committing armed robbery and murder. In accordance with Georgia procedure in capital cases, the trial was in two stages, a guilt stage and a sentencing stage. . . .

. . . The jury found the petitioner guilty of two counts of armed robbery and two counts of murder.

At the penalty stage, which took place before the same jury, . . . the trial judge instructed the jury that it could recommend either a death sentence or a life prison sentence on each count. . . . The jury returned verdicts of death on each count.

II

. . . The Georgia statute, as amended after our decision in *Furman* v. *Georgia* (1972), retains the death penalty for six categories of crime: murder, kidnaping for ransom or where the victim is harmed, armed robbery, rape, treason, and aircraft hijacking. . . .

III

We address initially the basic contention that the punishment of death for the crime of murder is, under all circumstances, "cruel and unusual" in violation of the Eighth and Fourteenth Amendments of the Constitution.

The Court on a number of occasions has both assumed and asserted the constitutionality of capital punishment. In several cases that assumption provided a necessary foundation for the decision, as the Court was asked to decide whether a particular method of carrying out a capital sentence would be allowed to stand under the Eighth Amendment. But until *Furman* v. *Georgia* (1972), the Court never confronted squarely the fundamental claim that the punishment of death always, regardless of the enormity of the offense or the procedure followed in imposing the sentence, is cruel and unusual punishment in violation of the Constitution. Although this issue was presented and addressed in *Furman,* it was not resolved by the Court. Four Justices would have held that capital punishment is not unconstitutional per se; two Justices would have reached the opposite conclusion; and three Justices, while agreeing that the statutes then before the Court were invalid as applied, left open the question whether such punishment may ever be imposed. We now hold that the punishment of death does not invariably violate the Constitution.

A

The history of the prohibition of "cruel and unusual" punishment already has been reviewed at length. The phrase first appeared in the English Bill of Rights of 1689, which was drafted by Parliament at the accession of William and Mary. The English version appears to have been directed against punishments unauthorized by statute and beyond the jurisdiction of the sentencing court, as well as those disproportionate to the offense involved. The American draftsmen, who adopted the English phrasing in drafting the Eighth Amendment, were primarily concerned, however, with proscribing "tortures" and other "barbarous" methods of punishment.

In the earliest cases raising Eighth Amendment claims, the Court focused on particular methods of execution to determine whether they were too cruel to pass constitutional muster. The constitutionality of the sentence of death itself was not at issue, and the criterion used to evaluate the mode of execution was its similarity to "torture" and other "barbarous" methods. . . .

But the Court has not confined the prohibition embodied in the Eighth Amendment to "barbarous" methods that were generally outlawed in the 18th century. Instead, the Amendment has been interpreted in a flexible and dynamic manner. The Court early recognized that "a principle to be vital must be capable of wider application than the mischief which gave it birth." Thus the Clause forbidding "cruel and unusual" punishments "is not fastened to the obsolete but may acquire meaning as public opinion becomes enlightened by a humane justice."

But our cases also make clear that public perceptions of standards of decency with respect to criminal sanctions are not conclusive. A penalty also must accord with "the dignity of man," which is the "basic concept underlying the Eighth Amendment." This means, at least, that the punishment not be "excessive." When a form of punishment in the abstract (in this case, whether capital punishment may ever be imposed as a sanction for murder) rather than in the particular (the propriety of death as a penalty to be applied to a specific defendant for a specific crime) is under consideration, the inquiry into "excessiveness" has two aspects. First, the punishment must not involve the unnecessary and wanton infliction of pain. Second, the punishment must not be grossly out of proportion to the severity of the crime. . . .

The imposition of the death penalty for the crime of murder has a long history of acceptance both in the United States and in England. . . .

It is apparent from the text of the Constitution itself that the existence of capital punishment was accepted by the Framers. At the time the Eighth Amendment was ratified, capital punishment was a common sanction in every State. Indeed, the First Congress of the United States enacted legislation providing death as the penalty for specified crimes. . . .

For nearly two centuries, this Court, repeatedly and often expressly, has recognized that capital punishment is not invalid per se. . . .

Four years ago, the petitioners in *Furman* and its companion cases predicated their argument primarily upon the asserted proposition that standards of decency had evolved to the point where capital punishment no longer could be tolerated. The petitioners in those cases said, in effect, that the evolutionary process had come to an end, and that standards of decency required that the Eighth Amendment be construed finally as prohibiting capital punishment for any crime regardless of its depravity and impact on society. This view was accepted by two Justices. Three other Justices were unwilling to go so far; focusing on the procedures by which convicted defendants were selected for the death penalty rather than on the actual punishment inflicted, they joined in the conclusion that the statutes before the Court were constitutionally invalid.

The petitioners in the capital cases before the Court today renew the "standards of decency" argument, but developments during the four years since *Furman* have undercut substantially the assumptions upon which their argument rested. Despite the continuing debate, dating back to the nineteenth century, over the morality and utility of capital punishment, it is now evident that a large proportion of American society continues to regard it as an appropriate and necessary criminal sanction.

The most marked indication of society's endorsement of the death penalty for murder is the legislative response to *Furman*. The legislatures of at least thirty-five States have enacted new statutes that provide for the death penalty for at least some crimes that result in the death of another person. And the Congress of the United States, in 1974, enacted a statute providing the death penalty for aircraft piracy that results in death. These recently adopted statutes have attempted to address the concerns expressed by the Court in *Furman* primarily (i) by specifying the factors to be weighed and the procedures to be followed in deciding when to impose a capital sentence, or (ii) by making the death penalty mandatory for specified crimes. But all of the post-*Furman* statutes make clear that capital punishment itself has not been rejected by the elected representatives of the people. . . .

The jury also is a significant and reliable objective index of contemporary values because it is so directly involved. The Court has said that "one of the most important functions any jury can perform in making . . . a selection [between life imprisonment and death for a defendant convicted in a capital case] is to maintain a link between contemporary community values and the penal system." It may be true that evolving standards have influenced juries in recent decades to be more discriminating in imposing the sentence of death. But the relative infrequency of jury verdicts imposing the death sentence does not indicate rejection of capital punishment per se. Rather, the reluctance of juries in many cases to impose the sentence may well reflect the humane feeling that this most irrevocable of sanctions should be reserved for a small number of extreme cases. Indeed, the actions of juries in many States since *Furman* are fully compatible with the legislative judgments, reflected in the new statutes, as to the continued utility and necessity of capital punishment in appropriate cases. At the close of 1974 at least 254 persons had been sentenced to death since *Furman,* and by the end of March 1976, more than 460 persons were subject to death sentences.

As we have seen, however, the Eighth Amendment demands more than that a challenged punishment be acceptable to contemporary society. The Court also must ask whether it comports with the basic concept of human dignity at the core of the Amendment. Although we cannot "invalidate a category of penalties because we deem less severe penalties, adequate to serve the ends of penology," the sanction imposed cannot be so totally without penological justification that it results in the gratuitous infliction of suffering.

The death penalty is said to serve two principal social purposes: retribution and deterrence of capital crimes by prospective offenders.

In part, capital punishment is an expression of society's moral outrage at particularly offensive conduct. This function may be unappealing to many, but it is essential in an ordered society that asks its citizens to rely on legal processes rather than self-help to vindicate their wrongs.

> The instinct for retribution is part of the nature of man, and channeling that instinct in the administration of criminal justice serves an important purpose in promoting the stability of a society governed by law. When people begin to believe that organized society is unwilling or unable to impose upon criminal offenders the punishment they "deserve," then there are sown the seeds of anarchy—of self-help, vigilante justice, and lynch law.
>
> *Furman v. Georgia* (Stewart, J., concurring).

"Retribution is no longer the dominant objective of the criminal law," but neither is it a forbidden objective nor one inconsistent with our respect for the dignity of men. Indeed, the decision that capital punishment may be the appropriate sanction in extreme cases is an expression of the community's belief that certain crimes are themselves so grievous an affront to humanity that the only adequate response may be the penalty of death.

Statistical attempts to evaluate the worth of the death penalty as a deterrent to crimes by potential offenders have occasioned a great deal of debate. The results simply have been inconclusive. . . .

Although some of the studies suggest that the death penalty may not function as a significantly greater deterrent than lesser penalties, there is no convincing empirical evidence either supporting or refuting this view. We may nevertheless assume safely that there are murderers, such as those who act in passion, for whom the threat of death has little or no deterrent effect. But for many others, the death penalty undoubtedly is a significant deterrent. There are carefully contemplated murders, such as murder for hire, where the possible penalty of death may well enter into the cold calculus that precedes the decision to act. And there are some categories of murder, such as murder by a life prisoner, where other sanctions may not be adequate.

The value of capital punishment as a deterrent of crime is a complex factual issue the resolution of which properly rests with the legislatures, which can evaluate the results of statistical studies in terms of their own local conditions and with a flexibility of approach that is not available to the courts. Indeed, many of the post-*Furman* statutes reflect just such a responsible effort to define those crimes and those criminals for which capital punishment is most probably an effective deterrent.

In sum, we cannot say that the judgment of the Georgia Legislature that capital punishment may be necessary in some cases is clearly wrong. Considerations of federalism, as well as respect for the ability of a legislature to evaluate, in terms of its particular State, the moral consensus concerning the death penalty and its social utility as a sanction, require us to conclude, in the absence of more convincing evidence, that the infliction of death as a punishment for murder is not without justification and thus is not unconstitutionally severe.

Finally, we must consider whether the punishment of death is disproportionate in relation to the crime for which it is imposed. There is no question that death as a punishment is unique in its severity and irrevocability. When a defendant's life is at stake, the Court has been particularly sensitive to insure that every safeguard is observed. But we are concerned here only with the imposition of capital punishment for the crime of murder, and when a life has been taken deliberately by the offender, we cannot say that the punishment is invariably disproportionate to the crime. It is an extreme sanction, suitable to the most extreme of crimes.

We hold that the death penalty is not a form of punishment that may never be imposed, regardless of the circumstances of the offense, regardless of the character of the offender, and regardless of the procedure followed in reaching the decision to impose it.

Minority Opinion

In *Furman* v. *Georgia* (1972) (concurring opinion), I set forth at some length my views on the basic issue presented to the Court in [this case]. The death penalty, I concluded, is a cruel and unusual punishment prohibited by the Eighth and Fourteenth Amendments. That continues to be my view.

I have no intention of retracing the "long and tedious journey" that led to my conclusion in *Furman.* My sole purposes here are to consider the suggestion that my conclusion in *Furman* has been undercut by developments since then, and briefly to evaluate the basis for my Brethren's holding that the extinction of life is a permissible form of punishment under the Cruel and Unusual Punishments Clause.

In *Furman* I concluded that the death penalty is constitutionally invalid for two reasons. First, the death penalty is excessive. And second, the American people, fully informed as to the purposes of the death penalty and its liabilities, would in my view reject it as morally unacceptable.

Since the decision in *Furman,* the legislatures of thirty-five States have enacted new statutes authorizing the imposition of the death sentence for certain crimes, and Congress has enacted a law providing the death penalty for air piracy resulting in death. I would be less than candid if I did not acknowledge that these developments have a significant bearing on a realistic assessment of the moral acceptability of the death penalty to the American people. But if the constitutionality of the death penalty turns, as I have urged, on the opinion of an *informed* citizenry, then even the enactment of new death statutes cannot be viewed as conclusive. In *Furman,* I observed that the American people are largely unaware of the information critical to a judgment on the morality of the death penalty, and concluded that if they were better informed they would consider it shocking, unjust, and unacceptable. A recent study, conducted after the enactment of the post-*Furman* statutes, has confirmed that the American people know little about the death penalty, and that the opinions of an informed public would differ significantly from those of a public unaware of the consequences and effects of the death penalty.

Even assuming, however, that the post-*Furman* enactment of statutes authorizing the death penalty renders the prediction of the views of an informed citizenry an uncertain basis for a constitutional decision, the enactment of those statutes has no bearing whatsoever on the conclusion that the death penalty is unconstitutional because it is excessive. An excessive penalty is invalid under the Cruel and Unusual Punishments Clause "even though popular sentiment may favor" it. The inquiry here, then, is simply whether the death penalty is necessary to accomplish the legitimate legislative purposes in punishment, or whether a less severe penalty—life imprisonment—would do as well.

The two purposes that sustain the death penalty as nonexcessive in the Court's view are general deterrence and retribution. In *Furman,* I canvassed the relevant data on the deterrent effect of capital punishment. The state of knowledge at that point, after literally centuries of debate, was summarized as follows by a United Nations Committee:

It is generally agreed between the retentionists and abolitionists, whatever their opinions about the validity of comparative studies of deterrence, that the data which now exist show no correlation between the existence of capital punishment and lower rates of capital crime.

The available evidence, I concluded in *Furman*, was convincing that "capital punishment is not necessary as a deterrent to crime in our society." . . .

The evidence I reviewed in *Furman* remains convincing, in my view, that "capital punishment is not necessary as a deterrent to crime in our society." The justification for the death penalty must be found elsewhere.

The other principal purpose said to be served by the death penalty is retribution. The notion that retribution can serve as a moral justification for the sanction of death finds credence in the opinion of my Brothers Stewart, Powell, and Stevens. . . . It is this notion that I find to be the most disturbing aspect of today's unfortunate [decision].

The concept of retribution is a multifaceted one, and any discussion of its role in the criminal law must be undertaken with caution. On one level, it can be said that the notion of retribution or reprobation is the basis of our insistence that only those who have broken the law be punished, and in this sense the notion is quite obviously central to a just system of criminal sanctions. But our recognition that retribution plays a crucial role in determining who may be punished by no means requires approval of retribution as a general justification for punishment. It is the question whether retribution can provide a moral justification for punishment—in particular, capital punishment—that we must consider.

My Brothers Stewart, Powell, and Stevens offer the following explanation of the retributive justification for capital punishment:

> The instinct for retribution is part of the nature of man, and channeling that instinct in the administration of criminal justice serves an important purpose in promoting the stability of a society governed by law. When people begin to believe that organized society is unwilling or unable to impose upon criminal offenders the punishment they "deserve," then there are sown the seeds of anarchy—of self-help, vigilante justice, and lynch law.

This statement is wholly inadequate to justify the death penalty. As my Brother Brennan stated in *Furman*, "[t]here is no evidence whatever that utilization of imprisonment rather than death encourages private blood feuds and other disorders." It simply defies belief to suggest that the death penalty is necessary to prevent the American people from taking the law into their own hands.

In a related vein, it may be suggested that the expression of moral outrage through the imposition of the death penalty serves to reinforce basic moral values—that it marks some crimes as particularly offensive and therefore to be avoided. The argument is akin to a deterrence argument, but differs in that it contemplates the individual's shrinking from antisocial conduct, not because he fears punishment, but because he has been told in the strongest possible way that the conduct is wrong. This contention, like the previous one, provides no support for the death penalty. It is inconceivable that any individual concerned about conforming his conduct to what society says is "right" would fail to realize that murder is "wrong" if the penalty were simply life imprisonment.

The foregoing contentions—that society's expression of moral outrage through the imposition of the death penalty preempts the citizenry from taking the law into its own hands and reinforces moral values—are not retributive in the purest sense. They are essentially utilitarian in that they portray the death penalty as valuable because of its beneficial results. These justifications for the death penalty are inadequate because the penalty is, quite clearly I think, not necessary to the accomplishment of those results.

There remains for consideration, however, what might be termed the purely retributive justification for the death penalty—that the death penalty is appropriate, not because of its beneficial effect on society, but because the taking of the murderer's life is itself morally good. Some of the language of the opinion of my Brothers Stewart, Powell, and Stevens . . . appears positively to embrace this notion of retribution for its own sake as a justification for capital punishment. They state:

> [T]he decision that capital punishment may be the appropriate sanction in extreme cases is an expression of the community's belief that certain crimes are themselves so grievous an affront to humanity that the only adequate response may be the penalty of death.

They then quote with approval from Lord Justice Denning's remarks before the British Royal Commission on Capital Punishment:

> The truth is that some crimes are so outrageous that society insists on adequate punishment, because the wrong-doer deserves it, irrespective of whether it is a deterrent or not.

Of course, it may be that these statements are intended as no more than observations as to the popular demands that it is thought must be responded to in order to prevent anarchy. But the implication of the statements appears to me to be quite different—namely, that society's judgment that the murderer "deserves" death must be respected not simply because the preservation of order requires it, but because it is appropriate that society make the judgment and carry it out. It is this latter notion, in particular, that I consider to be fundamentally at odds with the Eighth Amendment. The mere fact that the community demands the murderer's life in return for the evil he has done cannot sustain the death penalty, for as Justices Stewart, Powell, and Stevens remind us, "the Eighth Amendment demands more than that a challenged punishment be acceptable to contemporary society." To be sustained under the Eighth Amendment, the death penalty must "compor[t] with the basic concept of human dignity at the core of the Amendment"; the objective in imposing it must be "[consistent] with our respect for the dignity of [other] men." Under these standards, the taking of life "because the wrongdoer deserves it" surely must fail, for such a punishment has as its very basis the total denial of the wrongdoer's dignity and worth.

The death penalty, unnecessary to promote the goal of deterrence or to further any legitimate notion of retribution, is an excessive penalty forbidden by the Eighth and Fourteenth Amendments. I respectfully dissent from the Court's judgment upholding the [sentence] of death imposed upon the [petitioner in this case].

Hugo Bedau, "Against the Death Penalty," from "Capital Punishment" (1986)

Hugo Bedau (1926–) is one of the leading opponents of the death penalty, and he argues that its use is supported neither by considerations of deterrence nor by the supposed demand for retribution. He begins by agreeing, to get the argument going, that crime should be punished and that punishment should in some sense "fit" the crime. But neither of these principles is sufficient to justify the death penalty, which, he concludes, "only tends to add new injuries of its own to the catalogue of our inhumanity to each other." He points out that the death penalty has rarely been restricted to "a life for a life" and has often been employed to punish crimes other than murder, and murder itself is not always or even usually punished by death. The idea of retribution is rarely served by the death penalty, and perhaps most persuasive of all, there are the recently well-documented inequities in the application of the death penalty. Few, if any, white wealthy murderers have been executed, and a very large proportion of those executed are poor and members of racial minorities. Many of them had poor legal representation or faced an unusually ambitious prosecutor, and such misfortunes as these, rather than the severity of the crimes or the dangerousness of the criminals, sealed their fates. Capital punishment, Bedau concludes, cheapens and degrades human life rather than enhances respect for it.

There are two leading principles of retributive justice relevant to the capital-punishment controversy. One is the principle that crimes should be punished. The other is the principle that the severity of a punishment should be proportional to the gravity of the offense. (A corollary to the latter principle is the judgment that nothing so fits the crime of murder as the punishment of death.) Although these principles do not seem to stem from any concern over the worth, value, dignity, or rights of persons, they are moral principles of recognized weight and no discussion of the morality of capital punishment would be complete without them. Leaving aside all questions of social defense, how strong a case for capital punishment can be made on the basis if these principles? How reliable and persuasive are these principles themselves?

From Hugo Bedau, "Capital Punishment," in *Matters of Life and Death*, ed. Tom Regan, published by McGraw-Hill Publishing Co. Copyright © 1986 by McGraw-Hill Publishing Co. Reprinted by permission of the publisher.

Crime Must Be Punished

Given [a general rationale for punishment], there cannot be any dispute over this principle. In embracing it, of course, we are not automatically making a fetish of "law and order," in the sense that we would be if we thought that the most important single thing society can do with its resources is to punish crimes. In addition, this principle is not likely to be in dispute between proponents and opponents of the death penalty. Only those who completely oppose punishment for murder and other erstwhile capital crimes would appear to disregard this principle. Even defenders of the death penalty must admit that putting a convicted murderer in prison for years is a punishment of that criminal. The principle that crime must be punished is neutral to our controversy, because both sides acknowledge it and comply with it.

It is the other principle of retributive justice that seems to be a decisive one. Under the principle of retaliation, *lex talionis,* it must always have seemed that murderers ought to be put to death. Proponents of the death penalty, with rare exceptions, have insisted on this point, and it seems that even opponents of the death penalty must give it grudging assent. The strategy for opponents of the death penalty is to show either (a) that this principle is not really a principle of justice after all, or (b) that although it is, other principles outweigh or cancel its dictates. As we shall see, both these objections have merit.

Is Murder Alone to Be Punished by Death?

Let us recall, first, that not even the Biblical world limited the death penalty to the punishment of murder. Many other nonhomicidal crimes also carried this penalty (e.g., kidnapping, witchcraft, cursing one's parents). In our own recent history, persons have been executed for aggravated assault, rape, kidnapping, armed robbery, sabotage, and espionage. It is not possible to defend any of these executions (not to mention some of the more bizarre capital statutes, like the one in Georgia that used to provide an optional death penalty for desecration of a grave) on grounds of just retribution. This entails that either such executions are not justified or that they are justified on some ground other than retribution. In actual practice, few if any defenders of the death penalty have ever been willing to rest their case entirely on the moral principle of just retribution as formulated in terms of "a life for a life." Kant seems to have been a conspicuous exception. Most defenders of the death penalty have implied by their willingness to use executions to defend limb and property, as well as life, that they did not place much value on the lives of criminals when compared to the value of both lives and things belonging to innocent citizens.

Are All Murders to Be Punished by Death?

Our society for several centuries has endeavored to confine the death penalty to some criminal homicides. Even Kant took a casual attitude toward a mother's killing of her illegitimate child. ("A child born into the world outside marriage is outside the law . . . , and consequently it is also outside the protection of the law.") (Immanuel Kant, *The Metaphysical Elements of Justice* [1797].) In our society, the development nearly 200 years ago of the distinction between first- and second-degree murder was an attempt to narrow the class of criminal homicides deserving of the death penalty. Yet those dead owing to manslaughter, or to any kind of unintentional, accidental, unpremeditated, unavoidable, unmalicious killing are just as dead as the victims of the most ghastly murder. Both the law in practice and moral reflection show how difficult it is to identify all and only the criminal homicides that are appropriately punished by death (assuming that any are). Individual judges and juries differ in the conclusions they reach. The history of capital punishment for homicides reveals continual efforts, uniformly unsuccessful, to identify before the fact those homicides for which the slayer should die. Benjamin Cardozo, a justice of the United States Supreme Court fifty years ago, said of the distinction between degrees of murder that it was

> . . . so obscure that no jury hearing it for the first time can fairly be expected to assimilate and understand it. I am not at all sure that I understand it myself after trying to apply it for many years and after diligent study of what has been written in the books. Upon the basis of this fine distinction with its obscure and mystifying psychology, scores of men have gone to their death.
> (Benjamin Cardozo, "What Medicine Can Do for Law" [1928])

Similar skepticism has been registered on the reliability and rationality of death-penalty statutes that give the trial court the discretion to sentence to prison or to death. As Justice John Marshall Harlan of the Supreme Court observed a decade ago,

> Those who have come to grips with the hard task of actually attempting to draft means of channeling capital sentencing discretion have confirmed the lesson taught by history. . . . To identify before the fact those characteristics of criminal homicide and their perpetrators which call for the death penalty, and to express these characteristics in language which can be fairly understood and applied by the sentencing authority, appear to be tasks which are beyond present human ability.
> (*McGautha v. California*, 402 U.S. 183 [1971])

The abstract principle that the punishment of death best fits the crime of murder turns out to be extremely difficult to interpret and apply.

If we look at the matter from the standpoint of the actual practice of criminal justice, we can only conclude that "a life for a life" plays little or no role whatever. Plea bargaining (by means of which one of the persons involved in a crime agrees to accept a lesser sentence in exchange for testifying against the others to enable the prosecutor to get them all convicted), even where murder is concerned, is widespread. Studies of criminal justice reveal that what the courts (trial or appellate) decide on a given day is first-degree murder suitably punished by death in a given jurisdiction could just as well be decided in a neighboring jurisdiction on another day either as second-degree murder or as first-degree murder but without the death penalty. The factors that influence prosecutors in determining the charge under which they will prosecute go far beyond the simple principle of "a life for a life." Nor can it be objected that these facts show that our society does not care about justice. To put it succinctly, either justice in punishment does not consist of retribution, because there are other principles of justice; or there are other moral considerations besides justice that must be honored; or retributive justice is not adequately expressed in the idea of "a life for a life."

Is Death Sufficiently Retributive?

Given the reality of horrible and vicious crimes, one must consider whether there is not a quality of unthinking arbitrariness in advocating capital punishment for murder as the retributively just punishment. Why does death in the electric chair or the gas chamber or before a firing squad or on a gallows meet the requirements of retributive justice? When one thinks of the savage, brutal, wanton character of so many murders, how can retributive justice be served by anything less than equally savage methods of execution for the murderer? From a retributive point of view, the oft-heard exclamation, "Death is too good for him!," has a certain truth. Yet few defenders of the death penalty are willing to embrace this consequence of their own doctrine.

The reason they do not and should not is that, if they did, they would be stooping to the methods and thus to the squalor of the murderer. Where criminals set the limits of just methods of punishment, as they will do if we attempt to give exact and literal implementation to *lex talionis,* society will find itself descending to the cruelties and savagery that criminals employ. But society would be deliberately authorizing such acts, in the cool light of reason, and not (as is often true of vicious criminals) impulsively or in hatred and anger or with an insane or unbalanced mind. Moral restraints, in short, prohibit us from trying to make executions perfectly retributive. Once we grant the role of these restraints, the principle of "a life for a life" itself has been qualified and no longer suffices to justify the execution of murderers.

Other considerations take us in a different direction. Few murders, outside television and movie scripts, involve anything like an execution. An execution, after all, begins with a solemn pronouncement of the death sentence from a judge, is followed by long detention in maximum security awaiting the date of execution, various appeals, perhaps a final sanity hearing, and then "the last mile" to the execution chamber itself. As the French writer Albert Camus remarked,

> For there to be an equivalence, the death penalty would have to punish a criminal who had warned his victim of the date at which he would inflict a horrible death on him and who, from that moment onward, had confined him at his mercy for months. Such a monster is not encountered in private life.
>
> (Albert Camus, *Resistance, Rebellion, and Death* [1961])

Differential Severity Does Not Require Executions

What, then, emerges from our examination of retributive justice and the death penalty? If retributive justice is thought to consist in *lex talionis,* all one can say is that this principle has never exercised more than a crude and indirect effect on the actual punishments meted out. Other principles interfere with a literal and single-minded application of this one. Some murders seem improperly punished by death at all; other murders would require methods of execution too horrible to inflict; in still other cases any possible execution is too deliberate and monstrous given the nature of the motivation culminating in the murder. Proponents of the death penalty rarely confine themselves to reliance on this principle of just retribution and nothing else, since they rarely confine themselves to supporting the death penalty only for all murders.

But retributive justice need not be thought to consist of *lex talionis.* One may reject that principle as too crude and still embrace the retributive principle that the severity of punishments should be graded according to the gravity of the offense. Even though one need not claim that life imprisonment (or any kind of punishment other than death) "fits" the crime of murder, one can claim that this punishment is the proper one for murder. To do this, the schedule of punishments accepted by society must be arranged so that this mode of imprisonment is the most severe penalty used. Opponents of the death penalty need not reject this principle of retributive justice, even though they must reject a literal *lex talionis.*

Equal Justice and Capital Punishment

During the past generation, the strongest practical objection to the death penalty has been the inequities with which it has been applied. As Supreme Court Justice William O. Douglas once observed, "One searches our chronicles in vain for the execution of any member of the affluent strata of this society." (*Furman* v. *Georgia,* 408 U.S. 238 [1972]) One does not search our chronicles in vain for the crime of murder committed by the affluent. Every study of the death penalty for rape has confirmed that black male rapists (especially where the victim is a white female) are far more likely to be sentenced to death (and executed) than white male rapists. Half of all those under death sentence during 1976 and 1977 were black, and nearly half of all those executed since 1930 were black. All the sociological evidence points to the conclusion that the death penalty is the poor man's justice; as the current street saying has it, "Those without the capital get the punishment."

Let us suppose that the factual basis for such a criticism is sound. What follows for the morality of capital punishment? Many defenders of the death penalty have been quick to point out that since there is nothing intrinsic about the crime of murder or rape that dictates that only the poor or racial-minority males will commit it, and since there is nothing overtly racist about the statutes that authorize the death penalty for murder or rape, it is hardly a fault in the idea of capital punishment if in practice it falls with unfair impact on the poor and the black. There is, in short, nothing in the death penalty that requires it to be applied unfairly and with arbitrary or discriminatory results. It is at worst a fault in the system of administering criminal justice (and some, who dispute the facts cited above, would deny even this).

Presumably, both proponents and opponents of capital punishment would concede that it is a fundamental dictate of justice that a punishment should not be unfairly—inequitably or unevenly—enforced and applied. They should also be able to agree that when the punishment in question is the extremely severe one of death, then the requirement to be fair in using such a punishment becomes even more stringent. Thus, there should be no dispute in the death penalty controversy over these principles of justice. The dispute begins as soon as one attempts to connect these principles with the actual use of this punishment.

In this country, many critics of the death penalty have argued, we would long ago have got rid of it entirely if it had been a condition of its use that it be applied equally and fairly. In the words of the attorneys who argued against the death penalty in the Supreme Court during 1972, "It is a freakish aberration, a random extreme act of violence, visibly arbitrary and discriminatory—a penalty reserved for unusual application because, if it were usually used, it would affront universally shared standards of public decency." It is difficult to dispute this judgment, when one considers that there have been in the United States during the past fifty years about half a million criminal homicides but only about 4,000 executions (all but 50 of which were of men).

We can look at these statistics in another way to illustrate the same point. If we could be assured that the 4,000 persons executed were the worst of the worst repeated offenders without exception, the most dangerous murderers in captivity—the ones who had killed more than once and were likely to kill again, and the least likely to be confined in prison without imminent danger to other inmates and the staff—then one might accept half a million murders and a few thousand executions with a sense that rough justice had been done. But the truth is otherwise. Persons are sentenced to death and executed not because they have been found to be uncontrollably violent, hopelessly poor parole and release risks, or for other reasons. Instead, they are executed for entirely different reasons. They have a poor defense at trial; they have no funds to bring sympathetic witnesses to court; they are immigrants or strangers in the community where they were tried; the prosecuting attorney wants the publicity that goes with "sending a killer to the chair"; they have inexperienced or overworked counsel at trial; there are no funds for an appeal or for a transcript of the trial record; they are members of a despised racial minority. In short, the actual study of why particular persons have been sentenced to death and executed does not show any careful winnowing of the worst from the bad. It shows that the executed were usually the unlucky victims of prejudice and discrimination, the losers in an arbitrary lottery that could just as well have spared them as killed them, the victims of the disadvantages that almost always go with poverty. A system like this does not enhance respect for human life; it cheapens and degrades it. However heinous murder and other crimes are, the system of capital punishment does not compensate for or erase those crimes. It only tends to add new injuries of its own to the catalogue of our inhumanity to each other.

Ernest van den Haag, "For the Death Penalty," from "Deterrence and the Death Penalty" (1969)

Ernest van den Haag has long been a proponent of the death penalty, and in the following excerpt he defends the use of execution in the most serious criminal cases, despite the fact that statistics brought forward to show a correlation between use of the death penalty and deterrence of crime are inconclusive. Van den Haag points out that this uncertainty is to be found in any method of punishment, and there are no clear statistics to prove that (e.g.) the threat of a six-year prison term deters crime any more than the threat of a three-year term. In every case, there is uncertainty, and

Reprinted by special permission of Northwestern University School of Law, *Journal of Criminal Law, Criminology, and Police Science*, vol. 60, issue 2, 1969.

though in the case of the death penalty more evidence is demanded than for other penalties (because of capital punishment's irrevocability), the argument would still be that calculated risks favor the death penalty. It may be that there is no deterrent effect, but then again, there may be such an effect, and surely the life (or lives) of the murder's potential future victims (or other murderers' victims) should count for more in our policy judgments than the life of the murderer himself or herself.

— — —

. . . If we do not know whether the death penalty will deter others [in a uniquely effective way], we are confronted with two uncertainties. If we impose the death penalty, and achieve no deterrent effect thereby, the life of a convicted murderer has been expended in vain (from a deterrent viewpoint). There is a net loss. If we impose the death sentence and thereby deter some future murderers, we spared the lives of some future victims (the prospective murderers gain too; they are spared punishment because they were deterred). In this case, the death penalty has led to a net gain, unless the life of a convicted murderer is valued more highly than that of the unknown victim, or victims (and the non-imprisonment of the deterred non-murderer).

The calculation can be turned around, of course. The absence of the death penalty may harm no one and therefore produce a gain—the life of the convicted murderer. Or it may kill future victims of murderers who could have been deterred, and thus produce a loss—their life.

To be sure, we must risk something certain—the death (or life) of the convicted man, for something uncertain—the death (or life) of the victims of murderers who may be deterred. This is in the nature of uncertainty—when we invest, or gamble, we risk the money we have for an uncertain gain. Many human actions, most commitment—including marriage and crime—share this characteristic with the deterrent purpose of any penalization, and with its rehabilitative purpose (and even with the protective).

More proof is demanded for the deterrent effect of the death penalty than is demanded for the deterrent effect of other penalties. This is not justified by the absence of other utilitarian purposes such as protection and rehabilitation; they involve no less uncertainty than deterrence. Rehabilitation or protection are of minor importance in our penal system (though not in our theory). We confine many people who do not need rehabilitation and against whom we do not need protection (e.g., the exasperated husband who killed his wife); we release many unrehabilitated offenders against whom protection is needed. Certainly rehabilitation and protection are not, and deterrence is, the main actual function of legal punishment, if we disregard nonutilitarian purposes.

Irrevocability may support a demand for some reason to expect more deterrence than revocable penalties might produce, but not a demand for more proof of deterrence, as has been pointed out above. The reason for expecting more deterrence lies in the greater severity, the terrifying effect inherent in finality. Since it seems more important to spare victims than to spare murderers, the burden of proving that the greater severity inherent in irrevocability adds nothing to deterrence lies on those who oppose capital punishment. Proponents of the death penalty need show only that there is no more uncertainty about it than about greater severity in general.

The demand that the death penalty be proved more deterrent than alternatives cannot be satisfied any more than the demand that six years in prison be proved to be more deterrent than three. But the uncertainty which confronts us favors the death penalty as long as by imposing it we might save future victims of murder. This effect is as plausible as the general idea that penalties have deterrent effects which increase with their severity. Though we have no proof of the positive deterrence of the penalty, we also have no proof of zero, or negative effectiveness. I believe we have no right to risk additional future victims of murder for the sake of sparing convicted murderers; on the contrary, our moral obligation is to risk the possible ineffectiveness of executions. However rationalized, the opposite view appears to be motivated by the simple fact that executions are more subjected to social control than murder. However, this applies to all penalties and does not argue for the abolition of any.

Albert Camus, "The Unique Horror of the Death Penalty," from "Reflections on the Guillotine" (1957)

Albert Camus (1913–1960) was one of the great humanist writers of the mid-twentieth-century. Caught in the middle of the French-Algerian war (he was a French Algerian, or "*pied noir,*" by birth) and having lived in France during the Nazi occupation, he became the conscience and spokesman for those who found the ideologies of both the left and the right intolerably extreme. "Neither victims nor executioners," the well-chosen title of one of his essays, expresses a humanist sentiment shared by millions of his fellow French, and many more millions besides. He has long been identified with the "existentialist" movement in France, but he denied the affiliation and openly broke off his friendship with existentialist godfather Jean-Paul Sartre precisely on such political issues. Sartre was an ideologue of the left—albeit an unorthodox one; Camus refused to side with the left because of its inexcusable violence. It was in the same frame of mind, "neither victims nor executioners," that he wrote one of his most quoted essays, a long argument against capital punishment. A brief excerpt from it is included here.

———————————

From RESISTANCE, REBELLION, AND DEATH by Albert Camus, trans. J. O'Brien. Copyright © 1960 by Alfred A Knopf. Reprinted by permission of the publisher.

If there is a desire to maintain the death penalty, let us at least be spared the hypocrisy of a justification by example. Let us be frank about that penalty which can have no publicity, that intimidation which works only on respectable people, so long as they are respectable, which fascinates those who have ceased to be respectable and debases or deranges those who take part in it. It is a penalty, to be sure, a frightful torture, both physical and moral, but it provides no sure example except a demoralizing one. It punishes, but it forestalls nothing; indeed, it may even arouse the impulse to murder. It hardly seems to exist, except for the man who suffers it—in his soul for months and years, in his body during the desperate and violent hour when he is cut in two without suppressing his life. Let us call it by the name which, for lack of any other nobility, will at least give the nobility of truth, and let us recognize it for what it is essentially: a revenge.

A punishment that penalizes without forestalling is indeed called revenge. It is a quasi-arithmetical reply made by society to whoever breaks its primordial law. That reply is as old as man; it is called the law of retaliation. Whoever has done me harm must suffer harm; whoever has put out my eye must lose an eye; and whoever has killed must die. This is an emotion, and a particularly violent one, not a principle.

Retaliation is related to nature and instinct, not to law. Law, by definition, cannot obey the same rules as nature. If murder is in the nature of man, the law is not intended to imitate or reproduce that nature. It is intended to correct it. Now, retaliation does no more than ratify and confer the status of a law on a pure impulse of nature. We have all known that impulse, often to our shame, and we know its power, for it comes down to us from the primitive forests. In this regard, we French, who are properly indignant upon seeing the oil king in Saudi Arabia preach international democracy and call in a butcher to cut off a thief's hand with a cleaver, live also in a sort of Middle Ages without even the consolations of faith. We still define justice according to the rules of a crude arithmetic. Can it be said at least that that arithmetic is exact and that justice, even when elementary, even when limited to legal revenge, is safeguarded by the death penalty? The answer must be no.

Let us leave aside the fact that the law of retaliation is inapplicable and that it would seem just as excessive to punish the incendiary by setting fire to his house as it would be insufficient to punish the thief by deducting from his bank account a sum equal to his theft. Let us admit that it is just and necessary to compensate for the murder of the victim by the death of the murderer. But beheading is not simply death. It is just as different, in essence, from the privation of life as a concentration camp is from prison. It is a murder, to be sure, and one that arithmetically pays for the murder committed. But it adds to death a rule, a public premeditation known to the future victim, an organization, in short, which is in itself a source of moral sufferings more terrible than death. Hence there is no equivalence. Many laws consider a premeditated crime more serious than a crime of pure violence. But what then is capital punishment but the most premeditated of murders, to which no criminal's deed, however calculated it may be, can be compared? For there to be equivalence, the death penalty would have to punish a criminal who had warned his victim of the date at which he would inflict a horrible death on him and who, from that moment onward, had confined him at his mercy for months. Such a monster is not encountered in private life.

Part Five: The Current Debate on Distributive Justice

Today, the central debate about justice emerges from the text and strategy of John Rawls's monumental *A Theory of Justice*. Published in 1971, *A Theory of Justice* has been credited with almost singlehandedly reviving moribund political philosophy, and virtually nothing written today about justice manages to escape a direct confrontation with that work, whether the author intends to agree with or merely amend Rawls's work, tries to deny its basic principles or strategy or both, insists that Rawls's vision of justice is mistaken at its very foundation, or wants to counter Rawls's influence with an entirely different approach or conception. Ronald Dworkin and Thomas Nagel are certainly sympathetic critics of Rawls's work: while each of them is in basic agreement about the liberal account of justice that Rawls offers, each raises questions about particular features of Rawls's view, calling for clarifications or further defense (and, in Dworkin's case, offering a reconception of what is at the heart of Rawls's system). Robert Nozick would certainly seem to be offering an entirely different rival account of justice, for both his approach to social philosophy and his conception of justice are radically at odds with those of his colleague in Emerson Hall. But from a longer perspective it turns out that Rawls and Nozick may be more similar than different, and what they jointly presuppose and exclude from their theories may be more telling than their now famous disagreements over the justifiability of redistribution—or so argues Alasdair MacIntyre. Michael Sandel challenges the conception of the moral agent assumed by the Rawlsian account of justice, holding that to view all social institutions as justified by presocial persons in a social contract rules out the essential way that the human good can be found in community. Michael Walzer takes the flaw in the Rawlsian vision to be shared by any theory of justice that aims to provide an overriding master principle of distribution: on his view, different "spheres of justice" have different ground rules and different concerns, and there is no reason to suppose that there is an overarching conception of justice that embraces them all. Susan Moller Okin, a feminist critic of Rawls, Nozick, and MacIntyre, notes that the structure of Rawls's vision seems to make the family immune to criticism in terms of injustice, while noting that a theory like Rawls's might nevertheless be put to use as part of an effective critique of gendered society. And perhaps most interesting of all is a response to *A Theory of Justice* from Rawls himself. In recent work Rawls has argued that the proper task of the political philosopher in an age of pluralism—that is, an age in which a soci-

ety contains reasonable adherents of a number of diverse and irreconcilable philosophical and religious views—is not to provide yet another comprehensive philosophical theory but instead to provide a "freestanding" view, one that can be articulated
from the basic ideas of the public culture. The theory of justice articulated in 1971 as
an account of what all reasonable persons would agree to as a matter of the first principles of social justice is now put forward only as an account particularly suited for
those inhabiting modern democratic societies.

John Rawls, "Justice as Fairness," from "Justice as Fairness" (1958) and *A Theory of Justice* (1971)

In the two selections that follow, John Rawls (1921–) defends both his general approach to justice as a rational decision procedure and the two principles that define his theory. On Rawls's theory, which he calls "justice as fairness," the central idea is that a just distribution of social goods would be one that all members of society would agree on were they placed in a fair situation in which to make the agreement. This fair situation, as we saw in the selection from *A Theory of Justice* that appears in Part Two, is the "original position": each agent in the original position knows no particular information about himself or herself; he or she knows only general facts about human beings and human societies. Given so little information, how will the parties in the original position reach an agreement, and what principles of justice will they agree to? Rawls argues that they would agree to two principles of justice, the first of which requires equal liberty for all and the second of which requires that inequalities should work out to the advantage of all. (So if there are any departures from equal distributions of goods, these departures will have to make everyone better off.) They would choose these principles, Rawls argues, because in such a high-stakes decision—the parties in the original position are deciding on principles of justice that will determine their entire life prospects, but with almost no information to go on—the most reasonable decision procedure is that of "maximin," according to which one should choose the option that would leave one best off if the worst outcome were to occur. By following maximin, Rawls thinks, the parties in the original position would refuse to accept any but equal liberty and would—since each is worried about being the worst off—require a distribution of resources that would require that everyone gain from any social inequalities.

―――――◦◦◦―――――

From "Justice as Fairness"

1. It might seem at first sight that the concepts of justice and fairness are the same, and that there is no reason to distinguish them, or to say that one is more fundamental than the other.

I think that this impression is mistaken. In this paper I wish to show that the fundamental idea in the concept of justice is fairness; and I wish to offer an analysis of the concept of justice from this point of view. To bring out the force of this claim, and the analysis based upon it, I shall then argue that it is this aspect of justice for which utilitarianism, in its classical form, is unable to account, but which is expressed, even if misleadingly, by the idea of the social contract.

To start with I shall develop a particular conception of justice by stating and commenting upon two principles which specify it, and by considering the circumstances and conditions under which they may be thought to arise. The principles defining this conception, and the conception itself, are, of course, familiar. It may be possible, however, by using the notion of fairness as a framework, to assemble and to look at them in a new way. Before stating this conception, however, the following preliminary matters should be kept in mind.

Throughout I consider justice only as a virtue of social institutions, or what I shall call practices. The principles of justice are regarded as formulating restrictions as to how practices may define positions and offices, and assign thereto powers and liabilities, rights and duties. Justice as a virtue of particular actions or of persons I do not take up at all. It is important to distinguish these various subjects of justice, since the meaning of the concept varies according to whether it is applied to practices, particular actions, or persons. These meanings are, indeed, connected, but they are not identical. I shall confine my discussion to the sense of justice as applied to practices, since this sense is the basic one. Once it is understood, the other senses should go quite easily.

Justice is to be understood in its customary sense as representing but *one* of the many virtues of social institutions, for these may be antiquated, inefficient, degrading, or any number of other things, without being unjust. Justice is not to be confused with an all-inclusive vision of a good society; it is only one part of any such conception. It is important, for example, to distinguish that sense of equality which is an aspect of the concept of justice from that sense of equality which belongs to a more comprehensive social ideal. There may well be inequalities which one concedes are just, or at least not unjust, but which, nevertheless, one wishes on other grounds, to do away with. I shall focus attention, then, on the usual sense of justice in which it is essentially the elimination of arbitrary distinctions and the establishment, within the structure of a practice, of a proper balance between competing claims.

Finally, there is no need to consider the principles discussed below as *the* principles of justice. For the moment it is sufficient that they are typical of a family of principles normally associated with the concept of justice. The way in which the principles of this family resemble one another, as shown by the background against which they may be thought to arise, will be made clear by the whole of the subsequent argument.

2. The conception of justice which I want to develop may be stated in the form of two principles as follows: first, each person participating in a practice, or affected by it, has an equal right to the most extensive liberty compatible with a like liberty for all; and second, inequalities are arbitrary unless it is reasonable to expect that they will work out for everyone's advantage, and provided the positions and offices to which they attach, or from which they may be gained, are open to all. These principles express justice as a complex of three ideas: liberty, equality, and reward for services contributing to the common good. . . .

The first principle holds, of course, only if other things are equal: that is, while there must always be a justification for departing from the initial position of equal liberty (which is defined by the pattern of rights and duties, powers and liabilities, established by a practice), and the burden of proof is placed on him who would depart from it, nevertheless, there can be, and often there is, a justification for doing so. Now, that similar particular cases, as defined by a practice, should be treated similarly as they arise, is part of the very concept of a practice; it is involved in the notion of an activity in accordance with rules. The first principle expresses an analogous conception, but as applied to the structure of practices themselves. It holds, for example, that there is a presumption against the distinctions and classifications made by legal systems and other practices to the extent that they infringe on the original and equal liberty of the persons participating in them. The second principle defines how this presumption may be rebutted.

It might be argued at this point that justice requires only an equal liberty. If, however, a greater liberty were possible for all without loss or conflict, then it would be irrational to settle on a lesser liberty. There is no reason for circumscribing rights unless their exercise would be incompatible, or would render the practice defining them less effective. Therefore no serious distortion of the concept of justice is likely to follow from including within it the concept of the greatest equal liberty.

The second principle defines what sorts of inequalities are permissible; it specifies how the presumption laid down by the first principle may be put aside. Now by inequalities it is best to understand not *any* differences between offices and positions, but differences in the benefits and burdens attached to them either directly or indirectly, such as prestige and wealth, or liability to taxation and compulsory services. Players in a game do not protest against there being different positions, such as batter, pitcher, catcher, and the like, nor to there being various privileges and powers as specified by the rules; nor do the citizens of a country object to there being the different offices of government such as president, senator, governor, judge, and so on, each with their special rights and duties. It is not differences of this kind that are normally thought of as inequalities, but differences in the resulting distribution established by a practice, or made possible by it, of the things men strive to attain or avoid. Thus they may complain about the pattern of honors and rewards set up by a practice (e.g., the privileges and salaries of government officials) or they may object to the distribution of power and wealth which results from the various ways in which men avail themselves of the opportunities allowed by it (e.g., the concentration of wealth which may develop in a free price system allowing large entrepreneurial or speculative gains).

It should be noted that the second principle holds that an inequality is allowed only if there is reason to believe that the practice with the inequality, or resulting in it, will work for the advantage of *every* party engaging in it. Here it is important to stress that *every* party must gain from the inequality. Since the principle applies to practices, it implies that the representative man in every office or position defined by a practice, when he views it as a going concern, must find it reasonable to prefer his condition and prospects with the inequality to what they would be under the practice without it. The principle excludes, therefore, the justification of inequalities on the grounds that the disadvantages of those in one position are outweighed by the greater advantages of those in another position. This rather simple restriction is the main modification I wish to make in the utilitarian principle as usually understood. . . .

3. Given these principles one might try to derive them from a priori principles of reason, or claim that they were known by intuition. These are familiar enough steps and, at least in the case of the first principle, might be made with some success. Usually, however, such arguments, made at this point, are unconvincing. They are not likely to lead to an understanding of the basis of the principles of justice, not at least as principles of justice. I wish, therefore, to look at the principles in a different way.

Imagine a society of persons amongst whom a certain system of practices is *already* well established. Now suppose that by and large they are mutually self-interested; their allegiance to their established practices is normally founded on the prospect of self-advantage. One need not assume that, in all senses of the term "person," the persons in this society are mutually self-interested. If the characterization as mutually self-interested applies when the line of division is the family, it may still be true that members of families are bound by ties of sentiment and affection and willingly acknowledge duties in contradiction to self-interest. Mutual self-interestedness in the relations between families, nations, churches, and the like, is commonly associated with intense loyalty and devotion on the part of individual members. Therefore, one can form a more realistic conception of this society if one thinks of it as consisting of mutually self-interested families, or some other association. Further, it is not necessary to suppose that these persons are mutually self-interested under all circumstances, but only in the usual situations in which they participate in their common practices.

Now suppose also that these persons are rational: they know their own interests more or less accurately; they are capable of tracing out the likely consequences of adopting one practice rather than another; they are capable of adhering to a course of action once they have decided upon it; they can resist present temptations and the enticements of immediate gain; and the bare knowledge or perception of the difference between their condition and that of others is not, within certain limits and in itself, a source of great dissatisfaction. Only the last point adds anything to the usual definition of rationality. This definition should allow, I think, for the idea that a rational man would not be greatly downcast from knowing, or seeing, that others are in a better position than himself, unless he thought their being so was the result of injustice, or the consequence of letting chance work itself out for no useful common purpose, and so on. So if these persons strike us as unpleasantly egoistic, they are at least free in some degree from the fault of envy.

Finally, assume that these persons have roughly similar needs and interests, or needs and interests in various ways complementary, so that fruitful cooperation amongst them is possible; and suppose that they are sufficiently equal in power and ability to guarantee that in normal circumstances none is able to dominate the others. This condition (as well as the others) may seem excessively vague; but in view of the conception of justice to which the argument leads, there seems no reason for making it more exact here.

Since these persons are conceived as engaging in their common practices, which are already established, there is no question of our supposing them to come together to deliberate as to how they will set these practices up for the first time. Yet we can imagine that from time to time they discuss with one another whether any of them has a legitimate complaint against their established institutions. Such discussions are perfectly natural in any normal society. Now suppose that they have settled on doing this in the following way. They first try to arrive at the principles by which complaints, and so practices themselves, are to be judged. Their procedure for this is to let each person propose the principles upon which he wishes his complaints to be tried with the understanding that, if acknowledged, the complaints of others will be similarly tried, and that no complaints will be heard at all until everyone is roughly of one mind as to how complaints are to be judged. They each understand further that the principles proposed and acknowledged on this occasion are binding on future occasions. Thus each will be wary of proposing a principle which would give him a peculiar advantage, in his present circumstances, supposing it to be accepted. Each person knows that he will be bound by it in future circumstances the peculiarities of which cannot be known, and which might well be such that the principle is then to his disadvantage. The idea is that everyone should be required to make *in advance* a firm commitment, which others also may reasonably be expected to make, and that no one be given the opportunity to tailor the canons of a legitimate complaint to fit his own special condition, and then to discard them when they no longer suit his purpose. Hence each person will propose principles of a general kind which will, to a large degree, gain their sense from the various applications to be made of them, the particular circumstances of which being as yet unknown. These principles will express the conditions in accordance with which each is the least unwilling to have his interests limited in the design of practices, given the competing interests of the others, on the supposition that the interests of others will be limited likewise. The restrictions which would so arise might be thought of as those a person would keep in mind if he were designing a practice in which his enemy were to assign him his place.

The two main parts of this conjectural account have a definite significance. The character and respective situations of the parties reflect the typical circumstances in which questions of justice arise. The procedure whereby principles are proposed and acknowledged represents constraints, analogous to those of having a morality, whereby rational and mutually self-interested persons are brought to act reasonably. Thus the first part reflects the fact that questions of justice arise when conflicting claims are made upon the design of a practice and where it is taken for granted that each person will insist, as far as possible, on what he considers his rights. It is typical of cases of justice to involve persons who are pressing on one another their claims, between which a fair balance or equilibrium must be found. On the other hand, as expressed by the second part, having a morality must at least imply the acknowledgment of principles as impartially applying to one's own conduct as well as to another's, and moreover principles which may constitute a constraint, or limitation, upon the pursuit of one's own interests. There are, of course, other aspects of having a morality: the acknowledgment of moral principles must show itself in accepting a reference to them as reasons for limiting one's claims, in acknowledging the burden of providing a special explanation, or excuse, when one acts contrary to them, or else in showing shame and remorse and a desire to make amends, and so on. It is sufficient to remark here that having a morality is analogous to having made a firm commitment in advance; for one must acknowledge the principles of morality even when to one's disadvantage. A man whose moral judgments always coincided with his interests could be suspected of having no morality at all.

Thus the two parts of the foregoing account are intended to mirror the kinds of circumstances in which questions of justice arise and the constraints which having a morality would impose upon persons so situated. In this way one can see how the acceptance of the principles of justice might come about, for given all these conditions as described, it would be natural if the two principles of justice were to be acknowledged. Since there is no way for anyone to win special advantage for himself, each might consider it reasonable to acknowledge equality as an initial principle. There is, however, no reason why they should regard this position as final; for if there are inequalities which satisfy the second principle, the immediate gain which equality would allow can be considered as intelligently invested in view of its future return. If, as is quite likely, these inequalities work as incentives to draw out better efforts, the members of this society may look upon them as concessions to human nature: they, like us, may think that people ideally should want to serve one another. But as they are mutually self-interested, their acceptance of these inequalities is merely the acceptance of the relations in which they actually stand, and a recognition of the motives which lead them to engage in their common practices. *They* have no title to complain of one another. And so provided that the conditions of the principle are met, there is no reason why they should not allow such inequalities. Indeed, it would be short-sighted of them to do so, and could result, in most cases, only from their being dejected by the bare knowledge, or perception, that others are better situated. Each person will, however, insist on an advantage to himself, and so on a common advantage, for none is willing to sacrifice anything for the others.

From *A Theory of Justice*

It will be recalled that the general conception of justice as fairness requires that all primary social goods be distributed equally unless an unequal distribution would be to everyone's advantage. No restrictions are placed on exchanges of these goods and therefore a lesser liberty can be compensated for by greater social and economic benefits. Now looking at the situation from the standpoint of one person selected arbitrarily, there is no way for him to win special advantages for himself. Nor, on the other hand, are there grounds for his acquiescing in special disadvantages. Since it is not reasonable for him to expect more than an equal share in the division of social goods, and since it is not rational for him to agree to less, the sensible thing for him to do is to acknowledge as the first principle of justice one requiring an equal distribution. Indeed, this principle is so obvious that we would expect it to occur to anyone immediately.

Thus, the parties start with a principle establishing equal liberty for all, including equality of opportunity, as well as an equal distribution of income and wealth. But there is no reason why this acknowledgment should be final. If there are inequalities in the basic structure that work to make everyone better off in comparison with the benchmark of initial equality, why not permit them? The immediate gain which a greater equality might allow can be regarded as intelligently invested in view of its future return. If, for example, these inequalities set up various incentives which succeed in eliciting more productive efforts, a person in the original position may look upon them as necessary to cover the costs of training and to encourage effective performance. One might think that ideally individuals should want to serve one another. But since the parties are assumed not to take an interest in one another's interests, their acceptance of these inequalities is only the acceptance of the relations in which men stand in the circumstances of justice. They have no grounds for complaining of one another's motives. A person in the original position would, therefore, concede the justice of these inequalities. Indeed, it would be shortsighted of him not to do so. He would hesitate to agree to these regularities only if he would be dejected by the bare knowledge or perception that others were better situated; and I have assumed that the parties decide as if they are not moved by envy. In order to make the principle regulating inequalities determinate, one looks at the system from the standpoint of the least advantaged representative man. Inequalities are permissible when they maximize, or at least all contribute to, the long-term expectations of the least fortunate group in society. . . .

It seems clear from these remarks that the two principles are at least a plausible conception of justice. The question, though, is how one is to argue for them more systematically. Now there are several things to do. One can work out their consequences for institutions and note their implications for fundamental social policy. In this way they are tested by a comparison with our considered judgments of justice. . . . But one can also try to find arguments in their favor that are decisive from the standpoint of the original position. In order to see how this might be done, it is useful as a heuristic device to think of the two principles as the maximin solution to the problem of social justice. There is an analogy between the two principles and the maximin rule for choice under uncertainty. This is evident from the fact that the two principles are those a person would choose for the design of a society in which his enemy is to assign him his place. The maximin rule tells us to rank alternatives by their worst possible outcomes: we are to adopt the alternative the worst outcome of which is superior to the worst outcomes of the others. The persons in the original position do not, of course, assume that their initial place in society is decided by a malevolent opponent. As I note below, they should not reason from false premises. The veil of ignorance does not violate this idea, since an absence of information is not misinformation. But that the two principles of justice would be chosen if the parties were forced to protect themselves against such a contingency explains the sense in which this conception is the maximin solution. And this analogy suggests that if the original position has been described so that it is rational for the parties to adopt the conservative attitude expressed by this rule, a conclusive argument can indeed be constructed for these principles. Clearly the maximin rule is not, in general, a suitable guide for choices under uncertainty. But it is attractive in situations marked by certain special features. My aim, then, is to show that a good case can be made for the two principles based on the fact that the original position manifests these features to the fullest possible degree, carrying them to the limit, so to speak. . . .

Now there appear to be three chief features of situations that give plausibility to this unusual rule. First, since the rule takes no account of the likelihoods of the possible circumstances, there must be some reason for sharply discounting estimates of these probabilities. Offhand, the most natural rule of choice would seem to be to compute the expectation of monetary gain for each decision and then to adopt the course of action with the highest prospect. . . . Thus it must be, for example, that the situation is one in which a knowledge of likelihoods is impossible, or at best extremely insecure. In this case it is unreasonable not to be skeptical of probabilistic calculations unless there is no other way out, particularly if the decision is a fundamental one that needs to be justified to others.

The second feature that suggests the maximin rule is the following: the person choosing has a conception of the good such that he cares very little, if anything, for what he might gain above the minimum stipend that he can, in fact, be sure of by following the maximin rule. It is not worthwhile for him to take a chance for the sake of a further advantage, especially when it may turn out that he loses much that is important to him. This last provision brings in the third feature, namely, that the rejected alternatives have outcomes that one can hardly accept. The situation involves grave risks. Of course these features work most effectively in combination. The paradigm situation for following the maximin rule is when all three features are realized to the highest degree. This rule does not, then, generally apply, nor of course is it self-evident. Rather, it is a maxim, a rule of thumb, that comes into its own in special circumstances. Its application depends upon the qualitative structure of the possible gains and losses in relation to one's conception of the good, all this against a background in which it is reasonable to discount conjectural estimates of likelihoods. . . .

Finally, the third feature holds if we can assume that other conceptions of justice may lead to institutions that the parties would find intolerable. For example, it has sometimes been held that under some conditions the utility principle (in either form) justifies, if not slavery or serfdom, at any rate serious infractions of liberty for the sake of greater social benefits. We need not consider here the truth of this claim, or the likelihood that the requisite conditions obtain. For the moment, this contention is only to illustrate the way in which conceptions of justice may allow for outcomes which the parties may not be able to accept. And having the ready alternative of the two principles of justice which secure a satisfactory minimum, it seems unwise, if not irrational, for them to take a chance that these outcomes are not realized.

Ronald Dworkin, "Justice and Hypothetical Agreements," from "The Original Position" (1973)

Ronald Dworkin (1931–) is, like Rawls, a liberal in matters of social justice, and has from the beginning been extraordinarily sympathetic to Rawls's account. In the excerpt that follows, Dworkin raises an interesting and difficult question for Rawls's theory. On Rawls's view, justice is a matter of agreement. But it is not an actual agreement, but a hypothetical one; we are to ask what we *would* agree to *under different circumstances*. As Dworkin notes, though, in most cases hypothetical agreements are of no binding force. Why, then, should we be interested in what the parties in the original position agree to? Dworkin argues that we need to see the contract not as being at the foundation of Rawls's account but as a halfway point on the way to principles of justice; what is at the basis of Rawls's view is an assumed natural right, the natural right of all people to equal concern and respect. The design of the original position is a way of giving more vivid and concrete expression to this right so that we can generate specific political conclusions from it.

Suppose that men and women in the original position would in fact choose Rawls' two principles as being in their own best interest. Rawls seems to think that that fact would provide an argument in favor of these two principles as a standard of justice against which to test actual political institutions. But it is not immediately plain why this should be so.

If a group contracted in advance that disputes amongst them would be settled in a particular way, the fact of that contract would be a powerful argument that such disputes should be settled in that way when they do arise. The contract would be an argument in itself, independent of the forces of the reasons that might have led different people to enter the contract. Ordinarily, for example, each of the parties supposes that a contract he signs is in his own interest; but if someone has made a mistake in calculating his self-interest, the fact that he did contract is a strong reason for the fairness of holding him nevertheless to the bargain.

Rawls does not suppose that any group ever entered into a social contract of the sort he describes. He argues only that if a group of rational men did find themselves in the predicament of the original position, they would contract for the two principles. His contract is hypothetical, and hypothetical contracts do not supply an independent argument for

From "The Original Position," *University of Chicago Law Review* 40 (1973). Reprinted by permission of the University of Chicago Law Review.

the fairness of enforcing their terms. A hypothetical contract is not simply a pale form of an actual contract; it is no contract at all.

If, for example, I am playing a game, it may be that I would have agreed to any number of ground rules if I had been asked in advance of play. It does not follow that these rules may be enforced against me if I have not, in fact, agreed to them. There must be reasons, of course, why I would have agreed if asked in advance, and these may also be reasons why it is fair to enforce these rules against me even if I have not agreed. But my hypothetical agreement does not count as a reason, independent of these other reasons, for enforcing the rules against me, as my actual agreement would have.

Suppose that you and I are playing poker and we find, in the middle of a hand, that the deck is one card short. You suggest that we throw the hand in, but I refuse because I know I am going to win and I want the money in the pot. You might say that I would certainly have agreed to that procedure had the possibility of the deck being short been raised in advance. But your point is not that I am somehow committed to throwing the hand in by an agreement I never made. Rather you use the device of a hypothetical agreement to make a point that might have been made without that device, which is that the solution recommended is so obviously fair and sensible that only someone with an immediate contrary interest could disagree. Your main argument is that your solution is fair and sensible, and the fact that I would have chosen it myself adds nothing of substance to that argument. If I am able to meet the main argument nothing remains, rising out of your claim that I would have agreed, to be answered or excused. . . .

Rawls says that the contract is a powerful argument for his principles because it embodies philosophical principles that we accept, or would accept if we thought about them. We want to find out what these principles are, and we may put our problem this way. The two principles comprise a theory of justice that is built up from the hypothesis of a contract. But the contract cannot sensibly be taken as the fundamental premise or postulate of that theory. . . . It must be seen as a kind of halfway point in a larger argument, as itself the product of a deeper political theory that argues for the two principles *through* rather than *from* the contract. We must therefore try to identify the features of a deeper theory that would recommend the device of a contract as the engine of justice, rather than the other theoretical devices Rawls mentions, like the device of the impartial spectator.

We shall find the answer, I think, if we attend to and refine the familiar distinction philosophers make between two types of moral theories, which they call teleological theories and deontological theories. I shall argue that any deeper theory that would justify Rawls' use of the contract must be a particular form of deontological theory, a theory that takes the idea of rights so seriously as to make them fundamental in political morality. I shall try to show how such a theory would be distinguished, as a type, from other types of political theories, and why only such a theory could give the contract the role and prominence Rawls does.

I must begin this argument, however, by explaining how I shall use some familiar terms. (1) I shall say that some state of affairs is a *goal* within a particular political theory if it counts in favor of a political act, within that theory, that the act will advance or preserve that state of affairs, and counts against an act that will retard or threaten it. Goals may be relatively specific, like full employment or respect for authority, or relatively abstract, like improving the general welfare, advancing the power of a particular concept of human goodness or of the good life. (2) I shall say that an individual has a *right* to a particular political act, within a political theory, if the failure to provide that act, when he calls for it, would be unjustified within that theory even if the goals of the theory would, on the balance, be disserviced by that act. The strength of a particular right, within a particular theory, is a function of the degree of disservice to the goals of the theory, beyond a mere disservice on the whole, that is necessary to justify refusing an act called for under the right. In the popular political theory apparently prevailing in the United States, for example, individuals have rights to free public speech on political matters and to a certain minimum standard of living, but neither right is absolute and the former is much stronger than the latter. (3) I shall say that an individual has a *duty* to act in a particular way, within a political theory, if a political decision constraining such act is justified within that theory notwithstanding that no goal of the system would be served by that decision. A theory may provide, for example, that individuals have a duty to worship God, even though it does not stipulate any goal served by requiring them to do so.

The three concepts I have described work in different ways, but they all serve to justify or to condemn, at least *pro tanto,* particular political decisions. In each case, the justification provided by citing a goal, a right, or a duty is in principle complete, in the sense that nothing need be added to make the justification effective, if it is not undermined by some competing considerations. But, though such a justification is in this sense complete, it need not, within the theory, be ultimate. It remains open to ask why the particular goal, right, or duty is itself justified, and the theory may provide an answer by deploying a *more basic* goal, right, or duty that is served by accepting this less basic goal, right, or duty as a complete justification in particular cases.

A particular goal, for example, might be justified as contributing to a more basic goal; thus, full employment might be justified as contributing to greater average welfare. Or a goal might be justified as serving a more basic right or duty; a theory might argue, for · example, that improving the gross national product, which is a goal, is necessary to enable the state to respect the rights of individuals to a decent minimum standard of living, or that improving the efficiency of the police process is necessary to enforce various individual duties not to sin. On the other hand, rights and duties may be justified on the ground that, by acting as a complete justification on particular occasions, they in fact serve more fundamental goals; the duty of individuals to drive carefully may be justified, for example, as serving the more basic goal of improving the general welfare. This form of justification does not, of course, suggest that the less basic right or duty itself justifies political decisions only when these decisions, considered one by one, advance the more basic goal. The point is rather the familiar one of rule utilitarianism, that treating the right or duty as a complete justification in particular cases, without reference to the more basic goal, will in fact advance the goal in the long run.

So goals can be justified by other goals or by rights or duties, and rights or duties can be justified by goals. Rights and duties can also be justified, of course, by other, more fundamental duties or rights. Your duty to respect my privacy, for example, may be justified by my right to privacy. I do not mean merely that rights and duties may be correlated, as opposite sides of the same coin. That may be so when, for example, a right and the corresponding duty are justified as serving a more fundamental goal, as when your right to property and my corresponding duty not to trespass are together justified by the more fundamental goal of socially efficient land use. In many cases, however, corresponding rights and duties are not correlative, but one is derivative from the other, and it makes a difference which is derivative from which. There is a difference between the idea that you have a duty not to lie to me because I have a right not to be lied to, and the idea that I have a right that you do not lie to me because you have a duty not to tell lies. In the first case I justify a duty by calling attention to a right; if I intend any further justification it is the right that I must justify, and I cannot do so by calling attention to the duty. In the second case it is the other way around. The difference is important because, as I shall shortly try to show, a theory that takes rights as fundamental is a theory of a different character from one that takes duties as fundamental.

Political theories will differ from one another, therefore, not simply in the particular goals, rights, and duties each sets out, but also in the way each connects the goals, rights, and duties it employs. In a well-formed theory some consistent set of these, internally ranked or weighted, will be taken as fundamental or ultimate within the theory. It seems reasonable to suppose that any particular theory will give ultimate pride of place to just one of these concepts; it will take some overriding goal, or some set of fundamental rights, or some set transcendent duties, as fundamental, and show other goals, rights, and duties as subordinate and derivative.

We may therefore make a tentative initial classification of the political theories we might produce, on the constructive model, as deep theories that might contain a contract as an intermediate device. Such a theory might be *goal-based,* in which case it would take some goal, like improving the general welfare, as fundamental; it might be *right-based,* taking some right, like the right of all men to the greatest possible overall liberty, as fundamental; or it might be *duty-based,* taking some duty, like the duty to obey God's will as set forth in the Ten Commandments, as fundamental. It is easy to find examples of pure, or nearly pure, cases of each of these types of theory. Utilitarianism is, as my example suggested, a goal-based theory; Kant's categorical imperatives compose a duty-based theory; and Tom Paine's theory of revolution is right-based. . . .

. . . My point is . . . to suggest that these differences in the character of a political theory are important quite apart from the details of position that might distinguish one theory from another of the same character. It is for this reason that the social contract is so important a feature of Rawls' methodology. It signals that his deep theory is a right-based theory, rather than a theory of either of the other two types.

The social contract provides every potential party with a veto: unless he agrees, no contract is formed. The importance, and even the existence, of this veto is obscured in the particular interpretation of the contract that constitutes the original position. Since no one knows anything about himself that would distinguish him from anyone else, he cannot rationally pursue any interest that is different. In these circumstances nothing turns on each man having a veto, or, indeed, on there being more than one potential party to the contract in the first place. But the original position is only one interpretation of the contract, and in any other interpretation in which the parties do have some knowledge with which to distinguish their situation or ambitions from those of others, the veto that the contract gives each party becomes crucial. The force of the veto each individual has depends, of course, upon his knowledge, that is to say, the particular interpretation of the contract we in the end choose. But the fact that individuals should have any veto at all is in itself remarkable.

It can have no place in a purely goal-based theory, for example. I do not mean that the parties to a social contract could not settle on a particular social goal and make that goal henceforth the test of the justice of political decisions. I mean that no goal-based theory could make a contract the proper device for deciding upon a principle of justice in the first place; that is, the deep theory we are trying to find could not itself be goal-based. . . .

The contract does, however, make sense in a right-based deep theory. Indeed, it seems a natural development of such a theory. The basic idea of a right-based theory is that distinct individuals have interests that they are entitled to protect if they so wish. It seems natural, in developing such a theory, to try to identify the institutions an individual would veto in the exercise of whatever rights are taken as fundamental. The contract is an excellent device for this purpose, for at least two reasons. First, it allows us to distinguish between a veto in the exercise of these rights and a veto for the sake of some interest that is not so protected, a distinction we can make by adopting an interpretation of the contract that reflects our sense of what these rights are. Second, it enforces the requirements of the constructive model of argument. The parties to the contract face a practical problem; they must devise a constitution from the options available to them, rather than postponing their decision to a day of later moral insight, and they must devise a program that is both practical and public in the sense I have described.

It seems fair to assume, then, that the deep theory behind the original position must be a right-based theory of some sort. . . .

I said that the use of a social contract, in the way that Rawls uses it, presupposes a deep theory that assumes natural rights. I want now to describe, in somewhat more detail, how the device of a contract applies that assumption. It capitalizes on the idea, mentioned earlier, that some political arrangements might be said to be in the antecedent interest of every individual even though they are not, in the event, in his actual interest.

Everyone whose consent is necessary to a contract has a veto over the terms of that contract, but the worth of that veto, to him, is limited by the fact that his judgment must be one of antecedent rather than actual self-interest. He must commit himself, and so abandon his veto, at a time when his knowledge is sufficient only to allow him to estimate the best odds, not to be certain of his bet. So the contract situation is in one way structurally like the situation in which an individual with specific political rights confronts political decisions that may disadvantage him. He has a limited, political right to veto these, a veto limited by the scope of the rights he has. The contract can be used as a model for the political situation by shaping the degree or character of a party's ignorance in the contractual situation so that this ignorance has the same force on his decision as the limited nature of his rights would have in the political situation.

This shaping of ignorance to suit the limited character of political rights is most efficiently done simply by narrowing the individual goals that the parties to the contract know they wish to pursue. If we take Hobbes' deep theory, for example, to propose that men have a fundamental natural right to life, so that it is wrong to take their lives, even for social goals otherwise proper, we should expect a contract situation of the sort he describes. Hobbes' men and women, in Rawls' phrase, have lexically ordered security of life over all other individual goals; the same situation would result if they were simply ignorant of any other goals they might have and unable to speculate about the chances that they have any particular one or set of these.

The ignorance of the parties in the original position might thus be seen as a kind of limiting case of the ignorance that can be found, in the form of a distorted or eccentric ranking of interests, in classical contract theories and that is natural to the contract device. The original position is a limiting case because Rawls' men are not simply ignorant of interests beyond a chosen few; they are ignorant of all the interests they have. It would be wrong to suppose that this makes them incapable of any judgments of self-interest. But the judgments they make must nevertheless be very abstract; they must allow for any combination of interests, without the benefit of any supposition that some of these are more likely than others.

The basic right of Rawls' deep theory, therefore, cannot be a right to any particular individual goal, like a right to security of life, or a right to lead a life according to a particular conception of the good. Such rights to individual goals may be produced by the deep theory as rights that men in the original position would stipulate as being in their best interest. But the original position cannot itself be justified on the assumption of such a right, because the parties to the contract do not know that they have any such interest or rank it lexically ahead of others.

So the basic right of Rawls' deep theory must be an abstract right, that is, not a right to any particular individual goal. There are two candidates, within the familiar concepts of political theory, for this role. The first is the right to liberty, and it may strike many readers as both plausible and comforting to assume that Rawls' entire structure is based on the assumption of a fundamental natural right to liberty—plausible because the two principles that compose his theory of justice gave liberty an important and dominant place, and comforting because the argument attempting to justify that place seems uncharacteristically incomplete.

Nevertheless, the right to liberty cannot be taken as the fundamental right in Rawls' deep theory. Suppose we define general liberty as the overall minimum possible constraints, imposed by government or by other men, on what a man might want to do. We must then distinguish this general liberty from particular liberties, that is, freedom from such constraints on particular acts thought specially important, like participation in politics. The parties to the original position certainly have, and know that they have, an interest in general liberty, because general liberty will, *pro tanto*, improve their power to achieve any particular goals they later discover themselves to have. But the qualification is important because they have no way of knowing that general liberty will in fact improve this power overall, and every reason to suspect that it will not. They know that they might have other interests, beyond general liberty, that can be protected only by political constraints on acts of others.

So if Rawlsian men must be supposed to have a right to liberty of some sort, which the contract situation is shaped to embody, it must be a right to particular liberties. Rawls does name a list of basic liberties, and it is these that his men do choose to protect through their lexically ordered first principle of justice. But Rawls plainly casts this principle as the product of the contract rather than as a condition of it. He argues that the parties to the original position would select these basic liberties to protect the basic goods they decide to value, like self-respect, rather than taking these liberties as goals in themselves. Of course they might, in fact, value the activities protected as basic liberties for their own sake, rather than as a means to some other goal or interest. But they certainly do not know that they do.

The second familiar concept of political theory is even more abstract than liberty. This is equality, and in one way Rawlsian men and women cannot choose other than to protect it. The state of ignorance in the original position is so shaped that the antecedent interest of everyone must lie, as I said, in the same solution. The right of each man to be treated equally without regard to his person or character or tastes is enforced by the fact that no one else can secure a better position by virtue of being different in any such respect. In other contract situations, when ignorance is less complete, individuals who share the same goal may nevertheless have different antecedent interests. Even if two men value life above everything else, for example, the antecedent interest of the weaker might call for a state monopoly of force rather than some provision for private vengeance, but the antecedent interest of the stronger might not. Even if two men value political participation above all else, the knowledge that one's views are likely to be more unorthodox or unpopular than those of the other will suggest that his antecedent interests calls for different arrangements. In the original position no such discrimination of antecedent interests can be made.

It is true that, in two respects, the principles of justice that Rawls thinks men and women would choose in the original position may be said to fall short of an egalitarian ideal. First, they subordinate equality in material resources, when this is necessary, to liberty of political activity, by making demands of the first principle prior to those of the second. Second, they do not take account of relative deprivation, because they justify any inequality when those worse off are better off than they would be, in absolute terms, without that inequality.

Rawls makes plain that these inequalities are required, not by some competing notion of liberty or some overriding goal, but by a more basic sense of equality itself. He accepts a distinction between what he calls two conceptions of equality:

> Some writers have distinguished between equality as it is invoked in connection with the distribution of certain goods, some of which will almost certainly give higher status or prestige to those who are more favored, and equality as it applies to the respect which is owed to persons irrespective of their social position. Equality of the first kind is defined by the second principle of justice. . . . But equality of the second kind is fundamental.

We may describe a right to equality of the second kind, which Rawls says is fundamental, in this way. We might say that individuals have a right to equal concern and respect in the design and administration of the political institutions that govern them. This is a highly abstract right. Someone might argue, for example, that it is satisfied by political arrangements that provide equal opportunity, for office and position on the basis of merit. Someone else might argue, to the contrary, that it is satisfied only by a system that guarantees absolute equality of income and status, without regard to merit. A third man might argue that equal concern and respect is provided by that system, whatever it is, that improves the average welfare of all citizens counting the welfare of each on the same scale. A fourth might argue, in the name of this fundamental equality, for the priority of liberty, and for the other apparent inequalities of Rawls' two principles.

The right to equal concern and respect, then, is more abstract than the standard conceptions of equality that distinguish different political theories. It permits arguments that this more basic right requires one or another of these conceptions as a derivative right or goal.

The original position may now be seen as a device for testing these competing arguments. It supposes, reasonably, that political arrangements that do not display equal concern and respect are those that are established and administered by powerful men and women who, whether they recognize it or not, have more concern and respect for members of a particular class, or people with particular talents or ideals, than they have for others. It relies on this supposition in shaping the ignorance of the parties to the contract. Men who do not know to which class they belong cannot design institutions, consciously or unconsciously, to favor their own class. Men who have no idea of their own conception of the good cannot act to favor those who hold one ideal over those who hold another. The original position is well designed to enforce the abstract right to equal concern and respect, which must be understood to be the fundamental concept of Rawls' deep theory.

If this is right, then Rawls must not use the original position to argue for this right in the same way that he uses it, for example, to argue for the rights to basic liberties embodied in the first principle. The text confirms that he does not. It is true that he once says that equality of respect is "defined" by the first principle of justice. But he does not mean, and in any case he does not argue, that the parties choose to be respected equally in order to advance some more basic right or goal. On the contrary, the right to equal respect is not, on his account, a product of the contract, but a condition of admission to the original position. This right, he says, is "owed to human beings as moral persons," and follows from the moral personality that distinguishes humans from animals. It is possessed by all men who can give justice, and only such men can contract. This is one right, therefore, that does not emerge from the contract, but is assumed, as the fundamental right must be, in its design.

Thomas Nagel, "Internal Difficulties with Justice as Fairness," from "Rawls on Justice" (1973)

Thomas Nagel (1937–) was one of the first and one of the most thoughtful enthusiastic reviewers of *A Theory of Justice*. He had serious reservations about the book, nevertheless, anticipating much subsequent controversy. Rawls attempts to justify the constraints placed on the original position as being weak and uncontroversial; in tandem, though, they constrain the decision in such a way that the two principles of justice emerge. Nagel's criticism, however, is that the constraints are not so weak after all: ruling out knowledge of one's conception of the good, in particular, generates a bias in favor of those persons whose conception of the good is of a highly individualistic sort. Further, Nagel calls into question Rawls's strong egalitarianism, which endorses inequalities only if they are to the benefit of all. As Nagel argues, the points that Rawls makes in favor of using maximin reasoning in the original position seem to give the parties in the original position reason only to create a kind of "safety net" rather than to go for more full-blooded Rawlsian equality.

A Theory of Justice is a rich, complicated, and fundamental work. It offers an elaborate set of arguments and provides many issues for discussion. This review will focus on its contribution to the more abstract portions of ethical theory.

From *Philosophical Review* 82 (1973). Copyright © 1973 Cornell University. Reprinted by permission of the publisher.

The book contains three elements. One is a vision of men and society as they should be. Another is a conception of moral theory. The third is a construction that attempts to derive principles expressive of the vision, in accordance with methods that reflect the conception of moral theory. In that construction Rawls has pursued the contractarian tradition in moral and political philosophy. His version of the social contract, a hypothetical choice situation called the original position, was first presented in 1958 and is here developed in great and explicit detail. The aim is to provide a way of treating the basic problems of social choice, for which no generally recognized methods of precise solution exist, through the proxy of a specially constructed parallel problem of individual choice, which can be solved by the more reliable intuitions and decision procedures of rational prudence. . . .

Rawls's substantive doctrine is a rather pure form of egalitarian liberalism, whose controversial elements are its egalitarianism, its anti-perfectionism and anti-meritocracy, the primacy it gives to liberty, and the fact that it is more egalitarian about liberty than about other goods. The justice of social institutions is measured not by their tendency to maximize the sum or average of certain advantages, but by their tendency to counteract the natural inequalities deriving from birth, talent, and circumstance, pooling those resources in the service of the common good. The common good is measured in terms of a very restricted, basic set of benefits to individuals: personal and political liberty, economic and social advantages, and self-respect.

The justice of institutions depends on their conformity to two principles. The first requires the greatest equal liberty compatible with a like liberty for all. The second (the difference principle) permits only those inequalities in the distribution of primary economic and social advantages that benefit everyone, in particular the worst off. Liberty is prior in the sense that it cannot be sacrificed for economic and social advantages, unless they are so scarce or unequal as to prevent the meaningful exercise of equal liberty until material conditions have improved.

The view is firmly opposed to mere equality of opportunity, which allows too much influence to the morally irrelevant contingencies of birth and talent; it is also opposed to counting a society's advanced cultural or intellectual achievements among the gains which can make sacrifice of the more primary goods just. What matters is that everyone be provided with the basic conditions for the realization of his own aims, regardless of the absolute level of achievement that may represent.

When the social and political implications of this view are worked out in detail . . . , it is extremely appealing, but far from self-evident. In considering its theoretical basis, one should therefore ask whether the contractarian approach, realized in terms of the original position, depends on assumptions any less controversial than the substantive conclusions it is adduced to support.

The notion that a contract is the appropriate model for a theory of social justice depends on the view that it is fair to require people to submit to procedures and institutions only if, given the opportunity, they could in some sense have agreed in advance on the principles to which they must submit. That is why Rawls calls the theory "justice as fairness." (Indeed, he believes that a similar contractual basis can be found for the principles of individual morality, yielding a theory of rightness as fairness.) The fundamental attitude toward persons on which justice as fairness depends is a respect for their autonomy or freedom. Since social institutions are simply there and people are born into them, submission cannot be literally voluntary, but "A society satisfying the principles of justice as fairness comes as close as a society can to being a voluntary scheme, for it meets the principles which free and equal persons would assent to under circumstances that are fair."

Before considering whether the original position embodies these conditions, we must ask why respect for the freedom of others, and the desire to make society as near to voluntary as possible, should be taken as the mainspring of the sense of justice. That gives liberty a position of great importance from the very beginning, an importance that it retains in the resulting substantive theory. But we must ask how the respect for autonomy by itself can be expected to yield further results as well.

When one justifies a policy on the ground that the affected parties would have (or even have) agreed to it, much depends on the reasons for their agreement. If it is motivated by ignorance or fear or helplessness or a defective sense of what is reasonable, then actual or possible prior agreement does not sanction anything. In other cases, prior agreement for the right reasons can be obtained or presumed, but it is not the agreement that justifies what has been agreed to, but rather whatever justifies the agreement itself. If, for example, certain principles would be agreed to because they are just, that cannot be what makes them just. In many cases the appeal to hypothetical prior agreement is actually of this character. It is not a final justification, not a mark of respect for autonomy, but merely a way of recalling someone to the kind of *moral* judgment he would make in the absence of distorting influences derived from his special situation.

Actual or presumable consent can be the *source* of a justification only if it is already accepted that the affected parties are to be treated as certain reasons would incline each of them to want to be treated. The circumstances of consent are designed to bring those reasons into operation, suppressing irrelevant considerations, and the fact that the choice would have been made becomes a further reason for adhering to the result.

When the interests of the parties do not naturally coincide, a version of consent may still be preserved if they are able to agree in advance on a procedure for settling conflicts. They may agree unanimously that the procedure treats them equally in relevant respects, though they would not be able to agree in advance to any of the particular distributions of advantages that it might yield. (An example would be a lottery to determine the recipient of some indivisible benefit.)

For the result of such a choice to be morally acceptable, two things must be true: (*a*) the choice must be unanimous; (*b*) the circumstances that make unanimity possible must not undermine the equality of the parties in other respects. Presumably they must be deprived of some knowledge (for example, of who will win the lottery) in order to reach agreement, but it is essential that they not be unequally deprived (as would be the case, for example, if they agreed to submit a dispute to an arbitrator who, unknown to any of them, was extremely biased).

The more disparate the conflicting interests to be balanced, however, the more information the parties must be deprived of to insure unanimity, and doubts begin to arise whether any procedure can be relied on to treat everyone equally in respect of the relevant interests. There is then a real question whether hypothetical choice under conditions of ignorance, as a representation of consent, can by itself provide a moral justification for outcomes that could not be unanimously agreed to if they were known in advance. . . .

I do not believe that the assumptions of the original position are either weak or innocuous or uncontroversial. In fact, the situation thus constructed may not be fair. Rawls says that the aim of the veil of ignorance is "to rule out those principles that it would be rational to propose for acceptance, however little the chance of success, only if one knew certain things that are irrelevant from the standpoint of justice." Let us grant that the parties should be equal and should not be in possession of information which would lead them to seek advantages on morally irrelevant grounds like race, sex, parentage, or natural endowments.

But they are deprived also of knowledge of their particular conception of the good. It seems odd to regard that as morally irrelevant from the standpoint of justice. If someone favors certain principles because of his conception of the good, he will not be seeking special advantages for himself so long as he does not know who in the society he is. Rather he will be opting for principles that advance the good for everyone, as defined by that conception. (I assume a conception of the good is just that, and not simply a system of tastes or preferences.) Yet Rawls appears to believe that it would be as unfair to permit people to press for the realization of their conception of the good as to permit them to press for the advantage of their social class.

It is true that men's different conceptions of the good divide them and produce conflict, so allowing this knowledge to the parties in the original position would prevent unanimity. Rawls concludes that the information must be suppressed and a common idea substituted which will permit agreement without selecting any particular conception of the good. This is achieved by means of the class of primary goods that it is supposedly rational to want whatever else one wants. Another possible conclusion, however, is that the model of the original position will not work because in order to secure spontaneous unanimity and avoid the necessity of bargaining one must suppress information that is morally relevant, and moreover suppress it in a way that does not treat the parties equally.

What Rawls wishes to do, by using the notion of primary goods, is to provide an Archimedean point, as he calls it, from which choice is possible without unfairness to any of the fuller conceptions of the good that lead people to differ. A *theory* of the good is presupposed, but it is ostensibly neutral between divergent particular conceptions, and supplies a least common denominator on which a choice in the original position can be based without unfairness to any of the parties. Only later, when the principles of justice have been reached on this basis, will it be possible to rule out certain particular interests or aims as illegitimate because they are unjust. It is a fundamental feature of Rawls's conception of the fairness of the original position that it should not permit the choice of principles of justice to depend on a particular conception of the good over which the parties may differ.

The construction does not, I think, accomplish this, and there are reasons to believe that it cannot be successfully carried out. Any hypothetical choice situation which requires agreement among the parties will have to impose strong restrictions on the grounds of choice, and these restrictions can be justified only in terms of a conception of the good. It is one of those cases in which there is no neutrality to be had, because neutrality needs as much justification as any other position.

Rawls's minimal conception of the good does not amount to a weak assumption: it depends on a strong assumption of the sufficiency of that reduced conception for the purposes of justice. The refusal to rank particular conceptions of the good implies a very marked tolerance for individual inclinations. Rawls is opposed not only to teleological conceptions according to which justice requires adherence to the principles that will maximize the good. He is also opposed to the natural position that even in a nonteleological theory what is just must depend on what is good, at least to the extent that a correct conception of the good must be used in determining what counts as an advantage and what as a disadvantage, and how much, for purposes of distribution and compensation. I interpret him as saying that the principles of justice are objective and interpersonally recognizable in a way that conceptions of the good are not. The refusal to rank individual conceptions and the reliance on primary goods are intended to insure this objectivity.

Objectivity may not be so easily achieved. The suppression of knowledge required to achieve unanimity is not equally fair to all the parties, because the primary goods are not equally valuable in pursuit of all conceptions of the good. They will serve to advance many different individual life plans (some more efficiently than others), but they are less useful in implementing views that hold a good life to be readily achievable only in certain well-defined types of social structure, or only in a society that works concertedly for the realization of certain higher human capacities and the suppression of baser ones, or only given certain types of economic relations among men. The model contains a strong individualistic bias, which is further strengthened by the motivational assumptions of mutual disinterest and absence of envy. These assumptions have the effect of discounting the claims of conceptions of the good that depend heavily on the relation between one's own position and that of others (though Rawls is prepared to allow such considerations to enter in so far as they affect self-esteem). The original position seems to presuppose not just a neutral theory of the good, but a liberal, individualistic conception according to which the best that can be wished for someone is the unimpeded pursuit of his own path, provided it does not interfere with the rights of others. The view is persuasively developed in the later portions of the book, but without a sense of its controversial character.

Among different life plans of this general type the construction is neutral. But given that many conceptions of the good do not fit into the individualistic pattern, how can this be described as a fair choice situation for principles of justice? Why should parties in the original position be prepared to commit themselves to principles that may frustrate or contravene their deepest convictions, just because they are deprived of the knowledge of those convictions?

There does not seem to be any way of redesigning the original position to do away with a restrictive assumption of this kind. One might think it would be an improvement to allow the parties full information about everyone's preferences and conception of the good, merely depriving them of the knowledge of who they were. But this, as Rawls points out, would yield no result at all. For either the parties would retain their conceptions of the good and, choosing from different points of view, would not reach unanimity, or else they would possess no aims of their own and would be asked to choose in terms of the aims of all the people they might be—an unintelligible request which provides no basis for a unified choice, in the absence of a dominant conception. The reduction to a common ground of choice is therefore essential for the model to operate at all, and the selection of that ground inevitably represents a strong assumption.

Let us now turn to the argument leading to the choice of the two principles in the original position as constructed. The core of this argument appears intertwined with an argument against the choice of the principle of average utility. Rawls has gone to some lengths to defend his controversial claim that in the original position it is rational to adopt the maximin rule which leads one to choose principles that favor the bottom of the social hierarchy, instead of accepting a greater risk at the bottom in return for the possibility of greater benefits at the top (as might be prudentially rational if one had an equal chance of being anyone in the society).

Rawls states that three conditions which make maximin plausible hold in the original position to a high degree. (1) "There must be some reason for sharply discounting estimates of . . . probabilities." (2) "The person choosing has a conception of the good such that he cares very little, if anything, for what he might gain above the minimum stipend that he can, in fact, be sure of by following the maximin rule." (3) "The rejected alternatives have outcomes that one can hardly accept." Let us consider these in turn.

The first condition is very important, and the claim that it holds in the original position is not based simply on a general rejection of the principle of insufficient reason (that is, the principle that where probabilities are unknown they should be regarded as equal). For one could characterize the original position in such a way that the parties would be prudentially rational to choose as if they had an equal chance of being anyone in the society, and the problem is to see why this would be an inappropriate representation of the grounds for a choice of principles.

One factor mentioned by Rawls is that the subject matter of the choice is extremely serious, since it involves institutions that will determine the total life prospects for the parties and those close to them. It is not just a choice of alternatives for a single occasion. Now this would be a reason for a conservative choice even if one knew the relative probabilities of different outcomes. It would be irresponsible to accept even a small risk of dreadful life prospects for oneself and one's descendants in exchange for a good chance of wealth or power. But what is needed is an account of why probabilities should be totally discounted, and not just with regard to the most unacceptable outcomes. The difference principle, for example, is supposed to apply at all levels of social development, so it is not justified merely by the desire to avoid grave risks. The fact that total life prospects are involved does not seem an adequate explanation. There must be some reason against allowing probabilities (proportional, for instance, to the number of persons in each social position) to enter into the choice of distributions above an acceptable minimum. Let me stress that I am posing a question not about decision theory but about the design of the original position and the comprehensiveness of the veil of ignorance. Why should it be thought that a just solution will be reached only if these considerations are suppressed?

Their suppression is justified, I think, only on the assumption that the proportions of people in various social positions are regarded as morally irrelevant, and this must be because it is not thought acceptable to sum advantages and disadvantages over persons, so that a loss for some is compensated by a gain for others. This aspect of the design of the original position appears, therefore, to be motivated by the wish to avoid extending to society as a whole the principle of rational choice for one man. Now this is supposed to be one of the *conclusions* of the contract approach, not one of its presuppositions. Yet the constraints on choice in Rawls's version of the original position are designed to rule out the possibility of such an extension, by requiring that probabilities be discounted. I can see no way to avoid presupposing some definite view on this matter in the design of a contract situation. If that is true, then a contract approach cannot give any particular view very much support.

Consider next the second condition. Keeping in mind that the parties in the original position do not know the stage of development of their society, and therefore do not know what minimum will be guaranteed by a maximin strategy, it is difficult to understand how an individual can know that he "cares very little, if anything, for what he might gain above the minimum." The explanation Rawls offers seems weak. Even if parties in the original position accept the priority of liberty, and even if the veil of ignorance leaves them with skeletal conception of the good, it seems impossible that they should care very little for increases in primary economic and social goods above what the difference principle guarantees at any given stage of social development.

Finally, the third condition, that one should rule out certain possibilities as unacceptable, is certainly a ground for requiring a social minimum and the priority of basic personal liberties, but it is not a ground for adopting the maximin rule in that general form needed to justify the choice of the difference principle. That must rely on stronger egalitarian premises.

Robert Nozick, "The Entitlement Theory," from *Anarchy, State, and Utopia* (1974)

Robert Nozick (1938–) published *Anarchy, State, and Utopia* three years after *A Theory of Justice*, in part to offer a worked-out alternative conception of distributive justice to rival that of his Harvard colleague Rawls. What Nozick draws our attention to is the emphasis in Rawls's theory on distributive outcomes, or "end-states." What makes a distribution just, on Rawls's view, is simply the pattern that it displays. If it accords equal liberty to all and makes the least well off better off than any alternative end-state would, then the distribution is just. But, Nozick argues, surely distributive justice is largely, even entirely, not a matter of what a distribution looks like at a given time, but how it came about. In order to work out such an intuition, Nozick develops an entitlement theory of justice, on which the justice of a distribution is determined by rules of just acquisition and transfer. The selection concludes with Nozick's more direct criticism of Rawls's views.

The minimal state is the most extensive state that can be justified. Any state more extensive violates people's rights. Yet many persons have put forth reasons purporting to justify a more extensive state. . . . In this chapter we consider the claim that a more extensive state is justified, because necessary (or the best instrument) to achieve distributive justice. . . .

The term "distributive justice" is not a neutral one. Hearing the term "distribution," most people presume that some thing or mechanism uses some principle or criterion to give out a supply of things. Into this process of distributing shares some error may have crept. So it is an open question, at least, whether *redistribution* should take place; whether we should do again what has already been done once, though poorly. However, we are not in the position of children who have been given portions of pie by someone who now makes last minute adjustments to rectify careless cutting. There is no *central* distribution, no person or group entitled to control all the resources, jointly deciding how they are to be doled out. What each person gets, he gets from others who give to him in exchange for something, or as a gift. In a free society, diverse persons control different resources, and new holdings arise out of the voluntary exchanges and actions of persons. There is no more a distributing or distribution of shares than there is a distributing of mates in a society in which persons choose whom they shall marry. The total result is the product of many individual decisions which the different individuals involved are entitled to make. Some uses of the term "dis-

tribution," it is true, do not imply a previous distributing appropriately judged by some criterion (for example, "probability distribution"); nevertheless, despite the title of this chapter, it would be best to use a terminology that clearly is neutral. We shall speak of people's
holdings; a principle of justice in holdings describes (part of) what justice tells us (requires)
about holdings. . . .

The Entitlement Theory

The subject of justice in holdings consists of three major topics. The first is the *original
acquisition of holdings,* the appropriation of unheld things. This includes the issues of how
unheld things may come to be held, the process, or processes, by which unheld things may
come to be held, the things that may come to be held by these processes, the extent of what
comes to be held by a particular process, and so on. We shall refer to the complicated truth
about this topic, which we shall not formulate here, as the principle of justice in acquisition. The second topic concerns the *transfer of holdings* from one person to another. By
what processes may a person transfer holdings to another? How may a person acquire a
holding from another who holds it? Under this topic come general descriptions of voluntary exchange, and gift and (on the other hand) fraud, as well as reference to particular conventional details fixed upon in a given society. The complicated truth about this subject
(with placeholders for conventional details) we shall call the principle of justice in transfer.
(And we shall suppose it also includes principles governing how a person may divest himself of a holding, passing it into an unheld state.)

If the world were wholly just, the following inductive definition would exhaustively
cover the subject of justice in holdings.

> 1. A person who acquires a holding in accordance with the principle of justice in
> acquisition is entitled to that holding.
> 2. A person who acquires a holding in accordance with the principle of justice in
> transfer, from someone else entitled to the holding, is entitled to the holding.
> 3. No one is entitled to a holding except by (repeated) applications of 1 and 2.

The complete principle of distributive justice would say simply that a distribution is just if
everyone is entitled to the holdings they possess under the distribution.

A distribution is just if it arises from another just distribution by legitimate means. The
legitimate means of moving from one distribution to another are specified by the principle
of justice in transfer. The legitimate first "moves" are specified by the principle of justice
in acquisition. Whatever arises from a just situation by just steps is itself just. The means
of change specified by the principle of justice in transfer preserve justice. As correct rules
of inference are truth-preserving, and any conclusion deduced via repeated application of
such rules from only true premises is itself true, so the means of transition from one situation to another specified by the principle of justice in transfer are justice-preserving, and
any situation actually arising from repeated transitions in accordance with the principle
from a just situation is itself just. The parallel between justice-preserving transformations
and truth-preserving transformations illuminates where it fails as well as where it holds.
That a conclusion could have been deduced by truth-preserving means from premises that
are true suffices to show its truth. That from a just situation a situation *could* have arisen via
justice-preserving means does *not* suffice to show its justice. The fact that a thief's victims
voluntarily *could* have presented him with gifts does not entitle the thief to his ill-gotten

gains. Justice in holdings is historical; it depends upon what actually has happened. We shall return to this point later.

Not all actual situations are generated in accordance with the two principles of justice in holdings: the principle of justice in acquisition and the principle of justice in transfer. Some people steal from others, or defraud them, or enslave them, seizing their product and preventing them from living as they choose, or forcibly exclude others from competing in exchanges. None of these are permissible modes of transition from one situation to another. And some persons acquire holdings by means not sanctioned by the principle of justice in acquisition. The existence of past injustice (previous violations of the first two principles of justice in holdings) raises the third major topic under justice in holdings: the rectification of injustice in holdings. If past injustice has shaped present holdings in various ways, some identifiable and some not, what now, if anything, ought to be done to rectify these injustices? What obligations do the performers of injustice have toward those whose position is worse than it would have been had the injustice not been done? Or, than it would have been had compensation been paid promptly? How, if at all, do things change if the beneficiaries and those made worse off are not the direct parties in the act of injustice, but, for example, their descendants? Is an injustice done to someone whose holding was itself based upon an unrectified injustice? How far back must one go in wiping clean the historical slate of injustices? What may victims of injustice permissibly do in order to rectify the injustices being done to them, including the many injustices done by persons acting through their government? I do not know of a thorough or theoretically sophisticated treatment of such issues. Idealizing greatly, let us suppose theoretical investigation will produce a principle of rectification. This principle uses historical information about previous situations and injustices done in them (as defined by the first two principles of justice and rights against interference), and information about the actual course of events that flowed from these injustices, until the present, and it yields a description (or descriptions) of holdings in the society. The principle of rectification presumably will make use of its best estimate of subjunctive information about what would have occurred (or a probability distribution over what might have occurred, using the expected value) if the injustice had not taken place. If the actual description of holdings turns out not to be one of the descriptions yielded by the principle, then one of the descriptions yielded must be realized.

The general outlines of the theory of justice in holdings are that the holdings of a person are just if he is entitled to them by the principles of justice in acquisition and transfer, or by the principle of rectification of injustice (as specified by the first two principles). If each person's holdings are just, then the total set (distribution) of holdings is just.

Historical Principles and End-Result Principles

The general outlines of the entitlement theory illuminate the nature and defects of other conceptions of distributive justice. The entitlement theory of justice in distribution is *historical;* whether a distribution is just depends upon how it came about. In contrast, *current time-slice principles* of justice hold that the justice of a distribution is determined by how things are distributed (who has what) as judged by some *structural* principle(s) of just distribution. A utilitarian who judges between any two distributions by seeing which has the greater sum of utility and, if the sums tie, applies some fixed equality criterion to choose the more equal distribution, would hold a current time-slice principle of justice. As would someone who had a fixed schedule of trade-offs between the sum of happiness and equality. According to a current time-slice principle, all that needs to be looked at, in judging the justice of a distribution, is who ends up with what; in comparing any two distributions one need look only at the matrix presenting the distributions. No further information need be fed into a principle of justice. It is a consequence of such principles of justice that any two structurally identical distributions are equally just. (Two distributions are structurally identical if they present the same profile, but perhaps have different persons occupying the particular slots. My having ten and your having five, and my having five and your having ten are structurally identical distributions.) Welfare economics is the theory of current time-slice principles of justice. The subject is conceived as operating on matrices representing only current information about distribution. This, as well as some of the usual conditions (for example, the choice of distribution is invariant under relabeling of columns), guarantees that welfare economics will be a current time-slice theory, with all of its inadequacies.

Most persons do not accept current time-slice principles as constituting the whole story about distributive shares. They think it relevant in assessing the justice of a situation to consider not only the distribution it embodies, but also how that distribution came about. If some persons are in prison for murder or war crimes, we do not say that to assess the justice of the distribution in the society we must look only at what this person has, and that person has, and that person has, . . . at the current time. We think it relevant to ask whether someone did something so that he *deserved* to be punished, deserved to have a lower share. Most will agree to the relevance of further information with regard to punishments and penalties. Consider also desired things. One traditional socialist view is that workers are entitled to the product and full fruits of their labor; they have earned it; a distribution is unjust if it does not give the workers what they are entitled to. Such entitlements are based upon some past history. No socialist holding this view would find it comforting to be told that because the actual distribution A happens to coincide structurally with the one he desires D, A therefore is no less just than D; it differs only in that the "parasitic" owners of capital receive under A what the workers are entitled to under D, and the workers receive under A what the owners are entitled to under D, namely very little. This socialist rightly, in my view, holds onto the notions of earning, producing, entitlement, desert, and so forth, and he rejects current time-slice principles that look only to the structure of the resulting set of holdings. (The set of holdings resulting from what? Isn't it implausible that how holdings are produced and come to exist has no effect at all on who should hold what?) His mistake lies in his view of what entitlements arise out of what sorts of productive processes.

We construe the position we discuss too narrowly by speaking of *current* time-slice principles. Nothing is changed if structural principles operate upon a time sequence of current time-slice profiles and, for example, give someone more now to counterbalance the less he has had earlier. A utilitarian or an egalitarian or any mixture of the two over time will inherit the difficulties of his more myopic comrades. He is not helped by the fact that *some* of the information others consider relevant in assessing a distribution is reflected, unrecoverable, in past matrices. Henceforth, we shall refer to such unhistorical principles of distributive justice, including the current time-slice principles, as *end-result principles* or *end-state principles*.

In contrast to end-result principles of justice, *historical principles* of justice hold that past circumstances or actions of people can create differential entitlements or differential deserts to things. An injustice can be worked by moving from one distribution to another structurally identical one, for the second, in profile the same, may violate people's entitlements or deserts; it may not fit the actual history.

Patterning

The entitlement principles of justice in holdings that we have sketched are historical principles of justice. To better understand their precise character, we shall distinguish them from another subclass of the historical principles. Consider, as an example, the principle of distribution according to moral merit. This principle requires that total distributive shares vary directly with moral merit; no person should have a greater share than anyone whose moral merit is greater. (If moral merit could be not merely ordered but measured on an interval or ratio scale, stronger principles could be formulated.) Or consider the principle that results by substituting "usefulness to society" for "moral merit" in the previous principle. Or instead of "distribute according to moral merit," or "distribute according to usefulness to society," we might consider "distribute according to the weighted sum of moral merit, usefulness to society, and need," with the weights of the different dimensions equal. Let us call a principle of distribution *patterned* if it specifies that a distribution is to vary along with some natural dimension, weighted sum of natural dimensions, or lexicographic ordering of natural dimensions. And let us say a distribution is patterned if it accords with some patterned principle.

Almost every suggested principle of distributive justice is patterned: to each according to his moral merit, or needs, or marginal product, or how hard he tries, or the weighted sum of the foregoing, and so on. The principle of entitlement we have sketched is *not* patterned. There is no one natural dimension or weighted sum or combination of a small number of natural dimensions that yields the distributions generated in accordance with the principle of entitlement. The set of holdings that results when some persons receive their marginal products, others win at gambling, others receive a share of their mate's income, others receive gifts from admirers, others receive returns on investment, others make for themselves much of what they have, others find things, and so on, will not be patterned. Heavy strands of patterns will run through it; significant portions of the variance in holdings will be accounted for by pattern-variables. If most people most of the time choose to transfer some of their entitlements to others only in exchange for something from them, then a large part of what many people hold will vary with what they held that others wanted. More details are provided by the theory of marginal productivity. But gifts to relatives, charitable donations, bequests to children, and the like, are not best conceived, in the first instance, in this manner. Ignoring the strands of pattern, let us suppose for the moment that a distribution actually arrived at by the operation of the principle of entitlement is random with respect to any pattern. Though the resulting set of holdings will be unpatterned, it will not be incomprehensible, for it can be seen as arising from the operation of a small number of principles. These principles specify how an initial distribution may arise (the principle of acquisition of holdings) and how distributions may be transformed into others (the principle of transfer of holdings). The process whereby the set of holdings is generated will be intelligible, though the set of holdings itself that results from this process will be unpatterned.

The writings of F. A. Hayek focus less than is usually done upon what patterning distributive justice requires. Hayek argues that we cannot know enough about each person's situation to distribute to each according to his moral merit (but would justice demand we do so if we did have this knowledge?); and he goes on to say, "our objection is against all attempts to impress upon society a deliberately chosen pattern of distribution, whether it be an order of equality or of inequality." However, Hayek concludes that in a free society there will be distribution in accordance with value rather than moral merit; that is, in accordance with the perceived value of a person's actions and services to others. Despite his rejection of a patterned conception of distributive justice, Hayek himself suggests a pattern he thinks justifiable: distribution in accordance with the perceived benefits given to others, leaving room for the complaint that a free society does not realize exactly this pattern. Stating this patterned strand of a free capitalist society more precisely, we get "To each according to how much he benefits others who have the resources for benefiting those who benefit them." This will seem arbitrary unless some acceptable initial set of holdings is specified, or unless it is held that the operation of the system over time washes out any significant effects from the initial set of holdings. As an example of the latter, if almost anyone would have bought a car from Henry Ford, the supposition that it was an arbitrary matter who held the money then (and so bought) would not place Henry Ford's earnings under a cloud. In any event, *his* coming to hold it is not arbitrary. Distribution according to benefits to others *is* a major patterned strand in a free capitalist society, as Hayek correctly points out, but it is only a strand and does not constitute the whole pattern of a system of entitlements (namely, inheritance, gifts for arbitrary reasons, charity, and so on) or a standard that one should insist a society fit. Will people tolerate for long a system yielding distributions that they believe are unpatterned? No doubt people will not long accept a distribution they believe is *unjust*. People want their society to be and to look just. But must the look of justice reside in a resulting pattern rather than in the underlying generating principles? We are in no position to conclude that the inhabitants of a society embodying an entitlement conception of justice in holdings will find it unacceptable. Still, it must be granted that were people's reasons for transferring some of their holdings to others always irrational or arbitrary, we would find this disturbing. (Suppose people always determined what holdings they would transfer, and to whom, by using a random device.) We feel more comfortable upholding the justice of an entitlement system if most of the transfers under it are done for reasons. This does not mean necessarily that all deserve what holdings they receive. It means only that there is a purpose or point to someone's transferring a holding to one person rather than to another; that usually we can see what the transferrer thinks he's gaining, what cause he thinks he's serving, what goals he thinks he's helping to achieve, and so forth. Since in a capitalist society people often transfer holdings to others in accordance with how much they perceive these others benefiting them, the fabric constituted by the individual transactions and transfers is largely reasonable and intelligible. (Gifts to loved ones, bequests to children, charity to the needy also are nonarbitrary components of the fabric.) In stressing the large strand of distribution in accordance with benefits to others, Hayek shows the point of many transfers, and so shows that the system of transfer of entitlement is not just spinning its gears aimlessly. The system of entitlements is defensible when constituted by the individual aims of individual transactions. No overarching aim is needed, no distributional pattern is required.

To think that the task of a theory of distributive justice is to fill in the blank in "to each according to his———" is to be predisposed to search for a pattern; and the separate treatment of "from each according to his———" treats production and distribution as two separate and independent issues. On an entitlement view these are *not* two separate questions. Whoever makes something, having bought or contracted for all other held resources used in the process (transferring some of his holdings for these cooperating factors), is entitled to it. The situation is *not* one of something's getting made, and there being an open question of who is to get it. Things come into the world already attached to people having entitlements over them. From the point of view of the historical entitlement conception of justice in holdings, those who start afresh to complete "to each according to his————" treat objects as if they appeared from nowhere, out of nothing. A complete theory of justice might cover this limit case as well; perhaps here is a use for the usual conceptions of distributive justice.

So entrenched are maxims of the usual form that perhaps we should present the entitlement conception as a competitor. Ignoring acquisition and rectification, we might say:

> From each according to what he chooses to do, to each according to what he makes for himself (perhaps with the contracted aid of others) and what others choose to do for him and choose to give him of what they've been given previously (under this maxim) and haven't yet expended or transferred.

This, the discerning reader will have noticed, has its defects as a slogan. So as a summary and great simplification (and not as a maxim with any independent meaning) we have:

> *From each as they choose, to each as they are chosen.*

Rawls' Theory

Rawls holds, as we have seen, that

> since everyone's well-being depends upon a scheme of cooperation without which no one could have a satisfactory life, the division of advantages should be such as to draw forth the willing cooperation of everyone taking part in it, including those less well situated. Yet this can be expected only if reasonable terms are proposed. The two principles mentioned seem to be a fair agreement on the basis of which those better endowed or more fortunate in their social position . . . could expect the willing cooperation of others when some workable scheme is a necessary condition of the welfare of all.

No doubt, the difference principle presents terms on the basis of which those less well endowed would be willing to cooperate. (What *better* terms could they propose for themselves?) But is this a fair agreement on the basis of which those *worse* endowed could expect the *willing* cooperation of others? . . .

Rawls would have us imagine the worse-endowed persons say something like the following: "Look, better endowed: you gain by cooperating with us. If you want our cooperation you'll have to accept reasonable terms. We suggest these terms: We'll cooperate with you only if we get *as much as possible.* That is, the terms of our cooperation should give us that maximal share such that, if it was tried to give us more, we'd end up with less." How generous these proposed terms are might be seen by imagining that the better endowed make the almost symmetrical opposite proposal: "Look, worse endowed: you gain by cooperating with *us.* If you want our cooperation you'll have to accept reasonable terms. We propose these terms: We'll cooperate with you so long as *we* get as much as possible. That is, the terms of our cooperation should give us the maximal share such that, if it was tried to give us more, we'd end up with less." If these terms seem outrageous, as they are, why don't the terms proposed by those worse endowed seem the same? Why shouldn't the better endowed treat this latter proposal as beneath consideration, supposing someone to have the nerve explicitly to state it? . . .

How can it have been supposed that these terms offered by the less well endowed are fair? Imagine a social pie somehow appearing so that *no one* has any claim at all on any portion of it, no one has any more of a claim than any other person; yet there must be unanimous agreement on how it is to be divided. Undoubtedly, apart from threats or holdouts in bargaining, an equal distribution would be suggested and found plausible as a solution. (It is, in Schelling's sense, a focal point solution.) If *somehow* the size of the pie wasn't fixed, and it was realized that pursuing an equal distribution somehow would lead to a smaller total pie than otherwise might occur, the people might well agree to an unequal distribution which raised the size of the least share. But in any actual situation, wouldn't this realization reveal something about differential claims on parts of the pie? Who is it that could make the pie larger, and would do it if given a larger share, but not if given an equal share under the scheme of equal distribution? To whom is an incentive to be provided to make this larger contribution? (There's no talk here of inextricably entangled joint product; it's known *to whom* incentives are to be offered, or at least to whom a bonus is to be paid after the fact.) Why doesn't this identifiable differential contribution lead to some differential entitlement?

If things fell from heaven like manna, and no one had any special entitlement to any portion of it, and no manna would fall unless all agreed to a particular distribution, and somehow the quantity varied depending on the distribution, then it is plausible to claim that persons placed so they couldn't make threats, or hold out for specially large shares, would agree to the difference principle rule of distribution. But is *this* the appropriate model for thinking about how the things people produce are to be distributed? Why think the same results should obtain for situations where there *are* differential entitlements as for situations where there are not?

A procedure that founds principles of distributive justice on what rational persons who know nothing about themselves or their histories would agree to *guarantees that end-state principles of justice will be taken as fundamental.* Perhaps some historical principles of justice are derivable from end-state principles, as the utilitarian tries to derive individual rights, prohibitions on punishing the innocent, and so forth, from *his* end-state principle; perhaps such arguments can be constructed even for the entitlement principle. But no historical principle, it seems, could be agreed to in the first instance by the participants in Rawls' original position. For people meeting together behind a veil of ignorance to decide who gets what, knowing nothing about any special entitlements people may have, will treat anything to be distributed as manna from heaven.

Alasdair MacIntyre, "Justice, Tradition, and Desert," from *After Virtue* (1981)

Rawls and Nozick seem to be deeply at odds in matters of distributive justice. But according to Alasdair MacIntyre (1929–), the disagreement between the two perhaps covers up what is a deeper and much more significant set of similarities between justice as fairness and the entitlement theory. We find, MacIntyre notes, the arguments offered by Rawls and Nozick on the lips of ordinary citizens in ordinary political debates, but with one important difference: ordinary citizens make appeal to the concept of "desert" in arguing for a particular view of what justice requires. But desert is of no interest in either Rawls's or Nozick's theories: both reject the notion that desert is central to matters of distributive justice. The concept of desert had its place, argues MacIntyre, within communities with a shared conception of the good by reference to which just claims could be assessed. In the absence of such agreement, the concept of desert loses application, and we are left with disputes like that between Rawls and Nozick that we have little hope of rationally resolving.

When Aristotle praised justice as the first virtue of political life, he did so in such a way as to suggest that a community which lacks practical agreement on a conception of justice must also lack the necessary basis for political community. But the lack of such a basis must therefore threaten our own society. For the outcome of that history . . . has not only been an inability to agree upon a catalogue of the virtues and an even more fundamental inability to agree upon the relative importance of the virtue concepts within a moral scheme in which notions of rights and of utility also have a key place. It has also been an inability to agree upon the content and character of particular virtues. For since a virtue is now generally understood as a disposition or sentiment which will produce in us obedience to certain rules, agreement on what the relevant rules are to be is always a prerequisite for agreement upon the nature and content of a particular virtue. But this prior agreement in rules is . . . something which our individualist culture is unable to secure. Nowhere is this more marked and nowhere are the consequences more threatening than in the case of justice. Everyday life is pervaded by them and basic controversies cannot therefore be rationally resolved. Consider one such controversy, endemic in the politics of the United States today—I present it in the form of a debate between two ideal-typical characters unimaginatively named "A" and "B."

A, who may own a store or be a police officer or a construction worker, has struggled

From *After Virtue: A Study in Moral Theory,* second edition by Alasdair MacIntyre. © 1984 by University of Notre Dame Press. Used by permission of the publisher.

to save enough from his earnings to buy a small house, to send his children to the local college, to pay for some special type of medical care for his parents. He now finds all of his projects threatened by rising taxes. He regards this threat to his projects as *unjust;* he claims to have a right to what he has earned and that nobody else has a right to take away what he acquired legitimately and to which he has a just title. He intends to vote for candidates for political office who will defend his property, his projects *and* his conception of justice.

B, who may be a member of one of the liberal professions, or a social worker, or someone with inherited wealth, is impressed with the arbitrariness of the inequalities in the distribution of wealth, income and opportunity. He is, if anything, even more impressed with the inability of the poor and the deprived to do very much about their own condition as a result of inequalities in the distribution of power. He regards both these types of inequality as *unjust* and as constantly engendering further injustice. He believes more generally that all inequality stands in need of justification and that the only possible justification for inequality is to improve the condition of the poor and the deprived—by, for example, fostering economic growth. He draws the conclusion that in present circumstances redistributive taxation which will finance welfare and the social services is what justice demands. He intends to vote for candidates for political office who will defend redistributive taxation *and* his conception of justice.

It is clear that in the actual circumstances of our social and political order A and B are going to disagree about politics and politicians. But *must* they so disagree? The answer seems to be that under certain types of economic condition their disagreement need not manifest itself at the level of political conflict. If A and B belong to a society where economic resources are such, or are at least believed to be such, that B's public redistributive projects can be carried through at least to a certain point without threatening A's private life-plan projects, A and B might for some time vote for the same politicians and policies. Indeed they might on occasion be one and the same person. But if it is, or comes to be, the case that economic circumstances are such that either A's projects must be sacrificed to B's or vice versa, it at once becomes clear that A and B have views of justice which are not only logically incompatible with each other but which invoke considerations which are incommensurable with those advanced by the adversary party.

The logical incompatibility is not difficult to identify. A holds that principles of just acquisition and entitlement set limits to redistributive possibilities. If the outcome of the application of the principles of just acquisition and entitlement is gross inequality, the toleration of such inequality is a price that has to be paid for justice. B holds that principles of just distribution set limits to legitimate acquisition and entitlement. If the outcome of the application of the principles of just distribution is interference—by means of taxation or such devices as eminent domain—with what has up till now been regarded in this social order as legitimate acquisition and entitlement, the toleration of such interference is a price that has to be paid for justice. We may note in passing—it will not be unimportant later—that in the case of both A's principle and B's principle the price for one person or group of persons receiving justice is always paid by someone else. Thus different identifiable social groups have an interest in the acceptance of one of the principles and the rejection of the other. Neither principle is socially or politically neutral.

Moreover it is not simply that A and B advance principles which produce incompatible practical conclusions. The type of concept in terms of which each frames his claim is so different from that of the other that the question of how and whether the dispute between them may be rationally settled begins to pose difficulties. For A aspires to ground the notion of justice in some account of what and how a given person is entitled to in virtue of what he has acquired and earned; B aspires to ground the notion of justice in some account of the equality of the claims of each person in respect of basic needs and of the means to meet such needs. Confronted by a given piece of property or resource, A will be apt to claim that it is justly his because he owns it—he acquired it legitimately, he earned it; B will be apt to claim that it justly ought to be someone else's, because they need it much more, and if they do not have it, their basic needs will not be met. But our pluralist culture possesses no method of weighing, no rational criterion for deciding between claims based on legitimate entitlement against claims based on need. Thus these two types of claim are indeed, as I suggested, incommensurable, and the metaphor of "weighing" moral claims is not just inappropriate but misleading.

It is at this point that recent analytical moral philosophy makes important claims. For it aspires to provide rational principles to which appeal may be made by contending parties with conflicting interests. And the two most distinguished recent attempts to carry through this project have a special relevance for the argument between A and B. For Robert Nozick's account of justice is at least to some large degree a rational articulation of key elements in A's position, while John Rawls's account is in the same way a rational articulation of key elements in B's position. Thus if the philosophical considerations which either Rawls or Nozick urge upon us turn out to be rationally compelling, the argument between A and B will have been rationally settled one way or another and my own characterization of the dispute will in consequence turn out to be quite false. . . .

Many critics of Rawls have focused their attention on the ways in which Rawls derives his principles of justice from his statement of the initial position of the rational agent "situated behind the veil of ignorance." Such critics have made a number of telling points, but I do not intend to dwell on them, if only because I take it not only that a rational agent in *some such* situation as that of the veil of ignorance would indeed choose *some such* principles of justice as Rawls claims, but also that it is *only* a rational agent in such a situation who would choose such principles. Later in my argument this point will become important. . . .

What I want to argue is threefold: first, that the incompatibility of Rawls's and Nozick's accounts does up to a point genuinely mirror the incompatibility of A's position with B's, and that to this extent at least Rawls and Nozick successfully articulate at the level of moral philosophy the disagreement between such ordinary non-philosophical citizens as A and B; but that Rawls and Nozick also reproduce the very same type of incompatibility and incommensurability at the level of philosophical argument that made A's and B's debate unsettlable at the level of social conflict; and secondly, that there is nonetheless an element in the position of both A and B which neither Rawls's account nor Nozick's captures, an element which survives from that older classical tradition in which the virtues were central. When we reflect on both these points, a third emerges: namely, that in their conjunction we have an important clue to the social presuppositions which Rawls and Nozick to some degree share.

Rawls makes primary what is in effect a principle of equality with respect to needs. His conception of "the worst off" sector of the community is a conception of those whose needs are gravest in respect of income, wealth and other goods. Nozick makes primary what is a principle of equality with respect to entitlement. For Rawls how those who are now in grave need come to be in grave need is irrelevant; justice is made into a matter of present patterns of distribution to which the past is irrelevant. For Nozick only evidence about what has been legitimately acquired in the past is relevant; present patterns of distribution in themselves must be irrelevant to *justice* (although not perhaps to kindness or generosity).

To say even this much makes it clear how close Rawls is to B and how close Nozick is to A. For A appealed against distributive canons to a justice of entitlement, and B appealed against canons of entitlement to a justice which regards needs. Yet it is also at once clear not only that Rawls's priorities are incompatible with Nozick's in a way parallel to that in which B's position is incompatible with A's, but also that Rawls's position is incommensurable with Nozick's in a way similarly parallel to that in which B's is incommensurable with A's. For how can a claim that gives priority to equality of needs be rationally weighed against one which gives priority to entitlements? If Rawls were to argue that anyone *behind the veil of ignorance,* who knew neither whether and how his needs would be met nor what his entitlements would be, ought rationally to prefer a principle which respects needs to one which respects entitlements, invoking perhaps principles of rational decision theory to do so, the immediate answer must be not only that *we* are *never* behind such a veil of ignorance, but also that this leaves unimpugned Nozick's premise about inalienable rights. And if Nozick were to argue that any distributive principle, if enforced, could violate a freedom to which everyone of us is entitled—as he does indeed argue—the immediate answer must be that in so interpreting the inviolability of basic rights he begs the question in favor of his own argument and leaves unimpugned Rawls's premises.

Nonetheless there is something important, if negative, which Rawls's account shares with Nozick's. Neither of them make any reference to *desert* in their account of justice, nor could they consistently do so. And yet both A and B did make such a reference—and it is imperative here to notice that "A" and "B" are not the names of mere arbitrary constructions of my own; their arguments faithfully reproduce, for example, a good deal of what was actually said in recent fiscal debates in California, New Jersey and elsewhere. What A complains of on his own behalf is not merely that he is entitled to what he has earned, but that he *deserves* it in virtue of his life of hard work; what B complains of on behalf of the poor and deprived is that their poverty and deprivation is *undeserved* and therefore unwarranted. And it seems clear that in the case of the real-life counterparts of A and B it is the reference to desert which makes them feel strongly that what they are complaining about is injustice, rather than some other kind of wrong or harm.

Neither Rawls's account nor Nozick's allows this central place, or indeed any kind of place, for desert in claims about justice and injustice. Rawls allows that common sense views of justice connect it with desert, but argues first that we do not know what anyone deserves until we have already formulated the rules of justice (and hence we cannot base our understanding of justice upon desert), and secondly that when we have formulated the rules of justice it turns out that it is not desert that is in question anyway, but only legitimate expectations. He also argues that to attempt to apply notions of desert would be impracticable—the ghost of Hume walks in his pages at this point.

Nozick is less explicit, but his scheme of justice being based exclusively on entitlements can allow no place for desert. He does at one point discuss the possibility of a principle for the rectification of injustice, but what he writes on that point is so tentative and cryptic that it affords no guidance for amending his general viewpoint. It is in any case clear that for both Nozick and Rawls a society is composed of individuals, each with his or her own interest, who then have to come together and formulate common rules of life. In Nozick's case there is the additional negative constraint of a set of basic rights. In Rawls's case the only constraints are those that a prudent rationality would impose. Individuals are thus in both accounts primary and society secondary, and the identification of individual interests is prior to, and independent of, the construction of any moral or social bonds between them. But we have already seen that the notion of desert is at home only in the context of a community whose primary bond is a shared understanding both of the good for man and of the good of that community and where individuals identify their primary interests with reference to those goods. Rawls explicitly makes it a presupposition of his view that we must expect to disagree with others about what the good life for man is and must therefore exclude any understanding of it that we may have from our formulation of the principles of justice. Only those goods in which everyone, whatever their view of the good life, takes an interest are to be admitted to consideration. In Nozick's argument too, the concept of community required for the notion of desert to have application is simply absent. To understand this is to clarify two further points.

The first concerns the shared social presuppositions of Rawls and Nozick. It is, from both standpoints, as though we had been shipwrecked on an uninhabited island with a group of other individuals, each of whom is a stranger to me and to all the others. What have to be worked out are rules which will safeguard each one of us maximally in such a situation. Nozick's premise concerning rights introduces a strong set of constraints; we do know that certain types of interference with each other are absolutely prohibited. But there is a limit to the bonds between us, a limit set by our private and competing interests. This individualistic view has of course, as I noticed earlier, a distinguished ancestry: Hobbes, Locke (whose views Nozick treats with great respect), Machiavelli and others. And it contains within itself a certain note of realism about modern society; modern society is indeed often, at least in surface appearance, nothing but a collection of strangers, each pursuing his or her own interests under minimal constraints. We still of course, even in modern society, find it difficult to think of families, colleges and other genuine communities in this way; but even our thinking about those is now invaded to an increasing degree by individualist conceptions, especially in the law courts. Thus Rawls and Nozick articulate with great power a shared view which envisages entry into social life as—at least ideally—the voluntary act of at least potentially rational individuals with prior interests who have to ask the question 'What kind of social contract with others is it reasonable for me to enter into?' Not surprisingly it is a consequence of this that their views exclude any account of human community in which the notion of desert in relation to contributions to the common tasks of that community in pursuing shared goods could provide the basis for judgments about virtue and injustice.

Desert is ruled out too in another way. I have remarked upon how Rawls's distributive principles exclude reference to the past and so to claims to desert based on past actions and sufferings. Nozick too excludes that of the past on which such claims might be based, by making a concern for the legitimacy of entitlements the sole ground for taking an interest in the past in connection with justice. What makes this important is that Nozick's account serves the interest of a particular mythology about the past precisely by what it excludes from view. For central to Nozick's account is the thesis that all legitimate entitlements can be traced to legitimate acts of original acquisition. But, if that is so, there are in fact very few, and in some large areas of the world *no*, legitimate entitlements. The property-owners of the modern world are not the legitimate heirs of the Lockean individuals who performed quasi-Lockean ("quasi" to allow for Nozick's emendations of Locke) acts of original acquisition; they are the inheritors of those who, for example, stole, and used violence to steal the common lands of England from the common people, vast tracts of North America from the American Indian, much of Ireland from the Irish, and Prussia from the original non-German Prussians. This is the historical reality ideologically concealed behind any Lockean thesis. The lack of any principle of rectification is thus not a small side issue for a thesis such as Nozick's; it tends to vitiate the theory as a whole—even if we were to suppress the overwhelming objections to any belief in inalienable human rights.

A and B differ from Rawls and Nozick at the price of inconsistency. Each of them in conjoining either Rawls's principles or Nozick's with an appeal to desert exhibits an adherence to an older, more traditional, more Aristotelian and Christian view of justice. This inconsistency is thus a tribute to the residual power and influence of the tradition, a power and influence with two distinct sources. In the conceptual *mélange* of moral thought and practice today fragments from the tradition—virtue concepts for the most part—are still found alongside characteristically modern and individualist concepts such as those of rights or utility. But the tradition also survives in a much less fragmented, much less distorted form in the lives of certain communities whose historical ties with their past remain strong. So the older moral tradition is discernible in the United States and elsewhere among, for example, some Catholic Irish, some Orthodox Greeks and some Jews of an Orthodox persuasion, all of them communities that inherit their moral tradition not only through their religion, but also from the structure of the peasant villages and households which their immediate ancestors inhabited on the margins of modern Europe. Moreover it would be wrong to conclude from the stress that I have laid on the medieval background that Protestantism did not in some areas become the bearer of this very same moral tradition; in Scotland, for example, Aristotle's *Nicomachean Ethics* and *Politics* were the secular moral texts in the universities, coexisting happily with a Calvinist theology which was often elsewhere hostile to them, until 1690 and after. And there are today both black and white Protestant communities in the United States, especially perhaps those in or from the South, who will recognize in the tradition of the virtues a key part of their own cultural inheritance.

Even however in such communities the need to enter into public debate enforces participation in the cultural *mélange* in the search for a common stock of concepts and norms which all may employ and to which all may appeal. Consequently the allegiance of such marginal communities to the tradition is constantly in danger of being eroded, and this in search of what, if my argument is correct, is a chimaera. For what analysis of A's and B's position reveals once again is that we have all too many disparate and rival moral concepts, in this case rival and disparate concepts of justice, and that the moral resources of the culture allow us no way of settling the issue between them rationally. Moral philosophy, as it is dominantly understood, reflects the debates and disagreements of the culture so faithfully that its controversies turn out to be unsettlable in just the way that the political and moral debates themselves are.

It follows that our society cannot hope to achieve moral consensus. . . .

. . . This does not mean that there are not many tasks only to be performed in and through government which still require performing: the rule of law, so far as it is possible in a modern state, has to be vindicated, injustice and unwarranted suffering have to be dealt with, generosity has to be exercised, and liberty has to be defended, in ways that are sometimes only possible through the use of governmental institutions. But each particular task, each particular responsibility has to be evaluated on its own merits. Modern systematic politics, whether liberal, conservative, radical or socialist, simply has to be rejected from a standpoint that owes genuine allegiance to the tradition of the virtues; for modern politics itself expresses in its institutional forms a systematic rejection of that tradition.

Michael Sandel, "Justice and Community," from *Liberalism and the Limits of Justice* (1982)

Michael Sandel (1953–) provides in *Liberalism and the Limits of Justice* a reconstruction of Rawls's argument and a diagnosis of its deepest problems. Sandel takes Rawls's account of the original position to be an account of human nature, of what is essential to human beings; and given the fact that we are denied knowledge of our conceptions of the good and of the particular attachments that we possess, it must be, Sandel thinks, that the Rawlsian project involves taking our views on the good and our attachments to others to be inessential to us. But, Sandel says (echoing Hegel in Part Two), this conception of ourselves is ultimately unintelligible; we are not, and cannot be, the people that justice as fairness presupposes us to be.

What Really Goes on Behind the Veil of Ignorance

What goes on in the original position is first of all a choice, or more precisely, a choosing together, an agreement among parties. What the parties agree to are the principles of justice. Unlike most actual contracts, which cannot justify, the hypothetical contract the parties agree to does justify; the principles they choose are just in virtue of their choosing them. As the voluntarist account of justification would suggest, the principles of justice are the products of choice. . . .

Justice as fairness differs from traditional contract theories in that "the relevant agreement is not to enter a given society or to adopt a given form of government, but to accept certain moral principles." The result of the agreement is not a set of obligations applying to individuals, at least not directly, but principles of justice applying to the basic structure of society. Still, the voluntarist aspect of justification corresponds in some sense to the notion of society as a voluntary agreement. Rawls writes that living in a society governed by principles of justice derived from a voluntary account of justification is, in effect, the next best thing to living in a society we have actually chosen.

> No society can, of course, be a scheme of co-operation which men enter voluntarily in a literal sense; each person finds himself placed at birth in some particular position in some particular society, and the nature of this position materially affects his life prospects. Yet a society satisfying the principles of justice as fairness comes as close as a society can to being a *voluntary scheme*, for it meets the principles which free and equal persons *would assent to* under circumstances which are fair. In this sense its

members are autonomous and the obligations they recognize *self-imposed* [emphasis added].

As our reconstruction suggests, the voluntarist nature of Rawls' contract view is bound up with the essential plurality of human subjects and the need to resolve conflicting claims. Without plurality, contracts, and for that matter principles of justice, would be neither possible nor necessary. "Principles of justice deal with conflicting claims upon the advantages won by social co-operation; they apply to the relations among several persons or groups. The word 'contract' suggests this plurality as well as the condition that the appropriate division of advantages must be in accordance with principles acceptable to all parties."

As previously seen, justice as fairness differs from utilitarianism in its emphasis on the plurality and distinctiveness of individuals, and this difference is embodied in the role contract plays in justification.

> Whereas the utilitarian extends to society the principles of choice for one man, justice as fairness, *being a contract view,* assumes that the principles of social choice, and so the principles of justice, are themselves the object of an original *agreement* [emphasis added].

> From the standpoint of *contract theory* one cannot arrive at a principle of social choice merely by extending the principle of rational prudence to the system of desires constructed by the impartial spectator. To do this is not to take seriously the *plurality and distinctness of individuals,* nor to recognize as the basis of justice that to which men would *consent* [emphasis added].

In basing the principles of justice on an agreement among parties, Rawls emphasizes two characteristics that the hypothetical contract shares with actual ones, namely choice and plurality. But we have already seen that the ingredients of choice and plurality are not sufficient to make justice; actual contracts, which include both, cannot justify. This is due to the problems we have described as contingency and conventionalism. Actual agreements often turn out unfairly because of the various (coercive and non-coercive) contingencies associated with the inevitable differences of power and knowledge among persons differently situated. But in the original position, such contingencies are cured. Due to the veil of ignorance and other conditions of equality, all are similarly situated, and so none can take advantage, even inadvertently, of a more favorable bargaining position.

The original position is designed to overcome the problem of conventionalism as well. Where actual contracts are inescapably embedded in the practices and conventions of some particular society, the agreement in the original position is not implicated in the same way. It is not an actual contract, only a hypothetical one. Since it is imagined to occur before the principles of justice arrive on the scene, it may be thought of as "pre-situated" in the relevant sense, a status quo antecedent to the arrival of justice such that no prior moral principles are available by which its results might be impugned. In this way it is able to realize the ideal of pure procedural justice. (Ironically, where the hypothetical nature of the original agreement at first appeared to weaken its justificatory force, it now appears as a positive, perhaps indispensable, advantage. Where Rawls emphasizes that "nothing resembling [the original agreement] need ever have taken place," it might be the case that no such agreement ever *could* take place and still overcome the problem of conventionalism.)

> Since *all are similarly situated* and no one is able to design principles to favor his particular condition, the principles of justice are the result of a *fair* agreement or bargain [emphasis added].

> The original position is, one might say, the *appropriate initial status quo,* and thus the fundamental agreements reached in it are *fair.* This explains the propriety of the name "justice as fairness": it conveys the idea that the principles of justice are agreed to in *an initial situation that is fair* [emphasis added].

> It is a state of affairs in which the parties are equally represented as moral persons and *the outcome is not conditioned by arbitrary contingencies* or the relative balance of social forces. Thus justice as fairness is able to use the idea of pure procedural justice from the beginning [emphasis added].

By imposing the veil of ignorance it is possible to "nullify the effects of specific contingencies which put men at odds and tempt them to exploit social and natural circumstances to their own advantage."

> If a knowledge of particulars is allowed, then the outcome is biased by *arbitrary contingencies.* As already observed, to each according to his threat advantage is not a principle of justice. If the original position is to yield agreements that are just, the parties must be *fairly situated* and treated equally as moral persons. The arbitrariness of the world must be corrected for by adjusting the circumstances of the initial contractual situation [emphasis added].

Once the parties to an agreement are assumed to be similarly situated in all relevant respects, differences of power and knowledge disappear, and the possible sources of unfairness are thus eradicated. Since no one is able to choose on the basis of contingently-given attributes, the ideal of autonomy, implicit but imperfect in actual contracts, is fulfilled, the ideal of reciprocity is realized as a matter of course, and the vulnerability of contract to the "further question" ("But is it fair?") is eliminated. "The veil of ignorance deprives the persons in the original position of the knowledge that would enable them to choose heteronomous principles. The parties arrive at their choice together as free and equal rational persons knowing only that those circumstances obtain which give rise to the need for principles of justice."

Once the "further question" of fairness loses its independent moral force, owing to the fact that the parties are situated in such a way that no unfairness conceivably could result, any agreement reached becomes a case of pure procedural justice; its outcome is fair, "whatever it is," in virtue of its agreement alone. Under such conditions, a contract ceases to be a constitutive convention and becomes instead an instrument of justification.

> The aim is to characterize this situation so that the principles that would be chosen, *whatever they turn out to be,* are acceptable from a moral point of view. The original position is defined in such a way that it is a status quo in which *any agreements reached are fair* [emphasis added].

> The idea of the original position is to set up a fair procedure so that *any principles agreed to will be just.* The aim is to use the notion of pure procedural justice as a basis of theory [emphasis added].

But at this point a crucial ambiguity arises, for it is not clear what exactly it means "to use the notion of pure procedural justice as a basis of theory." Rawls claims that *once* the situation is appropriately characterized, *then* the principles chosen, *whatever they turn out to be,* are acceptable from a moral point of view; *once* the original position is properly defined, *then any agreements reached* in it are fair; *once* a fair procedure is established, *then any principles agreed to* will be just.

What is unclear is how generous these provisions are to the choosers. On one reading, the terms seem generous indeed, the very embodiment of the voluntarist provisions suggested above. Once the parties find themselves in a fair situation, anything goes; the scope for their choice is unlimited. The results of their deliberations will be morally acceptable "whatever they turn out to be." No matter what principles they choose, those principles will count as just.

But there is another, less expansive reading of their situation, which gives considerably less scope to their enterprise. On this interpretation, what it means to say that the principles chosen will be just "whatever they turn out to be" is simply that, given their situation, the parties are guaranteed to choose the *right* principles. While it may be true that, strictly speaking, they can choose any principles they wish, their situation is designed in such a way that they are guaranteed to "wish" to choose only certain principles. On this view, "any agreements reached" in the original position are fair, not because the procedure sanctifies just any outcome. But if the principles agreed to are just because only (the) just principles can be agreed to, the voluntarist aspect of the enterprise is not as spacious as would first appear. The distinction between pure and perfect procedural justice fades, and it becomes unclear whether the procedure "translates its fairness to the outcome," or whether the fairness of the procedure is given by the fact that it necessarily leads to the right result.

Rawls confirms the less voluntarist reading when he writes, "The acceptance of these principles is not conjectured as a psychological law or probability. Ideally anyway, I should like to show that their acknowledgement is the only choice [sic] consistent with the full description of the original position. The argument aims eventually to be strictly deductive." The notion that the full description of the original position determines a single "choice" which the parties cannot but acknowledge seems to introduce a cognitive element to justification after all and to call into question the priority of procedure over principle which the contract view—and the deontological project generally—seemed to require. But a more immediate consequence of this reading is that it complicates our account of what goes on in the original position. . . .

For Rawls, the consequences of taking seriously the distinction between persons are not directly moral but more decisively epistemological. What the bounds between persons confine is less the reach of our sentiments—this they do not prejudge—than the reach of our understanding, of our cognitive access to others. And it is this *epistemic* deficit (which derives from the nature of the subject) more than any shortage of benevolence (which is in any case variable and contingent) that requires justice for its remedy and so accounts for its pre-eminence. Where for Hume, we need justice because we do not *love* each other well enough, for Rawls we need justice because we cannot *know* each other well enough for even love to serve alone.

But as our discussion of agency and reflection suggests, we are neither as transparent to ourselves nor as opaque to others as Rawls' moral epistemology requires. If our agency is to consist in something more than the exercise in "efficient administration" which Rawls' account implies, we must be capable of deeper introspection than a "direct self-knowledge" of our immediate wants and desires allows. But to be capable of a more thoroughgoing reflection, we cannot be wholly unencumbered subjects of possession, individuated in advance and given prior to our ends, but must be subjects constituted in part by our central aspirations and attachments, always open, indeed vulnerable, to growth and transformation in the light of revised self-understandings. And in so far as our constitutive self-understandings comprehend a wider subject than the individual alone, whether a family or tribe or city or class or nation or people, to this extent they define a community in the constitutive sense. And what marks such a community is not merely a spirit of benevolence, or the prevalence of communitarian vocabulary of discourse and a background of implicit practices and understandings within which the opacity of the participants is reduced if never finally dissolved. In so far as justice depends for its pre-eminence on the separateness or boundedness of persons in the cognitive sense, its priority would diminish as that opacity faded and this community deepened.

Justice and Community

Of any society it can always be asked to what extent it is just, or "well-ordered" in Rawls' sense, and to what extent it is a community, and the answer can in neither case fully be given by reference to the sentiments and desires of the participants alone. As Rawls observes, to ask whether a particular society is just is not simply to ask whether a large number of its members happen to have among their various desires the desire to act justly—although this may be one feature of a just society—but whether the society is itself a society of a certain kind, ordered in a certain way, such that justice describes its "basic structure" and not merely the dispositions of persons within the structure. Thus Rawls writes that although we call the attitudes and dispositions of persons just and unjust, for justice as fairness the "primary subject of justice is the basic structure of society." For a society to be just in this strong sense, justice must be constitutive of its framework and not simply an attribute of certain of the participants' plans of life.

Similarly, to ask whether a particular society is a community is not simply to ask whether a large number of its members happen to have among their various desires the desire to associate with others or to promote communitarian aims—although this may be one feature of a community—but whether the society is itself a society of a certain kind, ordered in a certain way, such that community describes its basic structure and not merely the dispositions of persons within the structure. For a society to be a community in this strong sense, community must be constitutive of the shared self-understandings of the participants and embodied in their institutional arrangements, not simply an attribute of certain of the participants' plans of life.

Rawls might object that a constitutive conception of community such as this should be rejected "for reasons of clarity among others," or on the grounds that it supposes society to be "an organic whole with a life of its own distinct from and superior to that of all its members in their relations with one another." But a constitutive conception of community is no more metaphysically problematic than a constitutive conception of justice such as Rawls defends. For if this notion of community describes a framework of self-understandings that is distinguishable from and in some sense prior to the sentiments and dispositions of individuals within the framework, it is only in the same sense that justice as fairness describes a "basic structure" or framework that is likewise distinguishable from and prior to the sentiments and dispositions of individuals within it.

If utilitarianism fails to take seriously our distinctness, justice as fairness fails to take seriously our commonality. In regarding the bounds of the self as prior, fixed once and for all, it relegates our commonality to an aspect of the good, and relegates the good to a mere contingency, a product of indiscriminate wants and desires "not relevant from a moral standpoint." Given a conception of the good that is diminished in this way, the priority of right would seem an unexceptionable claim indeed. But utilitarianism gave the good a bad name, and in adopting it uncritically, justice as fairness wins for deontology a false victory.

Liberalism and the Limits of Justice

For justice to be the first virtue, certain things must be true of us. We must be creatures of a certain kind, related to human circumstance in a certain way. We must stand at a certain distance from our circumstance . . . as essentially unencumbered subject of possession. . . . Either way, we must regard ourselves as independent: independent from the interests and attachments we may have at any moment, never identified by our aims but always capable of standing back to survey and assess and possibly to revise them.

Deontology's Liberating Project

Bound up with the notion of an independent self is a vision of the moral universe this self must inhabit. Unlike classical Greek and medieval Christian conceptions, the universe of the deontological ethic is a place devoid of inherent meaning, a world "disenchanted" in Max Weber's phrase, a world without an objective moral order. Only in a universe empty of *telos,* such as seventeenth-century science and philosophy affirmed, is it possible to conceive a subject apart from and prior to its purposes and ends. Only a world ungoverned by a purposive order leaves principles of justice open to human construction and conceptions of the good to individual choice. In this the depth of opposition between deontological liberalism and teleological world views most fully appears. . . .

It is important to recall that, on the deontological view, the notion of a self barren of essential aims and attachments does not imply that we are beings wholly without purpose or incapable of moral ties, but rather that the values and relations we have are the products of choice, the possessions of a self given prior to its ends. It is similar with deontology's universe. Though it rejects the possibility of an objective moral order, this liberalism does not hold that just anything goes. It affirms justice, not nihilism. The notion of a universe empty of intrinsic meaning does not, on the deontological view, imply a world wholly ungoverned by regulative principles, but rather a moral universe inhabited by subjects capable of constituting meaning on their own—as agents of *construction* in case of the right, as agents of *choice* in the case of the good. *Qua* noumenal selves, or parties to the original position, we arrive at principles of justice; *qua* actual, individual selves, we arrive at conceptions of the good. And the principles we construct as noumenal selves constrain (but do not determine) the purposes we choose as individual selves. This reflects the priority of the right over the good.

The deontological universe and the independent self that moves within it, taken together, hold out a liberating vision. Freed from the dictates of nature and the sanction of social roles, the deontological subject is installed as sovereign, cast as the author of the only moral meanings there are. As inhabitants of a world without *telos,* we are free to construct principles of justice unconstrained by an order of value antecedently given. Although the principles of justice are not strictly speaking a matter of choice, the society they define "comes as close as a society can to being a voluntary scheme," for they arise from a pure will or act of construction not answerable to a prior moral order. And as independent selves, we are free to choose our purposes and ends unconstrained by such an order, or by custom or traditional or inherited status. So long as they are not unjust, our conceptions of the good carry weight, whatever they are, simply in virtue of our having chosen them. We are "self-originating sources of valid claims."

Now justice is the virtue that embodies deontology's liberating vision and allows it to unfold. It embodies this vision by describing those principles the sovereign subject is said to construct while situated prior to the constitution of all value. It allows the vision to unfold in that, equipped with these principles, the just society regulates each person's choice of ends in a way compatible with a similar liberty for all. Citizens governed by justice are thus enabled to realize deontology's liberating project—to exercise their capacity as "self-originating sources of valid claims"—as fully as circumstances permit. So the primacy of justice at once expresses and advances the liberating aspirations of the deontological world view and conception of the self.

But the deontological vision is flawed, both within its own terms and more generally as an account of our moral experience. Within its own terms, the deontological self, stripped of all possible constitutive attachments, is less liberated than disempowered. As we have seen, neither the right nor the good admits of the voluntarist derivation deontology requires. As agents of construction we do not really construct, and as agents of choice we do not really choose. What goes on behind the veil of ignorance is not a contract or an agreement but if anything a kind of discovery; and what goes on in "purely preferential choice" is less a choosing of ends than a matching of pre-existing desires, undifferentiated as to worth, with the best available means of satisfying them. For the parties to the original position, as for the parties to ordinary deliberative rationality, the liberating moment fades before it arrives; the sovereign subject is left at sea in the circumstances it was thought to command.

The moral frailty of the deontological self also appears at the level of first-order principles. Here we found that the independent self, being essentially dispossessed, was too thin to be capable of desert in the ordinary sense. For claims of desert presuppose thickly-constituted selves, beings capable of possession in the constitutive sense, but the deontological self is wholly without possessions of this kind. Acknowledging this lack, Rawls would found entitlements on legitimate expectations instead. If we are incapable of desert, at least we are entitled that institutions honor the expectations to which they give rise.

But the difference principle requires more. It begins with the thought, congenial to the deontological view, that the assets I have are only accidentally mine. But it ends by assuming that these assets are therefore common assets and that society has a prior claim on the fruits of their exercise. This either disempowers the deontological self or denies its independence. Either my prospects are left at the mercy of institutions established for "prior and independent social ends," ends which may or may not coincide with my own, or I must count myself a member of a community defined in part by those ends, in which case I cease to be unencumbered by constitutive attachments. Either way, the difference principle contradicts the liberating aspiration of the deontological project. We cannot be persons for whom justice is primary and also be persons for whom the difference principle is a principle of justice.

Character, Self-Knowledge, and Friendship

If the deontological ethic fails to redeem its own liberating promise, it also fails plausibly to account for certain indispensable aspects of our moral experience. For deontology insists that we view ourselves as independent selves, independent in the sense that our identity is never tied to our aims and attachments. Given our "moral power to form, to revise, and rationally to pursue a conception of the good," the continuity of our identity is unproblematically assured. No transformation of my aims and attachments could call into question the person I am, for no such allegiances, however deeply held, could possibly engage my identity to begin with.

But we cannot regard ourselves as independent in this way without great cost to those loyalties and convictions whose moral force consists partly in the fact that living by them is inseparable from understanding ourselves as the particular persons we are—as members of this family or community or nation or people, as bearers of this history, as sons and daughters of that revolution, as citizens of this republic. Allegiances such as these are more than values I happen to have or aims I "espouse at any given time." They go beyond the obligations I voluntarily incur and the "natural duties" I owe to human beings as such. They allow that to some I owe more than justice requires or even permits, not by reason of agreements I have made but instead in virtue of those more or less enduring attachments and commitments which taken together partly define the person I am.

To imagine a person incapable of constitutive attachments such as these is not to conceive an ideally free and rational agent, but to imagine a person wholly without character, without moral depth. For to have character is to know that I move in a history I neither summon nor command, which carries consequences none the less for my choices and conduct. It draws me closer to some and more distant from others; it makes some aims more appropriate, others less so. As a self-interpreting being, I am able to reflect on my history and in this sense to distance myself from it, but the distance is always precarious and provisional, the point of reflection never finally secured outside the history itself. A person with character thus knows that he is complicated in various ways even as he reflects, and feels the moral weight of what he knows.

This makes a difference for agency and self-knowledge. For, as we have seen, the deontological self, being wholly without character, is incapable of self-knowledge in any morally serious sense. Where the self is unencumbered and essentially dispossessed, no person is left for *self*-reflection to reflect upon. This is why, on the deontological view, deliberation about ends can only be an exercise in arbitrariness. In the absence of constitutive attachments, deliberation issues in "purely preferential choice," which means the ends we seek, being mired in contingency, "are not relevant from a moral standpoint."

When I act out of more or less enduring qualities of character, by contrast, my choice of ends is not arbitrary in the same way. In consulting my preferences, I have not only to weigh their intensity but also to assess their suitability to the person I (already) am. I ask, as I deliberate, not only what I really want but who I really am, and this last question takes me beyond an attention to my desires alone to reflect on my identity itself. While the contours of my identity will in some ways be open and subject to revision, they are not wholly without shape. And the fact that they are not enables me to discriminate among my more immediate wants and desires; some now appear essential, others merely incidental to my defining projects and commitments. Although there may be a certain ultimate contingency in my having wound up the person I am—only theology can say for sure—it makes a moral difference none the less that, being the person I am, I affirm these ends rather than those, turn this way rather than that. While the notion of constitutive attachments may at first seem an obstacle to agency—the self, now encumbered, is no longer strictly prior—some relative fixity of character appears essential to prevent the lapse into arbitrariness which the deontological self is unable to avoid.

The possibility of character in the constitutive sense is also indispensable to a certain kind of friendship, a friendship marked by mutual insight as well as sentiment. By any account, friendship is bound up with certain feelings. We like our friends; we have affection for them, and wish them well. We hope that their desires find satisfaction, that their plans meet with success, and we commit ourselves in various ways to advancing their ends.

But for persons presumed incapable of constitutive attachments, acts of friendship such as these face a powerful constraint. However much I might hope for the good of a friend and stand ready to advance it, only the friend himself can know what that good is. This restricted access to the good of others follows from the limited scope for self-reflection, which betrays in turn the thinness of the deontological self to begin with. Where deliberating about my good means no more than attending to wants and desires given directly to my awareness, I must do it on my own; it neither requires nor admits the participation of others. Every act of friendship thus becomes parasitic on a good identifiable in advance. "Benevolence and love are second-order notions: they seek to further the good of beloved individuals that is already given." Even the friendliest sentiments must await a moment of introspection itself inaccessible to friendship. To expect more of any friend, or to offer more, can only be a presumption against the ultimate privacy of self-knowledge.

For persons encumbered in part by a history they share with others, by contrast, knowing oneself is a more complicated thing. It is also a less strictly private thing. Where seeking my good is bound up with exploring my identity and interpreting my life history, the knowledge I seek is less transparent to me and less opaque to others. Friendship becomes a way of knowing as well as liking. Uncertain which path to take, I consult a friend who knows me well, and together we deliberate, offering and assessing by turns competing descriptions of the person I am, and of the alternatives I face as they bear on my identity. To take seriously such deliberation is to allow that my friend may grasp something I have missed, may offer a more adequate account of the way my identity is engaged in the alternatives before me. To adopt this new description is to see myself in a new way; my old self-image now seems partial or occluded, and I may say in retrospect that my friend knew me better than I knew myself. To deliberate with friends is to admit this possibility, which presupposes in turn a more richly-constituted self than deontology allows. While there will of course remain times when friendship requires deference to the self-image of a friend, however flawed, this too requires insight; here the need to defer implies the ability to know.

So to see ourselves as deontology would see us is to deprive us of those qualities of character, reflectiveness, and friendship that depend on the possibility of constitutive projects and attachments. And to see ourselves as given to commitments such as these is to admit a deeper commonality than benevolence describes, a commonality of shared self-understanding as well as "enlarged affections." As the independent self finds its limits in those aims and attachments from which it cannot stand apart, so justice finds its limits in those forms of community that engage the identity as well as the interests of the participants.

To all of this, deontology might finally reply with a concession and a distinction: it is one thing to allow that "citizens in their personal affairs . . . have attachments and loves that they believe they would not, or could not, stand apart from," that they "regard it as unthinkable . . . to view themselves without certain religious and philosophical convictions and commitment." But with public life it is different. There, no loyalty or allegiance could be similarly essential to our sense of who we are. Unlike our ties to family and friends, no devotion to city or nation, to party or cause, could possibly run deep enough to be defining. By contrast with our private identity, our "public identity" as moral persons "is not affected by changes over time" in our conceptions of the good. While we may be thickly-constituted selves in private, we must be wholly unencumbered selves in public, and it is there that the primacy of justice prevails.

But once we recall the special status of the deontological claim, it is unclear what the grounds for this distinction could be. It might seem at first glance a psychological distinction; detachment comes more easily in public life, where the ties we have are typically less compelling; I can more easily step back from, say, my partisan allegiances than certain personal loyalties and affections. But as we have seen from the start, deontology's claim for the independence of the self must be more than a claim of psychology or sociology. Otherwise, the primacy of justice would hang on the degree of benevolence and fellow-feeling any particular society managed to inspire. The independence of the self does not mean that I can, as a psychological matter, summon in this or that circumstance the detachment required to stand outside my values and ends, rather that I must regard myself as the bearer of a self distinct from my values and ends, whatever they may be. It is above all an epistemological claim, and has little to do with the relative intensity of feeling associated with public or private relations.

Understood as an epistemological claim, however, the deontological conception of the self cannot admit the distinction required. Allowing constitutive possibilities where "private" ends are at stake would seem unavoidably to allow at least the possibility that "public" ends could be constitutive as well. Once the bounds of the self are no longer fixed, individuated in advance and given prior to experience, there is no saying in principle what sorts of experiences could shape or reshape them, no guarantee that only "private" and never "public" events could conceivably be decisive.

Not egoists but strangers, sometimes benevolent, make for citizens of the deontological republic; justice finds its occasion because we cannot know each other, or our ends, well enough to govern by the common good alone. This condition is not likely to fade altogether, and so long as it does not, justice will be necessary. But neither is it guaranteed always to predominate, and in so far as it does not, community will be possible, and an unsettling presence for justice.

Liberalism teaches respect for the distance of self and ends, and when this distance is lost, we are submerged in a circumstance that ceases to be ours. But by seeking to secure this distance too completely, liberalism undermines its own insight. By putting the self beyond the reach of politics, it makes human agency an article of faith rather than an object of continuing attention and concern, a premise of politics rather than its precarious achievement. This misses the pathos of politics and also its most inspiring possibilities. It overlooks the danger that when politics goes badly, not only disappointments but also dislocations are likely to result. And it forgets the possibility that when politics goes well, we can know a good in common that we cannot know alone.

Michael Walzer, "Complex Equality," from *Spheres of Justice* (1983)

What is offered in Rawls's theory of justice—and, indeed, in Nozick's rival conception—is an all-embracing theory of justice, one that applies to all goods to be distributed within a society. Michael Walzer has us focus on the various considerations
that have been put forward as the decisive basis for distribution, and to note that
while as supreme principles of distribution they seem to be little more than self-serv-
ing ideologies, they often seem to be correct within a certain sphere of social life.
There are various spheres of life in which different criteria of justice are relevant;
tyranny, and inequality, are the result of one sphere's criteria coopting those of
another sphere.

Distribution is what social conflict is all about. Marx's heavy emphasis on productive
processes should not conceal from us the simple truth that the struggle for control of the
means of production is a distributive struggle. Land and capital are at stake, and these are
goods that can be shared, divided, exchanged, and endlessly converted. But land and capital are not the only dominant goods; it is possible (it has historically been possible) to come
to them by way of other goods—military or political power, religious office and charisma,
and so on. History reveals no single dominant good and no naturally dominant good, but
only different kinds of magic and competing bands of magicians.

The claim to monopolize a dominant good—when worked up for public purposes—
constitutes an ideology. Its standard form is to connect legitimate possession with some set
of personal qualities through the medium of a philosophical principle. So aristocracy, or the
rule of the best, is the principle of those who lay claim to breeding and intelligence: they
are commonly the monopolists of landed wealth and familial reputation. Divine supremacy
is the principle of those who claim to know the word of God: they are the monopolists of
grace and office. Meritocracy, or the career open to talents, is the principle of those who
claim to be talented: they are most often the monopolists of education. Free exchange is the
principle of those who are ready, or who tell us they are ready, to put their money at risk:
they are the monopolists of movable wealth. These groups—and others, too, similarly
marked off by their principles and possessions—compete with one another, struggling for
supremacy. One group wins, and then a different one; or coalitions are worked out, and
supremacy is uneasily shared. There is no final victory, nor should there be. But that is not
to say that the claims of the different groups are necessarily wrong, or that the principles
they invoke are of no value as distributive criteria; the principles are often exactly right

within the limits of a particular sphere. Ideologies are readily corrupted, but their corruption is not the most interesting thing about them.

It is in the study of these struggles that I have sought the guiding thread of my own argument. The struggles have, I think, a paradigmatic form. Some group of men and women—class, caste, strata, estate, alliance, or social formation—comes to enjoy a monopoly or a near monopoly of some dominant good; or, a coalition of groups comes to enjoy, and so on. This dominant good is more or less systematically converted into all sorts of other things—opportunities, powers, and reputations. So wealth is seized by the strong, honor by the wellborn, office by the well educated. Perhaps the ideology that justifies the seizure is widely believed to be true. But resentment and resistance are (almost) as pervasive as belief. There are always some people, and after a time there are a great many, who think the seizure is not justice but usurpation. The ruling group does not possess, or does not uniquely possess, the qualities it claims; the conversion process violates the common understanding of the goods at stake. Social conflict is intermittent, or it is endemic; at some point, counterclaims are put forward. Though these are of many different sorts, three general sorts are especially important:

> 1. The claim that the dominant good, whatever it is, should be redistributed so that it can be equally or at least more widely shared: this amounts to saying that monopoly is unjust.
> 2. The claim that the way should be opened for the autonomous distribution of all social goods: this amounts to saying that dominance is unjust.
> 3. The claim that some new good, monopolized by some new group, should replace the currently dominant good: this amounts to saying that the existing pattern of dominance and monopoly is unjust.

The third claim is, in Marx's view, the model of every revolutionary ideology—except, perhaps, the proletarian or last ideology. Thus, the French Revolution in Marxist theory: the dominance of noble birth and blood and of feudal landholding is ended, and bourgeois wealth is established in its stead. The original situation is reproduced with different subjects and objects (this is never unimportant), and then the class war is immediately renewed. It is not my purpose here to endorse or to criticize Marx's view. I suspect, in fact, that there is something of all three claims in every revolutionary ideology, but that, too, is not a position that I shall try to defend here. Whatever its sociological significance, the third claim is not philosophically interesting—unless one believes that there is a naturally dominant good, such that its possessors could legitimately claim to rule the rest of us. In a sense, Marx believed exactly that. The means of production is the dominant good throughout history, and Marxism is a historicist doctrine insofar as it suggests that whoever controls the prevailing means legitimately rules. After the communist revolution, we shall all control the means of production: at that point, the third claim collapses into the first. Meanwhile, Marx's model is a program for ongoing distributive struggle. It will matter, of course, who wins at this or that moment, but we won't know why or how it matters if we attend only to the successive assertions of dominance and monopoly.

Simple Equality

It is with the first two claims that I shall be concerned, and ultimately with the second alone, for that one seems to me to capture best the plurality of social meanings and the real complexity of distributive systems. But the first is the more common among philosophers; it matches their own search for unity and singularity; and I shall need to explain its difficulties at some length.

Men and women who make the first claim challenge the monopoly but not the dominance of a particular social good. This is also a challenge to monopoly in general; for if wealth, for example, is dominant and widely shared, no other good can possibly be monopolized. Imagine a society in which everything is up for sale and every citizen has as much money as every other. I shall call this the "regime of simple equality." Equality is multiplied through the conversion process, until it extends across the full range of social goods. The regime of simple equality won't last for long, because the further progress of conversion, free exchange in the market, is certain to bring inequalities in its train. If one wanted to sustain simple equality over time, one would require a "monetary law" like the agrarian laws of ancient times or the Hebrew sabbatical, providing for a periodic return to the original condition. Only a centralized and activist state would be strong enough to force such a return; and it isn't clear that state officials would actually be able or willing to do that, if money were the dominant good. In any case, the original condition is unstable in another way. It's not only that monopoly will reappear, but also that dominance will disappear.

In practice, breaking the monopoly of money neutralizes its dominance. Other goods come into play, and inequality takes on new forms. Consider again the regime of simple equality. Everything is up for sale, and everyone has the same amount of money. So everyone has, say, an equal ability to buy an education for his children. Some do that, and others don't. It turns out to be a good investment: other social goods are, increasingly, offered for sale only to people with educational certificates. Soon everyone invests in education; or, more likely, the purchase is universalized through the tax system. But then the school is turned into a competitive world within which money is no longer dominant. Natural talent or family upbringing or skill in writing examinations is dominant instead, and educational success and certification are monopolized by some new group. Let's call them (what they call themselves) the "group of the talented." Eventually the members of this group claim that the good they control should be dominant outside the school: offices, titles, prerogatives, wealth too, should all be possessed by themselves. This is the career open to talents, equal opportunity, and so on. This is what fairness requires; talent will out; and in any case, talented men and women will enlarge the resources available to everyone else. So Michael Young's meritocracy is born, with all its attendant inequalities.

What should we do now? It is possible to set limits to the new conversion patterns, to recognize but constrain the monopoly power of the talented. I take this to be the purpose of John Rawls's difference principle, according to which inequalities are justified only if they are designed to bring, and actually do bring, the greatest possible benefit to the least advantaged social class. More specifically, the difference principle is a constraint imposed on talented men and women, once the monopoly of wealth has been broken. It works in this way: Imagine a surgeon who claims more than his equal share of wealth on the basis of the skills he has learned and the certificates he has won in the harsh competitive struggles of college and medical school. We will grant the claim if, and only if, granting it is beneficial in the stipulated ways. At the same time, we will act to limit and regulate the sale of surgery—that is, the direct conversion of surgical skill into wealth.

This regulation will necessarily be the work of the state, just as monetary laws and agrarian laws are the work of the state. Simple equality would require continual state intervention to break up or constrain incipient monopolies and to repress new forms of dominance. But then state power itself will become the central object of competitive struggles.

Groups of men and women will seek to monopolize and then to use the state in order to consolidate their control of other social goods. Or, the state will be monopolized by its own agents in accordance with the iron law of oligarchy. Politics is always the most direct path to dominance, and political power (rather than the means of production) is probably the most important, and certainly the most dangerous, good in human history. Hence the need to constrain the agents of constraint, to establish constitutional checks and balances. These are limits imposed on political monopoly, and they are all the more important once the various social and economic monopolies have been broken.

One way of limiting political power is to distribute it widely. This may not work, given the well-canvassed dangers of majority tyranny; but these dangers are probably less acute than they are often made out to be. The greater danger of democratic government is that it will be weak to cope with re-emerging monopolies in society at large, with the social strength of plutocrats, bureaucrats, technocrats, meritocrats, and so on. In theory, political power is the dominant good in a democracy, and it is convertible in any way the citizens choose. But in practice, again, breaking the monopoly of power neutralizes its dominance. Political power cannot be widely shared without being subjected to the pull of all the other goods that the citizens already have or hope to have. Hence democracy is, as Marx recognized, essentially a reflective system, mirroring the prevailing and emerging distribution of social goods. Democratic decision making will be shaped by the cultural conceptions that determine or underwrite the new monopolies. To prevail against these monopolies, power will have to be centralized, perhaps itself monopolized. Once again, the state must be very powerful if it is to fulfill the purposes assigned to it by the difference principle or by any similarly interventionist rule.

Still, the regime of simple equality might work. One can imagine a more or less stable tension between emerging monopolies and political constraints, between the claim to privilege put forward by the talented, say, and the enforcement of the difference principle, and then between the agents of enforcement and the democratic constitution. But I suspect that difficulties will recur, and that at many points in time the only remedy for private privilege will be statism, and the only escape from statism will be private privilege. We will mobilize power to check monopoly, then look for some way of checking the power we have mobilized. But there is no way that doesn't open opportunities for strategically placed men and women to seize and exploit important social goods.

These problems derive from treating monopoly, and not dominance, as the central issue in distributive justice. It is not difficult, of course, to understand why philosophers (and political activists, too) have focused on monopoly. The distributive struggles of the modern age begin with a war against the aristocracy's singular hold on land, office, and honor. This seems an especially pernicious monopoly because it rests upon birth and blood, with which the individual has nothing to do, rather than upon wealth, or power, or education, all of which—at least in principle—can be earned. And when every man and woman becomes, as it were, a smallholder in the sphere of birth and blood, an important victory is indeed won. Birthright ceases to be a dominant good; henceforth, it purchases very little; wealth, power, and education come to the fore. With regard to these latter goods, however, simple equality cannot be sustained at all, or it can only be sustained subject to the vicissitudes I have just described. Within their own spheres, as they are currently understood, these three tend to generate natural monopolies that can be repressed only if state power is itself dominant and if it is monopolized by officials committed to the repression. But there is, I think, another path to another kind of equality.

Tyranny and Complex Equality

I want to argue that we should focus on the reduction of dominance—not, or not primarily, on the break-up or the constraint of monopoly. We should consider what it might mean to narrow the range within which particular goods are convertible and to vindicate the autonomy of distributive spheres. But this line of argument, though it is not uncommon historically, has never fully emerged in philosophical writing. Philosophers have tended to criticize (or to justify) existing or emerging monopolies of wealth, power, and education. Or, they have criticized (or justified) particular conversions—of wealth into education or of office into wealth. And all this, most often, in the name of some radically simplified distributive system. The critique of dominance will suggest instead a way of reshaping and then living with the actual complexity of distributions.

Imagine now a society in which different social goods are monopolistically held—as they are in fact and always will be, barring continual state intervention—but in which no particular good is generally convertible. As I go along, I shall try to define the precise limits on convertibility, but for now the general description will suffice. This is a complex egalitarian society. Though there will be many small inequalities, inequality will not be multiplied through the conversion process. Nor will it be summed across different goods, because the autonomy of distributions will tend to produce a variety of local monopolies, held by different groups of men and women. I don't want to claim that complex equality would necessarily be more stable than simple equality, but I am inclined to think that it would open the way for more diffused and particularized forms of social conflict. And the resistance to convertibility would be maintained, in large degree, by ordinary men and women within their own spheres of competence and control, without large-scale state action.

This is, I think, an attractive picture, but I have not yet explained just why it is attractive. The argument for complex equality begins from our understanding—I mean, our actual, concrete, positive, and particular understanding—of the various social goods. And then it moves on to an account of the way we relate to one another through those goods. Simple equality is a simple distributive condition, so that if I have fourteen hats and you have fourteen hats, we are equal. And it is all to the good if hats are dominant, for then our equality is extended through all the spheres of social life. On the view that I shall take here, however, we simply have the same number of hats, and it is unlikely that hats will be dominant for long. Equality is a complex relation of persons, mediated by the goods we make, share, and divide among ourselves; it is not an identity of possessions. It requires then, a diversity of distributive criteria that mirrors the diversity of social goods.

The argument of complex equality has been beautifully put by Pascal in one of his *Pensées*.

> The nature of tyranny is to desire power over the whole world and outside its own sphere.
>
> There are different companies—the strong, the handsome, the intelligent, the devout—and each man reigns in his own, not elsewhere. But sometimes they meet, and the strong and the handsome fight for mastery—foolishly, for their mastery is of different kinds. They misunderstand one another, and make the mistake of each aiming at universal dominion. Nothing can win this, not even strength, for it is powerless in the kingdom of the wise. . . .
>
> *Tyranny.* The following statements, therefore, are false and tyrannical: "Because I

am handsome, so I should command respect." "I am strong, therefore men should love me. . . ." "I am . . . et cetera."

Tyranny is the wish to obtain by one means what can only be had by another. We owe different duties to different qualities: love is the proper response to charm, fear to strength, and belief to learning.

Marx made a similar argument in his early manuscripts; perhaps he had this *pensée* in mind:

Let us assume man to be man, and his relation to the world to be a human one. Then love can only be exchanged for love, trust for trust, etc. If you wish to enjoy art you must be an artistically cultivated person; if you wish to influence other people, you must be a person who really has a stimulating and encouraging effect upon others. . . . If you love without evoking love in return, i.e., if you are not able, by the manifestation of yourself as a loving person, to make yourself a beloved person—then your love is impotent and a misfortune.

These are not easy arguments, and most of my book is simply an exposition of their meaning. But here I shall attempt something more simple and schematic: a translation of the arguments into the terms I have already been using.

The first claim of Pascal and Marx is that personal qualities and social goods have their own spheres of operation, where they work their effects freely, spontaneously, and legitimately. There are ready or natural conversions that follow from, and are intuitively plausible because of, the social meaning of particular goods. The appeal is to our ordinary understanding and, at the same time, against our common acquiescence in illegitimate conversion patterns. Or, it is an appeal from our acquiescence to our resentment. There is something wrong, Pascal suggests, with the conversion of strength into belief. In political terms, Pascal means that no ruler can rightly command my opinions merely because of the power he wields. Nor can he, Marx adds, rightly claim to influence my actions: if a ruler wants to do that, he must be persuasive, helpful, encouraging, and so on. These arguments depend for their force on some shared understanding of knowledge, influence, and power. Social goods have social meanings, and we find our way to distributive justice through an interpretation of those meanings. We search for principles internal to each distributive sphere.

The second claim is that the disregard of these principles is tyranny. To convert one good into another, when there is no intrinsic connection between the two, is to invade the sphere where another company of men and women properly rules. Monopoly is not inappropriate within the spheres. There is nothing wrong, for example, with the grip that persuasive and helpful men and women (politicians) establish on political power. But the use of political power to gain access to other goods is a tyrannical use. Thus, an old description of tyranny is generalized: princes become tyrants, according to medieval writers, when they seize the property or invade the family of their subjects. In political life—but more widely, too—the dominance of goods makes for the domination of people.

The regime of complex equality is the opposite of tyranny. It establishes a set of relationships such that domination is impossible. In formal terms, complex equality means that no citizen's standing in one sphere or with regard to one social good can be undercut by his standing in some other sphere, with regard to some other good. Thus, citizen X may be chosen over citizen Y for political office, and then the two of them will be unequal in the sphere of politics. But they will not be unequal generally so long as X's office gives him no advantages over Y in any other sphere—superior medical care, access to better schools for his children, entrepreneurial opportunities, and so on. So long as office is not a dominant good, is not generally convertible, office holders will stand, or at least can stand, in a relation of equality to the men and women they govern.

But what if dominance were eliminated, the autonomy of the spheres established—and the same people were successful in one sphere after another, triumphant in every company, piling up goods without the need for illegitimate conversions? This would certainly make for an inegalitarian society, but it would also suggest in the strongest way that a society of equals was not a lively possibility. I doubt that any egalitarian argument could survive in the face of such evidence. Here is a person whom we have freely chosen (without reference to his family ties or personal wealth) as our political representative. He is also a bold and inventive entrepreneur. When he was younger, he studied science, scored amazingly high grades in every exam, and made important discoveries. In war, he is surpassingly brave and wins the highest honors. Himself compassionate and compelling, he is loved by all who know him. Are there such people? Maybe so, but I have my doubts. We tell stories like the one I have just told, but the stories are fictions, the conversion of power or money or academic talent into legendary fame. In any case, there aren't enough such people to constitute a ruling class and dominate the rest of us. Nor can they be successful in every distributive sphere, for there are some spheres to which the idea of success doesn't pertain. Nor are their children likely, under conditions of complex equality, to inherit their success. By and large, the most accomplished politicians, entrepreneurs, scientists, soldiers, and lovers will be different people; and so long as the goods they possess don't bring other goods in train, we have no reason to fear their accomplishments.

The critique of dominance and domination points toward an open-ended distributive principle. *No social good x should be distributed to men and women who possess some other good y merely because they possess y and without regard to the meaning of x.* This is a principle that has probably been reiterated, at one time of another, for every y that has ever been dominant. But it has not often been stated in general terms. Pascal and Marx have suggested the application of the principle against all possible y's. . . .

The purpose of the principle is to focus our attention; it doesn't determine the shares or the division. The principle directs us to study the meaning of social goods, to examine the different distributive spheres from the inside.

Susan Moller Okin, "Justice as Fairness: For Whom?," from *Justice, Gender, and the Family* (1989)

In *Justice, Gender, and the Family*, Susan Moller Okin offers feminist critiques of a variety of prominent contemporary accounts of justice, including those of Rawls, Nozick, and MacIntyre. Okin notes that the assumptions that Rawls seems to make concerning the parties in the original position—that they are choosing "as heads of households," and that these heads of household are men—insulates the family from a critique in terms of justice: what goes on in a household is not up for discussion by the parties in the original position. Nonetheless, as Rawls recognizes, what goes on in families is crucial to the constitution and perseverance of a just, well-ordered society. While this is a serious gap in Rawls's theory, Okin does not dismiss the view outright: she thinks, instead, that the device of the original position is a powerful means to make clear the criticisms of a gendered society.

———————

There is strikingly little indication, throughout most of *A Theory of Justice*, that the modern liberal society to which the principles of justice are to be applied is deeply and pervasively gender-structured. Thus an ambiguity runs throughout the work, which is continually noticeable to anyone reading it from a feminist perspective. On the one hand, as I shall argue, a consistent and wholehearted application of Rawls's liberal principles of justice can lead us to challenge fundamentally the gender system of our society. On the other hand, in his own account of his theory, this challenge is barely hinted at, much less developed. After critiquing Rawls's theory for its neglect of gender, I shall ask two related questions: What effects does a feminist reading of Rawls have on some of his fundamental ideas (particularly those most attacked by critics); and what undeveloped potential does the theory have for feminist critique, and in particular for our attempts to answer the question, Can justice co-exist with gender?

Central to Rawls's theory of justice is a construct, or heuristic device, that is both his most important single contribution to moral and political theory and the focus of most of the controversy his theory still attracts, nearly twenty years after its publication. Rawls argues that the principles of justice that should regulate the basic institutions of society are those that would be arrived at by persons reasoning in what is termed "the original position." His specifications for the original position are that "the parties" who deliberate there are rational and mutually disinterested, and that while no limits are placed on the general information available to them, a "veil of ignorance" conceals from them all knowledge of their individual characteristics and their social position. Though the theory is presented as a contract theory, it is so only in an odd and metaphoric sense, since "no one knows his situation in society nor his natural assets, and therefore no one is in a position to tailor principles to his advantage." Thus they have "no basis for bargaining in the usual sense." This is how, Rawls explains, "the arbitrariness of the world . . . [is] corrected for," in order that the principles arrived at will be fair. Indeed, since no one knows who he is, all think identically and the standpoint of any one party represents that of all. Thus the principles of justice are arrived at unanimously. Later in this chapter, I shall address some of the criticisms that have been made of Rawls's original position and of the nature of those who deliberate there. I shall show that his theory can be read in a way that either obviates these objections or answers them satisfactorily. But first, let us see how the theory treats women, gender, and the family.

Justice for All?

Rawls, like almost all political theorists until very recently, employs in *A Theory of Justice* supposedly generic male terms of reference. *Men, mankind, he,* and *his* are interspersed with gender-neutral terms of reference such as *individual* and *moral person.* Examples of intergenerational concern are worded in terms of "fathers" and "sons," and the difference principle is said to correspond to "the principle of fraternity." This linguistic usage would perhaps be less significant if it were not for the fact that Rawls self-consciously subscribes to a long tradition of moral and political philosophy that has used in its arguments either such "generic" male terms or more inclusive terms of reference ("human beings," "persons," "all rational beings as such"), only to exclude women from the scope of its conclusions. Kant is a clear example. But when Rawls refers to the generality and universality of Kant's ethics, and when he compares the principles chosen in his own original position to those regulative of Kant's kingdom of ends, "acting from [which] expresses our nature as free and equal rational persons," he does not mention the fact that women were not included among those persons to whom Kant meant his moral theory to apply. Again, in a brief discussion of Freud's account of moral development, Rawls presents Freud's theory of the formation of the male superego in largely gender-neutral terms, without mentioning the fact that Freud considered women's moral development to be sadly deficient, on account of their incomplete resolution of the Oedipus complex. Thus there is a blindness to the sexism of the tradition in which Rawls is a participant, which tends to render his terms of reference more ambiguous than they might otherwise be. A feminist reader finds it difficult not to keep asking, Does this theory of justice apply to women?

This question is not answered in the important passages listing the characteristics that persons in the original position are not to know about themselves, in order to formulate impartial principles of justice. In a subsequent article, Rawls has made it clear that sex *is* one of those morally irrelevant contingencies that are hidden by the veil of ignorance. But throughout *A Theory of Justice,* while the list of things unknown by a person in the original position includes "his place in society, his class position or social status, . . . his fortune in the distribution of natural assets and abilities, his intelligence and strength, and the like, . . . his conception of the good, the particulars of his rational plan of life, even the special features of his psychology," "his" sex is not mentioned. Since the parties also "know the general facts about human society," presumably including the fact that it is gender-structured both by custom and still in some respects by law, one might think that whether or not they knew their sex might matter enough to be mentioned. Perhaps Rawls meant to cover it by his phrase "and the like," but it is also possible that he did not consider it significant.

The ambiguity is exacerbated by the statement that those free and equal moral persons in the original position who formulate the principles of justice are to be thought of not as "single individuals" but as "heads of families" or "representatives of families." Rawls says that it is not necessary to think of the parties as heads of families, but that he will generally do so. The reason he does this, he explains, is to ensure that each person in the original position cares about the well-being of some persons in the next generation. These "ties of sentiment" between generations, which Rawls regards as important for the establishment of intergenerational justice—his just savings principle—, would otherwise constitute a problem because of the general assumption that the parties in the original position are mutually disinterested. In spite of the ties of sentiment *within* families, then, "as representatives of families their interests are opposed as the circumstances of justice imply."

The head of a family need not necessarily, of course, be a man. Certainly in the United States, at least, there has been a striking growth in the proportion of female-headed households during the last several decades. But the very fact that, in common usage, the term "female-headed household" is used *only* in reference to households without resident adult males implies the assumption that any present male takes precedence over a female as the household or family head. Rawls does nothing to contest this impression when he says of those in the original position that "imagining themselves to be fathers, say, they are to ascertain how much they should set aside for their sons by noting what they would believe themselves entitled to claim of their fathers. He makes the "heads of families" assumption only in order to address the problem of justice between generations, and presumably does not intend it to be a sexist assumption. Nevertheless, he is thereby effectively trapped into the public/domestic dichotomy and, with it, the conventional mode of thinking that life within the family and relations between the sexes are not properly regarded as part of the subject matter of a theory of social justice.

Let me here point out that Rawls, for good reason, states at the outset of his theory that the family *is* part of the subject matter of a theory of social justice. "For us" he says, "the primary subject of justice is the basic structure of society, or more exactly, the way in which the major social institutions distribute fundamental rights and duties and determine the division of advantages from social cooperation." The political constitution and the principal economic and social arrangements are basic because "taken together as one scheme, [they] define men's rights and duties and influence their life prospects, what they can expect to be and how well they can hope to do. The basic structure is the primary subject of justice *because its effects are so profound and present from the start*" (emphasis added). Rawls specifies "the monogamous family" as an example of such major social institutions, together with the political constitution, the legal protection of essential freedoms, competitive markets, and private property. Although this initial inclusion of the family as a basic social institution to which the principles of justice should apply is surprising in the light of the history of liberal thought, with its dichotomy between domestic and public spheres, it is necessary, given Rawls's stated criteria for inclusion in the basic structure. It would scarcely be possible to deny that different family structures, and different distributions of rights and duties within families, affect men's "life prospects, what they can expect to be and how well they can hope to do," and even more difficult to deny their effects on the life prospects of women. There is no doubt, then, that in Rawls's initial definition of the sphere of social justice, the family is included and the public/domestic dichotomy momentarily cast in doubt. However, the family is to a large extent ignored, though assumed, in the rest of the theory. . . .

Rawls's Theory of Justice as a Tool for Feminist Criticism

The significance of Rawls's central, brilliant idea, the original position, is that it forces one to question and consider traditions, customs, and institutions from all points of view, and ensures that the principles of justice will be acceptable to everyone, regardless of what position "he" ends up in. The critical force of the original position becomes evident when one considers that some of the most creative critiques of Rawls's theory have resulted from more radical or broad interpretations of the original position than his own. The theory, in principle, avoids both the problem of domination that is inherent in theories of justice based on traditions or shared understandings and the partiality of libertarian theory to those who are talented or fortunate. For feminist readers, however, the problem of the theory as stated by Rawls himself is encapsulated in that ambiguous "he." As I have shown, while Rawls briefly rules out formal, legal discrimination on the grounds of sex (as on other grounds that he regards as "morally irrelevant"), he fails entirely to address the justice of the gender system, which, with its roots in the sex roles of the family and its branches extending into virtually every corner of our lives, is one of the fundamental structures of our society. If, however, we read Rawls in such a way as to take seriously both the notion that those behind the veil of ignorance do not know what sex they are and the requirement that the family and the gender system, as basic social institutions, are to be subject to scrutiny, constructive feminist criticism of these contemporary institutions follows. So, also, do hidden difficulties for the application of a Rawlsian theory of justice in a gendered society.

I shall explain each of these points in turn. But first, both the critical perspective and the incipient problems of a feminist reading of Rawls can perhaps be illuminated by a description of a cartoon I saw a few years ago. Three elderly, robed male justices are depicted, looking down with astonishment at their very pregnant bellies. One says to the others, without further elaboration: "Perhaps we'd better reconsider that decision." This illustration graphically demonstrates the importance, in thinking about justice, of a concept like Rawls's original position, which makes us adopt the positions of others—especially positions that we ourselves could never be in. It also suggests that those thinking in such a way might well conclude that more than formal legal equality of the sexes is required if justice is to be done. As we have seen in recent years, it is quite possible to enact and uphold "gender-neutral" laws concerning pregnancy, abortion, childbirth leave, and so on, that in effect discriminate against women. The United States Supreme Court decided in 1976, for example, that "an exclusion of pregnancy from a disability-benefits plan providing general coverage is not a gender-based discrimination at all." One of the virtues of the cartoon is its suggestion that one's thinking on such matters is likely to be affected by the knowledge that one might become "a pregnant person." The illustration also points out the limits of what is possible, in terms of thinking ourselves into the original position, as long as we live in a gender-structured society. While the elderly male justices can, in a sense, imagine themselves as pregnant, what is a much more difficult question is whether, in order to construct principles of justice, they can imagine themselves as women. This raises the question of whether, in fact, sex *is* a morally irrelevant and contingent characteristic in a society structured by gender.

Let us first assume that sex is contingent in this way, though I shall later question this assumption. Let us suppose that it is possible, as Rawls clearly considers it to be, to hypothesize the moral thinking of representative human beings, as ignorant of their sex as of all the other things hidden by the veil of ignorance. It seems clear that, while Rawls does not do this, we must consistently take the relevant positions of both sexes into account in formulating and applying principles of justice. In particular, those in the original position must take special account of the perspective of women, since their knowledge of "the general facts about human society" must include the knowledge that women have been and continue to be the less advantaged sex in a great number of respects. In considering the basic institutions of society, they are more likely to pay special attention to the family than virtually to ignore it. Not only is it potentially the first school of social justice, but its customary unequal assignment of responsibilities and privileges to the two sexes and its socialization of children into sex roles make it, in its current form, an institution of crucial importance for the perpetuation of sex inequality.

In innumerable ways, the principles of justice that Rawls arrives at are inconsistent with a gender-structured society and with traditional family roles. The critical impact of a feminist application of Rawls's theory comes chiefly from his second principle, which requires that inequalities be both "to the greatest benefit of the least advantaged" and "attached to offices and positions open to all." This means that if any roles or positions analogous to our current sex roles—including those of husband and wife, mother and father—were to survive the demands of the first requirement, the second requirement would prohibit any linkage between these roles and sex. Gender, with its ascriptive designation of positions and expectations of behavior in accordance with the inborn characteristic of sex, could no longer form a legitimate part of the social structure, whether inside or outside the family. . . .

There is, then, implicit in Rawls's theory of justice a potential critique of gender-structured social institutions, which can be developed by taking seriously the fact that those formulating the principles of justice do not know their sex. At the beginning of my brief account of this feminist critique, however, I made an assumption that I said would later be questioned—that a person's sex is, as Rawls at times indicates, a contingent and morally irrelevant characteristic, such that human beings really can hypothesize ignorance of this fact about them. First, I shall explain why, unless this assumption is a reasonable one, there are likely to be further feminist ramifications for a Rawlsian theory of justice, in addition to those I have just sketched out. I shall then argue that the assumption is very probably not plausible in any society that is structured along the lines of gender. I reach the conclusions not only that our current gender structure is incompatible with the attainment of social justice, but also that the disappearance of gender is a prerequisite for the *complete* development of a nonsexist, fully human theory of justice.

Although Rawls is clearly aware of the effects on individuals of their different places in the social system, he regards it as possible to hypothesize free and rational moral persons in the original position who, temporarily freed from the contingencies of actual characteristics and social circumstances, will adopt the viewpoint of the "representative" human being. He is under no illusions about the difficulty of this task: it requires a "great shift in perspective" from the way we think about fairness in everyday life. But with the help of the veil of ignorance, he believes that we can "take up a point of view that everyone can adopt on an equal footing," so that "we share a common standpoint along with others and do not make our judgments from a personal slant." The result of this rational impartiality or objectivity, Rawls argues, is that, all being convinced by the same arguments, agreement about the basic principles of justice will be unanimous. He does not mean that those in the original position will agree about *all* moral or social issues—"ethical differences are bound to remain"—but that complete agreement will be reached on all basic principles, or "essential understandings." A critical assumption of this argument for unanimity, however, is that all the parties have similar motivations and psychologies (for example, he assumes mutually disinterested rationality and an absence of envy) and have experienced similar patterns of moral development, and are thus presumed capable of a sense of justice. Rawls regards these assumptions as the kind of "weak stipulations" on which a general theory can safely be founded.

The coherence of Rawls's hypothetical original position, with its unanimity of representative human beings, however, is placed in doubt if the kinds of human beings we actually become in society differ not only in respect to interests, superficial opinions, prejudices, and points of view that we can discard for the purpose of formulating principles of justice, but also in their basic psychologies, conceptions of the self in relation to others, and experiences of moral development. A number of feminist theorists have argued in recent years that, in a gender-structured society, the different life experiences of females and males from the start in fact affect their respective psychologies, modes of thinking, and patterns of moral development in significant ways. Special attention has been paid to the effects on the psychological and moral development of both sexes of the fact, fundamental to our gendered society, that children of both sexes are reared primarily by women. It has been argued that the experience of individuation—of separating oneself from the nurturer with whom one is originally psychologically fused—is a very different experience for girls than for boys, leaving the members of each sex with a different perception of themselves and of their relations with others. . . . In addition, it has been argued that the experience of *being* primary nurturers (and of growing up with this expectation) also affects the psychological and moral perspective of women, as does the experience of growing up in a society in which members of one's sex are in many ways subordinate to the other sex. Feminist theorists have scrutinized and analyzed the different experiences we encounter as we develop, from our actual lived lives to our absorption of their ideological underpinnings, and have filled out in valuable ways Simone de Beauvoir's claim that "one is not born, but rather becomes, a woman."

What seems already to be indicated by these studies, despite their incompleteness so far, is that *in a gender-structured society* there is such a thing as the distinct standpoint of women, and that this standpoint cannot be adequately taken into account by male philosophers doing the theoretical equivalent of the elderly male justices depicted in the cartoon. The formative influence of female parenting on small children, especially, seems to suggest that sex difference is even more likely to affect one's thinking about justice in a gendered society than, for example, racial difference in a society in which race has social significance, or class difference in a class society. The notion of the standpoint of women, while not without its own problems, suggests that a fully human moral or political theory can be developed only with the full participation of both sexes. At the very least, this will require that women take their place with men in the dialogue in approximately equal numbers and in positions of comparable influence. In a society structured along the lines of gender, this cannot happen.

In itself, moreover, it is insufficient for the development of a fully human theory of justice. For if principles of justice are to be adopted unanimously by representative human beings ignorant of their particular characteristics and positions in society, they must be persons whose psychological and moral development is in all essentials identical. This means that the social factors influencing the differences presently found between the sexes—from female parenting to all the manifestations of female subordination and dependence—would have to be replaced by genderless institutions and customs. Only children who are equally mothered and fathered can develop fully the psychological and moral capacities that currently seem to be unevenly distributed between the sexes. Only when men participate equally in what have been principally women's realms of meeting the daily material and psychological needs of those close to them, and when women participate equally in what have been principally men's realms of larger scale production, government, and intellectual and artistic life, will members of both sexes be able to develop a more complete *human* personality than has hitherto been possible. Whereas Rawls and most other philosophers have assumed that human psychology, rationality, moral development, and other capacities are completely represented by the males of the species, this assumption itself has now been exposed as part of the male-dominated ideology of our gendered society.

What effect might consideration of the standpoint of women in gendered society have on Rawls's theory of justice? It would place in doubt some assumptions and conclusions, while reinforcing others. For example, the discussion of rational plans of life and primary goods might be focused more on relationships and less exclusively on the complex activities that he values most highly, if it were to take account of, rather than to take for granted, the traditionally more female contributions to human life. Rawls says that self-respect or self-esteem is "perhaps the most important primary good," and that "the parties in the original position would wish to avoid at almost any cost the social conditions that undermine [it]." Good early physical and especially psychological nurturance in a favorable setting is essential for a child to develop self-respect or self-esteem. Yet there is no discussion of this in Rawls's consideration of the primary goods. Since the basis of self-respect is formed in very early childhood, just family structures and practices in which it is fostered and in which parenting itself is esteemed, and high-quality, subsidized child care facilities to supplement them, would surely be fundamental requirements of a just society. On the other hand, as I indicated earlier, those aspects of Rawls's theory, such as the difference principle, that require a considerable capacity to identify with others, can be strengthened by reference to conceptions of relations between self and others that seem in gendered society to be more predominantly female, but that would in a gender-free society be more or less evenly shared by members of both sexes.

The arguments of this chapter have led to mixed conclusions about the potential usefulness of Rawls's theory of justice from a feminist viewpoint, and about its adaptability to a genderless society. Rawls himself neglects gender and, despite his initial statement about the place of the family in the basic structure, does not consider whether or in what form the family is a just institution. It seems significant, too, that whereas at the beginning of *A Theory of Justice* he explicitly distinguishes the institutions of the basic structure (*including* the family) from other "private associations" and "various informal conventions and customs of everyday life," [in his most recent work] he distinctly reinforces the impression that the family belongs with those "private" and therefore nonpolitical associations, for which he suggests the principles of justice are less appropriate or relevant. He does this, moreover, despite the fact that his own theory of moral development rests centrally on the early experience of persons within a family environment that is both loving and just. Thus the theory as it stands contains an internal paradox. Because of his assumptions about gender, he has not applied the principles of justice to the realm of human nurturance, a realm that is essential to the achievement and the maintenance of justice.

On the other hand, I have argued that the feminist *potential* of Rawls's method of thinking and his conclusions is considerable. The original position, with the veil of ignorance hiding from its participants their sex as well as their other particular characteristics, talents, circumstances, and aims, is a powerful concept for challenging the gender structure. Once we dispense with the traditional liberal assumptions about public versus domestic, political versus nonpolitical spheres of life, we can use Rawls's theory as a tool with which to think about how to achieve justice between the sexes both within the family and in society at large.

John Rawls, "Justice as Fairness as a Political Conception of Justice," from "Justice as Fairness: Political not Metaphysical" (1985)

A Theory of Justice has been the object of a tremendous amount of scholarly attention; it has set the agenda for discussions of distributive justice since its publication. (As Nozick wrote in 1974, those writing on justice must now work within Rawls's framework, or explain why not.) Not least among those suggesting modifications to the view put forward in *A Theory of Justice* has been Rawls himself, whose views on the aims of political philosophy and the methods for justifying an account of justice have undergone a number of transformations since 1971. As Rawls now sees it, the problem with *A Theory of Justice* was that it seemed to be built on too many controversial premises, premises that will not be shared within a pluralistic culture. How, though, can one defend a theory of justice in a way that can secure agreement in a political society with a number of rival views of the good life and how people ought to behave? Rawls's suggestion is to view justice as fairness as a "political" conception of justice: it is not derived from some set of philosophical propositions but rather is elaborated from the ideas implicit in the public culture of constitutional democracies. After seeing what results from such an undertaking—Rawls thinks that justice as fairness will be among the top contenders—we then turn to see whether citizens can, from their own particular points of view, affirm this political conception of justice as an appropriate criterion for deciding questions of basic justice.

In this discussion I shall make some general remarks about how I now understand the conception of justice that I have called "justice as fairness" (presented in my book *A Theory of Justice*). I do this because it may seem that this conception depends on philosophical claims I should like to avoid, for example, claims to universal truth, or claims about the essential nature and identity of persons. My aim is to explain why it does not. I shall first discuss what I regard as the task of political philosophy at the present time and then briefly survey how the basic intuitive ideas drawn upon in justice as fairness are combined into a political conception of justice for a constitutional democracy. Doing this will bring out how and why this conception of justice avoids certain philosophical and metaphysical claims. Briefly, the idea is that in a constitutional democracy the public conception of justice should be, so far as possible, independent of controversial philosophical and religious doctrines. Thus, to formulate such a conception, we apply the principle of toleration to philosophy itself: the public conception of justice is to be political, not metaphysical. Hence the title.

I want to put aside the question whether the text of *A Theory of Justice* supports different readings than the one I sketch here. Certainly on a number of points I have changed my views, and there are no doubt others on which my views have changed in ways that I am unaware of. I recognize further that certain faults of exposition as well as obscure and ambiguous passages in *A Theory of Justice* invite misunderstanding; but I think these matters need not concern us and I shan't pursue them beyond a few footnote indications. For our purposes here, it suffices first, to show how a conception of justice with the structure and content of justice as fairness can be understood, as political and not metaphysical, and second, to explain why we should look for such a conception of justice in a democratic society.

One thing I failed to say in *A Theory of Justice,* or failed to stress sufficiently, is that justice as fairness is intended as a political conception of justice. While a political conception of justice is, of course, a moral conception, it is moral conception worked out for a specific kind of subject, namely, for political, social, and economic institutions. In particular, justice as fairness is framed to apply to what I have called the "basic structure" of a modern constitutional democracy. (I shall use "constitutional democracy" and "democratic regime," and similar phrases interchangeably.) By this structure I mean such a society's main political, social, and economic institutions, and how they fit together into one unified system of social cooperation. Whether justice as fairness can be extended to a general political conception for different kinds of societies existing under different historical and social conditions, or whether it can be extended to a general moral conception, or a significant part thereof, are altogether separate questions. I avoid prejudging these larger questions one way or the other. . . .

. . . To conclude these introductory remarks, since justice as fairness is intended as a political conception of justice for a democratic society, it tries to draw solely upon basic intuitive ideas that are embedded in the political institutions of a constitutional democratic regime and the public traditions of their interpretation. Justice as fairness is a political conception in part because it starts from within a certain political tradition. We hope that this political conception of justice may at least be supported by what we may call an "overlapping consensus," that is, by a consensus that includes all the opposing philosophical and religious doctrines likely to persist and to gain adherents in a more or less just constitutional democratic society.

There are, of course, many ways in which political philosophy may be understood, and writers at different times, faced with different political and social circumstances, understand their work differently. Justice as fairness I would now understand as a reasonably systematic and practicable conception of justice for a constitutional democracy, a conception that offers an alternative to the dominant utilitarianism of our tradition of political thought. Its first task is to provide a more secure and acceptable basis for constitutional principles and basic rights and liberties than utilitarianism seems to allow. The need for such a political conception arises in the following way.

There are periods, sometimes long periods, in the history of any society during which certain fundamental questions give rise to sharp and divisive political controversy, and it seems difficult, if not impossible, to find any shared basis of political agreement. Indeed, certain questions may prove intractable and may never be fully settled. One task of political philosophy in a democratic society is to focus on such questions and to examine whether some underlying basis of agreement can be uncovered and a mutually acceptable way of resolving these questions publicly established. Or if these questions cannot be fully settled, as may well be the case, perhaps the divergence of opinion can be narrowed sufficiently so that political cooperation on a basis of mutual respect can still be maintained.

The course of democratic thought over the past two centuries or so makes plain that there is no agreement on the way basic institutions of a constitutional democracy should be arranged if they are to specify and secure the basic rights and liberties of citizens and answer to the claims of democratic equality when citizens are conceived as free and equal persons. . . . A deep disagreement exists as to how the values of liberty and equality are best realized in the basic structure of society. To simplify, we may think of this disagreement as a conflict within the tradition of democratic thought itself, between the tradition associated with Locke, which gives greater weight to what Constant called "the liberties of the moderns," freedom of thought and conscience, certain basic rights of the person and of property, and the rule of law, and the tradition associated with Rousseau, which gives greater weight to what Constant called "the liberties of the ancients," the equal political liberties and the values of public life. This is a stylized contrast and historically inaccurate, but it serves to fix ideas.

Justice as fairness tries to adjudicate between these contending traditions first, by proposing two principles of justice to serve as guidelines for how basic institutions are to realize the values of liberty and equality, and second, by specifying a point of view from which these principles can be seen as more appropriate than other familiar principles of justice to the nature of democratic citizens viewed as free and equal persons. . . .

. . . The two principles of justice (mentioned above) read as follows:

> 1. Each person has an equal right to a fully adequate scheme of equal basic rights and liberties, which scheme is compatible with a similar scheme for all.
> 2. Social and economic inequalities are to satisfy two conditions: first, they must be attached to offices and positions open to all under conditions of fair equality of opportunity; and second, they must be to the greatest benefit of the least advantaged members of society.

Each of these principles applies to a different part of the basic structure; and both are concerned not only with basic rights, liberties, and opportunities, but also with the claims of equality; while the second part of the second principle underwrites the worth of these institutional guarantees. The two principles together, when the first is given priority over the second, regulate the basic institutions which realize these values. But these details, although important, are not our concern here.

We must now ask: how might political philosophy find a shared basis for settling such a fundamental question as that of the most appropriate institutional forms for liberty and equality? Of course, it is likely that the most that can be done is to narrow the range of public disagreement. Yet even firmly held convictions gradually change: religious toleration is now accepted, and arguments for persecution are no longer openly professed; similarly, slavery is rejected as inherently unjust, and however much the aftermath of slavery may persist in social practices and unavowed attitudes, no one is willing to defend it. We collect such settled convictions as the belief in religious toleration and the rejection of slavery and try to organize the basic ideas and principles implicit in these convictions into a coherent conception of justice. We can regard these convictions as provisional fixed points which any conception of justice must account for if it is to be reasonable for us. We look, then, to our public political culture itself, including its main institutions and the historical traditions of their interpretation, as the shared fund of implicitly recognized basic ideas and principles. The hope is that these ideas and principles can be formulated clearly enough to be combined into a conception of political justice congenial to our most firmly held convictions. We express this by saying that a political conception of justice, to be acceptable, must be in accordance with our considered convictions, at all levels of generality, on due reflection . . .

Now suppose justice as fairness were to achieve its aim and a publicly acceptable political conception of justice is found. Then this conception provides a publicly recognized point of view from which all citizens can examine before one another whether or not their political and social institutions are just. It enables them to do this by citing what are recognized among them as valid and sufficient reasons singled out by that conception itself. Society's main institutions and how they fit together into one scheme of social cooperation can be examined on the same basis by each citizen, whatever that citizen's social position or more particular interests. It should be observed that, on this view, justification is not regarded simply as valid argument from listed premises, even should these premises be true. Rather, justification is addressed to others who disagree with us, and therefore it must always proceed from some consensus, that is, from premises that we and others publicly recognize as true; or better, publicly recognize as acceptable to us for the purpose of establishing a working agreement on the fundamental questions of political justice. It goes without saying that this agreement must be informed and uncoerced, and reached by citizens in ways consistent with their being viewed as free and equal persons.

Thus, the aim of justice as fairness as a political conception is practical, and not metaphysical or epistemological. That is, it presents itself not as a conception of justice that is true, but one that can serve as a basis of informed and willing political agreement between citizens viewed as free and equal persons. This agreement when securely founded in public political and social attitudes sustains the goods of all persons and associations within a just democratic regime. To secure this agreement we try, so far as we can, to avoid disputed philosophical, as well as disputed moral and religious, questions. We do this not because these questions are unimportant or regarded with indifference, but because we think them too important and recognize that there is no way to resolve them politically. The only alternative to a principle of toleration is the autocratic use of state power. Thus, justice as fairness deliberately stays on the surface, philosophically speaking. Given the profound differences in belief and conceptions of the good at least since the Reformation, we must recognize that, just as on questions of religious and moral doctrine, public agreement on the basic questions of philosophy cannot be obtained without the state's infringement of basic liberties. Philosophy as the search for truth about an independent metaphysical and moral order cannot, I believe, provide a workable and shared basis for a political conception of justice in a democratic society. . . .

I now take up the idea of the original position. This idea is introduced in order to work out which traditional conception of justice, or which variant of one of those conceptions, specifies the most appropriate principles for realizing liberty and equality once society is viewed as a system of cooperation between free and equal persons. Assuming we had this purpose in mind, let's see why we would introduce the idea of the original position and how it serves its purpose.

Consider again the idea of social cooperation. Let's ask: how are the fair terms of cooperation to be determined? Are they simply laid down by some outside agency distinct from the persons cooperating? Are they, for example, laid down by God's law? Or are these terms to be recognized by these persons as fair by reference to their knowledge of a prior and independent moral order? For example, are they regarded as required by natural law, or by a realm of values known by rational intuition? Or are these terms to be established by an undertaking among these persons themselves in the light of what they regard as their mutual advantage? Depending on which answer we give, we get a different conception of cooperation.

Since justice as fairness recasts the doctrine of the social contract, it adopts a form of the last answer: the fair terms of social cooperation are conceived as agreed to by those engaged in it, that is, by free and equal persons as citizens who are born into the society in which they lead their lives. But their agreement, like any other valid agreement, must be entered into under appropriate conditions. In particular, these conditions must situate free and equal persons fairly and must not allow some persons greater bargaining advantages than others. Further, threats of force and coercion, deception and fraud, and so on, must be excluded.

So far so good. The foregoing considerations are familiar from everyday life. But agreements in everyday life are made in some more or less clearly specified situation embedded within the background institutions of the basic structure. Our task, however, is to extend the idea of agreement to this background framework itself. Here we face a difficulty for any political conception of justice that uses the idea of a contract, whether social or otherwise. The difficulty is this: we must find some point of view, removed from and not distorted by the particular features and circumstances of the all-encompassing background framework, from which a fair agreement between free and equal persons can be reached. The original position, with the feature I have called "the veil of ignorance," is this point of view. And the reason why the original position must abstract from and not be affected by the contingencies of the social world is that the conditions for a fair agreement on the principles of political justice between free and equal persons must eliminate the bargaining advantages which inevitably arise within background institutions of any society as the result of cumulative social, historical, and natural tendencies. These contingent advantages and accidental influences from the past should not influence an agreement on the principles which are to regulate the institutions of the basic structure itself from the present into the future.

Here we seem to face a second difficulty, which is, however, only apparent. To explain: from what we have just said it is clear that the original position is to be seen as a device of representation and hence any agreement reached by the parties must be regarded as both hypothetical and nonhistorical. But if so, since hypothetical agreements cannot bind, what is the significance of the original position? The answer is implicit in what has already been said: it is given by the role of the various features of the original position as a device of representation. Thus, that the parties are symmetrically situated is required if they are to be seen as representatives of free and equal citizens who are to reach an agreement under conditions that are fair. Moreover, one of our considered convictions, I assume, is this: the fact that we occupy a particular social position is not a good reason for us to accept, or to expect others to accept, a conception of justice that favors those in this position. To model this conviction in the original position the parties are not allowed to know their social position; and the same idea is extended to other cases. This is expressed figuratively by saying that the parties are behind a veil of ignorance. In sum, the original position is simply a device of representation: it describes the parties, each of whom are responsible for the essential interests of a free and equal person, as fairly situated and as reaching an agreement subject to appropriate restrictions on what are to count as good reasons. . . .

To conclude: we introduce an idea like that of the original position because there is no better way to elaborate a political conception of justice for the basic structure from the fundamental intuitive idea of society as a fair system of cooperation between citizens as free and equal persons. There are, however, certain hazards. As a device of representation the original position is likely to seem somewhat abstract and hence open to misunderstanding. The description of the parties may seem to presuppose some metaphysical conception of the person, for example, that the essential nature of persons is independent of and prior to their contingent attributes, including their final ends and attachments, and indeed, their character as a whole. But this is an illusion caused by not seeing the original position as a device of representation. The veil of ignorance, to mention one prominent feature of that position, has no metaphysical implications concerning the nature of the self; it does not imply that the self is ontologically prior to the facts about persons that the parties are excluded from knowing. We can, as it were, enter this position any time simply by reasoning for principles of justice in accordance with the enumerated restrictions. When, in this way, we simulate being in this position, our reasoning no more commits us to a metaphysical doctrine about the nature of the self than our playing a game like Monopoly commits us to thinking that we are landlords engaged in a desperate rivalry, winner take all. We must keep in mind that we are trying to show how the idea of society as a fair system of social cooperation can be unfolded so as to specify the most appropriate principles for realizing the institutions of liberty and equality when citizens are regarded as free and equal persons. . . .

By contrast with liberalism as a comprehensive moral doctrine, justice as fairness tries to present a conception of political justice rooted in the basic intuitive ideas found in the public culture of a constitutional democracy. We conjecture that these ideas are likely to be affirmed by each of the opposing comprehensive moral doctrines influential in a reasonably just democratic society. Thus justice as fairness seeks to identify the kernel of an overlapping consensus, that is, the shared intuitive ideas which when worked up into a political conception of justice turn out to be sufficient to underwrite a just constitutional regime. This is the most we can expect, nor do we need more. We must note, however, that when justice as fairness is fully realized in a well-ordered society, the value of full autonomy is likewise realized. In this way justice as fairness is indeed similar to the liberalisms of Kant and Mill; but in contrast with them, the value of full autonomy is here specified by a political conception of justice, and not by a comprehensive moral doctrine.

It may appear that, so understood, the public acceptance of justice as fairness is no more than prudential; that is, that those who affirm this conception do so simply as a modus vivendi which allows the groups in the overlapping consensus to pursue their own good subject to certain constraints which each thinks to be for its advantage given existing circumstances. The idea of an overlapping consensus may seem essentially Hobbesian. But against this, two remarks: first, justice as fairness is a moral conception: it has conceptions of person and society, and concepts of right and fairness, as well as principles of justice with their complement of the virtues through which those principles are embodied in human character and regulate political and social life. This conception of justice provides an account of the cooperative virtues suitable for a political doctrine in view of the conditions and requirements of a constitutional regime. It is no less a moral conception because it is restricted to the basic structure of society, since this restriction is what enables it to serve as a political conception of justice given our present circumstances. Thus, in an overlapping consensus (as understood here), the conception of justice as fairness is not regarded merely as a modus vivendi.

Second, in such a consensus each of the comprehensive philosophical, religious, and moral doctrines accepts justice as fairness in its own way; that is, each comprehensive doctrine, from within its own point of view, is led to accept the public reasons of justice specified by justice as fairness. We might say that they recognize its concepts, principles, and virtues as theorems, as it were, at which their several views coincide. But this does not make these points of coincidence any less moral or reduce them to mere means. For, in general, these concepts, principles, and virtues are accepted by each as belonging to a more comprehensive philosophical, religious, or moral doctrine. Some may even affirm justice as fairness as a natural moral conception that can stand on its own feet. They accept this conception of justice as a reasonable basis for political and social cooperation, and hold that it is as natural and fundamental as the concepts and principles of honesty and mutual trust, and the virtues of cooperation in everyday life. The doctrines in an overlapping consensus differ in how far they maintain a further foundation is necessary and on what that further foundation should be. These differences, however, are compatible with a consensus on justice as fairness as a political conception of justice.

SELECTED BIBLIOGRAPHY

Ackerman, Bruce A. *Social Justice in the Liberal State.* New Haven, Conn.: Yale University Press, 1980.

Aristotle. *Nicomachean Ethics.* Translated by Terence Irwin. Indianapolis: Hackett, 1985.

Aristotle. *Politics.* Translated by Benjamin Jowett. New York: Modern Library, 1943.

Axelrod, Robert M. *The Evolution of Cooperation.* New York: Basic Books, 1984.

Baier, Annette. "Trust and Antitrust." *Ethics* 96 (1986):231–260.

Barber, Benjamin. *The Conquest of Politics.* Oxford: Oxford University Press, 1988.

Barker, Ernest, ed. *The Social Contract: Locke, Hume, and Rousseau.* Oxford: Oxford University Press, 1962.

Beccaria, Cesare. *On Crimes and Punishment.* Translated by H. Paolucci. Indianapolis: Bobbs-Merrill, 1963.

Becker, Carl. *The Declaration of Independence: A Study in the History of Political Ideas.* New York. Vintage Books, 1970.

Becker, Lawrence, *Reciprocity.* Boston: Routledge and Kegan Paul, 1986.

Bedau, Hugo. "Capital Punishment." In *Matters of Life and Death,* edited by Tom Regan. New York: McGraw-Hill, 1986.

Bentham, Jeremy. *Introduction to the Principles of Morals and Legislation.* New York: Hafner, 1948.

Buchanan, James M. *The Limits of Liberty: Between Anarchy and Leviathan.* Chicago: University of Chicago Press, 1975.

Calhoun, Cheshire. "Justice, Care, Gender Bias." *Journal of Philosophy* 85 (1988):451–463.

Camus, Albert. "Reflections on the Guillotine." In *Resistance, Rebellion, and Death,* translated by Justin O'Brien. New York: Vintage, 1961.

Coleman, Jules. *Risks and Wrongs.* Cambridge: Cambridge University Press, 1992.

Cupit, Geoffrey. *Justice as Fittingness.* New York: Oxford University Press, 1996.

Daniels, Norman, ed. *Reading Rawls.* New York: Basic Books, 1975.

Davis, Michael. *To Make the Punishment Fit the Crime: Essays in the Theory of Criminal Justice.* Boulder, Colo.: Westview Press, 1992.

Dworkin, Ronald. "The Original Position." *University of Chicago Law Review* 40 (1973):500–533.

Dworkin, Ronald. *Taking Rights Seriously.* Cambridge, Mass.: Harvard University Press, 1977.

Ellis, Anthony. "Recent Work on Punishment." *Philosophical Quarterly* 45 (1995):225–233.

Feinberg, Joel. *Doing and Deserving.* Princeton, N.J.: Princeton University Press, 1970.

Feinberg, Joel. *Social Philosophy.* Englewood Cliffs, N.J.: Prentice-Hall, 1973.

Finnis, John. *Natural Law and Natural Rights.* New York: Oxford University Press, 1980.

Fishkin, James. *Justice, Equal Opportunity, and the Family.* New Haven, Conn.: Yale University Press, 1983.

Fishkin, James. *The Dialogue of Justice: Toward a Self-Reflective Society.* New Haven, Conn.: Yale University Press, 1993.

Flew, Anthony. *The Politics of Procrustes.* Buffalo, N.Y.: Prometheus, 1981.

Galston, William. *Justice and the Human Good.* Chicago: University of Chicago Press, 1980.

Gauthier, David. "The Social Contract as Ideology." *Philosophy & Public Affairs* 6 (1977):130–164.

Gauthier, David. *Morals by Agreement.* New York: Oxford University Press, 1986.

Gilligan, Carol. *In a Different Voice: Psychological Theory and Women's Development.* Cambridge, Mass.: Harvard University Press, 1982.

Goodman, Lenn E. *On Justice: An Essay in Jewish Philosophy.* New Haven, Conn.: Yale University Press, 1991.

Hampton, Jean. "The Moral Education Theory of Punishment." *Philosophy & Public Affairs* 13 (1984):208–238.

Hampton, Jean. *Hobbes and the Social Contract Tradition.* Cambridge: Cambridge University Press, 1986.

Havelock, Eric. *The Greek Concept of Justice: From Its Shadow in Homer to Its Substance in Plato.* Cambridge: Cambridge University Press, 1978.

Hegel, G. W. F. *The Philosophy of Right.* Translated by T. M. Knox. New York: Oxford University Press, 1967.

Hegel, G. W. F. *The Phenomenology of Spirit.* Translated by A. V. Miller. Oxford: Oxford University Press, 1977.

Heller, Agnes. *Beyond Justice.* Oxford: Oxford University Press, 1981.

Heschel, Abraham. *The Prophets.* New York: Harper and Row, 1962.

Hobbes, Thomas. *Leviathan.* Edited by Edwin Curley. Indianapolis: Hackett, 1994.

Honderich, Ted. *Punishment: The Supposed Justification.* Harmondsworth, UK: Penguin, 1976.

Hume, David. *A Treatise of Human Nature.* Edited by L. A. Selby-Bigge. Oxford: Oxford University Press, 1978.

Hume, David. *Enquiries Concerning the Principles of Morals.* Edited by L. A. Selby-Bigge. Oxford: Oxford University Press, 1978.

Jackson, W. W. *Matters of Justice.* London: Croom Helm, 1986.

Jacoby, Susan. *Wild Justice.* New York: Harper and Row, 1983.

Kant, Immanuel. *Metaphysical Elements of Justice.* Translated by John Ladd. Indianapolis: Bobbs-Merrill, 1965.

Kant, Immanuel. *Grounding for the Metaphysics of Morals.* Translated by James Ellington. Indianapolis: Hackett, 1981.

Kaufmann, Walter. *Without Guilt and Justice.* New York: Wyden, 1973.

Kekes, John. *Against Liberalism.* Ithaca, N.Y.: Cornell University Press, 1997.

Locke, John. *Two Treatises on Government.* Edited by Peter Laslett. Cambridge: Cambridge University Press, 1988.

Lucash, Frank, ed. *Justice and Equality: Here and Now.* Ithaca, N.Y.: Cornell University Press, 1986.

MacIntyre, Alasdair. *After Virtue.* South Bend, Ind.: University of Notre Dame Press, 1981.

MacIntyre, Alasdair. *Whose Justice? Which Rationality?* South Bend, Ind.: University of Notre Dame Press, 1988.

Marongiu, Pietro, and Newman, Graeme. *Vengeance.* Totowa, N.J.: Rowman and Littlefield, 1987.

Martin, Rex. *Rawls and Rights.* Lawrence: Kansas University Press, 1985.

Marx, Karl, and Engels, Friedrich. *Basic Writings on Politics and Philosophy.* Edited by Lewis Feuer. New York: Doubleday, 1959.

McKerlie, Dennis. "Equality." *Ethics* 106 (1996):274–296.

Melden, A. *Rights and Persons.* Berkeley: University of California Press, 1977.

Mencius. *The Mind of Mencius.* Translated by D. C. Lau. New York: Penguin, 1970.

Mill, John Stuart. *On Liberty.* Edited by Elizabeth Rapaport. Indianapolis: Hackett, 1978.

Mill, John Stuart. *Utilitarianism.* Edited by George Sher. Indianapolis: Hackett, 1980.

Miller, David. *Social Justice.* Oxford: Oxford University Press, 1976.

Moore, Michael. "The Moral Worth of Retribution." In *Responsibility, Character, and the Emotions,* edited by Ferdinand Schoeman. Cambridge: Cambridge University Press, 1987.

Nagel, Thomas. *Mortal Questions.* Cambridge: Cambridge University Press, 1979.

Nagel, Thomas. *The View from Nowhere.* New York: Oxford University Press, 1986.

Nietzsche, Friedrich. *On the Genealogy of Morals.* Translated by Douglas Smith, New York: Oxford University Press, 1996.

Nozick, Robert, *Anarchy, State, and Utopia.* New York: Basic Books, 1974.

Nozick, Robert. *Philosophical Explanations.* Cambridge, Mass.: Belknap Press of Harvard University Press, 1981.

Nussbaum, Martha. *The Fragility of Goodness.* New York: Cambridge University Press, 1985.

Okin, Susan Moller. *Justice, Gender, and the Family.* New York: Basic Books, 1989.

Parfit, Derek. *Reasons and Persons.* Oxford: Oxford University Press, 1984.

Paul, Ellen Frankel, Miller, Fred, and Paul, Jeffrey, eds. *The Just Society.* New York: Cambridge University Press, 1995.

Pincoffs, Edmund. *Quandaries and Virtues.* Lawrence: University Press of Kansas, 1986.

Plato. *The Republic.* Translated by G. M. A. Grube. Indianapolis: Hackett, 1982.

Plato. *The Trial and Death of Socrates.* Translated by G. M. A. Grube. Indianapolis: Hackett, 1982.

Pojman, Louis P., and Reiman, Jeffrey. *The Death Penalty: For and Against.* Lanham, MD: Rowman and Littlefield, 1998.

Pojman, Louis, and Westmoreland, Robert, eds. *Equality: Selected Readings.* New York: Oxford University Press, 1997.

Posner, Richard. *The Economics of Justice.* Cambridge, Mass.: Harvard University Press, 1983.

Rapacynski, Andrzej. *Nature and Politics.* Ithaca, N.Y.: Cornell University Press, 1987.

Raphael, D. D. *Moral Philosophy.* Oxford: Opus Books, 1981.

Rawls, John. "Two Concepts of Rules." *Philosophical Review* 64 (1955): pp. 3–32.

Rawls, John. "Justice as Fairness." *Philosophical Review* 57 (1958):164–194.

Rawls, John. *A Theory of Justice.* Cambridge, Mass.: Belknap Press of Harvard University Press, 1971.

Rawls, John. "Justice as Fairness: Political not Metaphysical." *Philosophy & Public Affairs* 14 (1985):223–251.

Rawls, John. *Political Liberalism.* New York: Columbia University Press, 1993.

Rescher, Nicholas. *Unselfishness.* Pittsburgh: University of Pittsburgh Press, 1975.

Roemer, John E. *Theories of Distributive Justice.* Cambridge, Mass.: Harvard University Press, 1996.

Rousseau, Jean-Jacques. *Emile.* Translated by Allan Bloom. New York: Basic Books, 1979.

Rousseau, Jean-Jacques. *On the Social Contract, Discourse on the Origin of Inequality, and Discourse on Political Economy.* Translated by Donald Cress. Indianapolis: Hackett, 1983.

Sandel, Michael. *Liberalism and the Limits of Justice.* Cambridge: Cambridge University Press, 1982.

Sandel, Michael. *Democracy's Discontent.* Cambridge, Mass.: Belknap Press of Harvard University Press, 1996.

Sen, A. K. *Collective Choice and Social Welfare.* San Francisco: Holden-Day, 1970.

Sidgwick, Henry. *The Methods of Ethics.* Indianapolis: Hackett, 1981.

Singer, Peter. *Practical Ethics.* Cambridge: Cambridge University Press, 1979.

Slote, Michael. "The Justice of Caring." *Social Philosophy and Policy* 15 (1998):171–195.

Smith, Adam. *The Theory of Moral Sentiments.* London: George Bell and Sons, 1880.

Smith, Adam. *An Inquiry into the Nature and Causes of the Wealth of Nations.* Edited by R. H. Campbell and A. S. Skinner. Oxford: Oxford University Press, 1976.

Solomon, Robert C. *In the Spirit of Hegel.* New York: Oxford University Press, 1983.

Solomon, Robert C. *A Passion for Justice.* New York: Addison-Wesley, 1990.

Soltan, Karol. *The Causal Theory of Justice.* Berkeley: University of California Press, 1987.

Steiner, Hillel. *An Essay on Rights.* New York: Cambridge University Press, 1994.

Sterba, James. *The Demands of Justice.* South Bend, Ind.: University of Notre Dame Press, 1980.

Tawney, R. H. *Equality.* New York: Barnes and Noble, 1964.

Taylor, Charles. "The Nature and Scope of Distributive Justice." In *Justice and Equality: Here and Now,* edited by Frank Lucash. Ithaca, N.Y.: Cornell University Press, 1986.

Ten, C. L. *Guilt and Punishment: A Philosophical Introduction.* Oxford: Oxford University Press, 1987.

Torrance, John. *Karl Marx's Theory of Justice.* New York: Cambridge University Press, 1995.

van den Haag, Ernest. "Deterrence and the Death Penalty." *Journal of Criminal Law, Criminology, and Police Science* 60 (1969):141–147.

Vlastos, Gregory. "Justice and Equality." In *Social Justice,* edited by R. Brandt. Englewood Cliffs, N.J.: Prentice-Hall, 1962.

von Hayek, Friedrich. *Law, Legislation, and Liberty, Vol. II: The Mirage of Social Justice.* Chicago: University of Chicago Press, 1976.

Walzer, Michael. *Spheres of Justice.* New York: Basic Books, 1983.

Walzer, Michael. "Justice Here and Now." In *Justice and Equality: Here and Now,* edited by Frank Lucash. Ithaca, N.Y.: Cornell University Press, 1986.

Walzer, Michael. *Thick and Thin: Moral Argument at Home and Abroad.* South Bend, Ind.: University of Notre Dame Press, 1994.

Warnke, Georgia. *Justice and Interpretation.* Cambridge, Mass.: MIT Press, 1993.

Westermarck, Edward. *The Origin and Development of the Moral Ideas.* London: Macmillan, 1912.

Williams, Bernard. "The Idea of Equality." In *Problems of the Self.* New York: Cambridge University Press, 1973.

Williams, Bernard. *Ethics and the Limits of Philosophy.* Cambridge, Mass.: Harvard University Press, 1973.

Williams, Bernard. "Justice as a Virtue." In *Essays on Aristotle's Ethics,* edited by Amelie Rorty. Berkeley: University of California Press, 1980.

Wills, Garry. *Inventing America: Jefferson's Declaration of Independence.* Garden City, N.Y.: Doubleday, 1978.

Winfield, Richard. *Reason and Justice.* Buffalo: S.U.N.Y. Press, 1988.

Wolff, Robert Paul. *Understanding Rawls.* Princeton, N.J.: Princeton University Press, 1977.

Wolgast, Elizabeth. *The Grammar of Justice.* Ithaca, N.Y.: Cornell University Press, 1987.

Breinigsville, PA USA
18 January 2011
253547BV00003B/4/P